A HISTORY OF WITCHCRAFT IN ENGLAND FROM 1558 TO 1718

BY

Wallace Notestein

A HISTORY OF WITCHCRAFT IN ENGLAND FROM 1558 TO 1718

Published by Wallachia Publishers

New York City, NY

First published circa 1969

ABOUT WALLACHIA PUBLISHERS

<u>Wallachia Publishers</u> mission is to publish the world's finest European history texts. More information on our recent publications and catalog can be found on our website.

PREFACE.

In its original form this essay was the dissertation submitted for a doctorate in philosophy conferred by Yale University in 1908. When first projected it was the writer's purpose to take up the subject of English witchcraft under certain general political and social aspects. It was not long, however, before he began to feel that preliminary to such a treatment there was necessary a chronological survey of the witch trials. Those strange and tragic affairs were so closely involved with the politics, literature, and life of the seventeenth century that one is surprised to find how few of them have received accurate or complete record in history. It may be said, in fact, that few subjects have gathered about themselves so large concretions of misinformation as English witchcraft. This is largely, of course, because so little attention has been given to it by serious students of history. The mistakes and misunderstandings of contemporary writers and of the local historians have been handed down from county history to county history until many of them have crept into general works. For this reason it was determined to attempt a chronological treatment which would give a narrative history of the more significant trials along with some account of the progress of opinion. This plan has been adhered to somewhat strictly, sometimes not without regret upon the part of the writer. It is his hope later in a series of articles to deal with some of the more general phases of the subject, with such topics as the use of torture, the part of the physicians, the contagious nature of the witch alarms, the relation of Puritanism to persecution, the supposed influence of the Royal Society, the general causes for the gradual decline of the belief, and other like questions. It will be seen in the course of the narrative that some of these matters have been touched upon.

This study of witchcraft has been limited to a period of about one hundred and sixty years in English history. The year 1558 has been chosen as the starting point because almost immediately after the accession of Elizabeth there began the movement for a new law, a movement which resulted in the statute of 1563. With that statute the history of the persecution of witches gathers importance. The year 1718 has been selected as a concluding date because that year was marked by the publication of Francis Hutchinson's notable attack upon the belief. Hutchinson levelled a final and deadly blow at the dying superstition. Few men of intelligence dared after that avow any belief in the reality of witchcraft; it is probable that very few even secretly cherished such a belief. A complete history would of course include a full account both of the witch trials from Anglo-Saxon times to Elizabeth's accession and of the various witch-swimming incidents of the eighteenth century. The latter it has not seemed worth while here to consider. The former would involve an examination of all English sources from the earliest times and would mean a study of isolated and unrelated trials occurring at long intervals (at least, we have record only of such) and chiefly in church courts. The writer has not undertaken to treat this earlier period; he must confess to but small knowledge of it. In the few pages which he has given to it he has attempted nothing more than to sketch from the most obvious sources an outline of what is currently known as to English witches and witchcraft prior to the days of Elizabeth. It is to be hoped that some student of medieval society will at some time make a thorough investigation of the history of witchcraft in England to the accession of the great Queen.

For the study of the period to be covered in this monograph there exists a wealth of material. It would perhaps not be too much to say that everything in print and manuscript in England during the last half of the sixteenth and the entire seventeenth century should be read or at least glanced over. The writer has limited himself to certain kinds of material from which he could reasonably expect to glean information. These sources fall into seven principal categories. Most important of all are the pamphlets, or chapbooks, dealing with the history of particular alarms and trials and usually concluding with the details of confession and execution. Second only to them in importance are the local or municipal records, usually court files, but sometimes merely expense accounts. In the memoirs and diaries can be found many mentions of trials witnessed by the diarist or described to him. The newspapers of the time, in their eagerness to exploit the unusual, seize gloatingly upon the stories of witchcraft. The works of local historians and antiquarians record in their lists of striking and extraordinary events within their counties or boroughs the several trials and hangings for the crime. The writers, mainly theologians, who discuss the theory and doctrine of witchcraft illustrate the principles they lay down by cases that have fallen under their observation. Lastly, the state papers contain occasional references to the activities of the Devil and of his agents in the realm.

Besides these seven types of material there should be named a few others less important. From the pamphlet accounts of the criminal dockets at the Old Bailey and Newgate, leaflets which were published at frequent intervals after the Restoration, are to be gleaned mentions of perhaps half a dozen trials for witchcraft. The plays of Dekker, Heywood, and Shadwell must be used by the student, not because they add information omitted elsewhere, but because they offer some clue to the way in which the witches at Edmonton and Lancaster were regarded by the public. If the pamphlet narrative of the witch of Edmonton had been lost, it might be possible to reconstruct from the play of Dekker, Ford, and Rowley some of the outlines of the story. It would be at best a hazardous undertaking. To reconstruct the trials at Lancaster from the plays of Heywood and Brome or from that of Shadwell would be quite impossible. The ballads present a form of evidence much like that of the plays. Like the plays, they happen all to deal with cases about which we are already well informed. In general, they seem to follow the narratives and depositions faithfully.

No mention has been made of manuscript sources. Those used by the author have all belonged to one or other of the types of material described.

It has been remarked that there is current a large body of misinformation about English witchcraft. It would be ungrateful of the author not to acknowledge that some very good work has been done on the theme. The Reverend Francis Hutchinson, as already mentioned, wrote in 1718 an epoch-making history of the subject, a book which is still useful and can never be wholly displaced. In 1851 Thomas Wright brought out his Narratives of Sorcery and Magic, a work at once entertaining and learned. Wright wrote largely from original sources and wrote with a good deal of care. Such blunders as he made were the result of haste and of the want of those materials which we now possess. Mrs. Lynn Linton's Witch Stories, published first in

1861, is a better book than might be supposed from a casual glance at it. It was written with no more serious purpose than to entertain, but it is by no means to be despised. So far as it goes, it represents careful work. It would be wrong to pass over Lecky's brilliant essay on witchcraft in his History of Rationalism, valuable of course rather as an interpretation than as an historical account. Lecky said many things about witchcraft that needed to be said, and said them well. It is my belief that his verdicts as to the importance of sundry factors may have to be modified; but, however that be, the importance of his essay must always be recognized. One must not omit in passing James Russell Lowell's charming essay on the subject. Both Lecky and Lowell of course touched English witchcraft but lightly. Since Mrs. Lynn Linton's no careful treatment of English witchcraft proper has appeared. In 1907, however, Professor Kittredge published his Notes on Witchcraft, the sixty-seven pages of which with their footnotes contain a more scrupulous sifting of the evidence as to witchcraft in England than is to be found in any other treatment. Professor Kittredge is chiefly interested in English witchcraft as it relates itself to witchcraft in New England, but his work contains much that is fresh about the belief in England. As to the rôle and the importance of various actors in the drama and as to sundry minor matters, the writer has found himself forced to divergence of view. He recognizes nevertheless the importance of Professor Kittredge's contribution to the study of the whole subject and acknowledges his own indebtedness to the essay for suggestion and guidance.

The author cannot hope that the work here presented is final. Unfortunately there is still hidden away in England an unexplored mass of local records. Some of them no doubt contain accounts of witch trials. I have used chiefly such printed and manuscript materials as were accessible in London and Oxford. Some day perhaps I may find time to go the rounds of the English counties and search the masses of gaol delivery records and municipal archives. From the really small amount of new material on the subject brought to light by the Historical Manuscripts Commission and by the publication of many municipal records, it seems improbable that such a search would uncover so many unlisted trials as seriously to modify the narrative. Nevertheless until such a search is made no history of the subject has the right to be counted final. Mr. Charles W. Wallace, the student of Shakespeare, tells me that in turning over the multitudinous records of the Star Chamber he found a few witch cases. Professor Kittredge believes that there is still a great deal of such material to be turned up in private collections and local archives. Any information on this matter which any student of English local history can give me will be gratefully received.

I wish to express my thanks for reading parts of the manuscript to William Savage Johnson of Kansas University and to Miss Ada Comstock of the University of Minnesota. For general assistance and advice on the subject I am under obligations to Professor Wilbur C. Abbott and to Professor George Burton Adams of Yale University. It is quite impossible to say how very much I owe to Professor George L. Burr of Cornell. From cover to cover the book, since the award to it of the Adams Prize, has profited from his painstaking criticism and wise suggestion.

W. N.

Minneapolis, October 10, 1911.

CHAPTER I.: The Beginnings of English Witchcraft.

It has been said by a thoughtful writer that the subject of witchcraft has hardly received that place which it deserves in the history of opinions. There has been, of course, a reason for this neglect—the fact that the belief in witchcraft is no longer existent among intelligent people and that its history, in consequence, seems to possess rather an antiquarian than a living interest. No one can tell the story of the witch trials of sixteenth and seventeenth century England without digging up a buried past, and the process of exhumation is not always pleasant. Yet the study of English witchcraft is more than an unsightly exposure of a forgotten superstition. There were few aspects of sixteenth and seventeenth century life that were not affected by the ugly belief. It is quite impossible to grasp the social conditions, it is impossible to understand the opinions, fears, and hopes of the men and women who lived in Elizabethan and Stuart England, without some knowledge of the part played in that age by witchcraft. It was a matter that concerned all classes from the royal household to the ignorant denizens of country villages. Privy councillors anxious about their sovereign and thrifty peasants worrying over their crops, clergymen alert to detect the Devil in their own parishes, medical quacks eager to profit by the fear of evil women, justices of the peace zealous to beat down the works of Satan—all classes, indeed—believed more or less sincerely in the dangerous powers of human creatures who had surrendered themselves to the Evil One.

Witchcraft, in a general and vague sense, was something very old in English history. In a more specific and limited sense it is a comparatively modern phenomenon. This leads us to a definition of the term. It is a definition that can be given adequately only in an historical way. A group of closely related and somewhat ill defined conceptions went far back. Some of them, indeed, were to be found in the Old Testament, many of them in the Latin and Greek writers. The word witchcraft itself belonged to Anglo-Saxon days. As early as the seventh century Theodore of Tarsus imposed penances upon magicians and enchanters, and the laws, from Alfred on, abound with mentions of witchcraft. From these passages the meaning of the word witch as used by the early English may be fairly deduced. The word was the current English term for one who used spells and charms, who was assisted by evil spirits to accomplish certain ends. It will be seen that this is by no means the whole meaning of the term in later times. Nothing is yet said about the transformation of witches into other shapes, and there is no mention of a compact, implicit or otherwise, with the Devil; there is no allusion to the nocturnal meetings of the Devil's worshippers and to the orgies that took place upon those occasions; there is no elaborate and systematic theological explanation of human relations with demons.

But these notions were to reach England soon enough. Already there were germinating in southern Europe ideas out of which the completer notions were to spring. As early as the close of the ninth century certain Byzantine traditions were being introduced into the West. There were legends of men who had made written compacts with the Devil, men whom he promised to assist in this world in return for their souls in the next. But, while such stories were current throughout the Middle Ages, the notion behind them does not seem to have been connected with the other features of what was to make up the idea of witchcraft until about the middle of the fourteenth century. It was about that time that the belief in the "Sabbat" or nocturnal assembly of the witches made its appearance. The belief grew up that witches rode through the air to these meetings, that they renounced Christ and engaged in foul forms of homage to Satan. Lea tells us that towards the close of the century the University of Paris formulated the theory that a pact with Satan was inherent in all magic, and judges began to connect this pact with the old belief in night riders through the air. The countless confessions that resulted from the carefully framed questions of the judges served to develop and systematize the theory of the subject. The witch was much more than a sorcerer. Sorcerers had been those who, through the aid of evil spirits, by the use of certain words or of representations of persons or things produced changes above the ordinary course of nature. "The witch," says Lea, "has abandoned Christianity, has renounced her baptism, has worshipped Satan as her God, has surrendered herself to him, body and soul, and exists only to be his instrument in working the evil to her fellow creatures which he cannot accomplish without a human agent." This was the final and definite notion of a witch. It was the conception that controlled European opinion on the subject from the latter part of the fourteenth to the close of the seventeenth century. It was, as has been seen, an elaborate theological notion that had grown out of the comparatively simple and vague ideas to be found in the scriptural and classical writers.

It may well be doubted whether this definite and intricate theological notion of witchcraft reached England so early as the fourteenth century. Certainly not until a good deal later—if negative evidence is at all trustworthy—was a clear distinction made between sorcery and witchcraft. The witches searched for by Henry IV, the professor of divinity, the friar, the clerk, and the witch of Eye, who were hurried before the Council of Henry VI, that unfortunate Duchess of Gloucester who had to walk the streets of London, the Duchess of Bedford, the conspirators against Edward IV who were supposed to use magic, the unlucky mistress of Edward IV—none of these who through the course of two centuries were charged with magical misdeeds were, so far as we know, accused of those dreadful relations with the Devil, the nauseating details of which fill out the later narratives of witch history.

The truth seems to be that the idea of witchcraft was not very clearly defined and differentiated in the minds of ordinary Englishmen until after the beginning of legislation upon the subject. It is not impossible that there were English theologians who could have set forth the complete philosophy of the belief, but to the average mind sorcery, conjuration, enchantment, and witchcraft were but evil ways of mastering nature. All that was changed when laws were passed. With legislation came greatly increased numbers of accusations; with accusations and executions came treatises and theory. Continental writers were consulted, and the whole system and science of the subject were soon elaborated for all who read.

With the earlier period, which has been sketched merely by way of definition, this monograph cannot attempt to deal. It limits itself to a narrative of the witch trials, and incidentally of opinion as to witchcraft, after there was definite legislation by Parliament. The statute of the fifth year of Elizabeth's reign marks a point in the history of the judicial persecution at which an account may very naturally begin. The year 1558 has been selected as the date because from the very opening of the reign which was to be signalized by the passing of that statute and was to be characterized by a serious effort to enforce it, the persecution was preparing.

Up to that time the crime of sorcery had been dealt with in a few early instances by the common-law courts, occasionally (where politics were involved) by the privy council, but more usually, it is probable, by the church. This, indeed, may easily be illustrated from the works of law. Britton and Fleta include an inquiry about sorcerers as one of the articles of the sheriff's tourn. A note upon Britton, however, declares that it is for the ecclesiastical court to try such offenders and to deliver them to be put to death in the king's court, but that the king himself may proceed against them if he pleases. While there is some overlapping of procedure implied by this, the confusion seems to have been yet greater in actual practice. A brief narrative of some cases prior to 1558 will illustrate the strangely unsettled state of procedure. Pollock and Maitland relate several trials to be found in the early pleas. In 1209 one woman accused another of sorcery in the king's court and the defendant cleared herself by the ordeal. In 1279 a man accused of killing a witch who assaulted him in his house was fined, but only because he had fled away. Walter Langton, Bishop of Lichfield and treasurer of Edward I, was accused of sorcery and homage to Satan and cleared himself with the compurgators. In 1325 more than twenty men were indicted and tried by the king's bench for murder by tormenting a waxen image. All of them were acquitted. In 1371 there was brought before the king's bench an inhabitant of Southwark who was charged with sorcery, but he was finally discharged on swearing that he would never be a sorcerer.

It will be observed that these early cases were all of them tried in the secular courts; but there is no reason to doubt that the ecclesiastical courts were quite as active, and their zeal must have been quickened by the statute of 1401, which in cases of heresy made the lay power their executioner. It was at nearly the same time, however, that the charge of sorcery began to be frequently used as a political weapon. In such cases, of course, the accused was usually a person of influence and the matter was tried in the council. It will be seen, then, that the crime was one that might fall either under ecclesiastical or conciliar jurisdiction and the particular circumstances usually determined finally the jurisdiction. When Henry IV was informed that the diocese of Lincoln was full of sorcerers, magicians, enchanters, necromancers, diviners, and soothsayers, he sent a letter to the bishop requiring him to search for sorcerers and to commit them to prison after conviction, or even before, if it should seem expedient. This was entrusting the matter to the church, but the order was given by authority of the king, not improbably after the matter had been discussed in the council. In the reign of Henry VI conciliar and ecclesiastical authorities both took part at different times and in different ways. Thomas Northfield, a member of the Order of Preachers in Worcester and a professor of divinity, was brought before the council, together with all suspected matter belonging to him, and especially his books treating of sorcery. Pike does not tell us the outcome. In the same year there were summoned before the council three humbler sorcerers, Margery Jourdemain, John Virley, a cleric, and John Ashwell, a friar of the Order of the Holy Cross. It would be hard to say whether the three were in any way connected with political intrigue. It is possible that they were suspected of sorcery against the sovereign. They were all, however, dismissed on giving security. It was only a few years after this instance of conciliar jurisdiction that a much more important case was turned over to the clergy. The story of Eleanor Cobham, Duchess of Gloucester, is a familiar one. It was determined by the enemies of Duke Humphrey of Gloucester to attack him through his wife, who was believed to be influential with the young king. The first move was made by arresting a Roger Bolingbroke who had been connected with the duke and the duchess, and who was said to be an astronomer or necromancer. It was declared that he had cast the duchess's horoscope with a view to ascertaining her chances to the throne. Bolingbroke made confession, and Eleanor was then brought before "certayne bisshoppis of the kyngis." In the mean time several lords, members of the privy council, were authorized to "enquire of al maner tresons, sorcery, and alle othir thyngis that myghte in eny wise ... concerne harmfulli the kyngis persone." Bolingbroke and a clergyman, Thomas Southwell, were indicted of treason with the duchess as accessory. With them was accused that Margery Jourdemain who had been released ten years before. Eleanor was then reexamined before the Bishops of London, Lincoln, and Norwich, she was condemned as guilty, and required to walk barefoot through the streets of London, which she "dede righte mekely." The rest of her life she spent in a northern prison. Bolingbroke was executed as a traitor, and Margery Jourdemain was burnt at Smithfield.

The case of the Duchess of Bedford—another instance of the connection between sorcery and political intrigue—fell naturally into the hands of the council. It was believed by those who could understand in no other way the king's infatuation that he had been bewitched by the mother of the queen. The story was whispered from ear to ear until the duchess got wind of it and complained to the council against her maligners. The council declared her cleared of suspicion and ordered that the decision should be "enacted of record."

The charge of sorcery brought by the protector Richard of Gloucester against Jane Shore, who had been the mistress of Edward IV, never came to trial and in consequence illustrates neither ecclesiastical nor conciliar jurisdiction. It is worthy of note however that the accusation was preferred by the protector—who was soon to be Richard III—in the council chamber.

It will be seen that these cases prove very little as to procedure in the matter of sorcery and witchcraft. They are cases that arose in a disturbed period and that concerned chiefly people of note. That they were tried before the bishops or before the privy council does not mean that all such charges were brought into those courts. There must have been less important cases that were never brought before the council or the great ecclesiastical courts. It seems probable—to reason backward from later practice—that less important trials were conducted almost exclusively by the minor church courts.

This would at first lead us to suspect that, when the state finally began to legislate against witchcraft by statute, it was endeavoring to wrest jurisdiction of the crime out of the hands of the church and to put it into secular hands. Such a supposition, however, there is nothing to justify. It seems probable, on the contrary, that the statute enacted in the reign of Henry VIII was passed rather to support the church in its struggle against sorcery and witchcraft than to limit its jurisdiction in the matter. It was to assist in checking these practitioners that the state stepped in. At another point in this chapter we shall have occasion to note the great interest in sorcery and all kindred subjects that was springing up over England, and we shall at times observe some of the manifestations of this interest as well as some of the causes for it. Here it is necessary only to urge the importance of this interest as accounting for the passage of a statute.

Chapter VIII of 33 Henry VIII states its purpose clearly: "Where," reads the preamble, "dyvers and sundrie persones unlawfully have devised and practised Invocacions and conjuracions of Sprites, pretendyng by suche meanes to understande and get Knowlege for their owne lucre in what place treasure of golde and Silver shulde or mought be founde or had ... and also have used and occupied wichecraftes, inchauntmentes and sorceries to the distruccion of their neighbours persones and goodes." A description was given of the methods practised, and it was enacted that the use of any invocation or conjuration of spirits, witchcrafts, enchantments, or sorceries should be considered felony. It will be observed that the law made no graduation of offences. Everything was listed as felony. No later piece of legislation on the subject was so sweeping in its severity.

The law remained on the statute-book only six years. In the early part of the reign of Edward VI, when the protector Somerset was in power, a policy of great leniency in respect to felonies was proposed. In December of 1547 a bill was introduced into Parliament to repeal certain statutes for treason and felony. "This bill being a matter of great concern to every subject, a committee was appointed, consisting of the Archbishop of Canterbury, the lord chancellor, the lord chamberlain, the Marquis of Dorset, the Earls of Shrewsbury and Southampton, the Bishops of Ely, Lincoln, and Worcester, the Lords Cobham, Clinton, and Wentworth, with certain of the king's learned council; all which noblemen were appointed to meet a committee of the Commons ... in order to treat and commune on the purport of the said bill." The Commons, it seems, had already prepared a bill of their own, but this they were willing to drop and the Lords' measure with some amendments was finally passed. It was under this wide repeal of felonies that chapter VIII of 33 Henry VIII was finally annulled. Whether the question of witchcraft came up for special consideration or not, we are not informed. We do know that the Bishops of London, Durham, Ely, Hereford, and Chichester, took exception to some amendments that were inserted in the act of repeal, and it is not impossible that they were opposed to repealing the act against witchcraft. Certainly there is no reason to suppose that the church was resisting the encroachment of the state in the subject.

As a matter of fact it is probable that, in the general question of repeal of felonies, the question of witchcraft received scant attention. There is indeed an interesting story that seems to point in that direction and that deserves repeating also as an illustration of the protector's attitude towards the question. Edward Underhill gives the narrative in his autobiography: "When we hade dyned, the maior sentt to [two] off his offycers with me to seke Alene; whome we mett withalle in Poles, and toke hym with us unto his chamber, wheare we founde fygures sett to calke the nativetie off the kynge, and a jugementt gevyne off his deathe, wheroff this folyshe wreche thoughte hymselfe so sure thatt he and his conselars the papistes bruted it all over. The kynge laye att Hamtone courte the same tyme, and me lord protector at the Syone; unto whome I caryed this Alen, with his bokes off conejuracyons, cearkles, and many thynges beloungynge to thatt dyvlyshe art, wiche he affyrmed before me lorde was a lawfulle cyens [science], for the statute agaynst souche was repealed. 'Thow folyshe knave! (sayde me lorde) yff thou and all thatt be off thy cyens telle me what I shalle do to-morow, I wylle geve the alle thatt I have'; commaundynge me to cary hym unto the Tower." Alen was examined about his science and it was discovered that he was "a very unlearned asse, and a sorcerer, for the wiche he was worthye hangynge, sayde Mr. Recorde." He was however kept in the Tower "about the space off a yere, and then by frendshipe delyvered. So scapithe alwayes the weked."

But the wicked were not long to escape. The beginning of Elizabeth's reign saw a serious and successful effort to put on the statute-book definite and severe penalties for conjuration, sorcery, witchcraft, and related crimes. The question was taken up in the very first year of the new reign and a bill was draughted. It was not, however, until 1563 that the statute was finally passed. It was then enacted that those who "shall use, practise, or exercise any Witchecrafte, Enchantment, Charme or Sorcerie, whereby any person shall happen to bee killed or destroyed, ... their Concellors and Aidours, ... shall suffer paynes of Deathe as a Felon or Felons." It was further declared that those by whose practices any person was wasted, consumed, or lamed, should suffer for the first offence one year's imprisonment and should be put in the pillory four times. For the second offence death was the penalty. It was further provided that those who by witchcraft presumed to discover treasure or to find stolen property or to "provoke any person to unlawfull love" should suffer a year's imprisonment and four appearances in the pillory.

With this law the history of the prosecution of witchcraft in England as a secular crime may well begin. The question naturally arises, What was the occasion of this law? How did it happen that just at this particular time so drastic a measure was passed and put into operation? Fortunately part of the evidence exists upon which to frame an answer. The English churchmen who had been driven out of England during the Marian persecution had many of them sojourned in Zurich and Geneva, where the extirpation of witches was in full progress, and had talked over the matter with eminent Continental theologians. With the accession of Elizabeth these men returned to England in force and became prominent in church and state, many of them receiving bishoprics. It is not possible to show that they all were influential in putting through the statute of the fifth year of Elizabeth. It is clear that one of them spoke out plainly on the subject. It can hardly be doubted that he represented the opinions of many other ecclesiastics who had come under the same influences during their exile. John Jewel was an Anglican of Calvinistic sympathies who on his return to England at Elizabeth's accession had been appointed Bishop of Salisbury. Within a short time he came to occupy a prominent position in the court. He preached before the Queen and accompanied her on a visit to Oxford. It was in the course of one of his first sermons—somewhere between November of 1559 and March of 1560—that he laid before her his convictions on witchcraft. It is, he tells her, "the horrible using of your poor subjects," that forces him to speak. "This kind of people (I mean witches and sorcerers) within these few last years are marvellously increased within this your grace's realm. These eyes have seen most evident and manifest marks of their wickedness. Your grace's subjects pine away even unto death, their colour fadeth, their flesh rotteth, their speech is benumbed, their senses are bereft. Wherefore, your poor subjects' most humble petition unto your highness is, that the laws touching such malefactors may be put in due execution."

The church historian, Strype, conjectures that this sermon was the cause of the law passed in the fifth year of Elizabeth's reign, by which witchcraft was again made a felony, as it had been in the reign of Henry VIII. Whatever weight we may attach to Strype's suggestion, we have every right to believe that Jewel introduced foreign opinion on witchcraft. Very probably there were many returned exiles as well as others who brought back word of the crusade on the Continent; but Jewel's words put the matter formally before the queen and her government.

We can trace the effect of the ecclesiastic's appeal still further. The impression produced by it was responsible probably not only for the passage of the law but also for the issue of commissions to the justices of the peace to apprehend all the witches they were able to find in their jurisdictions.

It can hardly be doubted that the impression produced by the bishop's sermon serves in part to explain the beginning of the state's attack upon witches. Yet one naturally inquires after some other factor in the problem. Is it not likely that there were in England itself certain peculiar conditions, certain special circumstances, that served to forward the attack? To answer that query, we must recall the situation in England when Elizabeth took the throne. Elizabeth was a Protestant, and her accession meant the relinquishment of the Catholic hold upon England. But it was not long before the claims of Mary, Queen of Scots, began to give the English ministers bad dreams. Catholic and Spanish plots against the life of Elizabeth kept the government detectives on the lookout. Perhaps because it was deemed the hardest to circumvent, the use of conjuration against the life of the queen was most feared. It was a method too that appealed to conspirators, who never questioned its efficacy, and who anticipated little risk of discovery.

To understand why the English government should have been so alarmed at the efforts of the conjurers, we shall have to go back to the half-century that preceded the reign of the great queen and review briefly the rise of those curious traders in mystery. The earlier half of the fifteenth century, when the witch fires were already lighted in South Germany, saw the coming of conjurers in England. Their numbers soon evidenced a growing interest in the supernatural upon the part of the English and foreshadowed the growing faith in witchcraft. From the scattered local records the facts have been pieced together to show that here and there professors of magic powers were beginning to get a hearing. As they first appear upon the scene, the conjurers may be grouped in two classes, the position seekers and the treasure seekers. To the first belong those who used incantations and charms to win the favor of the powerful, and so to gain advancement for themselves or for their clients. It was a time when there was every encouragement to try these means. Men like Wolsey and Thomas Cromwell had risen from humble rank to the highest places in the state. Their careers seemed inexplicable, if not uncanny. It was easy to believe that unfair and unlawful practices had been used. What had been done before could be done again. So the dealers in magic may have reasoned. At all events, whatever their mental operations, they experimented with charms which were to gain the favor of the great, and some of their operations came to the ears of the court.

The treasure seekers were more numerous. Every now and then in the course of English history treasures have been unearthed, many of them buried in Roman times. Stories of lucky finds had of course gained wide circulation. Here was the opportunity of the bankrupt adventurer and the stranded promoter. The treasures could be found by the science of magic. The notion was closely akin to the still current idea that wells can be located by the use of hazel wands. But none of the conjurers—and this seems a curious fact to one familiar with the English stories of the supernatural—ever lit upon the desired treasure. Their efforts hardly aroused public interest, least of all alarm. Experimenters, who fifty years later would have been hurried before the privy council, were allowed to conjure and dig as they pleased. Henry VIII even sold the right in one locality, and sold it at a price which showed how lightly he regarded it.

Other forms of magic were of course practiced. By the time that Elizabeth succeeded to the throne, it is safe to say that the practice of forbidden arts had become wide-spread in England. Reginald Scot a little later declared that every parish was full of men and women who claimed to work miracles. Most of them were women, and their performances read like those of the gipsy fortune-tellers today. "Cunning women" they called themselves. They were many of them semi-medical or pseudo-medical practitioners who used herbs and extracts, and, when those failed, charms and enchantments, to heal the sick. If they were fairly fortunate, they became known as "good witches." Particularly in connection with midwifery were their incantations deemed effective. From such functions it was no far call to forecast the outcome of love affairs, or to prepare potions which would ensure love. They became general helpers to the distressed. They could tell where lost property was to be found, an undertaking closely related to that of the treasure seekers.

It was usually in the less serious diseases that these cunning folk were consulted. They were called upon often indeed—if one fragmentary evidence may be trusted—to diagnose the diseases and to account for the deaths of domestic animals. It may very easily be that it was from the necessity of explaining the deaths of animals that the practitioners of magic began to talk about witchcraft and to throw out a hint that some witch was at the back of the matter. It would be in line with their own pretensions. Were they not good witches? Was it not their province to overcome the machinations of the black witches, that is, witches who wrought evil rather than good? The disease of an animal was hard to prescribe for. A sick horse would hardly respond to the waving of hands and a jumble of strange words. The animal was, in all probability, bewitched.

At any rate, whether in this particular manner or not, it became shortly the duty of the cunning women to recognize the signs of witchcraft, to prescribe for it, and if possible to detect the witch. In many cases the practitioner wisely enough refused to name any one, but described the appearance of the guilty party and set forth a series of operations by which to expose her machinations. If certain herbs were plucked and treated in certain ways, if such and such words were said, the guilty party would appear at the door. At other times the wise woman gave a perfectly recognizable description of the guilty one and offered remedies that would nullify her maleficent influences. No doubt the party indicated as the witch was very often another of the "good witches," perhaps a rival. Throughout the records of the superstition are scattered examples of wise women upon whom suspicion suddenly lighted, and who were arraigned and sent to the gallows. Beyond question the suspicion began often with the ill words of a neighbor, perhaps of a competitor, words that started an attack upon the woman's reputation that she was unable to repel.

It is not to be supposed that the art of cunning was confined to the female sex. Throughout the reign of Elizabeth, the realm was alive with men who were pretenders to knowledge of mysteries. So closely was the occupation allied to that of the physician that no such strict line as now exists between reputable physicians and quack doctors separated the "good witches" from the regular practicers of medicine. It was so customary in Elizabethan times for thoroughly reputable and even eminent medical men to explain baffling cases as the results of witchcraft that to draw the line of demarcation between them and the pretenders who suggested by means of a charm or a glass a maleficent agent would be impossible. Granted the phenomena of conjuration and witchcraft as facts—and no one had yet disputed them—it was altogether easy to believe that good witches who antagonized the works of black witches were more dependable than the family physician, who could but suggest the cause of sickness. The regular practitioner must often have created business for his brother of the cunning arts.

One would like to know what these practicers thought of their own arts. Certainly some of them accomplished cures. Mental troubles that baffled the ordinary physician would offer the "good witch" a rare field for successful endeavor. Such would be able not only to persuade a community of their good offices, but to deceive themselves. Not all of them, however, by any means, were self-deceived. Conscious fraud played a part in a large percentage of cases. One witch was very naive in her confession of fraud. When suspected of sorcery and cited to court, she was said to have frankly recited her charm:

"My lofe in my lappe, My penny in my purse, You are never the better, I am never the worse." She was acquitted and doubtless continued to add penny to penny.

We need not, indeed, be surprised that the state should have been remiss in punishing a crime so vague in character and so closely related to an honorable profession. Except where conjuration had affected high interests of state, it had been practically overlooked by the government. Now and then throughout the fourteenth and fifteenth centuries there had been isolated plots against the sovereign, in which conjury had played a conspicuous part. With these few exceptions the crime had been one left to ecclesiastical jurisdiction. But now the state was ready to reclaim its jurisdiction over these crimes and to assume a very positive attitude of hostility towards them. This came about in a way that has already been briefly indicated. The government of the queen found itself threatened constantly by plots for making away with the queen, plots which their instigators hoped would overturn the Protestant regime and bring England back into the fold. Elizabeth had hardly mounted her throne when her councillors began to suspect the use of sorcery and conjuration against her life. As a result they instituted the most painstaking inquiries into all reported cases of the sort, especially in and about London and the neighboring counties. Every Catholic was suspected. Two cases that were taken up within the first year came to nothing, but a third trial proved more serious. In November of 1558 Sir Anthony Fortescue, member of a well known Catholic family, was arrested, together with several accomplices, upon the charge of casting the horoscope of the queen's life. Fortescue was soon released, but in 1561 he was again put in custody, this time with two brothers-in-law, Edmund and Arthur Pole, nephews of the famous cardinal of that name. The plot that came to light had many ramifications. It was proposed to marry Mary, Queen of Scots, to Edmund Pole, and from Flanders to proclaim her Queen of England. In the meantime Elizabeth was to die a natural death—at least so the conspirators claimed—prophesied for her by two conjurers, John Prestall and Edmund Cosyn, with the assistance of a "wicked spryte." It was discovered that the plot involved the French and Spanish ambassadors. Relations between Paris and London became strained. The conspirators were tried and sentenced to death. Fortescue himself, perhaps because he was a second cousin of the queen and brother of the Chancellor of the Exchequer, seems to have escaped the gallows.

The Fortescue affair was, however, but one of many conspiracies on foot during the time. Throughout the sixties and the seventies the queen's councillors were on the lookout. Justices of the peace and other prominent men in the counties were kept informed by the privy council of reported conjurers, and they were instructed to send in what evidence they could gather against them. It is remarkable that three-fourths of the cases that came under investigation were from a territory within thirty miles of London. Two-thirds of them were from Essex. Not all the conjurers were charged with plotting against the queen, but that charge was most common. It is safe to suppose that, in the cases where that accusation was not preferred, it was nevertheless the alarm of the privy council for the life of the queen that had prompted the investigation and arrest.

Between 1578 and 1582, critical years in the affairs of the Scottish queen, the anxiety of the London authorities was intense—their precautions were redoubled. Representatives of the government were sent out to search for conjurers and were paid well for their services. The Earl of Shrewsbury, a member of the council who had charge of the now captive Queen Mary, kept in his employ special detectors of conjuring. Nothing about Elizabeth's government was better organized than Cecil's detective service, and the state papers show that the ferreting out of the conjurers was by no means the least of its work. It was a service carried on, of course, as quietly as could be, and yet the cases now and again came to light and made clear to the public that the government was very fearful of conjurers' attacks upon the queen. No doubt the activity of the council put all conjurers under public suspicion and in some degree roused public resentment against them.

This brings us back to the point: What had the conjurers to do with witchcraft? By this time the answer is fairly obvious. The practisers of the magic arts, the charmers and enchanters, were responsible for developing the notions of witchcraft. The good witch brought in her company the black witch. This in itself might never have meant more than an increased activity in the church courts. But when Protestant England grew suddenly nervous for the life of the queen, when the conjurers became a source of danger to the sovereign, and the council commenced its campaign against them, the conditions had been created in which witchcraft became at once the most dangerous and detested of crimes. While the government was busy putting down the conjurers, the aroused popular sentiment was compelling the justices of the peace and then the assize judges to hang the witches.

This cannot be better illustrated than by the Abingdon affair of 1578-1579. Word had been carried to the privy council that Sir Henry Newell, justice of the peace, had committed some women near Abingdon on the charge of making waxen images. The government was at once alarmed and sent a message to Sir Henry and to the Dean of Windsor instructing them to find out the facts and to discover if the plots were directed against the queen. The precaution was unnecessary. There was no ground for believing that the designs of the women accused had included the queen. Indeed the evidence of guilt of any kind was very flimsy. But the excitement of the public had been stirred to the highest pitch. The privy council had shown its fear of the women and all four of them went to the gallows.

The same situation that brought about the attack upon witchcraft and conjuration was no doubt responsible for the transfer of jurisdiction over the crime. We have already seen that the practice of conjuration had probably been left largely to the episcopal hierarchy for punishment. The archdeacons were expected in their visitations to inquire into the practice of enchantment and magic within the parishes and to make report. In the reign of Elizabeth it became no light duty. The church set itself to suppress both the consulter and the consulted. By the largest number of recorded cases deal of course with the first class. It was very easy when sick or in trouble to go to a professed conjurer for help. It was like seeking a physician's service, as we have seen. The church frowned upon it, but the danger involved in disobeying the church was not deemed great. The cunning man or woman was of course the one who ran the great risk. When worst came to worst and the ecclesiastical power took cognizance of his profession, the best he could do was to plead that he was a "good witch" and rendered valuable services to the community. But a good end was in the eyes of the church no excuse for an evil means. The good witches were dealers with evil spirits and hence to be repressed.

Yet the church was very light in its punishments. In the matter of penalties, indeed, consulter and consulted fared nearly alike, and both got off easily. Public confession and penance in one or more specifically designated churches, usually in the nearest parish church, constituted the customary penalty. In a few instances it was coupled with the requirement that the criminal should stand in the pillory, taper in hand, at several places at stated times. The ecclesiastical records are so full of church penances that a student is led to wonder how effectual they were in shaming the penitent into better conduct. It may well be guessed that most of the criminals were not sensitive souls that would suffer profoundly from the disgrace incurred.

The control of matters of this kind was in the hands of the church by sufferance only. So long as the state was not greatly interested, the church was permitted to retain its jurisdiction. Doubtless the kings of England would have claimed the state's right of jurisdiction if it had become a matter of dispute. The church itself recognized the secular power in more important cases. In such cases the archdeacon usually acted with the justice of peace in conducting the examination, as in rendering sentence. Even then, however, the penalty was as a rule ecclesiastical. But, with the second half of the sixteenth century, there arose new conditions which resulted in the transfer of this control to the state. Henry VIII had broken with Rome and established a Church of England around the king as a centre. The power of the church belonged to the king, and, if to the king, to his ministers and his judges. Hence certain crimes that had been under the control of the church fell under the jurisdiction of the king's courts. In a more special way the same change came about through the attack of the privy council upon the conjurers. What had hitherto been a comparatively insignificant offence now became a crime against the state and was so dealt with.

The change, of course, was not sudden. It was not accomplished in a year, nor in a decade. It was going on throughout the first half of Elizabeth's reign. By the beginning of the eighties the church control was disappearing. After 1585 the state had practically exclusive jurisdiction.

We have now finished the attempt to trace the beginning of the definite movement against witchcraft in England. What witchcraft was, what it became, how it was to be distinguished from sorcery—these are questions that we have tried to answer very briefly. We have dealt in a cursory way with a series of cases extending from Anglo-Saxon days down to the fifteenth century in order to show how unfixed was the matter of jurisdiction. We have sought also to explain how Continental opinion was introduced into England through Jewel and other Marian exiles, to show what independent forces were operating in England, and to exhibit the growing influence of the charmers and their relation to the development of witchcraft; and lastly we have aimed to prove that the special danger to the queen had no little part in creating the crusade against witches. These are conclusions of some moment and a caution must be inserted. We have been treating of a period where facts are few and information fragmentary. Under such circumstances conclusions can only be tentative. Perhaps the most that can be said of them is that they are suggestions.

Benjamin Thorpe, Ancient Laws and Institutes of England (London, 1840), I, 41; Liebermann, Die Gesetze der Angelsachsen (Halle, 1906), and passages cited in his Wörterbuch under wiccan, wiccacræft; Thomas Wright, ed., A Contemporary Narrative of the Proceedings against Dame Alice Kyteler (Camden Soc., London, 1843), introd., i-iii.

George L. Burr, "The Literature of Witchcraft," printed in Papers of the Am. Hist. Assoc., IV (New York, 1890), 244.

Henry C. Lea, History of the Inquisition in Spain (New York, 1906-1907), IV, 207; cf. his History of the Inquisition of the Middle Ages (New York, 1888), III, chs. VI, VII. The most elaborate study of the rise of the delusion is that by J. Hansen, Zauberwahn, Inquisition und Hexenprozess im Mittelalter (Cologne, 1900).

Lea, Inquisition in Spain, IV, 206.

Pollock and Maitland, History of English Law (2d ed., Cambridge, 1898), II, 554.

Ibid. See also Wright, ed., Proceedings against Dame Alice Kyteler, introd., ix.

Ibid., x. Lincoln, not Norwich, as Wright's text (followed by Pollock and Maitland) has it. See the royal letter itself printed in his footnote, and cf. Rymer's Foedera (under date of 2 Jan. 1406) and the Calendar of the Patent Rolls (Henry IV, vol. III, p. 112). The bishop was Philip Repington, late the King's chaplain and confessor.

L. O. Pike, History of Crime in England (London, 1873), I, 355-356.

Ibid. Sir Harris Nicolas, Proceedings and Ordinances of the Privy Council (London, 1834-1837). IV, 114.

English Chronicle of the Reigns of Richard II, etc., edited by J. S. Davies (Camden Soc., London, 1856), 57-60.

Ramsay, Lancaster and York (Oxford, 1892), II, 31-35; Wright, ed., Proceedings against Dame Alice Kytcler, introd., xv-xvi, quoting the Chronicle of London; K. H. Vickers, Humphrey, Duke of Gloucester (London, 1907), 269-279.

Wright, ed., op. cit., introd., xvi-xvii.

James Gairdner, Life and Reign of Richard III (2d ed., London, 1879), 81-89. Jane Shore was finally tried before the court of the Bishop of London.

Sir J. F. Stephen, History of the Criminal Law of England (London, 1883), II, 410, gives five instances from Archdeacon Hale's Ecclesiastical Precedents; see extracts from Lincoln Episcopal Visitations in Archæologia (Soc. of Antiquaries, London), XLVIII, 254-255, 262; see also articles of visitation, etc., for 1547 and 1559 in David Wilkins, Concilia Magnae Britanniae (London, 1737), IV, 25, 186, 190.

An earlier statute had mentioned sorcery and witchcraft in connection with medical practitioners. The "Act concerning Phesicions and Surgeons" of 3 Henry VIII, ch. XI, was aimed against quacks. "Forasmoche as the science and connyng of Physyke and Surgerie to the perfecte knowlege wherof bee requisite bothe grete lernyng and ripe experience ys daily ... exercised by a grete multitude of ignoraunt persones ... soofarfurth that common Artificers as Smythes Wevers and Women boldely and custumably take upon theim grete curis and thyngys of great difficultie In the which they partely use socery and which crafte [sic] partely applie such medicyne unto the disease as be verey noyous," it was required that every candidate to practice medicine should be examined by the bishop of the diocese (in London by either the bishop or the Dean of St. Paul's).

Stephen, History of Criminal Law, II, 431, says of this act: "Hutchinson suggests that this act, which was passed two years after the act of the Six Articles, was intended as a 'hank upon the reformers,' that the part of it to which importance was attached was the pulling down of crosses, which, it seems, was supposed to be practised in connection with magic. Hutchinson adds that the act was never put into execution either against witches or reformers. The act was certainly passed during that period of Henry's reign when he was inclining in the Roman Catholic direction." The part of the act to which Hutchinson refers reads as follows: "And for execucion of their saide falce devyses and practises have made or caused to be made dyvers Images and pictures of men, women, childrene, Angelles or develles, beastes or fowles, ... and gyving faithe and credit to suche fantasticall practises have dygged up and pulled downe an infinite nombre of Crosses within this Realme."

Parliamentary History (London, 1751-1762), III, 229.

Ibid.

Autobiography of Edward Underhill (in Narratives of the Days of the Reformation, Camden Soc., London, 1859), 172-175.

The measure in fact reached the engrossing stage in the Commons. Both houses, however, adjourned early in April and left it unpassed.

Several of the bishops who were appointed on Elizabeth's accession had travelled in South Germany and Switzerland during the Marian period and had the opportunity of familiarizing themselves with the propaganda in these parts against witches. Thomas Bentham, who was to be bishop of Coventry and Lichfield, had retired from England to Zurich and had afterwards been preacher to the exiles at Basel. John Parkhurst, appointed bishop of Norwich, had settled in Zurich on Mary's accession. John Scory, appointed bishop of Hereford, had served as chaplain to the exiles in Geneva. Richard Cox, appointed bishop of Ely, had visited Frankfort and Strassburg. Edmund Grindall, who was to be the new bishop of London, had, during his exile, visited Strassburg, Speier, and Frankfort. Miles Coverdale, who had been bishop of Exeter but who was not reappointed, had been in Geneva in the course of his exile. There were many other churchmen of less importance who at one time or another during the Marian period visited Zurich. See Bullinger's Diarium (Basel, 1904) and Pellican's Chronikon (Basel, 1877), passim, as also Theodor Vetter, Relations between England and Zurich during the Reformation (London, 1904). At Strassburg the persecution raged somewhat later; but how thoroughly Bucer and his colleagues approved and urged it is clear from a letter of advice addressed by them in 1538 to their fellow pastor Schwebel, of Zweibrücken (printed as No. 88 in the Centuria Epistolarum appended to Schwebel's Scripta Theologica, Zweibrücken, 1605). That Bucer while in England (1549-1551) found also occasion to utter these views can hardly be doubted. These details I owe to Professor Burr.

Various dates have been assigned for Jewel's sermon, but it can be determined approximately from a passage in the discourse. In the course of the sermon he remarked: "I would wish that once again, as time should serve, there might be had a quiet and sober disputation, that each part might be required to shew their grounds without self will and without affection, not to maintain or breed contention, ... but only that the truth may be known.... For, at the last disputation that should have been, you know which party gave over and would not meddle." This is clearly an allusion to the Westminster disputation of the last of March, 1559; see John Strype, Annals of the Reformation (London, 1709-1731; Oxford, 1824), ed. of 1824, I, pt. i, 128. The sermon therefore was preached after that disputation. It may be further inferred that it was preached before Jewel's controversy with Cole in March, 1560. The words, "For at the last disputation ... you know which party gave over and would not meddle," were hardly written after Cole accepted Jewel's challenge. It was on the second Sunday before Easter (March 17), 1560, that Jewel delivered at court the discourse in which he challenged dispute on four points of church doctrine. On the next day Henry Cole addressed him a letter in which he asked him why he "yesterday in the Court and at all other times at Paul's Cross" offered rather to "dispute in these four points than in the chief matters that lie in question betwixt the Church of Rome and the Protestants." In replying to Cole on the 20th of March Jewel wrote that he stood only upon the negative and again mentioned his offer. On the 31st of March he repeated his challenge upon the four points, and upon this occasion went very much into detail in supporting them. Now, in the sermon which we are trying to date, the sermon in which allusion is made to the prevalence of witches, the four points are briefly named. It may be reasonably conjectured that this sermon anticipated the elaboration of the four points as well as the challenging sermon of March 17. It is as certain that it was delivered after Jewel's return to London from his visitation in the west country. On November 2, 1559, he wrote to Peter Martyr: "I have at last returned to London, with a body worn out by a most fatiguing journey." See Zurich Letters, I (Parker Soc., Cambridge, 1842), 44. It is interesting and significant that he adds: "We found in all places votive relics of saints, nails with which the infatuated people dreamed that Christ had been pierced, and I know not what small fragments of the sacred cross. The number of witches and sorceresses had everywhere become enormous." Jewel was consecrated Bishop of Salisbury in the following January, having been nominated in the summer of 1559 just before his western visitation. The sermon in which he alluded to witches may have been preached at any time after he returned from the west, November 2, and before March 17. It would be entirely natural that in a court sermon delivered by the newly appointed bishop of Salisbury the prevalence of witchcraft should be mentioned. It does not seem a rash guess that the sermon was preached soon after his return, perhaps in December, when the impression of what he had seen in the west was still fresh in his memory. But it is not necessary to make this supposition. Though the discourse was delivered some time after March 15, 1559, when the first bill "against Conjurations, Prophecies, etc.," was brought before the Commons (see Journal of the House of Commons, I, 57), it is not unreasonable to believe that there was some connection between the discourse and the fortunes of this bill. That connection seems the more probable on a careful reading of the Commons Journals for the first sessions of Elizabeth's Parliament. It is evident that the Elizabethan legislators were working in close cooperation with the ecclesiastical authorities. Jewel's sermon may be found in his Works (ed. for the Parker Soc., Cambridge, 1845-1850), II, 1025-1034. (For the correspondence with Cole see I, 26 ff.)

For assistance in dating this sermon the writer wishes to express his special obligation to Professor Burr.

Strype, Annals of the Reformation, I, pt. i, 11. He may, indeed, mean to ascribe it, not to the sermon, but to the evils alleged by the sermon.

In the contemporary account entitled A True and just Recorde of the Information, Examination, and Confession of all the Witches taken at St. Oses.... Written ... by W. W. (1582), next leaf after B 5, we read: "there is a man of great cunning and knowledge come over lately unto our Queenes Maiestie, which hath advertised her what a companie and number of witches be within Englande." This probably refers to Jewel.

See ibid., B 5 verso: "I and other of her Justices have received commission for the apprehending of as many as are within these limites." This was written later, but the event is referred to as following what must have been Bishop Jewel's sermon.

Thomas Wright, Narratives of Sorcery and Magic (ed. of N. Y., 1852), 126 ff.; see also his Elizabeth and her Times (London, 1838), I, 457, letter of Shrewsbury to Burghley.

Wright, Narratives, 130 ff.

Ibid., 134.

See Reginald Scot, The Discoverie of Witchcraft (London, 1584; reprinted, Brinsley Nicholson, ed., London, 1886), 4.

A very typical instance was that in Kent in 1597, see Archæologia Cantiana (Kent Archæological Soc., London), XXVI, 21. Several good instances are given in the Hertfordshire County Session Rolls (compiled by W. J. Hardy, London, 1905), I; see also J. Raine, ed., Depositions respecting the Rebellion of 1569, Witchcraft, and other Ecclesiastical Proceedings from the Court of Durham (Surtees Soc., London, 1845), 99, 100.

J. Raine, ed., Injunctions and other Ecclesiastical Proceedings of Richard Barnes, Bishop of Durham (Surtees Soc., London, 1850), 18; H. Owen and J. B. Blakeway, History of Shrewsbury (London, 1825), II, 364, art. 43.

Arch. Cant., XXVI, 19.

Hertfordshire Co. Sess. Rolls, I, 3.

See Depositions ... from the Court of Durham, 99; Arch. Cant., XXVI, 21; W. H. Hale, Precedents, etc. (London, 1847), 148, 185.

Hale, op. cit., 163; Middlesex County Records, ed. by J. C. Jeaffreson (London, 1892), I, 84, 94.

For an instance of how a "wise woman" feared this very thing, see Hale, op. cit., 147.

See Witches taken at St. Oses, E; also Dr. Barrow's opinion in the pamphlet entitled The most strange and admirable discoverie of the three Witches of Warboys, arraigned, convicted and executed at the last assizes at Huntingdon.... (London, 1593).

Folk Lore Soc. Journal, II, 157-158, where this story is quoted from a work by "Wm. Clouues, Mayster in Chirurgery," published in 1588. He only professed to have "reade" of it, so that it is perhaps just a pleasant tradition. If it is nothing more than that, it is at least an interesting evidence of opinion.

Strype, Annals of the Reformation, I, pt. i, 9-10; Dictionary of National Biography, article on Anthony Fortescue, by G. K. Fortescue.

Strype, op. cit., I, pt. i, 546, 555-558; also Wright, Elizabeth and her Times, I, 121, where a letter from Cecil to Sir Thomas Smith is printed.

The interest which the privy council showed in sorcery and witchcraft during the earlier part of the reign is indicated in the following references: Acts of the Privy Council, new series, VII, 6, 22, 200-201; X, 220, 382; XI, 22, 36, 292, 370-371, 427; XII, 21-22, 23, 26, 29, 34, 102, 251; Calendar of State Papers, Domestic, 1547-1580, 137, 142; id., 1581-1590, 29, 220, 246-247; id., Add. 1580-1625, 120-121; see also John Strype, Life of Sir Thomas Smith (London, 1698; Oxford, 1820), ed. of 1820, 127-129. The case mentioned in Cal. St. P., Dom., 1581-1590, 29, was probably a result of the activity of the privy council. The case in id., Add., 1580-1625, 120-121, is an instance of where the accused was suspected of both witchcraft and "high treason touching the supremacy." Nearly all of the above mentioned references to the activity of the privy council refer to the first half of the reign and a goodly proportion to the years 1578-1582.

Acts P. C., n. s., XI, 292.

Strype, Sir Thomas Smith, 127-129.

A Rehearsall both straung and true of hainous and horrible acts committed by Elizabeth Stile, etc. (for full title see appendix). This pamphlet is in black letter. Its account is confirmed by the reference in Acts P. C., n. s., XI, 22. See also Scot, Discoverie, 51, 543.

An aged widow had been committed to gaol on the testimony of her neighbors that she was "lewde, malitious, and hurtful to the people." An ostler, after he had refused to give her relief, had suffered a pain. So far as the account goes, this was the sum of the evidence against the woman. Unhappily she waited not on the order of her trial but made voluble confession and implicated five others, three of whom were without doubt professional enchanters. She had met, she said, with Mother Dutten, Mother Devell, and Mother Margaret, and "concluded several hainous and vilanous practices." The deaths of five persons whom she named were the outcome of their concerted plans. For the death of a sixth she avowed entire responsibility. This amazing confession may have been suggested to her piece by piece, but it was received at full value. That she included others in her guilt was perhaps because she responded to the evident interest aroused by such additions, or more likely because she had grudges unsatisfied. The women were friendless, three of the four were partially dependent upon alms, there was no one to come to their help, and they were convicted. The man that had been arraigned, a "charmer," seems to have gone free.

Injunctions ... of ... Bishop of Durham, 18, 84, 99; Visitations of Canterbury, in Arch. Cant., XXVI; Hale, Precedents, 1475-1640, 147, etc.

Arch. Cant., XXVI, passim; Hale, op. cit., 147, 148, 163, 185; Mrs. Lynn Linton, Witch Stories (London, 1861; new ed., 1883), 144.

See Hale, op. cit., 148, 157.

Hale, op. cit., 148; Depositions ... from the Court of Durham, 99; Arch. Cant., XXVI, 21.

Hale, op. cit., 148, 185.

Ibid., 157.

Denham Tracts (Folk Lore Soc., London), II, 332; John Sykes, Local Record ... of Remarkable Events ... in Northumberland, Durham, ... etc. (2d ed., Newcastle, 1833-1852), I, 79.

See, for example, Acts P. C., n. s., VII, 32 (1558).

Cal. St. P., Dom., 1547-1580, 173. Instance where the Bishop of London seems to have examined a case and turned it over to the privy council.

Rachel Pinder and Agnes Bridges, who pretended to be possessed by the Devil, were examined before the "person of St. Margarets in Lothberry," and the Mayor of London, as well as some justices of the peace. They later made confession before the Archbishop of Canterbury and some justices of the peace. See the black letter pamphlet, The discloysing of a late counterfeyted possession by the devyl in two maydens within the Citie of London [1574].

Francis Coxe came before the queen rather than the church. He narrates his experiences in A short treatise declaringe the detestable wickednesse of magicall sciences, ... (1561). Yet John Walsh, a man with a similar record, came before the commissary of the Bishop of Exeter. See *The Examination of John Walsh before Master Thomas Williams, Commissary to the Reverend father in God, William, bishop of Excester, upon certayne Interrogatories touchyng Wytch-crafte and Sorcerye, in the presence of divers gentlemen and others, the XX of August, 1566.*

We say "practically," because instances of church jurisdiction come to light now and again throughout the seventeenth century.

CHAPTER II.: Witchcraft under Elizabeth.

The year 1566 is hardly less interesting in the history of English witchcraft than 1563. It has been seen that the new statute passed in 1563 was the beginning of a vigorous prosecution by the state of the detested agents of the evil one. In 1566 occurred the first important trial known to us in the new period. That trial deserves note not only on its own account, but because it was recorded in the first of the long series of witch chap-books—if we may so call them. A very large proportion of our information about the execution of the witches is derived from these crude pamphlets, briefly recounting the trials. The witch chap-book was a distinct species. In the days when the chronicles were the only newspapers it was what is now the "extra," brought out to catch the public before the sensation had lost its flavor. It was of course a partisan document, usually a vindication of the worthy judge who had condemned the guilty, with some moral and religious considerations by the respectable and righteous author. A terribly serious bit of history it was that he had to tell and he told it grimly and without pity. Such comedy as lights up the gloomy black-letter pages was quite unintentional. He told a story too that was full of details trivial enough in themselves, but details that give many glimpses into the every-day life of the lower classes in town and country.

The pamphlet of 1566 was brief and compact of information. It was entitled The examination and confession of certaine Wytches at Chensforde in the Countie of Essex before the Quenes Maiesties Judges the XXVI daye of July anno 1566. The trial there recorded is one that presents some of the most curious and inexplicable features in the annals of English witchcraft. The personnel of the "size" court is mysterious. At the first examination "Doctor Cole" and "Master Foscue" were present. Both men are easily identified. Doctor Cole was the Reverend Thomas Cole, who had held several places in Essex and had in 1564 been presented to the rectory of Stanford Rivers, about ten miles from Chelmsford. Master Foscue was unquestionably Sir John Fortescue, later Chancellor of the Exchequer, and at this time keeper of the great wardrobe. On the second examination Sir Gilbert Gerard, the queen's attorney, and John Southcote, justice of the queen's bench, were present. Why Southcote should be present is perfectly clear. It is not so easy to understand about the others. Was the attorney-general acting as presiding officer, or was he conducting the prosecution? The latter hypothesis is of course more consistent with his position. But what were the rector of Stanford Rivers and the keeper of the great wardrobe doing there? Had Doctor Cole been appointed in recognition of the claims of the church? And the keeper of the wardrobe, what was the part that he played? One cannot easily escape the conclusion that the case was deemed one of unusual significance. Perhaps the privy council had heard of something that alarmed it and had delegated these four men, all known at Elizabeth's court, to examine into the matter in connection with the assizes.

The examinations themselves present features of more interest to the psychologist than to the historical student. Yet they have some importance in the understanding of witchcraft as a social phenomenon. Elizabeth Francis, when examined, confessed with readiness to various "vilanies." From her grandmother she said she had as a child received a white spotted cat, named Sathan, whom she had fed, and who gave her what she asked for. "She desired to have one Andrew Byles to her husband, which was a man of some welth, and the cat dyd promyse she shold." But the promise proved illusory. The man left her without marriage and then she "willed Sathan ... to touch his body, whych he forthewith dyd, whereof he died." Once again she importuned Satan for a husband. This time she gained one "not so rich as the other." She bore a daughter to him, but the marriage was an unhappy one. "They lived not so quietly as she desyred, beinge stirred to much unquietnes and moved to swearing and cursinge." Thereupon she employed the spirit to kill her child and to lame her husband. After keeping the cat fifteen years she turned it over to Mother Waterhouse, "a pore woman."

Mother Waterhouse was now examined. She had received the cat and kept it "a great while in woll in a pot." She had then turned it into a toad. She had used it to kill geese, hogs, and cattle of her neighbors. At length she had employed it to kill a neighbor whom she disliked, and finally her own husband. The woman's eighteen-year-old daughter, Joan, was now called to the stand and confirmed the fact that her mother kept a toad. She herself had one day been refused a piece of bread and cheese by a neighbor's child and had invoked the toad's help. The toad promised to assist her if she would surrender her soul. She did so. Then the toad haunted the neighbor's girl in the form of a dog with horns. The mother was again called to the stand and repeated the curious story told by her daughter.

Now the neighbor's child, Agnes Brown, was brought in to testify. Her story tallied in some of its details with that of the two Waterhouse women; she had been haunted by the horned dog, and she added certain descriptions of its conduct that revealed good play of childish imagination.

The attorney put some questions, but rather to lead on the witnesses than to entangle them. He succeeded, however, in creating a violent altercation between the Waterhouses on the one hand, and Agnes Brown on the other, over trifling matters of detail. At length he offered to release Mother Waterhouse if she would make the spirit appear in the court. The offer was waived. The attorney then asked, "When dyd thye Cat suck of thy bloud?" "Never," said she. He commanded the jailer to lift up the "kercher" on the woman's head. He did so and the spots on her face and nose where she had pricked herself for the evil spirit were exposed.

The jury retired. Two days later Agnes Waterhouse suffered the penalty of the law, not however until she had added to her confessions.

The case is a baffling one. We can be quite sure that the pamphlet account is incomplete. One would like to know more about the substance of fact behind this evidence. Did the parties that were said to have been killed by witchcraft really die at the times specified? Either the facts of their deaths were well known in the community and were fitted with great cleverness into the story Mother Waterhouse told, or the jurors and the judges neglected the first principles of common sense and failed to inquire about the facts. The questions asked by the queen's attorney reveal hardly more than an unintelligent curiosity to know the rest of the story. He shows just one saving glint of skepticism. He offered to release Mother Waterhouse if she would materialize her spirit.

Mother Waterhouse was her own worst enemy. Her own testimony was the principal evidence presented against her, and yet she denied guilt on one particular upon which the attorney-general had interrogated her. This might lead one to suppose that her answers were the haphazard replies of a half-witted woman. But the supposition is by no means consistent with the very definite and clear-cut nature of her testimony. It is useless to try to unravel the tangles of the case. It is possible that under some sort of duress—although there is no evidence of this—she had deliberately concocted a story to fit those of Elizabeth Francis and Agnes Brown, and that her daughter, hearing her mother's narrative in court—a very possible thing in that day—had fitted hers into it. It is conceivable too that Mother Waterhouse had yielded merely to the wish to amaze her listeners. It is a more probable supposition that the questions asked of her by the judge were based upon the accusations already made by Agnes Brown and that they suggested to her the main outlines of her narrative.

Elizabeth Francis, who had been the first accused and who had accused Mother Waterhouse, escaped. Whether it was because she had turned state's evidence or because she had influential friends in the community, we do not know. It is possible that the judges recognized that her confession was unsupported by the testimony of other witnesses. Such a supposition, however, credits the court with keener discrimination than seems ever to have been exhibited in such cases in the sixteenth century.

But, though Elizabeth Francis had escaped, her reputation as a dangerous woman in the community was fixed. Thirteen years later she was again put on trial before the itinerant justices. This brings us to the second trial of witches at Chelmsford in 1579. Mistress Francis's examination elicited less than in the first trial. She had cursed a woman "and badde a mischief to light uppon her." The woman, she understood, was grievously pained. She followed the course that she had taken before and began to accuse others. We know very little as to the outcome. At least one of the women accused went free because "manslaughter or murder was not objected against her." Three women, however, were condemned and executed. One of them was almost certainly Elleine Smith, daughter of a woman hanged as a witch,—another illustration of the persistence of suspicion against the members of a family.

The Chelmsford affair of 1579 was not unlike that of 1566. There were the same tales of spirits that assumed animal forms. The young son of Elleine Smith declared that his mother kept three spirits, Great Dick in a wicker bottle, Little Dick in a leathern bottle, and Willet in a wool-pack. Goodwife Webb saw "a thyng like a black Dogge goe out of her doore." But the general character of the testimony in the second trial bore no relation to that in the first. There was no agreement of the different witnesses. The evidence was haphazard. The witch and another woman had a falling out—fallings out were very common. Next day the woman was taken ill. This was the sort of unimpeachable testimony that was to be accepted for a century yet. In the affair of 1566 the judges had made some attempt at quizzing the witnesses, but in 1579 all testimony was seemingly rated at par. In both instances the proof rested mainly upon confession. Every woman executed had made confessions of guilt. This of course was deemed sufficient. Nevertheless the courts were beginning to introduce other methods of proving the accused guilty. The marks on Agnes Waterhouse had been uncovered at the request of the attorney-general; and at her execution she had been questioned about her ability to say the Lord's Prayer and other parts of the service. Neither of these matters was emphasized, but the mention of them proves that notions were already current that were later to have great vogue.

The Chelmsford cases find their greatest significance, however, not as illustrations of the use and abuse of evidence, but because they exemplify the continuity of the witch movement. That continuity finds further illustration in the fact that there was a third alarm at Chelmsford in 1589, which resulted in three more executions. But in this case the women involved seem, so far as we know, to have had no connection with the earlier cases. The fate of Elizabeth Francis and that of Elleine Smith are more instructive as proof of the long-standing nature of a community suspicion. Elleine could not escape her mother's reputation nor Elizabeth her own.

Both these women seem to have been of low character at any rate. Elizabeth had admitted illicit amours, and Elleine may very well have been guilty on the same count. All of the women involved in the two trials were in circumstances of wretched poverty; most, if not all, of them were dependent upon begging and the poor relief for support.

It is easy to imagine the excitement in Essex that these trials must have produced. The accused had represented a wide territory in the county. The women had been fetched to Chelmsford from towns as far apart as Hatfield-Peverel and Maldon. It is not remarkable that three years later than the affair of 1579 there should have been another outbreak in the county, this time in a more aggravated form. St. Oses, or St. Osyth's, to the northeast of Chelmsford, was to be the scene of the most remarkable affair of its kind in Elizabethan times. The alarm began with the formulation of charges against a woman of the community. Ursley Kemp was a poor woman of doubtful reputation. She rendered miscellaneous services to her neighbors. She acted as midwife, nursed children, and added to her income by "unwitching" the diseased. Like other women of the sort, she was looked upon with suspicion. Hence, when she had been refused the nursing of the child of Grace Thurlow, a servant of that Mr. Darcy who was later to try her, and when the child soon afterward fell out of its cradle and broke its neck, the mother suspected Ursley of witchcraft. Nevertheless she did not refuse her help when she "began to have a lameness in her bones." Ursley promised to unwitch her and seemingly kept her word, for the lameness disappeared. Then it was that the nurse-woman asked for the twelve-pence she had been promised and was refused. Grace pleaded that she was a "poore and needie woman." Ursley became angry and threatened to be even with her. The lameness reappeared and Grace Thurlow was thoroughly convinced that Ursley was to blame. When the case was carried before the justices of the peace, the accused woman denied that she was guilty of anything more than unwitching the afflicted. That she had learned, she said, ten or more years ago from a woman now deceased. She was committed to the assizes, and Justice Brian Darcy, whose servant Grace Thurlow had started the trouble, took the case in hand. He examined her eight-year-old "base son," who gave damning evidence against his mother. She fed four imps, Tyffin, Tittey, Piggen, and Jacket. The boy's testimony and the judge's promise that if she would confess the truth she "would have favour," seemed to break down the woman's resolution. "Bursting out with weeping she fell upon her knees and confessed that she had four spirits." Two of them she had used for laming, two for killing. Not only the details of her son's evidence, but all the earlier charges, she confirmed step by step, first in private confessions to the judge and then publicly at the court sessions. The woman's stories tallied with those of all her accusers and displayed no little play of imagination in the orientation of details. Not content with thus entangling herself in a fearful web of crime, she went on to point out other women guilty of similar witchcrafts. Four of those whom she named were haled before the justice. Elizabeth Bennett, who spun wool for a cloth-maker, was one of those most vehemently accused, but she denied knowledge of any kind of witchcraft. It had been charged against her that she kept some wool hidden in a pot under some stones in her house. She denied at first the possession of this potent and malignant charm; but, influenced by the gentle urgings of Justice Darcy, she gave way, as Ursley Kemp had done, and, breaking all restraint, poured forth wild stories of devilish crimes committed through the assistance of her imps.

But why should we trace out the confessions, charges, and counter-charges that followed? The stories that were poured forth continued to involve a widening group until sixteen persons were under accusation of the most awful crimes, committed by demoniacal agency. As at Chelmsford, they were the dregs of the lower classes, women with illegitimate children, some of them dependent upon public support. It will be seen that in some respects the panic bore a likeness to those that had preceded. The spirits, which took extraordinary and bizarre forms, were the offspring of the same perverted imaginations, but they had assumed new shapes. Ursley Kemp kept a white lamb, a little gray cat, a black cat, and a black toad. There were spirits of every sort, "two little thyngs like horses, one white, the other black'"; six "spirits like cowes ... as big as rattles"; spirits masquerading as blackbirds. One spirit strangely enough remained invisible. It will be observed by the reader that the spirits almost fitted into a color scheme. Very vivid colors were those preferred in their spirits by these St. Oses women. The reader can see, too, that the confessions showed the influence of the great cat tradition.

We have seen the readiness with which the deluded women made confession. Some of the confessions were poured forth as from souls long surcharged with guilt. But not all of them came in this way. Margerie Sammon, who had testified against one of her neighbors, was finally herself caught in the web of accusation in which a sister had also been involved. She was accused by her sister. "I defie thee," she answered, "though thou art my sister." But her sister drew her aside and "whyspered her in the eare," after which, with "great submission and many teares," she made a voluble confession. One wonders about that whispered consultation. Had her sister perhaps suggested that the justice was offering mercy to those who confessed? For Justice Darcy was very liberal with his promises of mercy and absolutely unscrupulous about breaking them. It is gratifying to be able to record that there was yet a remnant left who confessed nothing at all and stood stubborn to the last. One of them was Margaret Grevel, who denied the accusations against her. She "saith that shee herselfe hath lost severall bruings and bakings of bread, and also swine, but she never did complaine thereof: saying that shee wished her gere were at a stay and then shee cared not whether shee were hanged or burnt or what did become of her." Annis Herd was another who stuck to her innocence. She could recall various incidents mentioned by her accusers; it was true that she had talked to Andrew West about getting a pig, it was true that she had seen Mr. Harrison at his parsonage gathering plums and had asked for some and been refused. But she denied that she had any imps or that she had killed any one.

The use of evidence in this trial would lead one to suppose that in England no rules of evidence were yet in existence. The testimony of children ranging in age from six to nine was eagerly received. No objection indeed was made to the testimony of a neighbor who professed to have overheard what he deemed an incriminating statement. As a matter of fact the remark, if made, was harmless enough. Expert evidence was introduced in a roundabout way by the statement offered in court that a physician had suspected that a certain case was witchcraft. Nothing was excluded. The garrulous women had been give free rein to pile up their silly accusations against one another. Not until the trial was nearing its end does it seem to have occurred to Brian Darcy to warn a woman against making false charges.

It will be recalled that in the Chelmsford trials Mother Waterhouse had been found to have upon her certain marks, yet little emphasis had been laid upon them. In the trials of 1582 the proof drawn from these marks was deemed of the first importance and the judge appointed juries of women to make examination. No artist has yet dared to paint the picture of the gloating female inquisitors grouped around their naked and trembling victim, a scene that was to be enacted in many a witch trial. And it is well, for the scene would be too repellent and brutal for reproduction. In the use of these specially instituted juries there was no care to get unbiassed decisions. One of the inquisitors appointed to examine Cystley Celles had already served as witness against her.

It is hard to refrain from an indictment of the hopelessly prejudiced justice who gathered the evidence. To entrap the defendants seems to have been his end. In the account which he wrote he seems to have feared lest the public should fail to understand how his cleverness ministered to the conviction of the women.

"There is a man," he wrote, "of great cunning and knowledge come over lately unto our Queenes Maiestie, which hath advertised her what a companie and number of witches be within Englande: whereupon I and other of her Justices have received commission for the apprehending of as many as are within these limites." No doubt he hoped to attract royal notice and win favor by his zeal.

The Chelmsford affairs and that at St. Oses were the three remarkable trials of their kind in the first part of Elizabeth's reign. They furnish some evidence of the progress of superstition. The procedure in 1582 reveals considerable advance over that of 1566. The theory of diabolic agency had been elaborated. The testimony offered was gaining in complexity and in variety. New proofs of guilt were being introduced as well as new methods of testing the matter. In the second part of Elizabeth's reign we have but one trial of unusual interest, that at Warboys in Huntingdonshire. This, we shall see, continued the elaboration of the witch procedure. It was a case that attracted probably more notice at the time than any other in the sixteenth century. The accidental fancy of a child and the pronouncement of a baffled physician were in this instance the originating causes of the trouble. One of the children of Sir Robert Throckmorton, head of a prominent family in Huntingdonshire, was taken ill. It so happened that a neighbor, by name Alice Samuel, called at the house and the ailing and nervous child took the notion that the woman was a witch and cried out against her. "Did you ever see, sayd the child, one more like a witch then she is; take off her blacke thrumbd cap, for I cannot abide to looke on her." Her parents apparently thought nothing of this at the time. When Dr. Barrow, an eminent physician of Cambridge, having treated the child for two of the diseases of children, and without success, asked the mother and father if any witchcraft were suspected, he was answered in the negative. The Throckmortons were by no means quick to harbor a suspicion. But when two and then three other children in the family fell ill and began in the same way to designate Mother Samuel as a witch, the parents were more willing to heed the hint thrown out by the physician. The suspected woman was forcibly brought by Gilbert Pickering, an uncle of the children, into their presence. The children at once fell upon the ground "strangely tormented," and insisted upon scratching Mother Samuel's hand. Meantime Lady Cromwell visited at the Throckmorton house, and, after an interview with Alice Samuel, suffered in her dreams from her till at length she fell ill and died, something over a year later. This confirmed what had been suspicion. To detail all the steps taken to prove Mother Samuel guilty is unnecessary. A degree of caution was used which was remarkable. Henry Pickering, a relative, and some of his fellow scholars at Cambridge made an investigation into the case, but decided with the others that the woman was guilty. Mother Samuel herself laid the whole trouble to the children's "wantonness." Again and again she was urged by the children to confess. "Such were the heavenly and divine speeches of the children in their fits to this old woman ... as that if a man had heard it he would not have thought himself better edified at ten sermons." The parents pleaded with her to admit her responsibility for the constantly recurring sickness of their children, but she denied bitterly that she was to blame. She was compelled to live at the Throckmorton house and to be a witness constantly to the strange behavior of the children. The poor creature was dragged back and forth, watched and experimented upon in a dozen ways, until it is little wonder that she grew ill and spent her nights in groaning. She was implored to confess and told that all might yet be well. For a long time she persisted in her denial, but at length in a moment of weakness, when the children had come out of their fits at her chance exhortation to them, she became convinced that she was guilty and exclaimed, "O sir, I have been the cause of all this trouble to your children." The woman, who up to this time had shown some spirit, had broken down. She now confessed that she had given her soul to the Devil. A clergyman was hastily sent for, who preached a sermon of repentance, upon which the distracted woman made a public confession. But on the next day, after she had been refreshed by sleep and had been in her own home again, she denied her confession. The constable now prepared to take the woman as well as her daughter to the Bishop of Lincoln, and the frightened creature again made a confession. In the presence of the bishop she reiterated her story in detail and gave the names of her spirits. She was put in gaol at Huntingdon and with her were imprisoned her daughter Agnes and her husband John Samuel, who were now accused by the Throckmorton children, and all three were tried at the assizes in Huntingdon before Judge Fenner. The facts already narrated were given in evidence, the seizures of the children at the appearance of any of the Samuel family, the certainty with which the children could with closed eyes pick Mother Samuel out of a crowd and scratch her, the confessions of the crazed creature, all these evidences were given to the court. But the strongest proof was that given in the presence of the court. The daughter Agnes Samuel was charged to repeat, "As I am a witch and consenting to the death of Lady Cromwell, I charge thee, come out of her." At this charge the children would at once recover from their fits. But a charge phrased negatively, "As I am no witch," was ineffectual. And the affirmative charge, when tried by some other person, had no result. This was deemed conclusive proof. The woman was beyond doubt guilty. The same method was applied with equally successful issue to the father. When he refused to use the words of the charge he was warned by the judge that he would endanger his life. He gave way

It is needless to say that the grand jury arraigned all three of the family and that the "jury of life and death" found them guilty. It needed but a five hours' trial. The mother was induced to plead pregnancy as a delay to execution, but after an examination by a jury was adjudged not pregnant. The daughter had been urged to make the same defence, but spiritedly replied, "It shall never be said that I was both a witch and a whore." At the execution the mother made another confession, in which she implicated her husband, but refused to the end to accuse her daughter.

From beginning to end it had been the strong against the weak. Sir Robert Throckmorton, Sir Henry Cromwell, William Wickham, Bishop of Lincoln, the justices of the peace, Justice Fenner of the king's court, the Cambridge scholars, the "Doctor of Divinitie," and two other clergymen, all were banded together against this poor but respectable family. In some respects the trial reminds us of one that was to take place ninety-nine years later in Massachusetts. The part played by the children in the two instances was very similar. Mother Samuel had hit the nail on the head when she said that the trouble was due to the children's "wantonness." Probably the first child had really suffered from some slight ailment. The others were imitators eager to gain notice and pleased with their success; and this fact was realized by some people at the time. "It had been reported by some in the county, those that thought themselves wise, that this Mother Samuel ... was an old simple woman, and that one might make her by fayre words confesse what they would." Moreover the tone of the writer's defense makes it evident that others beside Mother Samuel laid the action of the Throckmorton children to "wantonness." And six years later Samuel Harsnett, chaplain to the Bishop of London and a man already influential, called the account of the affair "a very ridiculous booke" and evidently believed the children guilty of the same pretences as William Somers, whose confessions of imposture he was relating.

We have already observed that the Warboys affair was the only celebrated trial of its sort in the last part of Elizabeth's reign—that is, from the time of Reginald Scot to the accession of James I. This does not mean that the superstition was waning or that the trials were on the decrease. The records show that the number of trials was steadily increasing. They were more widely distributed. London was still the centre of the belief. Chief-Justice Anderson sent Joan Kerke to Tyburn and the Middlesex sessions were still occupied with accusations. The counties adjacent to it could still claim more than two-thirds of the executions. But a far wider area was infected with the superstition. Norfolk in East Anglia, Leicester, Nottingham and Derby in the Midlands, and York and Northumberland in the North were all involved.

The truth is that there are two tendencies that appear very clearly towards the last part of Elizabeth's reign. On the one hand the feeling of the people against witchcraft was growing in intensity, while on the other the administration at London was inclined to be more lenient. Pardons and reprieves were issued to women already condemned, while some attempt was made to curb popular excitement. The attitude of the queen towards the celebrated John Dee was an instance in point. Dee was an eminent alchemist, astrologer, and spiritualist of his time. He has left a diary which shows us his half mystic, half scientific pursuits. In the earlier part of Mary's reign he had been accused of attempting poison or magic against the queen and had been imprisoned and examined by the privy council and by the Star Chamber. At Elizabeth's accession he had cast the horoscope for her coronation day, and he was said to have revealed to the queen who were her enemies at foreign courts. More than once afterwards Dee was called upon by the queen to render her services when she was ill or when some mysterious design against her person was feared. While he dealt with many curious things, he had consistently refused to meddle with conjuring. Indeed he had rebuked the conjurer Hartley and had refused to help the bewitched Margaret Byrom of Cleworth in Lancashire. Sometime about 1590 Dee's enemies—and he had many—put in circulation stories of his success as a conjurer. It was the more easy to do, because for a long time he had been suspected by many of unlawful dealings with spirits. His position became dangerous. He appealed to Elizabeth for protection and she gave him assurance that he might push on with his studies. Throughout her life the queen continued to stand by Dee, and it was not until a new sovereign came to the throne that he again came into danger. But the moral of the incident is obvious. The privy council, so nervous about the conjurers in the days of Mary, Queen of Scots, and the Catholic and Spanish plots, was now resting easier and refused to be affrighted.

We have already referred to the pardons issued as one of the evidences of the more lenient policy of the government. That policy appeared too in the lessening rigor of the assize judges. The first half of Elizabeth's reign had been marked by few acquittals. Nearly half the cases of which we have record in the second part resulted in the discharge of the accused. Whether the judges were taking their cue from the privy council or whether some of them were feeling the same reaction against the cruelty of the prosecutions, it is certain that there was a considerable nullifying of the force of the belief. We shall see in the chapter on Reginald Scot that his Discoverie of Witchcraft was said to have "affected the magistracy and the clergy." It is hard to lay one's finger upon influences of this sort, but we can hardly doubt that there was some connection between Scot's brave indictment of the witch-triers and the lessening severity of court verdicts. When George Gifford, the non-conformist clergyman at Maiden, wrote his Dialogue concerning Witches, in which he earnestly deprecated the conviction of so many witches, he dedicated the book "to the Right Worshipful Maister Robert Clarke, one of her Maiesties Barons of her Highnesse Court of the Exchequer," and wrote that he had been "delighted to heare and see the wise and godly course used upon the seate of justice by your worship, when such have bene arraigned." Unfortunately there is not much evidence of this kind.

One other fact must not be overlooked. A large percentage of the cases that went against the accused were in towns judicially independent of the assize courts. At Faversham, at Lynn, at Yarmouth, and at Leicester the local municipal authorities were to blame for the hanging of witches. The regular assize courts had nothing to do with the matter. The case at Faversham in Kent was unusual. Joan Cason was indicted for bewitching to death a three-year-old child. Eight of her neighbors, seven of them women, "poore people," testified against her. The woman took up her own cause with great spirit and exposed the malicious dealings of her adversaries and also certain controversies betwixt her and them. "But although she satisfied the bench," says Holinshed, "and all the jurie touching hir innocencie ... she ... confessed that a little vermin, being of colour reddish, of stature lesse than a rat ... did ... haunt her house." She was willing too to admit illicit relations with one Mason, whose housekeeper she had been—probably the original cause of her troubles. The jury acquitted her of witchcraft, but found her guilty of the "invocation of evil spirits," intending to send her to the pillory. While the mayor was admonishing her, a lawyer called attention to the point that the invocation of evil spirits had been made a felony. The mayor sentenced the woman to execution. But, "because there was no matter of invocation given in evidence against hir, ... hir execution was staied by the space of three daies." Sundry preachers tried to wring confessions from her, but to no purpose. Yet she made so godly an end, says the chronicler, that "manie now lamented hir death which were before hir utter enimies." The case illustrates vividly the clumsiness of municipal court procedure. The mayor's court was unfamiliar with the law and utterly unable to avert the consequences of its own finding. In the regular assize courts, Joan Cason would probably have been sentenced to four public appearances in the pillory.

The differences between the first half and the second half of Elizabeth's reign have not been deemed wide enough by the writer to justify separate treatment. The whole reign was a time when the superstition was gaining ground. Yet in the span of years from Reginald Scot to the death of Elizabeth there was enough of reaction to justify a differentiation of statistics. In both periods, and more particularly in the first, we may be sure that some of the records have been lost and that a thorough search of local archives would reveal some trials of which we have at present no knowledge. It was a time rich in mention of witch trials, but a time too when but few cases were fully described. Scot's incidental references to the varied experiences of Sir Roger Manwood and of his uncle Sir Thomas Scot merely confirm an impression gained from the literature of the time that the witch executions were becoming, throughout the seventies and early eighties, too common to be remarkable. For the second period we have record of probably a larger percentage of all the cases. For the whole time from 1563, when the new law went into effect, down to 1603, we have records of nearly fifty executions. Of these just about two-thirds occurred in the earlier period, while of the acquittals two-thirds belong to the later period. It would be rash to attach too much significance to these figures. As a matter of fact, the records are so incomplete that the actual totals have little if any meaning and only the proportions can be considered. Yet it looks as if the forces which caused the persecution of witches in England were beginning to abate; and it may fairly be inquired whether some new factor may not have entered into the situation. It is time to speak of Reginald Scot and of the exorcists.

Who from a confession made in 1579 seems to have been her sister. See the pamphlet A Detection of damnable driftes, practised by three Witches arraigned at Chelmsforde in Essex at the last Assizes there holden, which were executed in Aprill, 1579 (London, 1579).

E. g.: "I was afearde for he [the dog with horns] skypped and leaped to and fro, and satte on the toppe of a nettle."

Whether Agnes Waterhouse had a "daggar's knife" and whether the dog had the face of an ape.

An offer which indicates that he was acting as judge.

She was questioned on her church habits. She claimed to be a regular attendant; she "prayed right hartely there." She admitted, however, that she prayed "in laten" because Sathan would not let her pray in English.

There is of course the further possibility that the pamphlet account was largely invented. A critical examination of the pamphlet tends to establish its trustworthiness. See appendix A, § 1.

Alice Chandler was probably hanged at this time. The failure to mention her name is easily explained when we remember that the pamphlet was issued in two parts, as soon as possible after the event. Alice Chandler's case probably did not come up for trial until the two parts of the pamphlet had already been published. See A Detection of damnable driftes.

Mother Staunton, who had apparently made some pretensions to the practice of magic, was arraigned on several charges. She had been refused her requests by several people, who had thereupon suffered some ills.

It is possible that the whole affair started from the whim of a sick child, who, when she saw Elleine Smith, cried, "Away with the witch."

A caution here. The pamphlets were hastily compiled and perhaps left out important facts.

Her eight-year-old boy was probably illegitimate.

Mother Waterhouse's knowledge of Latin, if that is more than the fiction of a Protestant pamphleteer, is rather remarkable.

Allowance must be made for a very prejudiced reporter, i. e., the judge himself.

These details were very probably suggested to her by the judge.

Who promised her also "favour."

The detestable methods of Justice Darcy come out in the case of a woman from whom he threatened to remove her imps if she did not confess, and by that means trapped her into the incriminating statement, "That shal ye not."

William Hooke had heard William Newman "bid the said Ales his wife to beate it away." Comparable with this was the evidence of Margerie Sammon who "sayeth that the saide widow Hunt did tell her that shee had harde the said Joan Pechey, being in her house, verie often to chide and vehemently speaking, ... and sayth that shee went in to see, ... shee founde no bodie but herselfe alone."

Reginald Scot, Discoverie of Witchcraft, 542, says of this trial, "In the meane time let anie man with good consideration peruse that booke published by W. W. and it shall suffie to satisfie him in all that may be required.... See whether the witnesses be not single, of what credit, sex, and age they are; namelie lewd miserable and envious poore people; most of them which speake to anie purpose being old women and children of the age of 4, 5, 6, 7, 8, or 9 yeares."

There can be no doubt that Brian Darcy either wrote the account himself or dictated it to "W. W." The frequent use of "me," meaning by that pronoun the judge, indicates that he was responsible.

It is some relief in this trial to read the testimony of John Tendering about William Byett. He had a cow "in a strange case." He could not lift it. He put fire under the cow, she got up and "there stood still and fell a byting of stickes larger than any man's finger and after lived and did well."

Second wife of Sir Henry Cromwell, who was the grandfather of Oliver.

The children were strangely inconsistent. At the first they had fits when Mother Samuel appeared. Later they were troubled unless Mother Samuel were kept in the house, or unless they were taken to her house.

This device seems to have been originally suggested by the children to try Mother Samuel's guilt.

The clergyman, "Doctor Dorrington," had been one of the leaders in prosecuting them.

Harsnett, Discovery of the Fraudulent Practises of John Darrel (London, 1599), 92, 97.

Among the manuscripts on witchcraft in the Bodleian Library are three such pardons of witches for their witchcraft—one of Jane Mortimer in 1595, one of Rosa Bexwell in 1600, and one of "Alice S.," without date but under Elizabeth.

In 1595 he was made warden of the Manchester Collegiate Church. Dee has in our days found a biographer. See John Dee (1527-1608), by Charlotte Fell Smith (London, 1909).

For the particular case, see Mary Bateson, ed., Records of the Borough of Leicester (Cambridge, 1899), III. 335; for the general letters patent covering such cases see id., II, 365, 366.

For this story see Ralph Holinshed, Chronicles of England, Scotland, and Ireland (London, 1577, reprinted 1586-1587 and 1807-1808), ed. of 1807-1808, IV, 891, 893. Faversham was then "Feversham."

Justice Anderson, when sentencing a witch to a year's imprisonment, declared that this was the twenty-fifth or twenty-sixth witch he had condemned. This is good evidence that the records of many cases have been lost. See Brit. Mus., Sloane MS. 831, f. 38.

CHAPTER III.: Reginald Scot.

From the chronicling of witch trials we turn aside in this chapter to follow the career of the first great English opponent of the superstition. We have seen how the attack upon the supposed creatures of the Devil was growing stronger throughout the reign of Elizabeth. We shall see how that attack was checked, at least in some degree, by the resistance of one man. Few men of so quiet and studious life have wrought so effectively as Reginald Scot. He came of a family well known in Kent, but not politically aggressive. As a young man he studied at Hart Hall in Oxford, but left without taking his degree and returned to Scots-Hall, where he settled down to the routine duties of managing his estate. He gave himself over, we are told, to husbandry and gardening and to a solid course of general reading in the obscure authors that had "by the generality been neglected." In 1574 his studies in horticulture resulted in the publication of A Perfect Platforme of a Hoppe-Garden and necessary instructions for the making and maintaining thereof. That the book ministered to a practical interest was evidenced by the call for three editions within five years. Whether he now applied himself to the study of that subject which was to be the theme of his Discoverie, we do not know. It was a matter which had doubtless arrested his attention even earlier and had enlisted a growing interest upon his part. Not until a decade after his Hoppe-Garden, however, did he put forth the epoch-making Discoverie. Nor does it seem likely that he had been engaged for a long period on the actual composition. Rather, the style and matter of the book seem to evince traces of hurry in preparation. If this theory be true—and Mr. Brinsley Nicholson, his modern commentator, has adduced excellent reasons for accepting it—there can be but one explanation, the St. Oses affair. That tragedy, occurring within a short distance of his own home, had no doubt so outraged his sense of justice, that the work which he had perhaps long been contemplating he now set himself to complete as soon as possible. Even he who runs may read in Scot's strong sentences that he was not writing for instruction only, to propound a new doctrine, but that he was battling with the single purpose to stop a detestable and wicked practice. Something of a dilettante in real life, he became in his writing a man with an absorbing mission. That mission sprang not indeed from indignation at the St. Oses affair alone. From the days of childhood his experience had been of a kind to encourage skepticism. He had been reared in a county where Elizabeth Barton, the Holy Maid of Kent, first came into prominence, and he had seen the downfall that followed her public exposure. In the year after he brought out his Hoppe-garden, his county was again stirred by performances of a supposedly supernatural character. Mildred Norrington, a girl of seventeen, used ventriloquism with such skill that she convinced two clergymen and all her neighbors that she was possessed. In answer to queries, the evil spirit that spoke through Mildred declared that "old Alice of Westwell" had sent him to possess the girl. Alice, the spirit admitted, stood guilty of terrible witchcrafts. The demon's word was taken, and Alice seems to have been "arraigned upon this evidence." But, through the justices' adroit management of the trial, the fraud of the accuser was exposed. She confessed herself a pretender and suffered "condign punishment." This case happened within six miles of Scot's home and opened his eyes to the possibility of humbug. In the very same year two pretenders, Agnes Bridges and Rachel Pinder, were convicted in London. By vomiting pins and straws they had convinced many that they were bewitched, but the trickery was soon found out and they were compelled to do public penance at St. Paul's. We are not told what was the fate of a detestable Mother Baker, who, when consulted by the parents of a sick girl at New Romney in Kent, accused a neighbor woman. She said that the woman had made a waxen heart and pricked it and by this means accomplished her evil purpose. In order to prove her accusation, she had in the mean time concealed the wax figure of a heart in the house of the woman she accused, and then pretended to find it. It is some satisfaction to know that the malicious creature—who, during the history of witchcraft, had many imitators—was caught and compelled to confess.

Scot learned, indeed, by observing marvels of this sort—what it is strange that many others did not learn—to look upon displays of the supernatural with a good deal of doubt. How much he had ever believed in them we do not know. It is not unlikely that in common with his generation he had, as a young man, held a somewhat ill-defined opinion about the Devil's use of witches. The belief in that had come down, a comparatively innocuous tradition, from a primitive period. It was a subject that had not been raised in speculation or for that matter in court rooms. But since Scot's early manhood all this had been changed. England had been swept by a tidal wave of suspicion. Hazy theological notions had been tightened into rigid convictions. Convictions had passed into legislative statutes and instructions to judges. The bench, which had at first acted on the new laws with caution and a desire to detect imposture, became infected with the fear and grew more ready to discover witchcraft and to punish it. It is unnecessary to recapitulate the progress of a movement already traced in the previous chapter. Suffice it to say that the Kentish gentleman, familiarized with accounts of imposture, was unwilling to follow the rising current of superstition. Of course this is merely another way of saying that Scot was unconventional in his mental operations and thought the subject out for himself with results variant from those of his own generation. Here was a new abuse in England, here was a wrong that he had seen spring up within his own lifetime and in his own part of England. He made it his mission as far as possible to right the wrong. "For so much," he says, "as the mightie helpe themselves together, and the poore widowes crie, though it reach to heaven, is scarse heard here upon earth: I thought good (according to my poore abilitie) to make intercession, that some part of common rigor, and some points of hastie judgement may be advised upon."

It was indeed a splendid mission and he was singularly well equipped for it. He had the qualifications—scholarly training and the power of scientific observation, a background of broad theological and scriptural information, a familiarity with legal learning and practice, as well as a command of vigorous and incisive language—which were certain to make his work effective towards its object.

That he was a scholar is true in more senses than one. In his use of deduction from classical writers he was something of a scholastic, in his willingness to venture into new fields of thought he was a product of the Renaissance, in his thorough use of research he reminds us of a modern investigator. He gives in his book a bibliography of the works consulted by him and one counts over two hundred Latin and thirty English titles. His reading had covered the whole field of superstition. To Cornelius Agrippa and to Wierus (Johann Weyer), who had attacked the tyranny of superstition upon the Continent, he owed an especial debt. He had not, however, borrowed enough from them to impair in any serious way the value of his own original contribution.

In respect to law, Scot was less a student than a man of experience. The Discoverie, however, bristled with references which indicated a legal way of thinking. He was almost certainly a man who had used the law. Brinsley Nicholson believes that he had been a justice of the peace. In any case he had a lawyer's sense of the value of evidence and a lawyer's way of putting his case.

No less practical was his knowledge of theology and scripture. Here he had to meet the baffling problems of the Witch of Endor. The story of the witch who had called up before the frightened King Saul the spirit of the dead Samuel and made him speak, stood as a lion in the path of all opponents of witch persecution. When Scot dared to explain this Old Testament tale as an instance of ventriloquism, and to compare it to the celebrated case of Mildred Norrington, he showed a boldness in interpretation of the Bible far in advance of his contemporaries.

His anticipation of present-day points of view cropped out perhaps more in his scientific spirit than in any other way. For years before he put pen to paper he had been conducting investigations into alleged cases of conjuring and witchcraft, attending trials, and questioning clergymen and magistrates. For such observation he was most favorably situated and he used his position in his community to further his knowledge. A man almost impertinently curious was this sixteenth-century student. When he learned of a conjurer whose sentence of death had been remitted by the queen and who professed penitence for his crimes, he opened a correspondence and obtained from the man the clear statement that his conjuries were all impostures. The prisoner referred him to "a booke written in the old Saxon toong by one Sir John Malborne, a divine of Oxenford, three hundred yeares past," in which all these trickeries are cleared up. Scot put forth his best efforts to procure the work from the parson to whom it had been entrusted, but without success. In another case he attended the assizes at Rochester, where a woman was on trial. One of her accusers was the vicar of the parish, who made several charges, not the least of which was that he could not enunciate clearly in church owing to enchantment. This explanation Scot carried to her and she was able to give him an explanation much less creditable to the clergyman of the ailment, an explanation which Scot found confirmed by an enquiry among the neighbors. To quiet such rumors in the community about the nature of the illness the vicar had to procure from London a medical certificate that it was a lung trouble.

Can we wonder that a student at such pains to discover the fact as to a wrong done should have used barbed words in the portrayal of injustice? Strong convictions spurred on his pen, already taught to shape vigorous and incisive sentences. Not a stylist, as measured by the highest Elizabethan standards of charm and mellifluence, he possessed a clearness and directness which win the modern reader. By his methods of analysis he displayed a quality of mind akin to and probably influenced by that of Calvin, while his intellectual attitude showed the stimulus of the Reformation.

He was indeed in his own restricted field a reformer. He was not only the protagonist of a new cause, but a pioneer who had to cut through the underbrush of opinion a pathway for speculation to follow. So far as England was concerned, Scot found no philosophy of the subject, no systematic defences or assaults upon the loosely constructed theory of demonic agency. It was for him to state in definite terms the beliefs he was seeking to overthrow. The Roman church knew fairly well by this time what it meant by witchcraft, but English theologians and philosophers would hardly have found common ground on any one tenet about the matter. Without exaggeration it may be asserted that Scot by his assault all along the front forced the enemy's advance and in some sense dictated his line of battle.

The assault was directed indeed against the centre of the opposing entrenchments, the belief in the continuance of miracles. Scot declared that with Christ and his apostles the age of miracles had passed, an opinion which he supported by the authority of Calvin and of St. Augustine. What was counted the supernatural assumed two forms—the phenomena exhibited by those whom he classed under the wide term of "couseners," and the phenomena said to be exhibited by the "poor doting women" known as witches. The tricks and deceits of the "couseners" he was at great pains to explain. Not less than one-third of his work is given up to setting forth the methods of conjurers, card tricks, sleight-of-hand performances, illusions of magic, materializations of spirits, and the wonders of alchemy and astrology. In the range of his information about these subjects, the discoverer was encyclopedic. No current form of dabbling with the supernatural was left unexposed.

In his attack upon the phenomena of witchcraft he had a different problem. He had to deal with phenomena the so-called facts of which were not susceptible of any material explanation. The theory of a Devil who had intimate relations with human beings, who controlled them and sent them out upon maleficent errands, was in its essence a theological conception and could not be absolutely disproved by scientific observation. It was necessary instead to attack the idea on its a priori grounds. This attack Scot attempted to base on the nature of spirits. Spirits and bodies, he urged, are antithetical and inconvertible, nor can any one save God give spirit a bodily form. The Devil, a something beyond our comprehension, cannot change spirit into body, nor can he himself assume a bodily form, nor has he any power save that granted him by God for vengeance. This being true, the whole belief in the Devil's intercourse with witches is undermined. Such, very briefly, were the philosophic bases of Scot's skepticism. Yet the more cogent parts of his work were those in which he denied the validity of any evidence so far offered for the existence of witches. What is witchcraft? he asked; and his answer is worth quoting. "Witchcraft is in truth a cousening art, wherin the name of God is abused, prophaned and blasphemed, and his power attributed to a vile creature. In estimation of the vulgar people, it is a supernaturall worke, contrived betweene a corporall old woman, and a spirituall divell. The maner thereof is so secret, mysticall, and strange, that to this daie there hath never beene any credible witnes thereof." The want of credible evidence was indeed a point upon which Scot continually insisted with great force. He pictured vividly the course which a witchcraft case often ran: "One sort of such as are said to bee witches are women which be commonly old, lame, bleare-eied, pale, fowle, and full of wrinkles; ... they are leane and deformed, shewing melancholie in their faces; ... they are doting, scolds, mad, divelish.... These miserable wretches are so odious unto all their neighbors, and so feared, as few dare offend them, or denie them anie thing they aske: whereby they take upon them, yea, and sometimes thinke, that they can doo such things as are beyond the abilitie of humane nature. These go from house to house, and from doore to doore for a pot of milke, yest, drinke, pottage, or some such releefe; without the which they could hardlie live.... It falleth out many times, that neither their necessities, nor their expectation is answered.... In tract of time the witch waxeth odious and tedious to hir neighbors; ... she cursseth one, and sometimes another; and that from the maister of the house, his wife, children, cattell, etc. to the little pig that lieth in the stie.... Doubtlesse (at length) some of hir neighbours die, or fall sicke." Then they suspect her, says Scot, and grow convinced that she is the author of their mishaps. "The witch, ... seeing things sometimes come to passe according to hir wishes, ... being called before a Justice, ... confesseth that she hath brought such things to passe. Wherein, not onelie she, but the accuser, and also the Justice are fowlie deceived and abused." Such indeed was the epitome of many cases. The process from beginning to end was never better described; the ease with which confessions were dragged from weak-spirited women was never pictured more truly. With quite as keen insight he displayed the motives that animated witnesses and described the prejudices and fears that worked on jurors and judges. It was, indeed, upon these factors that he rested the weight of his argument for the negative.

The affirmative opinion was grounded, he believed, upon the ignorance of the common people, "assotted and bewitched" by the jesting or serious words of poets, by the inventions of "lowd liers and couseners," and by "tales they have heard from old doting women, or from their mother's maids, and with whatsoever the grandfoole their ghostlie father or anie other morrow masse preest had informed them."

By the same method by which he opposed the belief in witchcraft he opposed the belief in possession by an evil spirit. The known cases, when examined, proved frauds. The instances in the New Testament he seemed inclined to explain by the assumption that possession merely meant disease.

That Scot should maintain an absolute negative in the face of all strange phenomena would have been too much to expect. He seems to have believed, though not without some difficulty, that stones had in them "certaine proper vertues which are given them of a speciall influence of the planets." The unicorn's horn, he thought, had certain curative properties. And he had heard "by credible report" and the affirmation of "many grave authors" that "the wound of a man murthered reneweth bleeding at the presence of a deere freend, or of a mortall enimie."

His credulity in these points may be disappointing to the reader who hopes to find in Scot a scientific rationalist. That, of course, he was not; and his leaning towards superstition on these points makes one ask, What did he really believe about witchcraft? When all the fraud and false testimony and self-deception were excluded, what about the remaining cases of witchcraft? Scot was very careful never to deny in toto the existence of witches. That would have been to deny the Bible. What were these witches, then? Doubtless he would have answered that he had already classified them under two heads: they were either "couseners" or "poor doting women"—and by "couseners" he seems to have meant those who used trickery and fraud. In other words, Scot distinctly implied that there were no real witches—with powers given them by the Devil. Would he have stood by this when pushed into a corner? It is just possible that he would have done so, that he understood his own implications, but hardly dared to utter a straighforward denial of the reality of witchcraft. It is more likely that he had not altogether thought himself out.

The immediate impression of Scot's book we know little about. Such contemporary comment as we have is neutral. That his book was read painstakingly by every later writer on the subject, that it shortly became the great support of one party in the controversy, that King James deemed it worth while to write an answer, and that on his accession to the throne he almost certainly ordered the book to be burned by the common hangman, these are better evidence than absolutely contemporary notices to show that the Discoverie exerted an influence.

We cannot better suggest how radical Scot's position must have seemed to his own time than by showing the point of view of another opponent of witchcraft, George Gifford, a non-conformist clergyman. He had read the Discoverie and probably felt that the theological aspect of the subject had been neglected. Moreover it had probably been his fortune, as Scot's, to attend the St. Oses trials. Three years after Scot's book he brought out A Discourse of the Subtill Practises of Devilles by Witches, and followed it six years later by A Dialogue concerning Witches, a book in which he expounded his opinions in somewhat more popular fashion. Like Scot, he wrote to end, so far as possible, the punishment of innocent women; like Scot, he believed that most of the evidence presented against them was worthless. But on other points he was far less radical. There were witches. He found them in the Bible. To be sure they were nothing more than pawns for the Devil. He uses them "onely for a colour," that is, puts them forward to cover his own dealings, and then he deludes them and makes them "beleeve things which are nothing so." In consequence they frequently at their executions falsely accuse others of dreadful witchcrafts. It is all the work of the Devil. But he himself cannot do anything except through the power of God, who, sometimes for vengeance upon His enemies and sometimes to try His own people, permits the Evil One to do harm.

Gifford of course never made the impression that Scot had made. But he represented the more conservative position and was the first in a long line of writers who deprecated persecution while they accepted the current view as to witchcraft; and therefore he furnishes a standard by which to measure Scot, who had nothing of the conservative about him. Scot had many readers and exerted a strong influence even upon those who disagreed with him; but he had few or none to follow in his steps. It was not until nearly a century later that there came upon the scene a man who dared to speak as Scot had spoken. Few men have been so far ahead of their time.

Where George Gifford, who wrote a little later on the subject, was also a student.

Discoverie of Witchcraft, Nicholson ed., introd., xxxv.

That at least a part of it was written in 1583 appears from his own words, where he speaks of the treatise of Leonardus Vairus on fascination as "now this present yeare 1583 newlie published," ibid., 124.

Elizabeth Barton (1506-1534) suffered from a nervous derangement which developed into a religious mania. She was taught by some monks, and then professed to be in communion with the Virgin Mary and performed miracles at stated times. She denounced Henry VIII's divorce and gained wide recognition as a champion of the queen and the Catholic church. She was granted interviews by Archbishop Warham, by Thomas More, and by Wolsey. She was finally induced by Cranmer to make confession, was compelled publicly to repeat her confession in various places, and was then executed; see Dict. Nat. Biog.

Illegitimate child.

That is, very probably, Alice Norrington, the mother of Mildred.

Discoverie of Witchcraft, 130.

Ibid., 132.

See The discloysing of a late counterfeyted possession by the devyl in two maydens within the Citie of London; see also Holinshed, Chronicles, ed. of 1807-1808, IV, 325, and John Stow, Annals ... of England (London, 1615), 678.

Discoverie of Witchcraft, 258, 259.

The spot she chose for concealing the token of guilt had been previously searched.

For another see Discoverie of Witchcraft, 132-133.

In his prefatory epistle "to the Readers."

An incidental reference to Weyer in "W. W.'s" account of the Witches taken at St. Oses is interesting: "... whom a learned Phisitian is not ashamed to avouche innocent, and the Judges that denounce sentence of death against them no better than hangmen."

E. g., Discoverie of Witchcraft, 5.

Ibid., 466-469.

Ibid., 5-6.

Ibid., 15: "Howbeit you shall understand that few or none are throughlie persuaded, resolved, or satisfied, that witches can indeed accomplish all these impossibilities; but some one is bewitched in one point, and some is coosened in another, untill in fine, all these impossibilities, and manie mo, are by severall persons affirmed to be true."

Discoverie, 472.

Ibid., 7-8.

Ibid., 8.

It was one of the points made by "witchmongers" that the existence of laws against witches proved there were witches. This argument was used by Sir Matthew Hale as late as 1664. Scot says on that point: "Yet I confesse, the customes and lawes almost of all nations doo declare, that all these miraculous works ... were attributed to the power of witches. The which lawes, with the executions and judicials thereupon, and the witches confessions, have beguiled almost the whole world." Ibid., 220.

Discoverie, 471, 472.

Ibid., 512.

Ibid., 303.

Thomas Nash in his Four Letters Confuted (London, 1593) refers to it in a non-committal way as a work treating of "the diverse natures and properties of Divels and Spirits." Gabriel Harvey's Pierces Supererogation (London, 1593), has the following mention of it: "Scottes discoovery of Witchcraft dismasketh sundry egregious impostures, and in certaine principall chapters, and special passages, hitteth the nayle on the head with a witnesse; howsoever I could have wished he had either dealt somewhat more curteously with Monsieur Bodine, or confuted him somewhat more effectually." Professor Burr informs me that there is in the British Museum (Harleian MSS. 2302) an incomplete and unpublished reply to Scot. Its handwriting shows it contemporary or nearly so. It is a series of "Reasons" why witches should be believed in—the MS. in its present state beginning with the "5th Reason" and breaking off in the midst of the 108th.

See Nicholson's opinion on this, pp. xxxvii-xxxix of his introduction to Scot's book.

George Gifford was a Church of England clergyman whose Puritan sympathies at length compelled him to identify himself publicly with the non-conformist movement in 1584. For two years previous to that time he had held the living of Maldon in Essex.

A second edition of this book appeared in 1603. It was reprinted for the Percy Society in 1842.

Dialogue, ed. of 1603, prefatory letter and L-M 2 verso.

Discourse, D 3 verso, G 4 verso; Dialogue, ed. of 1603, K 2-K 2 verso, L-L 2. See also ibid., K 4-K 4 verso: "As not long since a rugged water spaniell having a chaine, came to a mans doore that had a saut bitch, and some espied him in the darke, and said it was a thing as bigge as a colt, and had eyes as great as saucers. Hereupon some came to charge to him, and did charge him in the name of the Father, the Sonne, and the Holy Ghost, to tell what he was. The dogge at the last told them, for he spake in his language, and said, bowgh, and thereby they did know what he was."

Discourse, in the prefatory letter.

Ibid., F 4 verso, F 5.

Dialogue, ed of 1603, K 2 verso.

Ibid., D 3 verso; Discourse, G 3 verso, H 3 verso.

Ibid., D 2 verso.

Gifford grew very forceful when he described the progress of a case against a witch: "Some woman doth fal out bitterly with her neighbour: there followeth some great hurt.... There is a suspicion conceived. Within fewe yeares after shee is in some jarre with an other. Hee is also plagued. This is noted of all. Great fame is spread of the matter. Mother W. is a witch.... Wel, mother W. doth begin to bee very odious and terrible unto many, her neighbours dare say nothing but yet in their heartes they wish shee were hanged. Shortly after an other falleth sicke and doth pine.... The neighbors come to visit him. Well neighbour, sayth one, do ye not suspect some naughty dealing: did yee never anger mother W? truly neighbour (sayth he) I have not liked the woman a long tyme. I can not tell how I should displease her, unlesse it were this other day, my wife prayed her, and so did I, that shee would keepe her hennes out of my garden. Wee spake her as fayre as wee could for our lives. I thinke verely she hath bewitched me. Every body sayth now that mother W. is a witch in deede.... It is out of all doubt: for there were which saw a weasil runne from her housward into his yard even a little before hee fell sicke. The sicke man dieth, and taketh it upon his death that he is bewitched: then is mother W. apprehended, and sent to prison, shee is arrayned and condemned, and being at the gallows, taketh it upon her death that shee is not gylty." Discourse, G 4-G 4 verso. And so, Gifford explains, the Devil is pleased, for he has put innocent people into danger, he has caused witnesses to forswear themselves and jurymen to render false verdicts.

But his views were warmly seconded by Henry Holland, who in 1590 issued at Cambridge A Treatise against Witchcraft. Holland, however, was chiefly interested in warning "Masters and Fathers of families that they may learn the best meanes to purge their houses of all unclean spirits." It goes without saying that he found himself at variance with Scot, who, he declared, reduced witchcraft to a "cozening or poisoning art." In the Scriptures he found the evidence that witches have a real "confederacie with Satan himself," but he was frank to admit that the proof of bargains of the sort in his own time could not be given.

CHAPTER IV.: The Exorcists.

In the narrative of English witchcraft the story of the exorcists is a side-issue. Yet their performances were so closely connected with the operations of the Devil and of his agents that they cannot be left out of account in any adequate statement of the subject. And it is impossible to understand the strength and weakness of the superstition without a comprehension of the rôle that the would-be agents for expelling evil spirits played. That the reign which had seen pass in procession the bands of conjurers and witches should close with the exorcists was to be expected. It was their part to complete the cycle of superstition. If miracles of magic were possible, if conjurers could use a supernatural power of some sort to assist them in performing wonders, there was nothing very remarkable about creatures who wrought harm to their fellows through the agency of evil spirits. And if witches could send evil spirits to do harm, it followed that those spirits could be expelled or exorcised by divine assistance. If by prayer to the Devil demons could be commanded to enter human beings, they could be driven out by prayer to God. The processes of reasoning were perfectly clear; and they were easily accepted because they found adequate confirmation in the New Testament. The gospels were full of narratives of men possessed with evil spirits who had been freed by the invocation of God. Of these stories no doubt the most quoted and the one most effective in moulding opinion was the account of the dispossessed devils who had entered into a herd of swine and plunged over a steep place into the sea.

It must not be supposed that exorcism was a result of belief in witchcraft. It was as old as the Christian church. It was still made use of by the Roman church and, indeed, by certain Protestant groups. And just at this time the Roman church found it a most important instrument in the struggle against the reformed religions. In England Romanism was waging a losing war, and had need of all the miracles that it could claim in order to reestablish its waning credit. The hunted priests who were being driven out by Whitgift were not unwilling to resort to a practice which they hoped would regain for them the allegiance of the common people. During the years 1585-1586 they had conducted what they considered marvellous works of exorcism in Catholic households of Buckinghamshire and Middlesex. Great efforts had been made to keep news of these séances from reaching the ears of the government, but accounts of them had gained wide circulation and came to the privy council. That body was of course stimulated to greater activity against the Catholics.

As a phase of a suppressed form of religion the matter might never have assumed any significance. Had not a third-rate Puritan clergyman, John Darrel, almost by accident hit upon the use of exorcism, the story of its use would be hardly worth telling. When this young minister was not more than twenty, but already, as he says, reckoned "a man of hope," he was asked to cure a seventeen-year-old girl at Mansfield in Nottingham, Katherine Wright. Her disease called for simple medical treatment. That was not Darrel's plan of operation. She had an evil spirit, he declared. From four o'clock in the morning until noon he prayed over her spirit. He either set going of his own initiative the opinion that possessed persons could point out witches, or he quickly availed himself of such a belief already existing. The evil spirit, he declared, could recognize and even name the witch that had sent it as well as the witch's confederates. All of this was no doubt suggested to the possessed girl and she was soon induced to name the witch that troubled her. This was Margaret Roper, a woman with whom she was upon bad terms. Margaret Roper was at once taken into custody by the constable. She happened to be brought before a justice of the peace possessing more than usual discrimination. He not only discharged her, but threatened John Darrel with arrest.

This was in 1586. Darrel disappeared from view for ten years or so, when he turned up at Burton-upon-Trent, not very far from the scene of his first operations. Here he volunteered to cure Thomas Darling. The story is a curious one and too long for repetition. Some facts must, however, be presented in order to bring the story up to the point at which Darrel intervened. Thomas Darling, a young Derbyshire boy, had become ill after returning from a hunt. He was afflicted with innumerable fits, in which he saw green angels and a green cat. His aunt very properly consulted a physician, who at the second consultation thought it possible that the child was bewitched. The aunt failed to credit the diagnosis. The boy's fits continued and soon took on a religious character. Between seizures he conversed with godly people. They soon discovered that the reading of the Scriptures brought on attacks. This looked very like the Devil's work. The suggestion of the physician was more seriously regarded. Meanwhile the boy had overheard the discussion of witchcraft and proceeded to relate a story. He had met, he said, a "little old woman" in a "gray gown with a black fringe about the cape, a broad thrimmed hat, and three warts on her face." Very accidentally, as he claimed, he offended her. She angrily said a rhyming charm that ended with the words, "I wil goe to heaven, and thou shalt goe to hell," and stooped to the ground.

The story produced a sensation. Those who heard it declared at once that the woman must have been Elizabeth Wright, or her daughter Alse Gooderidge, women long suspected of witchcraft. Alse was fetched to the boy. She said she had never seen him, but her presence increased the violence of his fits. Mother and daughter were carried before two justices of the peace, who examined them together with Alse's husband and daughter. The women were searched for special marks in the usual revolting manner with the usual outcome, but only Alse herself was sent to gaol.

The boy grew no better. It was discovered that the reading of certain verses in the first chapter of John invariably set him off. The justices of the peace put Alse through several examinations, but with little result. Two good witches were consulted, but refused to help unless the family of the bewitched came to see them.

Meantime a cunning man appeared who promised to prove Alse a witch. In the presence of "manie worshipfull personages" "he put a paire of new shooes on her feete, setting her close to the fire till the shooes being extreame hot might constrayne her through increase of the paine to confesse." "This," says the writer, "was his ridiculous practice." The woman "being throghly heated desired a release" and offered to confess, but, as soon as her feet were cooled, refused. No doubt the justices of the peace would have repudiated the statement that the illegal process of torture was used. The methods of the cunning man were really nothing else.

The woman was harried day and night by neighbors to bring her to confess. At length she gave way and, in a series of reluctant confessions, told a crude story of her wrong-doings that bore some slight resemblance to the boy's tale, and involved the use of a spirit in the form of a dog.

Now it was that John Darrel came upon the ground eager to make a name for himself. Darling had been ill for three months and was not improving. Even yet some of the boy's relatives and friends doubted if he were possessed. Not so Darrel. He at once undertook to pray and fast for the boy. According to his own account his efforts were singularly blessed. At all events the boy gradually improved and Darrel claimed the credit. As for Alse Gooderidge, she was tried at the assizes, convicted by the jury, and sentenced by Lord Chief-Justice Anderson to imprisonment. She died soon after. This affair undoubtedly widened Darrel's reputation.

Not long after, a notable case of possession in Lancashire afforded him a new opportunity to attract notice. The case of Nicholas Starchie's children provoked so much comment at the time that it is perhaps worth while to go back and bring the narrative up to the point where Darrel entered. Two of Starchie's children had one day been taken ill most mysteriously, the girl "with a dumpish and heavie countenance, and with a certaine fearefull starting and pulling together of her body." The boy was "compelled to shout" on the way to school. Both grew steadily worse and the father consulted Edmund Hartley, a noted conjurer of his time. Hartley quieted the children by the use of charms. When he realized that his services would be indispensable to the father he made a pretence of leaving and so forced a promise from Starchie to pay him 40 shillings a year. This ruse was so successful that he raised his demands. He asked for a house and lot, but was refused. The children fell ill again. The perplexed parent now went to a physician of Manchester. But the physician "sawe no signe of sicknes." Dr. Dee, the famous astrologer and friend of Elizabeth, was summoned. He advised the help of "godlie preachers."

Meantime the situation in the afflicted family took a more serious turn. Besides Mr. Starchie's children, three young wards of his, a servant, and a visitor, were all taken with the mysterious illness. The modern reader might suspect that some contagious disease had gripped the family, but the irregular and intermittent character of the disease precludes that hypothesis. Darrel in his own pamphlet on the matter declares that when the parents on one occasion went to a play the children were quiet, but that when they were engaged in godly exercise they were tormented, a statement that raises a suspicion that the disease, like that of the Throckmorton children, was largely imaginary.

But the divines were at work. They had questioned the conjurer, and had found that he fumbled "verie ill favouredlie" in the repetition of the Lord's Prayer. He was haled before a justice of the peace, who began gathering evidence against him and turned him over to the assizes. There it came out that he had been wont to kiss the Starchie children, and had even attempted, although without success, to kiss a maid servant. In this way he had presumably communicated the evil spirit—a new notion. The court could find no law, however, upon which to hang him. He had bewitched the children, but he had bewitched none of them to death, and therefore had not incurred the death penalty. But the father leaped into the gap. He remembered that he had seen the conjurer draw a magic circle and divide it into four parts and that he had bidden the witness step into the quarters one after another. Making such circles was definitely mentioned in the law as felony. Hartley denied the charge, but to no purpose. He was convicted of felony—so far as we can judge, on this unsupported afterthought of a single witness—and was hanged. Sympathy, however, would be inappropriate. In the whole history of witchcraft there were few victims who came so near to deserving their fate.

This was the story up to the time of Darrel's arrival. With Darrel came his assistant, George More, pastor of a church in Derbyshire. The two at once recognized the supernatural character of the case they were to treat and began religious services for the stricken family. It was to no effect. "All or most of them joined together in a strange and supernatural loud whupping that the house and grounde did sounde therwith again."

But the exorcists were not by any means disheartened. On the following day, in company with another minister, they renewed the services and were able to expel six of the seven spirits. On the third day they stormed and took the last citadel of Satan. Unhappily the capture was not permanent. Darrel tells us himself that the woman later became a Papist and the evil spirit returned.

The exorcist now turned his skill upon a young apprenticed musician of Nottingham. According to Darrel's story of the affair, William Somers had nine years before met an old woman who had threatened him. Again, more than a year before Darrel came to Nottingham, Somers had had two encounters with a strange woman "at a deep cole-pit, hard by the way-side." Soon afterwards he "did use such strang and idle kinde of gestures in laughing, dancing and such like lighte behaviour, that he was suspected to be madd." He began to suffer from bodily distortions and to evince other signs of possession which created no little excitement in Nottingham.

Darrel had been sent for by this time. He came at once and with his usual precipitancy pronounced the case one of possession. Somers, he said, was suffering for the sins of Nottingham. It was time that something should be done. Prayer and fasting were instituted. For three days the youth was preached to and prayed over, while the people of Nottingham, or some of them at least, joined in the fast. On the third day came what was deemed a most remarkable exhibition. The preacher named slowly, one after another, fourteen signs of possession. As he named them Somers illustrated in turn each form of possession. Here was confirmatory evidence of a high order. The exorcist had outdone himself. He now held out promises of deliverance for the subject. For a quarter of an hour the boy lay as if dead, and then rose up quite well.

Darrel now took up again the witchfinder's rôle he had once before assumed. Somers was encouraged to name the contrivers of his bewitchment. Through him, Darrel is said to have boasted, they would expose all the witches in England. They made a most excellent start at it. Thirteen women were accused by the boy, who would fall into fits at the sight of a witch, and a general invitation was extended to prefer charges. But the community was becoming a bit incredulous and failed to respond. All but two of the accused women were released.

The witch-discoverer, who in the meantime had been chosen preacher at St. Mary's in

Nottingham, made two serious mistakes. He allowed accusations to be preferred against Alice Freeman, sister of an alderman, and he let Somers be taken out of his hands. By the contrivance of some citizens who doubted the possession, Somers was placed in the house of correction, on a trumped-up charge that he had bewitched a Mr. Sterland to death. Removed from the clergyman's influence, he made confession that his possessions were pretended. Darrel, he declared, had taught him how to pretend. The matter had now gained wide notoriety and was taken up by the Anglican church. The archdeacon of Derby reported the affair to his superiors, and the Archbishop of York appointed a commission to examine into the case. Whether from alarm or because he had anew come under Darrel's influence, Somers refused to confess before the commission and again acted out his fits with such success that the commission seems to have been convinced of the reality of his possession. This was a notable victory for the exorcist.

But Chief-Justice Anderson of the court of common pleas was now commencing the assizes at Nottingham and was sitting in judgment on the case of Alice Freeman. Anderson was a man of intense convictions. He believed in the reality of witchcraft and had earlier sent at least one witch to the gallows and one to prison. But he was a man who hated Puritanism with all his heart, and would at once have suspected Puritan exorcism. Whether because the arch-instigator against Alice Freeman was a Puritan, or because the evidence adduced against her was flimsy, or because Somers, again summoned to court, acknowledged his fraud, or for all these reasons, Anderson not only dismissed the case, but he wrote a letter about it to the Archbishop of Canterbury. Archbishop Whitgift called Darrel and More before the court of high commission, where the Bishop of London, two of the Lord Chief-Justices, the master of requests, and other eminent officials heard the case. It seems fairly certain that Bancroft, the Bishop of London, really took control of this examination and that he acted quite as much the part of a prosecutor as that of a judge. One of Darrel's friends complained bitterly that the exorcist was not allowed to make "his particular defences" but "was still from time to time cut off by the Lord Bishop of London." No doubt the bishop may have been somewhat arbitrary. It was his privilege under the procedure of the high commission court, and he was dealing with one whom he deemed a very evident impostor. In fine, a verdict was rendered against the two clergymen. They were deposed from the ministry and put in close prison. So great was the stir they had caused that in 1599 Samuel Harsnett, chaplain to the Bishop of London, published A Discovery of the Fraudulent Practises of John Darrel, a careful résumé of the entire case, with a complete exposure of Darrel's trickery. In this account the testimony of Somers was given as to the origin of his possession. He testified before the ecclesiastical court that he had known Darrel several years before they had met at Nottingham. At their first meeting he promised, declared Somers, "to tell me some thinges, wherein if I would be ruled by him, I should not be driven to goe so barely as I did." Darrel related to Somers the story of Katherine Wright and her possession, and remarked, "If thou wilt sweare unto me to keepe my counsell, I will teache thee to doe all those trickes which Katherine Wright did, and many others that are more straunge." He then illustrated some of the tricks for the benefit of his pupil and gave him a written paper of directions. From that time on there were meetings between the two at various places. The pupil, however, was not altogether successful with his fits and was once turned out of service as a pretender. He was then apprenticed to the musician already mentioned, and again met Darrel, who urged him to go and see Thomas Darling of Burton, "because," says Somers, "that seeing him in his fittes, I might the better learn to do them myselfe." Somers met Darrel again and went through with a series of tricks of possession. It was after all these meetings and practice that Somers began his career as a possessed person in Nottingham and was prayed over by Mr. Darrel. Such at least was his story as told to the ecclesiastical commission. It would be hazardous to say that the narrative was all true. Certainly it was accepted by Harsnett, who may be called the official reporter of the proceedings at Darrel's trial, as substantially true.

The publication of the Discovery by Harsnett proved indeed to be only the beginning of a pamphlet controversy which Darrel and his supporters were but too willing to take up. Harsnett himself after his first onslaught did not re-enter the contest. The semi-official character of his writing rendered it unnecessary to refute the statements of a convicted man. At any rate, he was soon occupied with another production of similar aim. In 1602 Bishop Bancroft was busily collecting the materials, in the form of sworn statements, for the exposure of Catholic pretenders. He turned the material over to his chaplain. Whether the several examinations of Roman exorcists and their subjects were the result of a new interest in exposing exorcism on the part of the powers which had sent Darrel to prison, or whether they were merely a phase of increased vigilance against the activity of the Roman priests, we cannot be sure. The first conclusion does not seem improbable. Be that as it may, the court of high commission got hold of evidence enough to justify the privy council in authorizing a full publication of the testimony. Harsnett was deputed to write the account of the Catholic exorcists which was brought out in 1603 under the title of A Declaration of Egregious Popish Impostures. We have not the historical materials with which to verify the claims made in the book. On the face of it the case against the Roman priests looks bad. A mass of examinations was printed which seem to show that the Jesuit Weston and his confreres in England had been guilty of a great deal of jugglery and pretence. The Jesuits, however, were wiser in their generation than the Puritans and had not made charges of witchcraft. For that reason their performances may be passed over.

Neither the pretences of the Catholics nor the refutation of them are very important for our purposes. The exposure of John Darrel was of significance, because it involved the guilt or innocence of the women he accused as witches, as well as because the ecclesiastical authorities took action against him and thereby levelled a blow directly at exorcism and possession and indirectly at loose charges of witchcraft. Harsnett's books were the outcome of this affair and the ensuing exposures of the Catholics, and they were more significant than anything that had gone before. The Church of England had not committed itself very definitely on witchcraft, but its spokesman in the attack upon the Catholic pretenders took no uncertain ground. He was skeptical not only about exorcism but about witchcraft as well. It is refreshing and inspiriting to read his hard-flung and pungent words. "Out of these," he wrote, "is shaped us the true Idea of a Witch, an old weather-beaten Croane, having her chinne and her knees meeting for age, walking like a bow leaning on a shaft, hollow-eyed, untoothed, furrowed on her face, having her lips trembling with the palsie, going mumbling in the streetes, one that hath forgotten her pater noster, and hath yet a shrewd tongue in her head, to call a drab, a drab. If shee have learned of an olde wife in a chimnies end: Pax, max, fax, for a spel: or can say Sir John of Grantams curse, for the Millers Eeles, that were stolne: ... Why then ho, beware, looke about you my neighbours; if any of you have a sheepe sicke of the giddies, or an hogge of the mumps, or an horse of the staggers, or a knavish boy of the schoole, or an idle girle of the wheele, or a young drab of the sullens, and hath not fat enough for her porredge, nor her father and mother butter enough for their bread; and she have a little helpe of the Mother, Epilepsie, or Cramp, ... and then with-all old mother Nobs hath called her by chaunce 'idle young huswife,' or bid the devil scratch her, then no doubt but mother Nobs is the witch.... Horace the Heathen spied long agoe, that a Witch, a Wizard, and a Conjurer were but bul-beggers to scare fooles.... And Geoffry Chaucer, who had his two eyes, wit, and learning in his head, spying that all these brainlesse imaginations of witchings, possessings, house-hanting, and the rest, were the forgeries, cosenages, Imposturs, and legerdemaine of craftie priests, ... writes in good plaine terms,"

It meant a good deal that Harsnett took such a stand. Scot had been a voice crying in the wilderness. Harsnett was supported by the powers in church and state. He was, as has been seen, the chaplain of Bishop Bancroft, now—from 1604—to become Archbishop of Canterbury. He was himself to become eminent in English history as master of Pembroke Hall (Cambridge), vice-chancellor of Cambridge University, Bishop of Chichester, Bishop of Norwich, and Archbishop of York. Whatever support he had at the time—and it is very clear that he had the backing of the English church on the question of exorcism—his later position and influence must have given great weight not only to his views on exorcism but to his skepticism about witchcraft.

His opinions on the subject, so far as can be judged by his few direct statements and by implications, were quite as radical as those of his predecessor. As a matter of fact he was a man who read widely and had pondered deeply on the superstition, but his thought had been colored by Scot. His assault, however, was less direct and studied than that of his master. Scot was a man of uncommonly serious temperament, a plain, blunt-spoken, church-going Englishman who covered the whole ground of superstition without turning one phrase less serious than another. His pupil, if so Harsnett may be called, wrote earnestly, even aggressively, but with a sarcastic and bitter humor that entertained the reader and was much less likely to convince. The curl never left his lips. If at times a smile appeared, it was but an accented sneer. A writer with a feeling indeed for the delicate effects of word combination, if his humor had been less chilled by hate, if his wit had been of a lighter and more playful vein, he might have laughed superstition out of England. When he described the dreadful power of holy water and frankincense and the book of exorcisms "to scald, broyle and sizzle the devil," or "the dreadful power of the crosse and sacrament of the altar to torment the devill and to make him roare," or "the astonishable power of nicknames, reliques and asses ears," he revealed a faculty of fun-making just short of effective humor.

It would not be fair to leave Harsnett without a word on his place as a writer. In point of literary distinction his prose style maintains a high level. In the use of forceful epithet and vivid phrase he is excelled by no Elizabethan prose writer. Because his writings deal so largely with dry-as-dust reports of examinations, they have never attained to that position in English literature which parts of them merit.

Harsnett's book was the last chapter in the story of Elizabethan witchcraft and exorcism. It is hardly too much to say that it was the first chapter in the literary exploitation of witchcraft. Out of the Declaration Shakespeare and Ben Jonson mined those ores which when fused and refined by imagination and fancy were shaped into the shining forms of art. Shakespearean scholars have pointed out the connection between the dramatist and the exposer of exorcism. It has indeed been suggested by one student of Shakespeare that the great playwright was lending his aid by certain allusions in Twelfth Night to Harsnett's attempts to pour ridicule on Puritan exorcism. It would be hard to say how much there is in this suggestion. About Ben Jonson we can speak more certainly. It is clearly evident that he sneered at Darrel's pretended possessions. In the third scene of the fifth act of The Devil is an Ass he makes Mere-craft say:

It is the easiest thing, Sir, to be done. As plaine as fizzling: roule but wi' your eyes, And foame at th' mouth. A little castle-soape Will do 't, to rub your lips: And then a nutshell, With toe and touchwood in it to spit fire, Did you ner'e read, Sir, little Darrel's tricks, With the boy o' Burton, and the 7 in Lancashire, Sommers at Nottingham? All these do teach it. And wee'l give out, Sir, that your wife ha's bewitch'd you.

This is proof enough, not only that Jonson was in sympathy with the Anglican assailants of Puritan exorcism, but that he expected to find others of like opinion among those who listened to his play. And it was not unreasonable that he should expect this. It is clear enough that the powers of the Anglican church were behind Harsnett and that their influence gave his views weight. We have already observed that there were some evidences in the last part of Elizabeth's reign of a reaction against witch superstition. Harsnett's book, while directed primarily against exorcism, is nevertheless another proof of that reaction.

Sir George Peckham of Denham near Uxbridge and Lord Vaux of Hackney were two of the most prominent Catholics who opened their homes for these performances. See Samuel Harsnett, Declaration of Egregious Popish Impostures (London, 1603), 7, 8.

For a discussion of the Catholic exorcists see T. G. Law, "Devil Hunting in Elizabethan England," in the Nineteenth Century for March, 1894. Peckham's other activities in behalf of his church are discussed by Dr. R. B. Merriman in "Some Notes on the Treatment of English Catholics in the Reign of Elizabeth," in the Am. Hist. Rev., April, 1908. Dr. Merriman errs, however, in supposing that John Darrel cooperated with Weston and the Catholic exorcists; ibid., note 51. Darrel was a Puritan and had nothing to do with the Catholic performances.

It is quite possible to suppose, however, that its course would have been run in much the same way at a later time.

For Harsnett's account of Katherine Wright see his Discovery of the Fraudulent Practises of John Darrel (London, 1599), 297-315. For Darrel's story see The Triall of Maist. Dorrel, or A Collection of Defences against Allegations ... (1599), 15-21.

See Harsnett, Discovery, 310.

Katherine Wright's evil spirit returned later.

"I have seene her begging at our doore," he declared, "as for her name I know it not."

Harsnett, Discovery, 41, 265, deals briefly with the Darling case and Alse Gooderidge. See also John Darrel, A Detection of that sinnful, shamful, lying, and ridiculous discours of Samuel Harshnet (1600), 38-40. But the fullest account is a pamphlet at the Lambeth Palace library. It is entitled The most wonderfull and true Storie of a certaine Witch named Alse Gooderidge of Stapenhill.... As also a true Report of the strange Torments of Thomas Darling.... (London, 1597). For a discussion of this pamphlet see appendix A, § 1.

The boy was visited by a stranger who tried to persuade him that there were no witches. But this Derbyshire disciple of Scot had come to the wrong place and his efforts were altogether useless.

Meantime her mother Elizabeth Wright was also being worried. She was found on her knees in prayer. No doubt the poor woman was taking this method of alleviating her distress; but her devotion was interpreted as worship of the Devil.

So Darrel says. The pamphleteer Denison, who put together the story of Alse Gooderidge, wrote "she should have been executed but that her spirit killed her in prison."

Darrel gives an extended account of this affair in A True Narration of the strange and grevous Vexation by the Devil of seven persons in Lancashire (1600; reprinted in Somers Tracts, III), 170-179. See also George More, A true Discourse concerning the certaine possession and dispossession of 7 persons in one familie in Lancashire ... (1600), 9 ff.

Certain matters in connection with this case are interesting. George More tells us that Mrs. Starchie was an "inheritrix." Some of her kindred, Papists, prayed for the perishing of her issue. Four of her children pined away. Mrs. Starchie, when told of their prayers, conveyed all her property to her husband. She had two children afterwards, the two that were stricken. It is possible that all this may present some key to the case, but it is hard to see just how. See More, A true Discourse, 11-12.

George More, A true Discourse, 15; Harsnett, Discovery, 22. While Dee took no part in the affair except that he "sharply reproved and straitly examined" Hartley, he lent Mr. Hopwood, the justice of the peace before whom Hartley was brought, his copy of the book of Wierus, then the collections of exorcisms known as the Flagellum Dæmonum and the Fustis Dæmonum, and finally the famous Malleus Maleficarum. See Dee's Private Diary (Camden Soc., London, 1843), entries for March 19, April 15, and August 6, 1597.

George More, A true Discourse, 21; Darrel, A True Narration (Somers Tracts, III), 175.

Harsnett, Discovery, tells us that "certain Seminarie priests" got hold of her and carried her up and down the country and thereby "wonne great credit."

Darrel's account of this affair is in A True Narration (Somers Tracts, III), 179-186. Harsnett takes it up in his Discovery, 78-264.

See deposition of Cooper, in Harsnett, Discovery, 114.

Depositions of Somers and Darrel, ibid., 124-125. It must be recalled that when this was first tried before a commission they were convinced that it was not imposture. A layman cannot refrain from suspecting that Darrel had hypnotic control over Somers.

Ibid., 141-142.

Ibid., 141. Harsnett quotes Darrel for this statement.

Ibid., 5; John Darrel, An Apologie, or defence of the possession of William Sommers ... (1599?), L verso.

Darrel, A True Narration (Somers Tracts, III), 184; see also his A brief Apologie proving the possession of William Sommers ... (1599), 17.

Harsnett, Discovery, 7.

Ibid.

Ibid., 8; Darrel, An Apologie, or defence, 4; Darrel, A True Narration (Somers Tracts, III), 185.

Triall of Maist. Dorrel, narrative in back of pamphlet.

Darrel, A Detection of that sinnful ... discours of Samuel Harshnet, 40. And see above, p. 56, note.

Harsnett, Discovery, 8.

Ibid., 320-322; Darrel, An Apologie, or defence, L III, says that the third jury acquitted her. Harsnett refers to the fact that he was found guilty by the grand inquest.

The Triall of Maist. Dorrel, preface "To the Reader."

Harsnett, Discovery, 9.

Ibid., 78-98.

Yet Darrel must have realized that he had the worst of it. There is a pathetic acknowledgment of this in the "Preface to the Reader" of his publication, A Survey of Certaine Dialogical Discourses, written by John Deacon and John Walker ... (1602): "But like a tried and weather-beaten bird [I] wish for quiet corner to rest myself in and to drye my feathers in the warme sun."

T. G. Law, "Devil Hunting in Elizabethan England," in Nineteenth Century, March, 1894.

On the matter of exorcism the position of the Church of England became fixed by 1604. The question had been a cause of disagreement among the leaders of the Reformation. The Lutherans retained exorcism in the baptismal ritual and rivalled the Roman clergy in their exorcism of the possessed. It was just at the close of the sixteenth century that there arose in Lutheran Germany a hot struggle between the believers in exorcism and those who would oust it as a superstition. The Swiss and Genevan reformers, unlike Luther, had discarded exorcism, declaring it to have belonged only to the early church, and charging modern instances to Papist fraud; and with them seem to have agreed their South German friends. In England baptismal exorcism was at first retained in the ritual under Edward VI, but in 1552, under Bucer's influence, it was dropped. Under Elizabeth the yet greater influence of Zurich and Geneva must have discredited all exorcism, and one finds abundant evidence of this in the writings of Jewel and his followers. An interesting letter of Archbishop Parker in 1574 shows his utter incredulity as to possession in the case of Agnes Bridges and Rachel Pinder of Lothbury; see Parker's Correspondence (Parker Soc., Cambridge, 1856), 465-466. His successor, the Calvinistic Whitgift, was almost certainly of the same mind. Bancroft, the next archbishop of Canterbury, drew up or at least inspired that epoch-making body of canons enacted by Convocation in the spring of 1604, the 72d article of which forbids any Anglican clergyman, without the express consent of his bishop obtained beforehand, to use exorcism in any fashion under any pretext, on pain of being counted an impostor and deposed from the ministry. This ended the matter so far as the English church was concerned. For this résumé of the Protestant and the Anglican attitude toward exorcism I am indebted to Professor Burr.

Harsnett, A Declaration of Egregious Popish Impostures (London, 1605), 136-138.

It is not impossible that Harsnett was acting as a mouth-piece for Bancroft. Darrel wrote: "There is no doubt but that S. H. stand for Samuell Harsnet, chapline to the Bishop of London, but whither he alone, or his lord and hee, have discovered this counterfeyting and cosonage there is the question. Some thinke the booke to be the Bishops owne doing: and many thinke it to be the joynt worke of them both." A Detection of that sinnful ... discours of Samuel Harshnet, 7, 8.

From 1602 until 1609 he was archdeacon of Essex; see Victoria History of Essex, II, (London, 1907), 46.

There is a statement by the Reverend John Swan, who wrote in 1603, that Harsnett's book had been put into the hands of King James, presumably after his coming to England; see John Swan, A True and Breife Report of Mary Glover's Vexation, and of her deliverance ... (1603), "Dedication to the King," 3. One could wish for some confirmation of this statement. Certainly James would not at that time have sympathized with Harsnett's views about witches, but his attitude on several occasions toward those supposed to be possessed by evil spirits would indicate that he may very well have been influenced by a reading of the Discovery.

On page 36 of the Discovery Harsnett wrote: "Whether witches can send devils into men and women (as many doe pretende) is a question amongst those that write of such matters, and the learneder and sounder sort doe hold the negative." One does not need to read far in Harsnett to understand what he thought.

His scholarship, evident from his books, is attested by Thomas Fuller, who calls him "a man of great learning, strong parts, and stout spirit" (Worthies of England, ed. of London, 1840, I, 507).

See his Declaration of Egregious Popish Impostures, 134-136; his Discovery also shows the use of Scot.

Harsnett, Declaration of Egregious Popish Impostures, 98, 123, 110.

Read ibid., 131-140.

Joseph Hunter, New Illustrations of the Life, Studies and Writings of Shakespeare (London, 1845), I, 380-390.

CHAPTER V.: James I and Witchcraft.

Some one has remarked that witchcraft came into England with the Stuarts and went out with them. This offhand way of fixing the rise and fall of a movement has just enough truth about it to cause misconception. Nothing is easier than to glance at the alarms of Elizabeth's reign and to see in them accidental outbreaks with little meaning, isolated affairs presaging a new movement rather than part of it. As a matter of fact, any such view is superficial. In previous chapters the writer has endeavored to show just how foreign ideas and conditions at home gave the impulse to a movement which within a single reign took very definite form.

Yet so much was the movement accelerated, such additional impetus was given it by James I, that the view that James set the superstition going in England, however superficial, has some truth in it. If Elizabeth had ever given the matter thought, she had not at least given it many words. James had very definite opinions on the subject and hesitated not at all to make them known. His views had weight. It is useless to deny that the royal position swayed the courts. James's part in the witch persecution cannot be condoned, save on the ground that he was perfectly honest. He felt deeply on the matter. It was little wonder. He had grown up in Scotland in the very midst of the witch alarms. His own life, he believed, had been imperilled by the machinations of witches. He believed he had every reason to fear and hate the creatures, and we can only wonder that he was so moderate as we shall later find him to have been. The story of the affair that stirred up the Scottish king and his people has often been told, but it must be included here to make his attitude explicable. In 1589 he had arranged for a marriage with the Princess Anne of Denmark. The marriage had been performed by proxy in July, and it was then provided that the princess was to come to England. She set out, but was driven on to the coast of Norway by a violent storm, and detained there by the continuance of the storms. James sailed to Upsala, and, after a winter in the north of the Continent, brought his bride to Scotland in the spring, not without encountering more rough weather. To the people of the time it was quite clear that the ocean was unfriendly to James's alliance. Had Scotland been ancient Greece, no doubt Neptune would have been propitiated by a sacrifice. But it was Scotland, and the ever-to-be-feared Satan was not so easily propitiated. He had been very active of late in the realm.

Moreover it was a time when Satanic and other conspiracies were likely to come to light. The kingdom was unsettled, if not discontented. There were plots, and rumors of plots. The effort to expose them, as well as to thwart the attacks of the evil one on the king, led to the conception and spread of the monstrous story of the conspiracy of Dr. Fian. Dr. Fian was nothing less than a Scottish Dr. Faustus. He was a schoolmaster by profession. After a dissolute youth he was said to have given soul to the Devil. According to the story he gathered around him a motley crowd, Catholic women of rank, "wise women," and humble peasant people; but it was a crew ready for evil enterprise. It is not very clear why they were supposed to have attacked the king; perhaps because of his well known piety, perhaps because he was a Protestant. In any case they set about, as the story went, to destroy him, and thought to have found their opportunity in his trip to Denmark. They would drown him in a storm at sea. There was a simple expedient for raising a storm, the throwing of cats into the sea. This Scottish method of sacrificing to Neptune was duly carried out, and, as we have seen, just fell short of destroying the king. It was only the piety of the king, as Dr. Fian admitted in his confession, that overmatched the power of the evil one.

Such is the story that stirred Scotland from end to end. It is a story that is easily explained. The confessions were wrung from the supposed conspirators by the various forms of torture "lately provided for witches in that country." Geillis Duncane had been tried with "the torture of the pilliwinkes upon her fingers, which is a grievous torture, and binding or wrinching her head with a cord or roape." Agnes Sampson had suffered terrible tortures and shameful indignities until her womanly modesty could no longer endure it and she confessed "whatsoever was demanded of her." Dr. Fian was put through the ordinary forms of torture and was then "put to the most severe and cruel pain in the world, called the bootes," and thereby was at length induced to break his silence and to incriminate himself. At another time, when the king, who examined him in person, saw that the man was stubborn and denied the confessions already made, he ordered him to be tortured again. His finger nails were pulled off with a pair of pincers, and under what was left of them needles were inserted "up to the heads." This was followed by other tortures too terrible to narrate.

It is a little hard to understand how it was that the king "took great delight to be present at the examinations," but throughout the whole wretched series of trials he was never wanting in zeal. When Barbara Napier, sister-in-law to the laird of Carshoggil, was to be executed, a postponement had been granted on account of her approaching accouchement. Afterwards, "nobody insisting in the pursute of her, she was set at libertie." It seems also that the jury that had before condemned her had acquitted her of the main charge, that of treasonable witchcraft against the king. The king was angered at the default of justice, went to the Tolbooth, and made an address on the subject. He spoke of "his own impartiality, the use of witchcraft, the enormity of the crime, ... the ignorance of thinking such matters mere fantasies, the cause of his own interference in the matter, the ignorance of the assizes in the late trial, his own opinion of what witches really are."

It was only a few years later that James put that opinion into written form. All the world knows that the king was a serious student. With unremitting zeal he studied this matter, and in 1597, seven years after the Dr. Fian affair, he published his Dæmonologie. It was expressly designed to controvert the "damnable opinions of two principally in our age"—Scot, who "is not ashamed in publick Print to deny that there can be such a thing as witchcraft," and Wierus, "a German physician," who "sets out a publicke apologie for all these craft-folkes whereby ... he plainly bewrayes himself to have been one of that profession."

It was to be expected that James would be an exponent of the current system of belief. He had read diligently, if not widely, in the Continental lore of the subject and had assimilated much of it. He was Scotch enough to be interested in theology and Stuart enough to have very definite opinions. James had, too, his own way of putting things. There was a certain freshness about his treatment, in spite of the fact that he was ploughing old fields. Nothing illustrates better his combination of adherence to tradition, of credulity, and of originality than his views on the transportation of witches, a subject that had long engaged the theorists in demonology. Witches could be transported, he believed, by natural means, or they could be carried through the air "by the force of the spirit which is their conducter," as Habakkuk was carried by the angel. This much he could accept. But that they could be transformed into a "little beast or foule" and pierce through "whatsoever house or Church, though all ordinarie passages be closed," this he refused to believe. So far, however, there was nothing original about either his belief or his disbelief. But his suggestion on another matter was very probably his own. There had been long discussion as to how far through the air witches could go. It was James's opinion that they could go only so far as they could retain their breath.

But it was seldom that the royal demonologist wandered far from the beaten road. He was a conformist and he felt that the orthodox case needed defence: so he set about to answer the objectors. To the argument that it was a strange thing that witches were melancholy and solitary women (and so, he would have explained, offer the easiest object of attack) he interposed a flat denial: they are "some of them rich and worldly-wise, some of them fat or corpulent in their bodies." To the point that if witches had the power ascribed to them no one but themselves would be left alive in the world, he answered that such would be the case, were not the power of the Devil bridled by God. To the plea that God would not allow his children to be vexed by the Devil, he replied that God permits the godly who are sleeping in sin to be troubled; that He even allows the Evil One to vex the righteous for his own good—a conventional argument that has done service in many a theological controversy.

It is a curious circumstance that James seemingly recognized the reliability of the Romish exorcisms which the Church of England was about that time beginning to attack. His explanation of them is worthy of "the wisest fool in Christendom." The Papists could often effect cures of the possessed, he thought, because "the divell is content to release the bodily hurting of them, ... thereby to obtain the perpetual hurt of the soules."

That James should indulge in religious disquisitions rather than in points of evidence was to be expected. Although he had given up the Scottish theology, he never succeeded in getting it thoroughly out of his system. As to the evidence against the accused, the royal writer was brief. Two sorts of evidence he thought of value, one "the finding of their marke, and the trying the insensiblenes thereof, the other is their fleeting [floating] on the water." The latter sign was based, he said, on the fact that the water refuses to receive a witch—that is to say, the pure element would refuse to receive those who had renounced their baptism. We shall see that the influence of the Dæmonologie can be fairly appraised by measuring the increased use of these two tests of guilt within his own reign and that of his son. Hitherto the evidence of the mark had been of rather less importance, while the ordeal by water was not in use.

The alleged witch-mark on the body had to do with the contracts between witches and the Devil. This loathsome side of witch belief we cannot go into. Suffice it to say that James insisted on the reality of these contracts and consequently upon the punishment that should be meted to those who had entered into them. All witches except children should be sentenced to death. The king shows a trace of conventional moderation, however, and admits that the magistrates should be careful whom they condemned. But, while he holds that the innocent should not be condemned, he warns officials against the sin of failing to convict the guilty. We shall see that throughout his reign in England he pursued a course perfectly consistent with these principles.

A critical estimate of James's book it is somewhat hard to give. Students of witchcraft have given utterance to the most extravagant but widely divergent opinions upon it. The writer confesses that he has not that acquaintance with the witch literature of the Continent which would enable him to appraise the Dæmonologie as to its originality. So good an authority as Thomas Wright has declared that it is "much inferior to the other treatises on the subject," and that it was compiled from foreign works. Doubtless a study of the Continental literature would warrant, at least in part, this opinion. Yet one gets the impression, from what may be learned of that great body of writing through the historians of witchcraft, that James's opinions were in some respects his own. He had, of course, absorbed the current belief, but he did not hesitate to give his own interpretation and explanation of phenomena. That interpretation is not wanting in shrewdness. It seems to one who has wandered through many tedious defences of the belief in witchcraft that James's work is as able as any in English prior to the time of Joseph Glanvill in 1668. One who should read Glanvill and James together would get a very satisfactory understanding of the position of the defenders of the superstition. Glanvill insisted upon what he believed were well authenticated facts of experience. James grounded his belief upon a course of theoretical reasoning.

We have already indicated that James's book was influential in its time. It goes without saying that his position as a sovereign greatly enhanced its influence. This was particularly true after he took the throne of England. The dicta that emanated from the executive of the English nation could not fail to find a wide audience, and especially in England itself. His work offered a text-book to officials. It was a key to the character and methods of the new ruler, and those who hoped for promotion were quick to avail themselves of it. To prosecute witches was to win the sovereign's approval. The judges were prompted to greater activity. Moreover, the sanction of royalty gave to popular outbreaks against suspicious women greater consideration at the hands of the gentry. And it was in the last analysis the gentry, in the persons of the justices of the peace, who decided whether or no neighborhood whispering and rumors should be followed up.

But the king's most direct influence was in the passing of a new law. His first Parliament had been in session but eight days when steps were taken by the House of Lords towards strengthening the statute against witchcraft. The law in force, passed in the fifth year of Elizabeth's reign, imposed the death penalty for killing by witchcraft, and a year's imprisonment for injuring by witchcraft or by allied means. James would naturally feel that this law was merely one version of the statute against murder and did not touch the horrible crime of contract with the Devil and the keeping of imps. Here was a sin beside which the taking of life was a light offence. It was needful that those who were guilty of it should suffer the severest penalty of the law, even if they had not caused the loss of a single life. It was to remedy this defect in the criminal code that a new statute was introduced.

It is not worth while to trace the progress of that bill from day to day. It can be followed in the journals of the Lords and Commons. The bill went to a large committee that included six earls and twelve bishops. Perhaps the presence of the bishops was an evidence that witchcraft was still looked upon as a sin rather than as a crime. It was a matter upon which the opinion of the church had been received before and might well be accepted again. It was further arranged that the Lord Chief-Justice of the common pleas, Sir Edmund Anderson, and the attorney-general, the later so famous Sir Edward Coke, along with other eminent jurists, were to act with the committee. Anderson, it will be recalled, had presided over numerous trials and had both condemned and released witches. As to Coke's attitude towards this subject, we know not a thing, save that he served on this committee. The committee seems to have found enough to do. At any rate the proposed statute underwent revision. Doubtless the privy council had a hand in the matter; indeed it is not unlikely that the bill was drawn up under its direction. On the 9th of June, about two months and a half after its introduction, the statute passed its final reading in the Lords. It repealed the statute of Elizabeth's reign and provided that any one who "shall use, practise or exercise any Invocation or Conjuration of any evill and wicked Spirit, or shall consult, covenant with, entertaine, employe, feede, or rewarde any evill and wicked Spirit to or for any intent or purpose; or take up any dead man, woman, or child, ... to be imployed or used in any manner of Witchcrafte" should suffer death as a felon. It further provided that any one who should "take upon him or them by Witchcrafte ... to tell or declare in what place any treasure of Golde or Silver should or might be founde ... or where Goods or Things loste or stollen should be founde or become, or to the intent to provoke any person to unlawfull love, or wherebie any Cattell or Goods of any person shall be destroyed, wasted, or impaired, or to hurte or destroy any person in his or her bodie, although the same be not effected and done," should for the first offence suffer one year's imprisonment with four appearances in the pillory, and for the second offence, death. The law explains itself. Not only the killing of people by the use of evil spirits, but even the using of evil spirits in such a way as actually to cause hurt was a capital crime. The second clause punished white magic and the intent to hurt, even where it "be not effected," by a year's imprisonment and the pillory. It can be easily seen that one of the things which the framers of the statute were attempting to accomplish in their somewhat awkward wording was to make the fact of witchcraft as a felony depend chiefly upon a single form of evidence, the testimony to the use of evil spirits.

We have seen why people with James's convictions about contracts with the Devil might desire to rest the crime upon this kind of proof. It can be readily understood, too, how the statute would work in practice. Hitherto it had been possible to arraign a witch on the accusations of her neighbors, but it was not possible to send her to the gallows unless some death in the vicinity could be laid to her charge. The community that hustled a suspicious woman to court was likely to suffer the expense of her imprisonment for a year. It had no assurance that it could be finally rid of her.

Under the new statute it was only necessary to prove that the woman made use of evil spirits, and she was put out of the way. It was a simpler thing to charge a woman with keeping a "familiar" than to accuse her of murder. The stories that the village gossips gathered in their rounds had the keeping of "familiars" for their central interest. It was only necessary to produce a few of these gossips in court and the woman was doomed.

To be sure, this is theory. The practical question is, not how would the law operate, but how did it operate? This brings us again into the dangerous field of statistics. Now, if we may suppose that the witch cases known to us are a safe basis of comparison, the reign of James, as has already been intimated, shows a notable increase in witch executions over that of Elizabeth. We have records of between forty and fifty people who suffered for the crime during the reign of James, all but one of them within the first fifteen years. It will be seen that the average per year is nearly double that of the executions known to us in the first part of Elizabeth's rule, and of course several times that of those known in the last part. This increased number we are at once inclined to assign to the direct and indirect influence of the new king. But it may very fairly be asked whether the new statute passed at the king's suggestion had not been in part responsible for the increased number. This question can be answered from an examination of those cases where we have the charges given. Of thirty-seven such cases in the reign of James I, where the capital sentence was given, seventeen were on indictments for witchcrafts that had not caused death. In the other twenty cases, the accused were charged with murder.

This means that over two-fifths of those who are known to have been convicted under the new law would have escaped death under the Elizabethan statute. With all due allowance for the incompleteness of our statistics, it seems certain that the new law had added very considerably to the number of capital sentences. Subtract the seventeen death sentences for crimes of witchcraft that were not murder from the total number of such sentences, and we have figures not so different from those of Elizabeth's reign.

This is a sufficient comment on the effectiveness of the new law as respects its particularly novel features. A study of the character of the evidence and of the tests of guilt employed at the various trials during the reign will show that the phrasing of the law, as well as the royal directions for trying guilt, influenced the forms of accusation and the verdicts of the juries. In other words the testimony rendered in some of the well known trials of the reign offers the best commentary upon the statute as well as upon the Dæmonologie. This can be illustrated from three of the processes employed to determine guilt. The king had recommended the water ordeal. Up to this time it had not been employed in English witch cases, so far as we know. The first record of its use was in 1612, nine years after James ascended the English throne. In that year there was a "discoverie" of witches at Northampton. Eight or nine women were accused of torturing a man and his sister and of laming others. One of them was, at the command of a justice of the peace, cast into the water with "her hands and feete bound," but "could not sink to the bottome by any meanes." The same experiment was applied to Arthur Bill and his parents. He was accused of bewitching a Martha Aspine. His father and mother had long been considered witches. But the "matter remaining doubtful that it could not be cleerly tryed upon him," he (and his parents) were tied with "their thumbes and great toes ... acrosse" and thrown into the water. The suspicion that was before not well grounded was now confirmed. To be sure, this was done by the justices of the peace and we do not know how much it influenced the assize court.

These are the only instances given us by the records of James's reign where this test was employed by the authorities. But in the very next year after the Northampton affair it was used in the adjoining county of Bedford by private parties. A land-owner who had suffered ills, as he thought, from two tenants, Mother Sutton and her daughter, took matters into his own hands. His men were ordered to strip the two women "in to their smocks," to tie their arms together, and to throw them into the water. The precaution of a "roape tyed about their middles" was useless, for both floated. This was not enough. The mother, tied toe and thumb, was thrown into the water again. She "sunke not at all, but sitting upon the water turned round about like a wheele.... And then being taken up, she as boldly as if she had beene innocent asked them if they could doe any more to her."

The use of marks as evidence was not as new as the water ordeal. But it is a rather curious thing that in the two series of cases involving water ordeal the other process was also emphasized. In these two instances it would seem as if the advice of the Dæmonologie had been taken very directly by the accusers. There was one other instance of this test. The remarkable thing, however, is that in the most important trial of the time, that at Lancaster in 1612, there was an utter absence, at least so far as the extant record goes, of female juries or of reports from them. This method of determining guilt was not as yet widely accepted in the courts. We can hardly doubt that it had been definitely forbidden at Lancaster. The evidence of the use of evil spirits, against which the statute of the first year of James I had been especially framed, was employed in such a large proportion of trials that it is not worth while to go over the cases in detail.

The law forbade to take up any dead person or the skin, bone, or other part thereof for use in witchcraft. Presumably some instance of this form of witchcraft had been responsible for the phrase, but we have on record no case of the sort until a few years after the passage of the statute. It was one of the principal charges against Johanna Harrison of Royston in 1606 that the officers found in her possession "all the bones due to the Anatomy of man and woman." This discovery brought out other charges and she was hanged. At the famous Lancashire trials in 1612 the arch-witch Chattox was declared to have had in her possession three scalps and eight teeth. She was guilty on other counts, but she escaped the executioner by death.

These are illustrations of the point that the Dæmonologie and the statute of James I find their commentary in the evidence offered at the trials. It goes without saying that these illustrations represent only a few of the forms of testimony given in the courts. It may not, therefore, be amiss to run over some other specimens of the proof that characterized the witch trials of the reign. With most of them we are already familiar. The requirement that the witch should repeat certain words after the justice of the peace was used once in the reign of James. It was an unusual method at best. A commoner form of proof was that adduced from the finding or seeing clay or waxen images in the possession of the accused. The witness who had found such a model on the premises of the defendant or had seen the defendant handling it, jumped readily to the conclusion that the image represented some individual. If it should be asked how we are to account for this sort of evidence, the answer is an easy one. Every now and then in the annals of witchcraft it came out that a would-be accuser had hidden a waxen or clay figure in the house of the person he wished to accuse and had then found it. No doubt some cases started in this way. No doubt, too, bitter women with grudges to satisfy did experiment with images and were caught at it. But this was rare. In the greater number of cases the stories of images were pure fabrications. To that category belong almost certainly the tales told at Lancaster.

"Spectral evidence" we have met with in the Elizabethan period. That reign saw two or three instances of its employment, and there were more examples of it in the reign of James. Master Avery of Northampton, who with his sister was the principal accuser in the trials there, saw in one of his fits a black wart on the body of Agnes Brown, a wart which was actually found "upon search." Master Avery saw other spectres, but the most curious was that of a bloody man desiring him to have mercy on his Mistress Agnes and to cease impeaching her. At Bedford, Master Enger's servant had a long story to tell, but the most thrilling part concerned a visit which the young Mary Sutton (whom he was accusing) made to him. On a "moonshine night" she came in at the window in her "accustomed and personall habite and shape" and knitted at his side. Then drawing nearer, she offered him terms by which he could be restored to his former health, terms which we are to understand the virtuous witness refused. It is pleasant to know that Master Enger was "distrustfull of the truth" of this tale. One fears that these spectres were not the products of overwrought imagination, as were many others, but were merely fabrics of elaborate fiction. In any case they were not the groundwork of the proof. In the Fairfax prosecutions at York in 1622 the charges against the six women accused rested entirely upon a great tissue of spectral evidence. The three children had talked to the spectres, had met them outdoors and at church and in the kitchen. The spectres were remarkably wise and named visitors whom the family did not know. They struggled with the children, they rolled over them in bed, they followed them to the neighbors.

Somewhat akin to the evidence from apparitions was that from the effect of a witch's glance. This is uncommonly rare in English witchcraft, but the reign of James offers two instances of it. In Royston, Hertfordshire, there was "an honest fellow and as boone a companion ... one that loved the pot with the long necke almost as well as his prayers." One day when he was drinking with four companions Johanna Harrison came in and "stood gloating upon them." He went home and at once fell sick. At Northampton the twelve-year-old Hugh Lucas had looked "stark" upon Jane Lucas at church and gone into convulsions when he returned home.

One other form of proof demands notice. In the trial of Jennet Preston at York it was testified that the corpse of Mr. Lister, whom she was believed to have slain by witchcraft, had bled at her presence. The judge did not overlook this in summarizing the evidence. It was one of three important counts against the woman, indeed it was, says the impressive Mr. Potts, quoting the judge, of more consequence than all the rest. Of course Mistress Preston went to the gallows.

It will occur to the reader to ask whether any sort of evidence was ruled out or objected to. On this point we have but slight knowledge. In reporting the trial of Elizabeth Sawyer of Edmonton in 1621 the Reverend Henry Goodcole wrote that a piece of thatch from the accused woman's house was plucked and burned, whereupon the woman presently came upon the scene. Goodcole characterized this method as an "old ridiculous custome" and we may guess that he spoke for the judge too. In the Lancashire cases, Justice Altham, whose credulity knew hardly any bounds, grew suddenly "suspitious of the accusation of this yong wench, Jennet Device," who had been piling up charges against Alice Nutter. The girl was sent out of the room, the witches were mixed up, and Jennet was required on coming in again to pick out Alice Nutter. Of course that proved an easy matter. At another time, when Jennet was glibly enumerating the witches that had assembled at the great meeting at Malking Tower, the judge suddenly asked her if Joane-a-Downe were there. But the little girl failed to rise to the bait and answered negatively, much to the satisfaction of everybody, and especially of the righteous Mr. Potts.

This is all we know directly about any tendency to question evidence at Lancaster in 1612, but a good deal more may be inferred from what is not there. A comparison of that trial with other contemporary trials will convince any one that Justices Altham and Bromley must have ruled out certain forms of evidence. There were no experiments made of any sort nor any female juries set inspecting. This, indeed, is not to say that all silly testimony was excluded. There is enough and more of sheer nonsense in the testimony to prove the contrary.

We turn now from the question of evidence to a brief consideration of several less prominent features of Jacobean witchcraft. We shall note the character of the sentences, the distribution of the trials, the personnel and position in life of the accused, and lastly the question of jurisdiction.

We have in another connection indicated the approximate number of executions of which we have record in James's reign. That number, we saw, was certainly over forty and probably approached fifty. It represented, however, not quite half the total number of cases of accusation recorded. In consequence the other verdicts and sentences have significance. Especially is this true of the acquittals. They amounted to thirty, perhaps to forty. When we add the trials of which we do not know the outcome, we can guess that the number was close to the sum total of executions. Legally only one other outcome of a trial was possible, a year's imprisonment with quarterly appearances in the pillory. There were three or four instances of this penalty as well as one case where bond of good behavior was perhaps substituted for imprisonment. Five pardons were issued, three of them by the authorities at London, two of them by local powers apparently under compulsion.

We come now to consider the personnel, sex, occupations, and positions in life of the accused. On certain of these matters it is possible to give statistical conclusions, but such conclusions must be accepted with great caution. By a count as careful as the insufficient evidence permits it would seem that about six times as many women were indicted as men. This was to be expected. It is perhaps less in accord with tradition that twice as many married women as spinsters seem to have figured in the witch trials of the Jacobean era. The proportion of widows to unmarried women was about the same, so that the proportion of unmarried women among the whole number accused would seem to have been small. These results must be accepted guardedly, yet more complete statistics would probably show that the proportion of married women was even greater.

The position in life of these people was not unlike that of the same class in the earlier period.

In the account of the Lancashire trials we shall see that the two families whose quarrels started the trouble were the lowest of low hill-country people, beggars and charmers, lax in their morals and cunning in their dealings. The Flower women, mother and daughter, had been charged with evil living; it was said that Agnes Brown and her daughter of Northampton had very doubtful reputations; Mother Sutton of Bedford was alleged to have three illegitimate children. The rest of the witches of the time were not, however, quite so low in the scale. They were household servants, poor tenants, "hog hearders," wives of yeomen, broomsellers, and what not.

Above this motley peasant crew were a few of various higher ranks. A schoolmaster who had experimented with sorcery against the king, a minister who had been "busy with conjuration in his youth," a lady charged with sorcery but held for other sin, a conjurer who had rendered professional services to a passionate countess, these make up a strange group of witches, and for that matter an unimportant one. None of their cases were illustrations of the working of witch law; they were rather stray examples of the connection between superstition, on the one hand, and politics and court intrigue on the other. Not so, however, the prosecution of Alice Nutter in the Lancashire trials of 1612. Alice Nutter was a member of a well known county family. "She was," says Potts, "a rich woman, had a great estate and children of good hope." She was moreover "of good temper, free from envy and malice." In spite of all this she was accused of the most desperate crimes and went to the gallows. Why family connections and influences could not have saved her is a mystery.

In another connection we spoke of two witches pardoned by local authorities at the instance of the government. This brings us to the question of jurisdiction. The town of Rye had but recently, it would seem, been granted a charter and certain judicial rights. But when the town authorities sentenced one woman to death and indicted another for witchcraft, the Lord Warden interfered with a question as to their power. The town, after some correspondence, gave way and both women were pardoned. This was, however, the only instance of disputed jurisdiction. The local powers in King's Lynn hanged a witch without interference, and the vicar-general of the Bishop of Durham proceeded against a "common charmer" with impunity, as of course he had every right to do.

There is, in fact, a shred of evidence to show that the memory of ecclesiastical jurisdiction had not been lost. In the North Riding of Yorkshire the quarter sessions sentenced Ralph Milner for "sorcerie, witchcraft, inchantment and telling of fortunes" to confess his fault at divine service, "that he hath heighlie offended God and deluded men, and is heartily sorie." There is nothing, of course, in the statute to authorize this form of punishment, and it is only accounted for as a reversion to the original ecclesiastical penalty for a crime that seemed to belong in church courts.

What we call nowadays mob law had not yet made its appearance—that is, in connection with witchcraft. We shall see plenty of it when we come to the early part of the eighteenth century. But there was in 1613 one significant instance of independence of any jurisdiction, secular or ecclesiastical. In the famous case at Bedford, Master Enger, whom we have met before, had been "damnified" in his property to the round sum of £200. He was at length persuaded that Mother Sutton was to blame. Without any authority whatsoever he brought her forcibly to his house and caused her to be scratched. Not only so, but he threw the woman and her daughter, tied and bound, into his mill-pond to prove their guilt. In the mean time the wretched creatures had been stripped of their clothes and examined for marks, under whose oversight we are not told, but Master Enger was responsible. He should have suffered for all this, but there is no record of his having done so. On the contrary he carried the prosecution of the women to a successful issue and saw them both hanged.

We now turn to the question of the distribution of witchcraft in the realm during James's reign. From the incidental references already given, it will be evident that the trials were distributed over a wide area. In number executed, Lancashire led with ten, Leicester had nine, Northampton five or more, Middlesex four, Bedford, Lincoln, York, Bristol, and Hertford each two; Derby had several, the exact number we can not learn. These figures of the more serious trials seem to show that the alarm was drifting from the southeast corner of England towards the midlands. In the last half of Elizabeth's rule the centre had been to the north of London in the southern midlands. Now it seems to have progressed to the northern midlands. Leicester, Derby, and Nottingham may be selected as the triangle of counties that would fairly represent the centre of the movement. If the matter were to be determined with mathematical accuracy, the centre would need to be placed perhaps a little farther west, for Stafford, Cheshire, Bristol, and the remote Welsh Carnarvon all experienced witch alarms. In the north, York and Durham had their share of trials.

It will be easier to realize what had happened when we discover that, so far as records go, Kent and Essex were entirely quiet during the period, and East Anglia almost so. We shall later see that these counties had not at all forgotten to believe in witchcraft, but the witchfinders had ceased their activities for a while.

To be sure, this reasoning from the distribution of trials is a dangerous proceeding. Witch alarms, on they face of things, seem haphazard outbursts of excitement. And such no doubt they are in part; yet one who goes over many cases in order cannot fail to observe that an outbreak in one county was very likely to be followed by one in the next county. This is perfectly intelligible to every one familiar with the essentially contagious character of these scares. The stories spread from village to village as fast as that personified Rumor of the poet Vergil, "than which nothing is fleeter"; nor did they halt with the sheriffs at the county boundaries.

We have now traced the growth of James's opinions until they found effect in English law, have seen the practical operation of that law, and have gone over the forms of evidence, as well as some other features of the witch trials of his reign. In the next chapter we shall take up some of the more famous Jacobean cases in detail as examples of witch alarms. We shall seek to find out how they started and what were the real causes at work.

I have not attempted to give more than a brief résumé of this story, and have used Thomas Wright, Narratives of Sorcery and Magic (London, 1851), I, 181-190, and Mrs. Lynn Linton, Witch Stories, 21-34. The pamphlet about Dr. Fian is a rare one, but may be found in several libraries. It has been reprinted by the Gentleman's Magazine, vol. XLIX (1779), by the Roxburghe Club (London, 1816), by Robert Pitcairn, in his Criminal Trials in Scotland (Edinburgh, 1829-1833), vol. I, and doubtless in many other places. Pitcairn has also printed a part of the records of his trial.

This is all based upon the contemporary accounts mentioned above.

Register of the Privy Council of Scotland, IV (Edinburgh, 1881), 644-645, note.

A fresh edition was brought out at London in 1603. In 1616 it appeared again as a part of the handsome collection of his Workes compiled by the Bishop of Winchester.

This story is to be found in the apocryphal book of Bel and the Dragon. It played a great part in the discussions of the writers on witchcraft.

H. C. Lea, Superstition and Force (4th ed., Philadelphia, 1892), 325 ff., gives some facts about the water ordeal on the Continent. A sharp dispute over its use in witch cases was just at this time going on there.

He recommended torture in finding out the guilty: "And further experience daily proves how loth they are to confesse without torture, which witnesseth their guiltinesse," Dæmonologie, bk. ii, ch. i.

Wright, Narratives of Sorcery and Magic, I, 197.

Edward Fairfax, A Discourse of Witchcraft As it was acted in the Family of Mr. Edward Fairfax ... in the year 1621 (Philobiblon Soc., Miscellanies, V, ed. R. Monckton Milnes, London, 1858-1859), "Preface to the Reader," 26, explains the king's motive: His "Majesty found a defect in the statutes, ... by which none died for Witchcraft but they only who by that means killed, so that such were executed rather as murderers than as Witches."

Journals of the House of Lords, II, 269; Wm. Cobbett, Parliamentary History, I, 1017, 1018.

Lords' Journal, II, 271, 316; Commons' Journal, I, 203-204.

Cal. St. P., Dom., 1603-1610, 117.

It had passed the third reading in the Commons on June 7; Commons' Journal, I, 234.

It can hardly be doubted that the change in the wording of the law was dictated not only by the desire to simplify the matter of proof but by a wish to satisfy those theologians who urged that any use of witchcraft was a "covenant with death" and "an agreement with hell" (Isaiah xxviii, 18).

See Southworth case in Thomas Potts, The Wonderfull Discoverie of Witches in the countie of Lancaster ... (London, 1613; reprinted, Chetham Soc., 1845), L 2 verso. Cited hereafter as Potts.

See, below, appendix B. It should be added that six others who had been condemned by the judges for bewitching a boy were released at James's command.

The Witches of Northamptonshire ... C 2 verso. The writer of this pamphlet, who does not tell the story of the ordeal so fully as the author of the MS. account, "A briefe abstract of the arraignment of nine witches at Northampton, July 21, 1612" (Brit. Mus., Sloane, 972), gives, however, proof of the influence of James in the matter. He says that the two ways of testing witches are by the marks and "the trying of the insensiblenesse thereof," and by "their fleeting on the water," which is an exact quotation from James, although not so indicated.

The mother and father were apparently not sent to the assize court.

The female jury was used at Northampton ("women sworn"), also at Bedford, but by a private party.

It was used in 1621 on Elizabeth Sawyer of Edmonton. In this case it was done clearly at the command of the judge who tried her at the Old Bailey.

Elizabeth Device, however, confessed that the "said Devill did get blood under her left arme," which raises a suspicion that this confession was the result of accusations against her on that score.

See account in next chapter of the trial at Lancaster.

This case must be used with hesitation; see below, appendix A, § 3.

At Warboys the Samuels had been required to repeat: "If I be a witch and consenting to the death" of such and such a one. Alice Wilson, at Northampton in 1612, was threatened by the justice with execution, if she would not say after the minister "I forsake the Devil." She is said to have averred that she could not say this. See MS. account of the witches of Northampton.

Well known is the practice ascribed to witches of making a waxen image, which was then pricked or melted before the fire, in the belief that the torments inflicted upon it would be suffered by the individual it represented.

Potts, E 3 verso, F 4, G 2; also The Wonderful Discoverie of the Witchcrafts of Margaret and Phillip Flower, ... (London, 1619), 21.

See MS. account of the Northampton witches.

Ibid.: "Sundry other witches appeared to him.... Hee heard many of them railing at Jane Lucas, laying the fault on her that they were thus accused."

There was practically no spectral evidence in the Lancashire cases. Lister on his death-bed had cried out against Jennet Preston, and John Law was tormented with a vision of Alizon Device "both day and night"; Potts, Y 2 verso. But these were exceptional.

See The Most Cruell and Bloody Murther committed by ... Annis Dell.... With the Severall Witch-crafts ... of one Johane Harrison and her Daughter (London, 1606).

MS. account of the Northampton witches.

See Potts, Z 2.

The dramatist Dekker made use of this; see his Witch of Edmonton, act IV, scene I (Mermaid edition, London, 1904):

1st Countreyman.—This thatch is as good as a jury to prove she is a witch.

* * * * * * * *

Justice.—Come, come: firing her thatch? ridiculous!

Take heed, sirs, what you do; unless your proofs

Come better aimed, instead of turning her

Into a witch, you'll prove yourselves stark fools.

See Potts, P 2.

See ibid., Q verso. This, however, was the second time that the judge had tried this ruse; see ibid., P 2.

See above, note 21.

North Riding Record Soc., Quarter Sessions Records (London, 1883, etc.), III, 181.

Two of them, however, were issued to the same woman, one in 1604 and one in 1610.

Hist. MSS. Comm. Reports, XIII, 4 (Rye), pp. 136-137, 139-140, 144, 147-148.

The term "spinster" was sometimes used of a married woman.

Cal. St. P., Dom., 1619-1623, 125, Chamberlain to Carleton, February 26, 1620: "Peacock, a schoolmaster, committed to the Tower and tortured for practising sorcery upon the King, to infatuate him in Sir Thos. Lake's business." This is one of those rare cases in which we know certainly that torture was used.

Sir Thomas Lake to Viscount Cranbourne, January 20, 1604, Brit. Mus., Add. MSS., 6177, fol. 403.

Cal. St. P., Dom., 1623-1625, 474, 485, 497.

T. B. and T. J. Howell, State Trials (London, 1809-1818), II.

See Potts, O 3 verso.

See Hist. MSS. Comm. Reports, XIII, 4 (Rye), pp. 136-137, 139-140, 144, 147-148.

See Alexander Roberts, A Treatise of Witchcraft ... (London, 1616), dedicated to the "Maior and Aldermen."

M. A. Richardson, Table Book (London, 1841-1846), I, 245.

North Riding Record Soc., Quarter Sessions Records, I, 58.

"... neither had they authoritie to compell her to goe without a Constable."

Brit. Mus., Add. MSS., 36,674, fol. 148. This is a brief description of "how to discover a witch." It recommends the water ordeal and cites the case of Mr. Enger and Mary Sutton.

In the case of three of these four we know only that they were sentenced.

Before the Flower case at Lincoln came the Willimot-Baker cases at Leicester. The Bedford trial resembled much the Northampton trial of the previous year.

CHAPTER VI.: Notable Jacobean Cases.

It is possible to sift, to analyze, and to reconstruct the material derived from witch trials until some few conclusions about a given period can be ventured. A large proportion of cases can be proved to belong in this or that category, a certain percentage of the women can be shown to possess these or those traits in common. Yet it is quite thinkable that one might be armed with a quiver full of generalizations, and fail, withal, to comprehend Jacobean witchcraft. If one could have asked information on the subject from a Londoner of 1620, he would probably have heard little about witchcraft in general, but a very great deal about the Lancashire, Northampton, Leicester, Lincoln, and Fairfax trials. The Londoner might have been able to tell the stories complete of all those famous cases. He would have been but poorly informed could he not have related some of them, and the listener would have caught the surface drift of those stories. But a witch panic is a subtle thing, not to be understood by those who do not follow all its deeper sequences. The springs of the movement, the interaction of cause and effect, the operation of personal traits, these are factors that must be evaluated, and they are not factors that can be fitted into a general scheme, labelled and classified.

This does not mean that the cases should be examined in chronological sequence. That is not necessary; for the half-dozen cases that we shall run over had little or no cause-and-effect connection with one another. It is convenient, indeed, to make some classification, and the simplest is that by probable origin, especially as it will enable us to emphasize that important feature of the trials. Now, by this method the six or more trials of note may be grouped under three headings: cases that seem to have originated in the actual practice of magic, cases where the victims of convulsions and fits started the furor, and cases that were simply the last stage of bitter quarrels or the result of grudges.

To the first group belongs the Lancastrian case of 1612, which, however, may also be classed under the last heading. No case in the course of the superstition in England gained such wide fame. Upon it Shadwell founded in part a well-known play, The Lancashire Witches, while poets and writers of prose have referred to it until the two words have been linked in a phrase that has given them lasting association. It was in the lonely forest of Pendle among the wild hills of eastern Lancashire that there lived two hostile families headed by Elizabeth Southerns, or "Old Demdike," and by Anne Chattox. The latter was a wool carder, "a very old, withered, spent, and decreped creature," "her lippes ever chattering"; the former a blind beggar of four-score years, "a generall agent for the Devell in all these partes," and a "wicked fire-brand of mischiefe," who had brought up her children and grandchildren to be witches. Both families professed supernatural practices. Both families no doubt traded on the fear they inspired. Indeed Dame Chattox was said to have sold her guarantee to do no harm in return for a fixed annual payment of "one aghen-dole of meale."

That there was a feud between the two clans was to be expected. They were at once neighbors and competitors, and were engaged in a career in which they must plot each against the other, and suspect each other. There are hints of other difficulties. Years before there had been a quarrel over stolen property. Demdike's daughter had missed clothes and food to the value of 20 shillings, and had later found some of the clothing in the possession of Chattox's daughter. A more serious difficulty involved a third family: a member of the Nutter family, well-to-do people in Lancashire, had sought to seduce old Chattox's married daughter, and, when repelled, had warned her that when he inherited the property where she lived she should be evicted. Chattox had retaliated by seeking to kill Nutter by witchcraft, and had been further incited thereto by three women, who wished to be rid of Nutter, in order that "the women, their coosens, might have the land." As a consequence Nutter had died within three months. The quarrel, indeed, was three-cornered. It was said that Demdike's daughter had fashioned a clay picture of a Nutter woman.

We have all the elements here of a mountain feud; but, in place of the revolvers and Kentucky moonshine of to-day, we have clay images and Satanic banquets. The battles were to be fought out with imps of Hell as participants and with ammunition supplied by the Evil One himself. It was this connection with a reservoir of untouched demoniacal powers that made the quarrel of the miserable mountaineers the most celebrated incident in Lancashire story. Here were charmers and "inchanters," experienced dealers in magic, struggling against one another. Small wonder that the community became alarmed and that Roger Nowell, justice of the peace, suddenly swooped down upon the Pendle families. It was but a short time before he had four women cooped up in Lancaster castle. In a few days more he was able to get confessions out of them. They admitted acquaintance with the Devil and implicated one another.

Now comes the strange part of the story. According to confessions made later, Elizabeth Device, not yet shut up, but likely to be at any time, called a meeting on Good Friday of all the witches in Pendle forest. They were to come to her home at Malking Tower to plot the delivery of the imprisoned women by the blowing up of Lancaster castle. The affair took the form of a dinner; and beef, bacon, and roasted mutton were served. "All the witches went out of the said House in their owne shapes and likenesses. And they all, by that they were forth of the dores, gotten on Horsebacke, like unto Foales, some of one colour, some of another; and Preston's wife was the last; and, when shee got on Horsebacke, they all presently vanished out of ... sight." This was the story, and the various witnesses agreed remarkably well as to its main details. Those who believed in the "sabbath" of witches must have felt their opinions confirmed by the testimony of the witnesses at Lancaster. Even the modern reader, with his skepticism, is somewhat daunted by the cumulative force of what purports to be the evidence and would fain rationalize it by supposing that some sort of a meeting actually did take place at Malking Tower and that some Pendle men and women who had delved in magic arts till they believed in them did formulate plans for revenge. But this is not a probable supposition. The concurring evidence in the Malking Tower story is of no more compelling character than that to be found in a multitude of Continental stories of witch gatherings which have been shown to be the outcome of physical or mental pressure and of leading questions. It seems unnecessary to accept even a substratum of fact. Probably one of the accused women invented the story of the witch feast after the model of others of which she had heard, or developed it under the stimulus of suggestive questions from a justice. Such a narrative, once started, would spread like wildfire and the witnesses and the accused who were persuaded to confess might tell approximately the same story. A careful re-reading of all this evidence suggests that the various testimonies may indeed have been echoes of the first narrative. They seem to lack those characteristic differences which would stamp them as independent accounts. Moreover, when the story was once started, it is not improbable that the justices and the judges would assist the witnesses by framing questions based upon the narrative already given. It cannot be said that the evidence exists upon which to establish this hypothesis. There is little to show that the witnesses were adroitly led into their narratives. But we know from other trials that the method was so often adopted that it is not a far cry to suspect that it was used at Lancaster.

It is not worth while to trace out the wearisome details that were elicited by confession. Those already in prison made confessions that implicated others, until the busy justices of the peace had shut up sixteen women and four men to be tried at the assizes. Sir Edward Bromley and Sir James Altham, who were then on the northern circuit, reached Lancaster on the sixteenth of August. In the meantime, "Old Demdike," after a confession of most awful crimes, had died in prison. All the others were put on trial. Thomas Potts compiled a very careful abstract of all the testimony taken, perhaps the most detailed account of a witch trial written in the English language, with the possible exception of the St. Oses affair. The evidence was in truth of a somewhat similar type. Secret interviews with the Evil One, promises of worldly riches, a contract sealed with blood, little shapes of dogs, cats, and hares, clay pictures that had been dried and had crumpled, threats and consequent "languishing" and death, these were the trappings of the stories. The tales were old. Only the Malking Tower incident was new. But its very novelty gave a plausibility to the stories that were woven around it. There was not a single person to interpose a doubt. The cross-examinations were nothing more than feeble attempts to bring out further charges.

Though there is in the record little suggestion of the use of pressure to obtain the confessions, the fact that three were retracted leads to a suspicion that they had not been given quite freely. There was doubtless something contagious about the impulse to confess. It is, nevertheless, a curious circumstance that five members of the two rival Pendle families made confession, while all the others whom their confessions had involved stuck to it that they were innocent. Among those who persisted in denying their guilt Alice Nutter merits special note. We have already mentioned her in the last chapter as an example of a well-to-do and well connected woman who fell a victim to the Lancashire excitement. The evidence against the woman was perhaps the flimsiest ever offered to a court. Elizabeth Device, daughter of "Old Demdike," and her two children were the chief accusers. Elizabeth had seen her present at the Malking Tower meeting. Moreover, she stated that Alice had helped her mother ("Old Demdike") bewitch a man to death. Her son had heard his grandmother Demdike narrate the incident. This testimony and his sister's definite statement that Alice Nutter attended the Malking Tower meeting established Mistress Nutter's guilt. The judge, indeed, was "very suspicious of the accusation of this yong wench, Jennet Device," and, as we have already seen, caused her to be sent out of the court room till the accused lady could be placed among other prisoners, when the girl was recalled and required before the great audience present to pick out the witch, as, of course, she easily did, and as easily escaped another transparent trap.

The two children figured prominently from this on. The nine-year-old girl gave evidence as to events of three years before, while the young man, who could hardly have been out of his teens, recounted what had happened twelve years earlier. It was their testimony against their mother that roused most interest. Although of a circumstantial character, it fitted in most remarkable fashion into the evidence already presented. The mother, says the nonchalant pamphleteer, indignantly "cryed out against the child," cursing her so outrageously that she was removed from the room while the child kept the stand. It is useless to waste sympathy upon a mother who was getting at the hands of her children the same treatment she had given her own mother Demdike. The Chattox family held together better. Mistress Redfearne had been carefully shielded in the testimony of her mother Chattox, but she fell a victim to the accusations of the opposing family. The course of her trial was remarkable. Denying her guilt with great emphasis, she had by some wonder been acquitted. But this verdict displeased the people in attendance upon the trial. Induced by the cries of the people, the court was persuaded to try her again. The charge against her was exactly the same, that eighteen years before she had participated in killing Christopher Nutter with a clay figure. "Old Demdike" had seen her in the act of making the image, and there was offered also the testimony of the sister and brother of the dead man, who recalled that Robert Nutter on his death-bed had accused Anne of his bewitchment. It does not seem to have occurred to the court that the principle that a person could not twice be put in jeopardy for the same offence was already an old principle in English law. The judges were more concerned with appeasing the people than with recalling old precedents, and sent the woman to the gallows.

The Pendle cases were interrupted on the third day by the trial of three women from Salmesbury, who pleaded not guilty and put themselves "upon God and their Countrey." The case against them rested upon the testimony of a single young woman, Grace Sowerbutts, who declared that for the three years past she had been vexed by the women in question, who "did violently draw her by the haire of the head, and layd her on the toppe of a Hay-mowe." This delightfully absurd charge was coupled with some testimony about the appearances of the accused in animal form. Three men attempted to bolster up the story; but no "matter of witchcraft" was proved, says the for once incredulous Mr. Potts. The women seized the decisive moment. They kneeled before the judge and requested him to examine Grace Sowerbutts as to who set her on. The judge—who had seemingly not thought of this before—followed the suggestion. The girl changed countenance and acknowledged that she had been taught her story. At the order of the judge she was questioned by a clergyman and two justices of the peace, who found that she had been coached to tell her story by a Master Thompson, alias Southworth, a "seminarie priest." So ended the charges against the Salmesbury witches.

One would suppose that this verdict might have turned the tide in the other cases. But the evidence, as Potts is careful to show, lest the reader should draw a wrong conclusion, was of very different character in the other trials. They were all finished on the third day of court and turned over to the jury. Five of the accused, exclusive of those at Salmesbury, were acquitted, one condemned to a year's imprisonment, and ten sentenced to death. To this number should be added Jennet Preston, who had in the preceding month been tried at York for the killing of a Mr. Lister, and who was named by the Lancaster witnesses as one of the gang at Malking Tower.

So ended the Lancashire trials of 1612. The most remarkable event of the sort in James's reign, they were clearly the outcome of his writings and policy. Potts asks pointedly: "What hath the King's Maiestie written and published in his Dæmonologie by way of premonition and prevention, which hath not here by the first or last beene executed, put in practice, or discovered?"

Our second group of cases includes those where convulsive and "possessed" persons had started the alarm. The Northampton, Leicester, and Lichfield cases were all instances in point. The last two, however, may be omitted here because they will come up in another connection. The affair at Northampton in 1612, just a month earlier than the Lancashire affair, merits notice. Elizabeth Belcher and her brother, "Master Avery," were the disturbing agents. Mistress Belcher had long been suffering with an illness that baffled diagnosis. It was suggested to her that the cause was witchcraft. A list of women reputed to be witches was repeated to her. The name of Joan Brown seemed to impress her. "Hath shee done it?" she asked. The name was repeated to her and from that time she held Joan guilty. Joan and her mother were shut up. Meantime Master Avery began to take fits and to aid his sister in making accusation. Between them they soon had accused six women for their afflictions. The stir brought to the surface the hidden suspicions of others. There was a witch panic and the justices of the peace scurried hither and thither till they had fourteen witches locked up in Northampton. When the trial came off at Northampton, Master Avery was the hero. He re-enacted the rôle of the Throckmorton children at Warboys with great success. When he came to court—he came in a "coch"—he was at once stricken with convulsions. His torments in court were very convincing. It is pleasant to know that when he came out of his seizure he would talk very "discreetly, christianly, and charitably." Master Avery was versatile, however. His evidence against the women rested by no means alone on his seizures. He had countless apparitions in which he saw the accused; he had been mysteriously thrown from a horse; strangest of all, he had foretold at a certain time that if any one should go down to the gaol and listen to the voices of the witches, he could not understand a word. Whereupon a Master of Arts of Trinity College, Oxford, went off to the prison at the uncanny hour of two in the morning and "heard a confused noise of much chattering and chiding, but could not discover a ready word."

Master Avery had a great deal more to tell, but the jury seem not to have fully credited him. They convicted Joan Brown and her mother, however, on the charges of Elizabeth and her brother. Three others were found guilty upon other counts. None of them, so far as the records go, and the records were careful on this point, admitted any guilt. The one young man among those who were hanged bitterly resisted his conviction from the beginning and died declaring that authority had turned to tyranny. He might well feel so. His father and mother had both been tortured by the water ordeal, and his mother had been worried till she committed suicide in prison.

This brings us to the third sort of cases, those that were the outcome of quarrels or grudges. It has already been observed that the Lancashire affair could very well be reckoned under this heading. It is no exaggeration to say that a goodly percentage of all other witch trials in the reign of James could be classified in the same way. Most notable among them was the famous trial of the Belvoir witches at Lincoln in 1618-1619. The trial has received wide notice because it concerned a leading family—perhaps the wealthiest in England—the great Catholic family of Manners, of which the Earl of Rutland was head. The effort to account for the mysterious illness of his young heir and for that which had a few years earlier carried off the boy's elder brother led to a charge of witchcraft against three humble women of the neighborhood. The Rutland affair shows how easily a suspicion of witchcraft might involve the fortunes of the lowly with those of the great. Joan Flower and her two daughters had been employed as charwomen in Belvoir Castle, the home of the Rutlands. One of the daughters, indeed, had been put in charge of "the poultrey abroad and the washhouse within dores." But this daughter seems not to have given satisfaction to the countess in her work, some other causes of disagreement arose which involved Mother Flower, and both Mother Flower and her daughter were sent away from the castle. This was the beginning of the trouble. Mother Flower "cursed them all that were the cause of this discontentment." Naturally little heed was paid to her grumblings. Such things were common enough and it did not even occur to any one, when the eldest son of the earl sickened and died, that the event was in any way connected with the malice of the Flowers. It was not until about five years later, when the younger son Francis fell sick of an illness to prove fatal, that suspicion seems to have lighted upon the three women. The circumstances that led to their discharge were then recalled and along with them a mass of idle gossip and scandal against the women. It was remembered that Mother Joan was "a monstrous malicious woman, full of oathes, curses, and imprecations irreligious." Some of her neighbors "dared to affirme that she dealt with familiar spirits, and terrified them all with curses and threatning of revenge." At length, in February of 1618/19, on the return of the earl from attending His Majesty "both at Newmarket before Christmas and at Christmas at Whitehall," the women were fetched before justices of the peace, who bound them over to the assizes at Lincoln. Mother Flower died on the way to Lincoln, but the two daughters were tried there before Sir Edward Bromley, who had been judge at the Lancashire trials, and before Sir Henry Hobart. The women made a detailed confession of weird crimes. There were tales of gloves belonging to the two young sons of the earl, gloves that had been found in uncanny places and had been put in hot water and rubbed upon Rutterkin the cat— or spirit. There were worse stories that will not bear repetition. Needless to say, Margaret and Philippa Flower were convicted and hanged.

The Rutland cases have been used to illustrate how the witch accusation might arise out of a grudge or quarrel. There were three or four other cases that illustrate this origin of the charge. The first is that of Johanna Harrison—she has been mentioned in the previous chapter—who had an "altercation" with a neighbor. Of course she threatened him, he fell ill, and he scratched her. But here the commonplace tale takes a new turn. She had him arrested and was awarded five shillings damages and her costs of suit. No wonder the man fell sick again. Perhaps—but this cannot be certain—it was the same man who was drinking his ale one day with his fellows when she entered and stood "gloating" over him. He turned and said, "Doe you heare, Witch, looke tother waies." The woman berated him with angry words, and, feeling ill the next morning—he had been drinking heavily the night before—he dragged her off to the justice. A few weeks later she and her daughter were hanged at Hertford.

The story of Mother Sutton and Master Enger has been referred to in several connections, but it will bear telling in narrative form. Mother Sutton was a poor tenant of Master Enger's, "a gentleman of worship," who often bestowed upon her "food and cloathes." On account of her want she had been chosen village "hog-heard," and had for twenty years fulfilled the duties of her office "not without commendations." But it happened that she quarreled one day with her benefactor, and then his difficulties began. The tale is almost too trivial for repetition, but is nevertheless characteristic. Master Enger's servants were taking some corn to market, when they met "a faire black sowe" grazing. The wayward beast began turning round "as readily as a Windmill sail at worke; and as sodainly their horses fell to starting and drawing some one way, some another." They started off with the cart of corn, but broke from it and ran away. The servants caught them and went on to Bedford with the load. But the sow followed. When the corn had been sold, one of the servants went home, the other stayed with his "boone companions." When he rode home later, he found the sow grazing outside of town. It ran by his side, and the horses ran away again. But the servants watched the sow and saw it enter Mother Sutton's house. Master Enger made light of the story when it was told to him, and, with remarkable insight for a character in a witch story, "supposed they were drunke." But a few days later the same servant fell into conversation with Mother Sutton, when a beetle came and struck him. He fell into a trance, and then went home and told his master. The next night the servant said that Mary Sutton entered his room—the vision we have already described.

The rest of the story the reader knows from the last chapter. Mother Sutton and her daughter were put to various ordeals and at length hanged. Doubtless the imaginative servant, who had in some way, perhaps, been involved in the original quarrel, gained favor with his master, and standing in the community.

The tale of the Bakewell witches is a very curious one and, though not to be confidently depended upon, may suggest how it was possible to avail oneself of superstition in order to repay a grudge. A Scotchman staying at a lodging-house in Bakewell fell in debt to his landlady, who retained some of his clothes as security. He went to London, concealed himself in a cellar, and was there found by a watchman, who arrested him for being in an unoccupied house with felonious intent. He professed to be dazed and declared that he was at Bakewell in Derbyshire at three o'clock that morning. He explained it by the fact that he had repeated certain words which he had heard his lodging-house keeper and her sister say. The judge was amazed, the man's depositions were taken down, and he was sent to the justices of Derby.

All that we really know about the Bakewell affair is that several witches probably suffered death there in 1607. A local antiquarian has given this tale of how the alarm started. While it is unlike any other narrative of witchcraft, it is not necessarily without foundation.

The reader has doubtless observed that the cases which we have been describing occurred, all of them with one exception, between 1603 and 1619. In discussing the matter of the distribution of witchcraft in the last chapter we noted that not only executions for the crime, but even accusations and indictments, were nearly altogether limited to the first fifteen years of James's rule. If it is true that there was a rather sudden falling off of prosecution in the reign of the zealous James, the fact merits explanation. Fortunately the explanation is not far to seek. The king's faith in the verity of many of the charges made against witches had been rudely shaken. As a matter of fact there had always been a grain of skepticism in his make-up. This had come out even before he entered England. In 1597 he had become alarmed at the spread of trials in Scotland and had revoked all the commissions then in force for the trial of the offence. At the very time when he became king of England, there were special circumstances that must have had weight with him. Throughout the last years of Elizabeth's reign there had been, as we have seen, a morbid interest in demoniacal possession, an interest to which sensation-mongers were quickly minded to respond. We saw that at the end of the sixteenth century the Anglican church stepped in to put down the exorcizing of spirits, largely perhaps because it had been carried on by Catholics and by a Puritan clergyman. Yet neither Harsnett's book nor Darrel's imprisonment quite availed to end a practice which offered at all times to all comers a path to notoriety. James had not been on the English throne a year when he became interested in a case of this kind. Mary Glover, a girl alleged to have been bewitched by a Mother Jackson, was at the king's wish examined by a skilled physician, Dr. Edward Jorden, who recognized her fits as disease, brought the girl to a confession, published an account of the matter, and so saved the life of the woman whom she had accused.

In the very next year there was a case at Cambridge that gained royal notice. It is not easy to straighten out the facts from the letters on the matter, but it seems that two Cambridge maids had a curious disease suggesting bewitchment. A Franciscan and a Puritan clergyman were, along with others, suspected. The matter was at once referred to the king and the government. James directed that examinations be made and reported to him. This was done. James wormed out of the "principal" some admission of former dealing with conjuration, but turned the whole thing over to the courts, where it seems later to have been established that the disease of the bewitched maidens was "naturall."

These were but the first of several impostures that interested the king. A girl at Windsor, another in Hertfordshire, were possessed by the Devil, two maids at Westminster were "in raptures from the Virgin Mary and Michael the Archangel," a priest of Leicestershire was "possessed of the Blessed Trinity." Such cases—not to mention the Grace Sowerbutts confessions at Lancaster that were like to end so tragically—were the excrescences of an intensely religious age. The reader of early colonial diaries in America will recognize the resemblance of these to the wonders they report. James took such with extreme seriousness. The possessed person was summoned to court for exhibition, or the king went out of his way to see him. It is a matter of common information that James prided himself on his cleverness. Having succeeded in detecting certain frauds, he became an expert detective. In one instance "he ordered it so that a proper courtier made love to one of these bewitched maids" and soon got her over her troubles. In another case a woman "strangely affected" by the first verse of John's Gospel failed to recognize it when read in Greek, proof positive that the omniscient Devil did not possess her.

Three instances of exposure of imposture were most notable, those of Grace Sowerbutts, the boy at Leicester, and the "Boy of Bilston." The first of these has already been sufficiently discussed in connection with the Lancashire trials. The second had nothing remarkable about it. A twelve or thirteen-year-old boy had fits which he said were caused by spirits sent by several women whom he accused as witches. Nine women were hanged, while six more were under arrest and would probably have met the same end, had not the king in his northward progress, while stopping at Leicester, detected the shamming. Whether or no the boy was punished we are not told. It is some satisfaction that the judges were disgraced.

The boy of Bilston was, if Webster may be believed, the most famous, if not the most successful, fraud of all. The case was heralded over the entire realm and thousands came to see. The story is almost an exact duplicate of earlier narratives of possession. A thirteen-year-old boy of Bilston in Staffordshire, William Perry, began to have fits and to accuse a Jane Clarke, whose presence invariably made him worse. He "cast out of his mouth rags, thred, straw, crooked pins." These were but single deceptions in a repertoire of varied tricks. Doubtless he had been trained in his rôle by a Roman priest. At any rate the Catholics tried exorcism upon him, but to no purpose. Perhaps some Puritans experimented with cures which had like result. The boy continued his spasms and his charges against the witch and she was brought into court at the July assizes. But Bishop Morton, before whose chancellor the boy had first been brought, was present, and the judges turned the boy over to him for further investigation. Then, with the help of his secretary, he set about to test the boy, and readily exposed his deception—in most curious fashion too. The boy, like one we have met before, could not endure the first verse of John's Gospel, but failed to recognize it when read in the Greek. After that he was secretly watched and his somewhat elaborate preparations for his pretences were found out. He was persuaded to confess his trickery in court before Sir Peter Warburton and Sir Humphrey Winch, "and the face of the County and Country there assembled," as well as to beg forgiveness of the women whom he had accused.

It will be seen that the records of imposture were well on their way to rival the records of witchcraft, if not in numbers, at least in the notice that they received. And the king who had so bitterly arraigned Reginald Scot was himself becoming the discoverer-general of England. It is not, then, without being forewarned that we read Fuller's remarkable statement about the king's change of heart. "The frequency of such forged possessions wrought such an alteration upon the judgement of King James that he, receding from what he had written in his 'Dæmonology,' grew first diffident of, and then flatly to deny, the workings of witches and devils, as but falsehoods and delusions." In immediate connection with this must be quoted what Francis Osborne has to say. He was told, he writes, that the king would have gone as far as to deny any such operations, but out of reasons of state and to gratify the church.

Such a conversion is so remarkable that we could wish we had absolutely contemporary statements of it. As a matter of fact, the statements we have quoted establish nothing more than a probability, but they certainly do establish that. Fuller, the church historian, responsible for the first of the two statements, was a student in Queen's College at Cambridge during the last four years of James's reign; Osborne was a man of thirty-two when the king died, and had spent a part of his young manhood at the court. Their testimony was that of men who had every opportunity to know about the king's change of opinion. In the absence of any evidence to the contrary, we must accept, at least provisionally, their statements. And it is easier to do so in view of the marked falling off of prosecutions that we have already noted. This indeed is confirmation of a negative sort; but we have one interesting bit of affirmative proof, the outcome of the trials at York in 1622. In that year the children of Mr. Edward Fairfax, a member of the historic Fairfax family of Yorkshire, were seized with some strange illness, in which they saw again and again the spectres of six different women. These women were examined by the justices of the peace and committed to the assizes. In the mean time they had found able and vigorous defenders in the community. What happened at the April assizes we no not know, but we know that four of the women were released, two of them on bond. This was probably a compromise method of settling the matter. Fairfax was not satisfied. Probably through his influence the women were again brought up at the August assizes. Then, at least, as we know beyond a doubt, they were formally tried, this time upon indictments preferred by Fairfax himself. The judge warned the jury to be very careful, and, after hearing some of the evidence, dismissed the women on the ground that the evidence "reached not to the point of the statute." This seems significant. A man of a well known county family was utterly baffled in pressing charges in a case where his own children were involved. It looks as if there were judges who were following the king's lead in looking out for imposture. In any case there was, in certain quarters, a public sentiment against the conviction of witches, a sentiment that made itself felt. This we shall have occasion to note again in following out the currents and fluctuations of opinions.

Of course the proof that some of the accused really made pretensions to magic rests upon their own confessions and their accusations of one another, and might be a part of an intricate tissue of falsehood. But, granting for the moment the absolute untrustworthiness of the confessions and accusations there are incidental statements which imply the practice of magic. For example, Elizabeth Device's young daughter quoted a long charm which she said her mother had taught her and which she hardly invented on the spur of the moment. And Demdike was requested to "amend a sick cow."

The gunpowder plot, seven years earlier, no doubt gave direction to this plan, or, perhaps it would be better to say, gave the idea to those who confessed the plan.

James Crossley seems to believe that there was "some scintilla of truth" behind the story. See his edition of Potts, notes, p. 40.

Among those who never confessed seems to have been Chattox's daughter, Anne Redfearne. See above, p. 116.

It is a satisfaction to know that Alice died "impenitent," and that not even her children could "move her to confesse."

See above, pp. 112-113, and Potts, Q-Q verso.

See Potts, I.

It can hardly be doubted that the children had been thoroughly primed with the stories in circulation against their mother.

Other witnesses charged her with "many strange practises."

The principle that a man's life may not twice be put in jeopardy for the same offence had been pretty well established before 1612. See Darly's Case, 25 Eliz. (1583), Coke's Reports (ed. Thomas and Fraser, London, 1826), IV, f. 40; Vaux's Case, 33 Eliz. (1591), ibid., f. 45; Wrote vs. Wiggs, 33 Eliz. (1591), ibid., f. 47. This principle had been in process of development for several centuries. See Bracton (ed. Sir Travers Twiss, London, 1878-1883), II, 417, 433, 437; Britton (ed. F. M. Nichols, Oxford, 1865), bk. I, cap. xxiv, 5, f. 44 b.

It must be noted, however, that the statute of 3 Hen. VII, cap. II, provides that indictments shall be proceeded in, immediately, at the king's suit, for the death of a man, without waiting for bringing an appeal; and that the plea of antefort acquit in an indictment shall be no bar to the prosecuting of an appeal. This law was passed to get around special legal inconvenience and related only to homicide and to the single case of prosecution by appeal. In general, then, we may say that the former-jeopardy doctrine was part of the common law, (1) an appeal of felony being a bar to subsequent appeal or indictment, (2) an indictment a bar to a subsequent indictment, and (3) an indictment to a subsequent appeal, except so far as the statute of 3 Hen. VII., cap. II, changed the law as respects homicides. For this brief statement I am indebted to Professor William Underhill Moore of the University of Wisconsin.

What Potts has to say about Anne Redfearne's case hardly enables us to reach a conclusion about the legal aspect of it.

This is the story in the MS. account (Brit. Mus., Sloane, 972). The printed narrative of the origin of the affair is somewhat different. Joan had on one occasion been struck by Mistress Belcher for unbecoming behavior and had cherished a grudge. No doubt this was a point recalled against Joan after suspicion had been directed against her.

In John Cotta's The Triall of Witchcraft ... (London, 1616), 66-67, there is a very interesting statement which probably refers to this case. Cotta, it will be remembered, was a physician at Northampton. He wrote: "There is a very rare, but true, description of a Gentlewoman, about sixe yeares past, cured of divers kinds of convulsions, ... After she was almost cured, ... but the cure not fully accomplished, it was by a reputed Wisard whispered ... that the Gentlewoman was meerely bewitched, supposed Witches were accused and after executed.... In this last past seventh yeare ... fits are critically again returned." Cotta says six years ago and the Northampton trials were in 1612, four years before. It is quite possible, however, that Mistress Belcher began to be afflicted in 1610.

One of these was Sir Gilbert Pickering of Tichmarsh, almost certainly the Gilbert Pickering mentioned as an uncle of the Throckmorton children at Warboys. See above, pp. 47-48. His hatred of witches had no doubt been increased by that affair.

See what is said of spectral evidence in chapter V, above.

At least there is no evidence that Alice Abbott, Catherine Gardiner, and Alice Harris, whom he accused, were punished in any way.

It seems, however, that Arthur Bill, while he sturdily denied guilt, had been before trapped into some sort of an admission. He had "unawares confest that he had certaine spirits at command." But this may mean nothing more than that something he had said had been grossly misinterpreted.

Three women of Leicestershire, Anne Baker, Joan Willimot, and Ellen Greene, who in their confessions implicated the Flowers (they belonged to parishes neighbor to that of Belvoir, which lies on the shire border) and whose testimony against them figured in their trials, were at the same time (Feb.-March, 1618/19) under examination in that county. Whether these women were authors or victims of the Belvoir suspicions we do not know. As we have their damning confessions, there is small doubt as to their fate.

The women were tried in March, 1618/19, Henry, the elder son of the earl, was buried at Bottesford, September 26, 1613. John Nichols, History and Antiquities of the County of Leicester (London, 1795-1815), II, pt. i, 49, note 10. Francis, the second, lingered till early in 1620. His sister, Lady Katherine, whose delicate health had also been ascribed to the witches, was now the heiress, and became in that year the bride of Buckingham, the king's favorite. There is one aspect of this affair that must not be overlooked. The accusation against the Flowers cannot have been unknown to the king, who was a frequent visitor at the seat of the Rutlands. It is hard to believe that under such circumstances the use of torture, which James had declared essential to bring out the guilt of the accused witches, was not after some fashion resorted to. The weird and uncanny confessions go far towards supporting such an hypothesis.

The Most Cruell and Bloody Murther committed by ... Annis Dell, ... with the severall Witch-crafts ... of one Johane Harrison and her Daughter, 63.

This story must be accepted with hesitation; see below, appendix A, §3.

See above, pp. 110-111.

The trial of Elizabeth Sawyer at Edmonton in 1621 had to do with similar trivialities. Agnes Ratcliffe was washing one day, when a sow belonging to Elizabeth licked up a bit of her washing soap. She struck it with a "washing beetle." Of course she fell sick, and on her death-bed accused Mistress Elizabeth Sawyer, who was afterwards hanged.

See T. Tindall Wildridge, in William Andrews, Bygone Derbyshire (Derby, 1892), 180-184. It has been impossible to locate the sources of this story. J. Charles Cox, who explored the Derby records, seems never to have discovered anything about the affair.

See F. Legge, "Witchcraft in Scotland," in the Scottish Review, XVIII, 264.

See above, ch. IV, especially note 36.

On Mary Glover see also appendix A, § 2. On other impostures see Thomas Fuller, Church History of Britain (London, 1655; Oxford, ed. J. S. Brewer, 1845), ed. of 1845, V, 450; letters given by Edmund Lodge, Illustrations of British History, Biography and Manners ... (London, 1791), III, 275, 284, 287-288; also King James, His Apothegms, by B. A., Gent. (London, 1643),

8-10.

Cal. St. P., Dom., 1603-1610, 218.

Fuller, op. cit., V, 450.

Ibid.; John Gee, The Foot out of the Snare, or Detection of Practices and Impostures of Priests and Jesuits in England ... (London, 1624), reprinted in Somers Tracts, III, 72.

Ibid.; Fuller, op. cit., V, 450.

How much more seriously than his courtiers is suggested by an anecdote of Sir John Harington's: James gravely questioned Sir John why the Devil did work more with ancient women than with others. "We are taught thereof in Scripture," gaily answered Sir John, "where it is told that the Devil walketh in dry places." See his Nugæ Antiquæ (London, 1769), ed. of London, 1804, I, 368-369.

Fuller, op. cit., V, 451.

Ibid.

The story of the hangings at Leicester in 1616 has to be put together from various sources. Our principal authority, however, is in two letters written by Robert Heyrick of Leicester to his brother William in 1616, which are to be found in John Nichols, History and Antiquities of the County of Leicester (London, 1795-1815), II, pt. ii, 471, and in the Annual Register for 1800. See also William Kelly, Royal Progresses to Leicester (Leicester, 1884), 367-369. Probably this is the case referred to by Francis Osborne, where the boy was sent to the Archbishop of Canterbury for further examination. Osborne, who wrote a good deal later than the events, apparently confused the story of the Leicester witches with that of the Boy of Bilston—their origins were similar—and produced a strange account; see his Miscellany of Sundry Essays, Paradoxes and Problematicall Discourses (London, 1658-1659), 6-9.

For the disgrace of the judges see Cal. St. P., Dom., 1611-1618, 398.

Webster knew Bishop Morton, and also his secretary, Baddeley, who had been notary in the case and had written an account of it. See John Webster, The Displaying of Supposed Witchcraft (London, 1677), 275.

The Catholics declared that the Puritans tried "syllabub" upon him. This was perhaps a sarcastic reference to their attempts to cure him by medicine.

Then of Lichfield.

Baddeley, who was Bishop Morton's secretary and who prepared the narrative of the affair for the printer, says that the woman was freed by the inquest; Ryc. Baddeley, The Boy of Bilson ... (London, 1622), 61. Arthur Wilson, who tells us that he heard the story "from the Bishop's own mouth almost thirty years before it was inserted here," says that the woman was found guilty and condemned to die; Arthur Wilson, Life and Reign of James I (London, 1653), 107. It is evident that Baddeley's story is the more trustworthy. It is of course possible, although not probable, that there were two trials, and that Baddeley ignored the second one, the outcome of which would have been less creditable to the bishop.

Webster, Displaying of Supposed Witchcraft, 275.

See Fairfax, A Discourse of Witchcraft (Philobiblon Soc.): "and those whose impostures our wise King so lately laid open." See also an interesting letter from James himself in J. O. Halliwell, Letters of the Kings of England (London, 1846), II, 124-125.

Fuller, Church History of Britain, V, 452 (ch. X, sect. 4). It is worthy of note that Peter Heylyn, who, in his Examen Historicum (London, 1659), sought to pick Fuller to pieces, does not mention this point.

See Francis Osborne, Miscellany, 4-9. Lucy Aikin, Memoirs of the Court of King James the First (London, 1823), II, 398-399, gives about the same story as Fuller and Osborne, and, while the wording is slightly different, it is probable that they were her sources.

Arthur Wilson, op. cit., 111, tells us: "The King took delight by the line of his reason to sound the depth of such brutish impostors, and he discovered many " A writer to the Gentleman's Magazine (LIV, pt. I, 246-247), in 1784, says that he has somewhere read that King James on his death-bed acknowledged that he had been deceived in his opinion respecting witchcraft and expressed his concern that so many innocent persons had suffered on that account. But, as he has forgotten where he read it, his evidence is of course of small value.

The college where an annual sermon was preached on the subject of witchcraft since the Warboys affair.

Osborne's statement should perhaps be discounted a little on account of his skepticism. On the other hand he was not such an admirer of James I as to have given him undue credit. Fuller's opinion was divided.

James still believed in witchcraft in 1613, when the malodorous divorce trial of Lady Essex took place. A careful reading of his words at that time, however, leaves the impression that he was not nearly so certain about the possibilities of witchcraft as he had been when he wrote his book. His position was clearly defensive. It must be remembered that James in 1613 had a point to be gained and would not have allowed a possible doubt as to witchcraft to interfere with his wish for the divorce. See Howell, State Trials, II, 806.

One of them was publicly searched by command of a justice. See Fairfax, op. cit., 138-139.

Ibid., 205. Two of the women had gone home before, ibid., 180.

Ibid., 225-234.

Ibid., 234.

Ibid., 237-238. If the women were tried twice, it seems a clear violation of the principle of former jeopardy. See above, note 11. The statute of 3 Hen. VII, cap. I, that the plea of antefort acquit was no bar to the prosecution of an appeal, would not apply in this instance, as that statute was limited to cases of homicide.

Fairfax was moreover a man for whom the king had a high personal regard.

At the August assizes there had been an effort to show that the children were "counterfeiting." See the Discourse, 235-237.

CHAPTER VII.: The Lancashire Witches and Charles I.

In his attitude towards superstition, Charles I resembled the later rather than the earlier James I. No reign up to the Revolution was marked by so few executions. It was a time of comparative quiet. Here and there isolated murmurs against suspected creatures of the Devil roused the justices of the peace to write letters, and even to make inquiries that as often as not resulted in indefinite commitments, or brought out the protests of neighbors in favor of the accused. But, if there were not many cases, they represented a wide area. Middlesex, Wilts, Somerset, Leicestershire, Staffordshire, Lancashire, Durham, Yorkshire, and Northumberland were among the counties infested. Yet we can count but six executions, and only four of them rest upon secure evidence. This is of course to reckon the reign of Charles as not extending beyond 1642, when the Civil War broke out and the Puritan leaders assumed responsibility for the government.

Up to that time there was but one really notable witch alarm in England. But it was one that illustrated again, as in Essex, the continuity of the superstition in a given locality. The Lancashire witches of 1633 were the direct outcome of the Lancashire witches of 1612. The story is a weird one. An eleven-year-old boy played truant one day to his cattle-herding, and, as he afterwards told the story, went plum-gathering. When he came back he had to find a plausible excuse to present to his parents. Now, the lad had been brought up in the Blackburn forest, close to Pendle Hill; he had overheard stories of Malking Tower from the chatter of gossipping women; he had shivered as suspected women were pointed out to him; he knew the names of some of them. His imagination, in search for an excuse, caught at the witch motive and elaborated it with the easy invention of youth. He had seen two greyhounds come running towards him. They looked like those owned by two of his neighbors. When he saw that no one was following them, he set out to hunt with them, and presently a hare rose very near before him, at the sight whereof he cried "Loo, Loo," but the dogs would not run. Being very angry, he tied them to a little bush in the hedge and beat them, and at once, instead of the black greyhound, "one Dickonson's wife" stood up, and instead of the brown greyhound "a little boy whom this informer knoweth not." He started to run away, but the woman stayed him and offered him a piece of silver "much like to a faire shillinge" if he would not betray her. The conscientious boy answered "Nay, thou art a witch," "whereupon shee put her hand into her pocket againe and pulled out a stringe like unto a bridle that gingled, which shee put upon the litle boyes heade that stood up in the browne greyhounds steade, whereupon the said boy stood up a white horse." In true Arabian Nights fashion they mounted and rode away. They came to a new house called Hoarstones, where there were three score or more people, and horses of several colors, and a fire with meat roasting. They had flesh and bread upon a trencher and they drank from glasses. After the first taste the boy "refused and would have noe more, and said it was nought." There were other refreshments at the feast. The boy was, as he afterwards confessed, familiar with the story of the feast at Malking Tower.

The names of those present he did not volunteer at first; but, on being questioned, he named eighteen whom he had seen. The boy confessed that he had been clever enough to make most of his list from those who were already suspected by their neighbors.

It needed but a match to set off the flame of witch-hatred in Lancashire. The boy's story was quite sufficient. Whether his narrative was a spontaneous invention of his own, concocted in emergency, as he asserted in his confession at London, or whether it was a carefully constructed lie taught him by his father in order to revenge himself upon some hated neighbors, and perhaps to exact blackmail, as some of the accused later charged, we shall never know. In later life the boy is said to have admitted that he had been set on by his father, but the narrative possesses certain earmarks of a story struck out by a child's imagination. It is easy enough to reconcile the two theories by supposing that the boy started the story of his own initiative and that his father was too shrewd not to realize the opportunity to make a sensation and perhaps some money. He took the boy before justices of the peace, who, with the zeal their predecessors had displayed twenty-two years before, made many arrests. The boy was exhibited from town to town in Lancashire as a great wonder and witch-detector. It was in the course of these exhibitions that he was brought to a little town on the Lancashire border of Yorkshire and was taken to the afternoon church service, where a young minister, who was long afterwards to become a famous opponent of the superstition, was discoursing to his congregation. The boy was held up by those in charge as if to give him the chance to detect witches among the audience. The minister saw him, and at the end of the service at once came down to the boy, and without parley asked him, "Good boy, tell me truly, and in earnest, didst thou see and hear such things of the meeting of the witches as is reported by many that thou dost relate?" The boy, as Webster has told the story, was not given time for reply by the men in charge of him, who protested against such questions. The lad, they said, had been before two justices of the peace, and had not been catechized in that fashion.

A lone skeptic had little chance to beat back the wave of excitement created by the young Robinson's stories. His success prompted him to concoct new tales. He had seen Lloynd's wife sitting on a cross-bar in his father's chimney; he had called to her; she had not come down but had vanished in the air. Other accounts the boy gave, but none of them revealed the clear invention of his first narrative.

He had done his work. The justices of the peace were bringing in the accused to the assizes at Lancaster. There Robinson was once more called upon to render his now famous testimony. He was supported by his father, who gave evidence that on the day he had sent his boy for the cattle he had gone after him and as he approached had heard him cry and had found him quite "distracted." When the boy recovered himself, he had related the story already told. This was the evidence of the father, and together with that of the son it constituted the most telling piece of testimony presented. But it served, as was usual in such cases, as an opening for all those who, for any reason, thought they had grounds of suspicion against any of their neighbors. It was recalled by one witness that a neighbor girl could bewitch a pail and make it roll towards her. We shall later have occasion to note the basis of fact behind this curious accusation. There was other testimony of an equally damaging character. But in nearly all the cases stress was laid upon the bodily marks. In one instance, indeed, nothing else was charged. The reader will remember that in the Lancaster cases of 1612 the evidence of marks on the body was notably absent, so notably that we were led to suspect that it had been ruled out by the judge. That such evidence was now reckoned important is proof that this particularly dark feature of the witch superstition was receiving increasing emphasis.

How many in all were accused we do not know. Webster, writing later, said that seventeen were found guilty. It is possible that even a larger number were acquitted. Certainly some were acquitted. A distinction of some sort was made in the evidence. This makes it all the harder to understand why the truth of Robinson's stories was not tested in the same way in which those of Grace Sowerbutts had been tested in 1612. Did that detection of fraud never occur to the judges, or had they never heard of the famous boy at Bilston? Perhaps not they but the juries were to blame, for it seems that the court was not altogether satisfied with the jury's verdict and delayed sentence. Perhaps, indeed, the judges wrote to London about the matter. Be that as it may, the privy council decided to take cognizance of an affair that was already the talk of the realm. Secretaries Coke and Windebank sent instructions to Henry Bridgeman, Bishop of Chester and successor to that Morton who had exposed the boy of Bilston, to examine seven of the condemned witches and to make a report. Bridgeman doubtless knew of his predecessor's success in exposing fraudulent accusations. Before the bishop was ready to report, His Majesty sent orders that three or four of the accused should be brought up to London by a writ of habeas corpus. Owing to a neglect to insert definite names, there was a delay. It was during this interval, probably, that Bishop Bridgeman was able to make his examination. He found three of the seven already dead and one hopelessly ill. The other three he questioned with great care. Two of them, Mary Spencer, a girl of twenty, and Frances Dickonson, the first whom Robinson had accused, made spirited denials. Mary Spencer avowed that her accusers had been actuated by malice against her and her parents for several years. At the trial, she had been unable, she said, to answer for herself, because the noise of the crowd had been so great as to prevent her from hearing the evidence against her. As for the charge of bewitching a pail so that it came running towards her of its own accord, she declared that she used as a child to roll a pail down-hill and to call it after her as she ran, a perfectly natural piece of child's play. Frances Dickonson, too, charged malice upon her accusers, especially upon the father of Edmund Robinson. Her husband, she said, had been unwilling to sell him a cow without surety and had so gained his ill-will. She went on to assert that the elder Robinson had volunteered to withdraw the charges against her if her husband would pay him forty shillings. This counter charge was supported by another witness and seemed to make a good deal of an impression on the ecclesiastic.

The third woman to be examined by the bishop was a widow of sixty, who had not been numbered among the original seventeen witches. She acknowledged that she was a witch, but was, wrote the bishop, "more often faulting in the particulars of her actions as one having a strong imagination of the former, but of too weak a memory to retain or relate the latter." The woman told a commonplace story of a man in black attire who had come to her six years before and made the usual contract. But very curiously she could name only one other witch, and professed to know none of those already in gaol.

Such were the results of the examinations sent in by the bishop. In the letter which he sent along, he expressed doubt about the whole matter. "Conceit and malice," he wrote, "are so powerful with many in those parts that they will easily afford an oath to work revenge upon their neighbour." He would, he intimated, have gone further in examining the counter charges brought by the accused, had it not been that he hesitated to proceed against the king, that is, the prosecution.

This report doubtless confirmed the fears of the government. The writs to the sheriff of Lancaster were redirected, and four of the women were brought up to London and carried to the "Ship Tavern" at Greenwich, close to one of the royal residences. Two of His Majesty's surgeons, Alexander Baker and Sir William Knowles, the latter of whom was accustomed to examine candidates for the king's touch, together with five other surgeons and ten certificated midwives, were now ordered to make a bodily examination of the women, under the direction of the eminent Harvey, the king's physician, who was later to discover the circulation of the blood. In the course of this chapter we shall see that Harvey had long cherished misgivings about witchcraft. Probably by this time he had come to disbelieve it. One can but wonder if Charles, already probably aware of Harvey's views, had not intended from his first step in the Lancashire case to give his physician a chance to assert his opinion. In any case his report and that of his subordinates was entirely in favor of the women, except that in the case of Margaret Johnson (who had confessed) they had found a mark, but one to which they attached little significance. The women seem to have been carried before the king himself. We do not know, however, that he expressed any opinion on the matter.

The whole affair has one aspect that has been entirely overlooked. Whatever the verdict of the privy council and of the king may have been—and it was evidently one of caution—they gave authorization from the highest quarters for the use of the test of marks on the body. That proof of witchcraft had been long known in England and had slowly won its way into judicial procedure until now it was recognized by the highest powers in the kingdom. To be sure, it was probably their purpose to annul the reckless convictions in Lancashire, and to break down the evidence of the female juries; but in doing so they furnished a precedent for the witch procedure of the civil-war period.

In the mean time, while the surgeons and midwives were busy over these four women, the Robinsons, father and son, had come to London at the summons of the privy council. There the boy was separated from his father. To a Middlesex justice of the peace appointed by Secretary Windebank to take his statements he confessed that his entire story was an invention and had no basis of fact whatever. Both father and son were imprisoned and proceedings seem to have been instituted against them by one of the now repentant jurymen who had tried the case. How long they were kept in prison we do not know.

One would naturally suppose that the women would be released on their return to Lancaster, but the sheriff's records show that two years later there were still nine witches in gaol. Three of them bore the same names as those whom Robinson pretended to have seen at Hoarstones. At least one other of the nine had been convicted in 1634, probably more. Margaret Johnson, the single one to confess, so far as we know, was not there. She had probably died in prison in the mean time. We have no clue as to why the women were not released. Perhaps public sentiment at home made the sheriff unwilling to do it, perhaps the wretched creatures spent two or more years in prison—for we do not know when they got out—as a result of judicial negligence, a negligence of which there are too many examples in the records of the time. More likely the king and the privy council, while doubting the charges against the women, had been reluctant to antagonize public sentiment by declaring them innocent.

It is disagreeable to have to state that Lancaster was not yet through with its witches. Early in the next year the Bishop of Chester was again called upon by the privy council to look into the cases of four women. There was some delay, during which a dispute took place between the bishop and the sheriff as to where the bishop should examine the witches, whether at Wigan, as he proposed, or at Lancaster. One suspects that the civil authorities of the Duchy of Lancaster may have resented the bishop's part in the affair. When Bridgeman arrived in Lancaster he found two of the women already dead. Of the other two, the one, he wrote, was accused by a man formerly "distracted and lunatic" and by a woman who was a common beggar; the other had been long reputed a witch, but he saw no reason to believe it. He had, he admitted, found a small lump of flesh on her right ear. Alas that the Bishop of Chester, like the king and the privy council, however much he discounted the accusations of witchcraft, had not yet wholly rid himself of one of the darkest and most disagreeable forms of the belief that the Evil One had bodily communication with his subjects.

In one respect the affair of 1633-1634 in northern England was singular. The social and moral character of those accused was distinctly high. Not that they belonged to any but the peasant class, but that they represented a good type of farming people. Frances Dickonson's husband evidently had some property. Mary Spencer insisted that she was accustomed to go to church and to repeat the sermon to her parents, and that she was not afraid of death, for she hoped it would make an entrance for her into heaven. Margaret Johnson was persuaded that a man and his wife who were in the gaol on Robinson's charges were not witches, because the man "daily prays and reads and seems a godly man." With this evidence of religious life, which must have meant something as to the status of the people in the community, should be coupled the entire absence of stories of threats at beggars and of quarrels between bad-tempered and loose-lived women, stories that fill so many dreary pages of witchcraft records. Nor is there any mention of the practice of pretended magic.

In previous chapters we have had occasion to observe the continuity of superstition in certain localities. It is obvious that Lancashire offers one of the best illustrations of that principle. The connection between the alarms of 1612 and 1633-1634 is not a matter of theory, but can be established by definite proof. It is perhaps not out of order to inquire, then, why Lancashire should have been so infested with witches. It is the more necessary when we consider that there were other witch cases in the country. Nicholas Starchie's children gave rise to the first of the scares. It seems likely that a certain Utley was hanged at Lancaster in 1630 for bewitching a gentleman's child. During Commonwealth days, as we shall find, there was an alarm at Lancaster that probably cost two witches their lives. No county in England except Essex had a similar record. No explanation can be offered for the records of these two counties save that both had been early infected with a hatred of witches, and that the witches came to be connected, in tradition, with certain localities within the counties and with certain families living there. This is, indeed, an explanation that does not explain. It all comes back to the continuity of superstition.

We have already referred to the widespread interest in the Lancashire witches. There are two good illustrations of this interest. When Sir William Brereton was travelling in Holland in June of 1634, a little while before the four women had been brought to London, he met King Charles's sister, the Queen of Bohemia, and at once, apparently, they began to talk about the great Lancashire discovery. The other instance of comment on the case was in England. It is one which shows that playwrights were quite as eager then as now to be abreast of current topics. Before final judgment had been given on the Lancashire women, Thomas Heywood and Richard Brome, well known dramatists, had written a play on the subject which was at once published and "acted at the Globe on the Bankside by His Majesty's Actors." By some it has been supposed that this play was an older play founded on the Lancashire affair of 1612 and warmed over in 1634; but the main incidents and the characters of the play are so fully copied from the depositions of the young Robinson and from the charges preferred against Mary Spencer, Frances Dickonson, and Margaret Johnson, that a layman would at once pronounce it a play written entirely to order from the affair of 1634. Nothing unique in the stories was left out. The pail incident—of course without its rational explanation—was grafted into the play and put upon the stage. Indeed, a marriage that afforded the hook upon which to hang a bundle of indecencies, and the story of a virtuous husband who discovers his wife to be a witch, were the only added motives of importance. For our purpose the significance of the play lies of course in its testimony to the general interest—the people of London were obviously familiar with the details, even, of the charges—and its probable reflection of London opinion about the case. Throughout the five acts there were those who maintained that there were no witches, a recognition of the existence of such an opinion. Of course in the play they were all, before the curtain fell, convinced of their error. The authors, who no doubt catered to public sentiment, were not as earnest as the divines of their day, but they were almost as superstitious. Heywood showed himself in another work, The Hierarchie of the Blessed Angels, a sincere believer in witchcraft and backed his belief by the Warboys case. Probably he had read Scot, but he was not at all the type of man to set himself against the tide. The late Lancashire Witches no doubt expressed quite accurately London opinion. It was written, it will be remembered, before the final outcome of the case could be foreseen. Perhaps Heywood foresaw it, more probably he was sailing close to the wind of opinion when he wrote in the epilogue,

... "Perhaps great mercy may, After just condemnation, give them day Of longer life."

It is easy in discussing the Lancashire affair to miss a central figure. Frances Dickonson, Mary Spencer, and the others, could they have known it, owed their lives in all probability to the intellectual independence of William Harvey. There is a precious story about Harvey in an old manuscript letter by an unknown writer, that, if trustworthy, throws a light on the physician's conduct in the case. The letter seems to have been written by a justice of the peace in southwestern England about 1685. He had had some experience with witches—we have mentioned them in another connection—and he was prompted by them to tell a story of Dr. Harvey, with whom he was "very familiarly acquainted." "I once asked him what his opinion was concerning witchcraft; whether there was any such thing. Hee told mee he believed there was not." Asked the reasons for his doubt, Harvey told him that "when he was at Newmercat with the King [Charles I] he heard there was a woman who dwelt at a lone house on the borders of the Heath who was reputed a Witch, that he went alone to her, and found her alone at home.... Hee said shee was very distrustful at first, but when hee told her he was a vizard, and came purposely to converse with her in their common trade, then shee easily believed him; for say'd hee to mee, 'You know I have a very magicall face.'" The physician asked her where her familiar was and desired to see him, upon which she brought out a dish of milk and made a chuckling noise, as toads do, at which a toad came from under the chest and drank some of the milk. Harvey now laid a plan to get rid of the woman. He suggested that as fellow witches they ought to drink together, and that she procure some ale. She went out to a neighboring ale-house, half a mile away, and Harvey availed himself of her absence to take up the toad and cut it open. Out came the milk. On a thorough examination he concluded that the toad "no ways differed from other toades," but that the melancholy old woman had brought it home some evening and had tamed it by feeding and had so come to believe it a spirit and her familiar. When the woman returned and found her "familiar" cut in pieces, she "flew like a Tigris" at his face. The physician offered her money and tried to persuade her that her familiar was nothing more than a toad. When he found that this did not pacify her he took another tack and told her that he was the king's physician, sent to discover if she were a witch, and, in case she were, to have her apprehended. With this explanation, Harvey was able to get away. He related the story to the king, whose leave he had to go on the expedition. The narrator adds: "I am certayne this for an argument against spirits or witchcraft is the best and most experimentall I ever heard."

Who the justice of the peace was that penned this letter, we are unable even to guess, nor do we know upon whose authority it was published. We cannot, therefore, rest upon it with absolute certainty, but we can say that it possesses several characteristics of a bona fide letter. If it is such, it gives a new clue to Harvey's conduct in 1634. We of course cannot be sure that the toad incident happened before that time; quite possibly it was after the interest aroused by that affair that the physician made his investigation. At all events, here was a man who had a scientific way of looking into superstition.

The advent of such a man was most significant in the history of witchcraft, perhaps the most significant fact of its kind in the reign of Charles I. That reign, in spite of the Lancashire affair, was characterized by the continuance and growth of the witch skepticism, so prevalent in the last years of the previous reign. Disbelief was not yet aggressive, it did not block prosecutions, but it hindered their effectiveness. The gallows was not yet done away with, but its use had been greatly restrained by the central government. Superstition was still a bird of prey, but its wings were being clipped.

The writer of the Collection of Modern Relations (London, 1693) speaks of an execution at Oxford, but there is nothing to substantiate it in the voluminous publications about Oxford; a Middlesex case rests also on doubtful evidence (see appendix C, 1641).

Cal. St. P., Dom., 1634-1635, 152.

Ibid., 141.

This is of course theory; cf. Daudet's story of his childhood in "Le Pape est mort."

There seem to be five different sources for the original deposition of young Robinson. Thomas D. Whitaker, History ... of Whalley (3d ed., 1818), 213, has an imperfect transcript of the deposition as given in the Bodleian, Dodsworth MSS., 61, ff. 45-46. James Crossley in his introduction to Potts, Wonderfull Discoverie of Witches in the countie of Lancaster (Chetham Soc.), lix-lxxii, has copied the deposition given by Whitaker. Thomas Wright, Narratives of Sorcery and Magic, II, 112-114, has given the story from a copy of this and of other depositions in Lord Londesborough's MSS. Webster prints a third copy, Displaying of Supposed Witchcraft, 347-349. A fourth is in Edward Baines, History of the ... county ... of Lancaster, ed. of 1836, I, 604, and is taken from Brit. Mus., Harleian MSS., cod. 6854, f. 26 b. A fifth is in the Bodleian, Rawlinson MSS., D, 399, f. 211. Wright's source we have not in detail, but the other four, while differing slightly as to punctuation, spelling, and names, agree remarkably well as to the details of the story.

Cal. St. P., Dom., 1634-1635, 152.

John Stearne, A Confirmation and Discovery of Witchcraft ... together with the Confessions of many of those executed since May 1645 (London, 1648), 11, says that in Lancashire "nineteene assembled." Robinson's deposition as printed by Webster, Displaying of Supposed Witchcraft, gives nineteen names.

Webster, op. cit., 277.

The boy, in his first examinations at London, said he had made up the story himself.

It is a curious thing that one of the justices of the peace was John Starchie, who had been one of the bewitched boys of the Starchie family at Cleworth in 1597. See above, ch. IV. See Baines, Lancaster, ed. of 1868-1870, I, 204.

This incident is related by Webster, op. cit., 276-278. Webster tells us that the boy was yet living when he wrote, and that he himself had heard the whole story from his mouth more than once. He appends to his volume the original deposition of the lad (at Padiham, February 10 1633/4).

These are given in the same deposition, but the deposition probably represents the boy's statement at the assizes.

The father had been a witness at the Lancashire trials in 1612. See Baines, Lancaster, ed. of 1868-1870, I, 204-205.

That is, of course, so far as we have evidence. It is a little dangerous to hold to absolute negatives.

Webster, op. cit., 277. Pelham on May 16, 1634, wrote: "It is said that 19 are condemned and ... 60 already discovered." Cal. St. P., Dom., 1634-1635, 26.

It had been reported in London that witches had raised a storm from which Charles had suffered at sea. Pelham's letter, ibid.

Ibid., 77. See also Council Register (MS.), Charles I, vol. IV, p. 658.

Hist. MSS. Comm. Reports, XII, 2, p. 53. The chancellor of the Duchy of Lancaster wrote in the meantime that the judges had been to see him. What was to be done with the witches?

See Hist. MSS. Comm. Reports, X, 2, p. 147; and Cal. St. P., Dom., 1634-1635, 98.

Cal. St. P., Dom., 1634-1635, 98, 129. See also Council Register (MS.), Chas. I, vol. V, p. 56.

Cal. St. P., Dom., 1634-1635, 129.

Webster, op. cit., 277, says that they were examined "after by His Majesty and the Council." See Council Register (MS.), Charles I, vol. IV, p. 657.

Cal. St. P., Dom., 1634-1635, 141.

Ibid., 152.

Farington Papers (Chetham Soc, no. 39, 1856), 27.

Hist. MSS. Comm. Reports, XII, 2, p. 77.

Ibid., p. 80.

Baines, Lancaster, ed. of 1868-1870, II, 12. Utley, who was a professed conjurer, was alleged to have bewitched to death one Assheton.

Travels in Holland, the United Provinces, England, Scotland and Ireland, 1634-1635, by Sir William Brereton, Bart. (Chetham Soc., no. 1. 1844), 33.

(London, 1635.) As to Heywood see also chapter X.

The correspondent who sent a copy of the MS. to the Gentleman's Magazine signs himself "B. C. T." I have been unable to identify him. For his account of the MS. and for its contents see Gentleman's Magazine, 1832, pt. I, 405-410, 489-492.

John Aubrey, Letters written by Eminent Persons (London, 1813), II, 379, says that Harvey "had made dissections of froggs, toads and a number of other animals, and had curious observations on them." This fits in well with the story, and in some measure goes to confirm it.

For example, in 1637 the Bishop of Bath and Wells sent Joice Hunniman to Lord Wrottesley to examine her and exonerate her. He did so, and the bishop wrote thanking him and abusing "certain apparitors who go about frightening the people." See Hist. MSS. Comm. Reports, II, app., p. 48. For a case of the acquittal of a witch and the exposure of the pretended convulsions of her accuser, see Cal. St. P., Dom., 1635, 477. For example of suits for slander see North Riding Rec. Soc, IV, 182, session July 9, 1640.

A solitary pamphlet of this period must be mentioned. It was entitled: Fearefull Newes from Coventry, or A true Relation and Lamentable Story of one Thomas Holt of Coventry a Musitian who through Covetousnesse and immoderate love of money, sold himselfe to the Devill, with whom he had made a contract for certaine yeares—And also of his Lamentable end and death, on the 16 day of February 1641 (London, 1642). The "sad subject of this little treatise" was a musician with nineteen children. Fearing that he would not be able to provide for them, he is alleged to have made a contract with the Devil, who finally broke his neck.

CHAPTER VIII.: Matthew Hopkins.

In the annals of English witchcraft Matthew Hopkins occupies a place by himself. For more than two years he was the arch-instigator in prosecutions which, at least in the numbers of those executed, mark the high tide of the delusion. His name was one hardly known by his contemporaries, but he has since become a figure in the annals of English roguery. Very recently his life has found record among those of "Twelve Bad Men."

What we know of him up to the time of his first appearance in his successful rôle about March of 1644/5 is soon told. He was the son of James Hopkins, minister of Wenham in Suffolk. He was "a lawyer of but little note" at Ipswich, thence removing to Manningtree. Whether he may have been the Matthew Hopkins of Southwark who complained in 1644 of inability to pay the taxes is more than doubtful, but there is reason enough to believe that he found the law no very remunerative profession. He was ready for some new venture and an accidental circumstance in Manningtree turned him into a wholly new field of endeavor. He assumed the rôle of a witchfinder and is said to have taken the title of witchfinder-general.

He had made little or no preparation for the work that now came to his hand. King James's famous Dæmonologie he was familiar with, but he may have studied it after his first experiences at Manningtree. It seems somewhat probable, too, that he had read, and indeed been much influenced by, the account of the Lancashire witches of 1612, as well as by Richard Bernard's Advice to Grand Jurymen. But, if he read the latter book, he seems altogether to have misinterpreted it. As to his general information and education, we have no data save the hints to be gained from his own writings. His letter to John Gaule and the little brochure which he penned in self-defence reveal a man able to express himself with some clearness and with a great deal of vigor. There were force of character and nervous energy behind his defiant words. It is no exaggeration, as we shall see in following his career, to say that the witch crusader was a man of action, who might in another field have made his mark.

To know something of his religious proclivities would be extremely interesting. On this point, however, he gives us no clue. But his fellow worker, John Stearne, was clearly a Puritan and Hopkins was surely of the same faith. It can hardly be proved, however, that religious zeal prompted him in his campaign. For a time of spiritual earnestness his utterances seem rather lukewarm.

It was in his own town that his attention was first directed towards the dangers of witchcraft. The witches, he tells us, were accustomed to hold their meetings near his house. During one of their assemblies he overheard a witch bid her imps to go to another witch. The other witch, whose name was thus revealed to him—Elizabeth Clarke, a poor one-legged creature—was promptly taken into custody on Hopkins's charge. Other accusations poured in. John Rivet had consulted a cunning woman about the illness of his wife, and had learned that two neighbors were responsible. One of these, he was told, dwelt a little above his own home; "whereupon he beleeved his said wife was bewitched by ... Elizabeth Clarke, ... for that the said Elizabeth's mother and some other of her kinsfolke did suffer death for witchcraft." The justices of the peace accordingly had her "searched by women who had for many yeares known the Devill's marks," and, when these were found on her, they bade her custodians "keep her from sleep two or three nights, expecting in that time to see her familiars."

Torture is unknown to English law; but, in our day of the "third degree," nobody needs to be told that what is put out at the door may steal in at the window. It may be that, in the seventeenth century, the pious English justices had no suspicion that enforced sleeplessness is a form of physical torture more nerve-racking and irresistible than the thumb-screw. Three days and nights of "watching" brought Elizabeth Clarke to "confess many things"; and when, on the fourth night, her townsmen Hopkins and Stearne dropped in to fill out from her own lips the warrants against those she had named as accomplices, she told them that, if they would stay and do her no hurt, she would call one of her imps.

Hopkins told her that he would not allow it, but he stayed. Within a quarter of an hour the imps appeared, six of them, one after another. The first was a "white thing in the likeness of a Cat, but not altogether so big," the second a white dog with some sandy spots and very short legs, the third, Vinegar Tom, was a greyhound with long legs. We need not go further into the story. The court records give the testimony of Hopkins and Stearne. Both have related the affair in their pamphlets. Six others, four of whom were women, made oath to the appearances of the imps. In this respect the trial is unique among all in English history. Eight people testified that they had seen the imps. Two of them referred elsewhere to what they had seen, and their accounts agreed substantially. It may be doubted if the supporting evidence offered at any trial in the seventeenth century in England went so far towards establishing the actual appearance of the so-called imps of the witches.

How are we to account for these phenomena? What was the nature of the delusion seemingly shared by eight people? It is for the psychologist to answer. Two explanations occur to the layman. It is not inconceivable that there were rodents in the gaol—the terrible conditions in the gaols of the time are too well known to need description—and that the creatures running about in the dark were easily mistaken by excited people for something more than natural. It is possible, too, that all the appearances were the fabric of imagination or invention. The spectators were all in a state of high expectation of supernatural appearances. What the over-alert leaders declared they had seen the others would be sure to have seen. Whether those leaders were themselves deceived, or easily duped the others by calling out the description of what they claimed to see, would be hard to guess. To the writer the latter theory seems less plausible. The accounts of the two are so clearly independent and yet agree so well in fact that they seem to weaken the case for collusive imposture. With that a layman may be permitted to leave the matter. What hypnotic possibilities are inherent in the story he cannot profess to know. Certainly the accused woman was not a professed dealer in magic and it is not easy to suspect her of having hypnotized the watchers.

Upon Elizabeth Clarke's confessions five other women—"the old beldam" Anne West, who had "been suspected as a witch many yeers since, and suffered imprisonment for the same," her daughter Rebecca, Anne Leech, her daughter Helen Clarke, and Elizabeth Gooding—were arrested. As in the case of the first, there was soon abundance of evidence offered about them. One Richard Edwards bethought himself and remembered that while crossing a bridge he had heard a cry, "much like the shrieke of a Polcat," and had been nearly thrown from his horse. He had also lost some cattle by a mysterious disease. Moreover his child had been nursed by a goodwife who lived near to Elizabeth Clarke and Elizabeth Gooding. The child fell sick, "rowling the eyes," and died. He believed that Anne Leech and Elizabeth Gooding were the cause of its death. His belief, however, which was offered as an independent piece of testimony, seems to have rested on Anne Leech's confession, which had been made before this time and was soon given to the justices of the peace. Robert Taylor charged Elizabeth Gooding with the death of his horse, but he too had the suggestion from other witnesses. Prudence Hart declared that, being in her bed in the night, "something fell down on her right side." "Being dark she cannot tell in what shape it was, but she believeth Rebecca West and Anne West the cause of her pains."

But the accusers could hardly outdo the accused. No sooner was a crime suggested than they took it upon themselves. It seemed as if the witches were running a race for position as high criminal. With the exception of Elizabeth Gooding, who stuck to it that she was not guilty, they cheerfully confessed that they had lamed their victims, caused them to "languish," and even killed them. The meetings at Elizabeth Clarke's house were recalled. Anne Leech remembered that there was a book read "wherein shee thinks there was no goodnesse."

So the web of charges and counter-charges was spun until twenty-three or more women were caught in its meshes. No less than twelve of them confessed to a share in the most revolting crimes. But there was one who, in court, retracted her confession. At least five utterly denied their guilt. Among them was a poor woman who had aroused suspicion chiefly because a young hare had been seen in front of her house. She was ready to admit that she had seen the hare, but denied all the more serious charges. Another of those who would not plead guilty sought to ward off charges against herself by adding to the charges accumulated against her mother. Hers was a damning accusation. Her mother had threatened her and the next night she "felt something come into the bed about her legges, ... but could not finde anything." This was as serious evidence as that of one of the justices of the peace, who testified from the bench that a very honest friend of his had seen three or four imps come out of Anne West's house in the moonlight. Hopkins was not to be outshone by the other accusers. He had visited Colchester castle to interview Rebecca West and had gained her confession that she had gone through a wedding ceremony with the Devil.

But why go into details? The evidence was all of a kind. The female juries figured, as in the trials at Lancaster in 1633, and gave the results of their harrowing examinations. What with their verdicts and the mass of accusations and confessions, the justices of the peace were busy during March, April, and May of 1645. It was not until the twenty-ninth of July that the trial took place. It was held at Chelmsford before the justices of the peace and Robert Rich, Earl of Warwick. Warwick was not an itinerant justice, nor was he, so far as we know, in any way connected with the judicial system. One of the most prominent Presbyterians in England, he had in April of this year, as a result of the "self-denying ordinance," laid down his commission as head of the navy.

He disappears from view until August, when he was again given work to do. In the mean time occurred the Chelmsford trial. We can only guess that the earl, who was appointed head of the Eastern Association less than a month later (August 27), acted in this instance in a military capacity. The assizes had been suspended. No doubt some of the justices of the peace pressed upon him the urgency of the cases to be tried. We may guess that he sat with them in the quarter sessions, but he seems to have played the rôle of an itinerant justice.

No narrative account of the trial proper is extant. Some one who signs himself "H. F." copied out and printed the evidence taken by the justices of the peace and inserted in the margins the verdicts. In this way we know that at least sixteen were condemned, probably two more, and possibly eleven or twelve more. Of the original sixteen, one was reprieved, one died before execution, four were hanged at Manningtree and ten at Chelmsford.

The cases excited some comment, and it is comment that must not be passed over, for it will prove of some use later in analyzing the causes of the outbreak. Arthur Wilson, whom we have mentioned as an historian of the time, has left his verdict on the trial. "There is nothing," he wrote, "so crosse to my temper as putting so many witches to death." He saw nothing, in the women condemned at Chelmsford, "other than poore mellenchollie ... ill-dieted atrabilious constitutions, whose fancies working by grosse fumes and vapors might make the imagination readie to take any impression." Wilson wrestled long with his God over the matter of witches and came at length to the conclusion that "it did not consist with the infinite goodnes of the Almightie God to let Satan loose in so ravenous a way."

The opinion of a parliamentary journal in London on the twenty-fourth of July, three days before the Essex executions, shows that the Royalists were inclined to remark the number of witches in the counties friendly to Parliament: "It is the ordinary mirth of the Malignants in this City to discourse of the Association of Witches in the Associated Counties, but by this they shall understand the truth of the old Proverbe, which is that where God hath his Church, the Devill hath his Chappell." The writer goes on, "I am sory to informe you that one of the cheifest of them was a Parsons Wife (this will be good news with the Papists).... Her name was Weight.... This Woman (as I heare) was the first apprehended." It seems, however, that Mrs. "Weight" escaped. Social and religious influences were not without value. A later pamphleteer tells us that the case of Mrs. Wayt, a minister's wife, was a "palpable mistake, for it is well knowne that she is a gentle-woman of a very godly and religious life."

Meantime Hopkins had extended his operations into Suffolk. Elizabeth Clarke and Anne Leech had implicated certain women in that county. Their charges were carried before the justices of the peace and were the beginning of a panic which spread like wildfire over the county.

The methods which the witchfinder-general used are illuminating. Four searchers were appointed for the county, two men and two women. "In what Town soever ... there be any person or persons suspected to be witch or Witches, thither they send for two or all of the said searchers, who take the partie or parties so suspected into a Roome and strip him, her, or them, starke naked." The clergyman Gaule has given us further particulars: "Having taken the suspected Witch, shee is placed in the middle of a room upon a stool, or Table, crosse-legg'd, or in some other uneasie posture, to which if she submits not, she is then bound with cords; there is she watcht and kept without meat or sleep for the space of 24 hours.... A little hole is likewise made in the door for the Impe to come in at; and lest it might come in some lesse discernible shape, they that watch are taught to be ever and anon sweeping the room, and if they see any spiders or flyes, to kill them. And if they cannot kill them, then they may be sure they are her Impes." Hutchinson tells a story of one woman, who, after having been kept long fasting and without sleep, confessed to keeping an imp called Nan. But a "very learned ingenious gentleman having indignation at the thing" drove the people from the house, gave the woman some food, and sent her to bed. Next morning she knew of no Nan but a pullet she had.

The most sensational discovery in Suffolk was that John Lowes, pastor of Brandeston, was a witch. The case was an extraordinary one and throws a light on the witch alarms of the time. Lowes was eighty years old, and had been pastor in the same place for fifty years. He got into trouble, undoubtedly as a result of his inability to get along with those around him. As a young man he had been summoned to appear before the synod at Ipswich for not conforming to the rites of the Established Church. In the first year of Charles's reign he had been indicted for refusing to exhibit his musket, and he had twice later been indicted for witchcraft and once as a common imbarritor. The very fact that he had been charged with witchcraft before would give color to the charge when made in 1645. We have indeed a clue to the motives for this accusation. A parishioner and a neighboring divine afterwards gave it as their opinion that "Mr. Lowes, being a litigious man, made his parishioners (too tenacious of their customs) very uneasy, so that they were glad to take the opportunity of those wicked times to get him hanged, rather than not get rid of him." Hopkins had afforded them the opportunity. The witchfinder had taken the parson in hand. He had caused him to be kept awake several nights together, and had run him backwards and forwards about the room until he was out of breath. "Then they rested him a little and then ran him again, and this they did for several days and nights together, till he was weary of his life and scarce sensible of what he said or did." He had, when first accused, denied all charges and challenged proof, but after he had been subjected to these rigorous methods he made a full confession. He had, he said, sunk a sailing vessel of Ipswich, making fourteen widows in a quarter of an hour. The witchfinder had asked him if it did not grieve him to see so many men cast away in a short time, and he answered: "No, he was joyfull to see what power his Impes had." He had, he boasted, a charm to keep him out of gaol and from the gallows. It is too bad that the crazed man's confidence in his charm was misplaced. His whole wild confession is an illustration of the effectiveness of the torture. His fate is indicative of the hysteria of the times and of the advantages taken of it by malicious people. It was his hostility to the ecclesiastical and political sympathies of his community that caused his fall.

The dementia induced by the torture in Lowes's case showed itself in the case of others, who made confessions of long careers of murder. "These and all the rest confessed that cruell malice ... was their chiefe delight." The accused were being forced by cruel torture to lend their help to a panic which exceeded any before or after in England. From one hundred and thirty to two hundred people were soon under accusation and shut up in Bury gaol.

News of this reached a Parliament in London that was very much engrossed with other matters. We cannot do better than to quote the Puritan biographer Clarke. "A report was carried to the Parliament ... as if some busie men had made use of some ill Arts to extort such confession; ... thereupon a special Commission of Oyer and Terminer was granted for the trial of these Witches." Care was to be used, in gathering evidence, that confessions should be voluntary and should be backed by "many collateral circumstances." There were to be no convictions except upon proof of express compact with the Devil, or upon evidence of the use of imps, which implied the same thing. Samuel Fairclough and Edmund Calamy (the elder), both of them Non-Conformist clergymen of Suffolk, together with Serjeant John Godbolt and the justices of the peace, were to compose this special court. The court met about the end of August, a month after the sessions under Warwick at Chelmsford, and was opened by two sermons preached by Mr. Fairclough in Bury church. One of the first things done by the special court, quite possibly at the instigation of the two clergymen, was to put an end to the swimming test, which had been used on several of the accused, doubtless by the authority of the justices of the peace. This was of course in some sense a blow at Hopkins. Nevertheless a great deal of the evidence which he had gathered must have been taken into account. Eighteen persons, including two men, were condemned to be hanged. On the night before their execution, they were confined in a barn, where they made an agreement not to confess a word at the gallows the following day, and sang a psalm in confirmation. Next day they "dyed ... very desperately." But there were still one hundred and twenty others in gaol awaiting trial. No doubt many forthwith would have met the same end, had it not been for a lucky chance of the wars. The king's forces were approaching and the court hastened to adjourn its sessions.

But this danger was soon over, and within three weeks' time the court seems to have resumed its duties. Of this second session we know nothing at all, save that probably forty or fifty more witches were condemned, and doubtless executed. What became of the others we can only guess. Perhaps some were released, some left in gaol indefinitely.

These things were not done in a corner. Yet so great was the distraction in England that, if we can trust negative evidence, they excited not a great deal of notice. Such comments as there were, however, were indicative of a division of opinion. During the interval between the two sessions, the Moderate Intelligencer, a parliamentary organ that had sprung up in the time of the Civil War, came out in an editorial on the affair. "But whence is it that Devils should choose to be conversant with silly Women that know not their right hands from their left, is the great wonder.... They will meddle with none but poore old Women: as appears by what we received this day from Bury.... Divers are condemned and some executed and more like to be. Life is precious and there is need of great inquisition before it is taken away."

This was the sole newspaper reference of which we know, as well as the only absolutely contemporary mention of these trials. What other expressions of opinion there were came later. James Howell, a popular essayist of his time, mentioned the trials in his correspondence as new proof of the reality of witchcraft. The pious Bishop Hall saw in them the "prevalency of Satan in these times." Thomas Ady, who in 1656 issued his Candle in the Dark, mentioned the "Berry

Assizes" and remarked that some credulous people had published a book about it. He thought criticism deserved for taking the evidence of the gaoler, whose profit lay in having the greatest possible number executed.

We have already described Hopkins as a man of action. Nothing is better evidence of it than the way in which he hurried back and forth over the eastern counties. During the last part of May he had probably been occupied with collecting the evidence against the accused at Bury. Long before they were tried he was busy elsewhere. We can trace his movements in outline only, but we know enough of them to appreciate his tremendous energy. Some time about the beginning of June he must have gone to Norfolk. Before the twenty-sixth of July twenty witches had been executed in that county. None of the details of these trials have been left us. From the rapidity with which they were carried to completion we may feel fairly certain that the justices of the peace, seeing no probability of assize sessions in the near future, went ahead to try cases on their own initiative. On the fifteenth of August the corporation of Great Yarmouth, at the southern extremity of the Norfolk coast line, voted to send for Mr. Hopkins, and that he should have his fee and allowance for his pains, "as he hath in other places." He came at two different times, once in September and once in December. Probably the burden of the work was turned over to the four female assistants, who were granted a shilling a day apiece. Six women were condemned, one of whom was respited. Later three other women and one man were indicted, but by this time the furor against them seems to have abated, and they probably went free.

Hopkins's further course can be traced with some degree of certainty. From Yarmouth he probably went to Ipswich, where Mother Lakeland was burned on September 9 at the instance of the justices of the peace. Mother Lakeland's death by burning is the second instance we have, during the Hopkins panic, of this form of sentence. It is explained by the fact that it was the law in England to burn women who murdered their husbands. The chief charge against Mother Lakeland, who, by the way, was a woman quite above the class from which witches were ordinarily recruited, was that she had bewitched her husband to death. The crime was "petty treason."

It is not a wild guess that Hopkins paused long enough in his active career to write an account of the affair, so well were his principles of detection presented in a pamphlet soon issued from a London press. But, at any rate, before Mother Lakeland had been burned he was on his way to Aldeburgh, where he was already at work on the eighth of September collecting evidence. Here also he had an assistant, Goody Phillips, who no doubt continued the work after he left. He was back again in Aldeburgh on the twentieth of December and the seventh of January, and the grand result of his work was summarized in the brief account: "Paid ... eleven shillings for hanging seven witches."

From Aldeburgh, Hopkins may have journeyed to Stowmarket. We do not know how many servants of the evil one he discovered here; but, as he was paid twenty-three pounds for his services, and had received but six pounds in Aldeburgh, the presumption is that his work here was very fruitful in results.

We now lose track of the witchfinder's movements for a while. Probably he was doubling on his track and attending court sessions. In December we know that he made his second visit to Yarmouth. From there he may have gone to King's Lynn, where two witches were hanged this year, and from there perhaps returned early in January to Aldeburgh and other places in Suffolk. It is not to be supposed for a moment that his activities were confined to the towns named. At least fifteen other places in Suffolk are mentioned by Stearne in his stories of the witches' confessions. While Hopkins's subordinates probably represented him in some of the villages, we cannot doubt that the witchfinder himself visited many towns.

From East Anglia Hopkins went westward into Cambridgeshire. His arrival there must have been during either January or February. His reputation, indeed, had gone ahead of him, and the witches were reported to have taken steps in advance to prevent detection. But their efforts were vain. The witchfinder found not less than four or five of the detested creatures, probably more. We know, however, of only one execution, that of a woman who fell under suspicion because she kept a tame frog.

From Cambridgeshire, Hopkins's course took him, perhaps in March of 1645/6, into Northamptonshire. There he found at least two villages infested, and he turned up some remarkable evidence. So far in his crusade, the keeping of imps had been the test infallible upon which the witchfinder insisted. But at Northampton spectral evidence seems to have played a considerable part. Hopkins never expresses his opinion on this variety of evidence, but his co-worker declares that it should be used with great caution, because "apparitions may proceed from the phantasie of such as the party use to fear or at least suspect."

But it was a case in Northamptonshire of a different type that seems to have made the most lasting impression on Stearne. Cherrie of Thrapston, "a very aged man," had in a quarrel uttered the wish that his neighbor's tongue might rot out. The neighbor thereupon suffered from something which we should probably call cancer of the tongue. Perhaps as yet the possibilities of suggestion have not been so far sounded that we can absolutely discredit the physical effects of a malicious wish. It is much easier, however, to believe the reported utterance imagined after its supposed effect. At all events, Cherrie was forced to confess that he had been guilty and he further admitted that he had injured Sir John Washington, who had been his benefactor at various times. He was indicted by the grand jury, but died in gaol, very probably by suicide, on the day when he was to have been tried.

From Northamptonshire Hopkins's course led him into Huntingdonshire, a county that seems to have been untroubled by witch alarms since the Warboys affair of 1593. The justices of the peace took up the quest eagerly. The evidence that they gathered had but little that was unusual. Mary Chandler had despatched her imp, Beelzebub, to injure a neighbor who had failed to invite her to a party. An accused witch who was questioned about other possible witches offered in evidence a peculiar piece of testimony. He had a conversation with "Clarke's sonne of Keiston," who had said to him (the witness): "I doe not beleeve you die a Witch, for I never saw you at our meetings." This would seem to have been a clever fiction to ward off charges against himself. But, strangely enough, the witness declared that he answered "that perhaps their meetings were at severall places."

Hopkins did not find it all smooth sailing in the county of Huntingdon. A clergyman of Great Staughton became outraged at his work and preached against it. The witchfinder had been invited to visit the town and hesitated. Meantime he wrote this blustering letter to one of John Gaule's parishioners.

"My service to your Worship presented, I have this day received a Letter, &c.—to come to a Towne called Great Staughton to search for evil disposed persons called Witches (though I heare your Minister is farre against us through ignorance) I intend to come (God willing) the sooner to heare his singular Judgment on the behalfe of such parties; I have known a Minister in Suffolke preach as much against their discovery in a Pulpit, and forc'd to recant it (by the Committee) in the same place. I much marvaile such evill Members should have any (much more any of the Clergy) who should daily preach Terrour to convince such Offenders, stand up to take their parts against such as are Complainants for the King, and sufferers themselves with their Families and Estates. I intend to give your Towne a Visite suddenly, I am to come to Kimbolton this weeke, and it shall bee tenne to one but I will come to your Town first, but I would certainely know afore whether your Town affords many Sticklers for such Cattell, or willing to give and afford us good welcome and entertainment, as other where I have beene, else I shall wave your Shire (not as yet beginning in any part of it my selfe) And betake me to such places where I doe and may persist without controle, but with thankes and recompence."

This stirred the fighting spirit of the vicar of Great Staughton, and he answered the witchfinder in a little book which he published shortly after, and which he dedicated to Colonel Walton of the House of Commons. We shall have occasion in another chapter to note its point of view.

In spite of opposition, Hopkins's work in Huntingdonshire prospered. The justices of the peace were occupied with examinations during March and April. Perhaps as many as twenty were accused. At least half that number were examined. Several were executed—we do not know the exact number—almost certainly at the instance of the justices of the peace. It is pleasant to know that one was acquitted, even if it was after she had been twice searched and once put through the swimming ordeal.

From Huntingdonshire it is likely that Hopkins and Stearne made their next excursion into Bedfordshire. We know very little about their success here. In two villages it would seem that they were able to track their prey. But they left to others the search which they had begun.

The witchfinder had been active for a little over a year. But during the last months of that time his discoveries had not been so notable. Was there a falling off in interest? Or was he meeting with increased opposition among the people? Or did the assize courts, which resumed their proceedings in the summer of 1646, frown upon him? It is hard to answer the question without more evidence. But at any rate it is clear that during the summer and autumn of 1646 he was not actively engaged in his profession. It is quite possible, indeed, that he was already suffering from the consumption which was to carry him off in the following year. And, with the retirement of its moving spirit, the witch crusade soon came to a close. Almost a twelvemonth later there was a single discovery of witches. It was in the island of Ely; and the church courts, the justices of the peace, and the assize courts, which had now been revived, were able, between them, to hang a few witches.

We do not know whether Hopkins participated in the Ely affair or not. It seems certain that his co-worker, Stearne, had some share in it. But, if so, it was his last discovery. The work of the two men was ended. They had been pursuing the pack of witches in the eastern counties since March of 1644/5. Even the execrations of those who opposed them could not mar the pleasure they felt in what they had done. Nay, when they were called upon to defend themselves, they could hardly refrain from exulting in their achievements. They had indeed every right to exult. When we come to make up the roll of their victims, we shall see that their record as witch discoverers surpassed the combined records of all others.

It is a mistake to suppose that they had acted in any haphazard way. The conduct of both men had been based upon perfectly logical deductions from certain premises. King James's Dæmonologie had been their catechism, the statute against the feeding of imps their book of rules. Both men started with one fundamental notion, that witchcraft is the keeping of imps. But this was a thing that could be detected by marks on the bodies. Both were willing to admit that mistakes could be made and were often made in assuming that natural bodily marks were the Devil's marks. There were, however, special indications by which the difference between the two could be recognized. And the two witchfinders, of course, possessed that "insight" which was necessary to make the distinction. The theories upon which they worked we need not enter into. Suffice it to say that when once they had proved, as they thought, the keeping of imps, the next step was to watch those accused of it. "For the watching," says Stearne, "it is not to use violence or extremity to force them to confess, but onely the keeping is, first to see whether any of their spirits, or familiars come to or neere them." It is clear that both Hopkins and Stearne recognized the fact that confessions wrung from women by torture are worthless and were by this explanation defending themselves against the charge of having used actual torture. There seems to be no adequate reason for doubting the sincerity of their explanation. Stearne tells us that the keeping the witches separate is "also to the end that Godly Divines might discourse with them." "For if any of their society come to them to discourse with them, they will never confess." Here, indeed, is a clue to many confessions. Several men arrayed against one solitary and weak woman could break her resolution and get from her very much what they pleased.

As for starving the witches and keeping them from sleep, Stearne maintained that these things were done by them only at first. Hopkins bore the same testimony. "After they had beat their heads together in the Gaole, and after this use was not allowed of by the Judges and other Magistrates, it was never since used, which is a yeare and a halfe since." In other words, the two men had given up the practice because the parliamentary commission had compelled them to do so.

The confessions must be received with great caution, Hopkins himself declared. It is so easy to put words into the witch's mouth. "You have foure Imps, have you not? She answers affirmatively. 'Yes'.... 'Are not their names so and so'? 'Yes,' saith she. 'Did you not send such an Impe to kill my child'? 'Yes,' saith she." This sort of thing has been too often done, asserted the virtuous witchfinder. He earnestly did desire that "all Magistrates and Jurors would, a little more than ever they did, examine witnesses about the interrogated confessions." What a cautious, circumspect man was this famous witchfinder! The confessions, he wrote, in which confidence may be placed are when the woman, without any "hard usages or questions put to her, doth of her owne accord declare what was the occasion of the Devil's appearing to her."

The swimming test had been employed by both men in the earlier stages of their work. "That hath been used," wrote Stearne, "and I durst not goe about to cleere my selfe of it, because formerly I used it, but it was at such time of the yeare as when none tooke any harme by it, neither did I ever doe it but upon their owne request." A thoughtful man was this Stearne! Latterly he had given up the test—since "Judge Corbolt" stopped it—and he had come to believe that it was a way of "distrusting of God's providence."

It can be seen that the men who had conducted the witch crusade were able to present a consistent philosophy of their conduct. It was, of course, a philosophy constructed to meet an attack the force of which they had to recognize. Hopkins's pamphlet and Stearne's Confirmation were avowedly written to put their authors right in the eyes of a public which had turned against them. It seems that this opposition had first shown itself at their home in Essex. A woman who was undergoing inquisition had found supporters, and, though she was condemned in spite of their efforts, was at length reprieved. Her friends turned the tables by indicting Stearne and some forty others of conspiracy, and apparently succeeded in driving them from the county. In Bury the forces of the opposition had appealed to Parliament, and the Commission of Oyer and Terminer, which, it will be noticed, is never mentioned by the witchfinders, was sent out to limit their activities. In Huntingdonshire, we have seen how Hopkins roused a protesting clergyman, John Gaule. If we may judge from the letter he wrote to one of Gaule's parishioners, Hopkins had by this time met with enough opposition to know when it was best to keep out of the way. His boldness was assumed to cover his fear.

But it was in Norfolk that the opposition to the witchfinders reached culmination. There most pungent "queries" were put to Hopkins through the judges of assize. He was charged with all those cruelties, which, as we have seen, he attempts to defend. He was further accused of fleecing the country for his own profit. Hopkins's answer was that he took the great sum of twenty shillings a town "to maintaine his companie with 3 horses." That this was untrue is sufficiently proved by the records of Stowmarket where he received twenty-three pounds and his traveling expenses. At such a rate for the discoveries, we can hardly doubt that the two men between them cleared from three hundred to a thousand pounds, not an untidy sum in that day, when a day's work brought six pence.

What further action was taken in the matter of the queries "delivered to the Judges of assize" we do not know. Both Hopkins and Stearne, as we have seen, went into retirement and set to work to exonerate themselves. Within the year Hopkins died at his old home in Manningtree. Stearne says that he died "peaceably, after a long sicknesse of a Consumption." But tradition soon had it otherwise. Hutchinson says that the story, in his time, was that Hopkins was finally put to the swimming test himself, and drowned. According to another tale, which seems to have lingered in Suffolk, he offered to show the Devil's roll of all the witches in England and so was detected. Butler, in his Hudibras, said of him:

"Who after proved himself a witch, And made a rod for his own breech."

Butler's lines appeared only fifteen years after Hopkin's death, and his statement is evidence enough that such a tradition was already current. The tradition is significant. It probably means, not that Hopkins really paid such a penalty for his career—Stearne's word is good enough proof to the contrary—but that within his own generation his name had become an object of detestation.

John Stearne did not return to Manningtree—he may have been afraid to—but settled down near Bury, the scene of his greatest successes.

If the epitaphs of these two men were to be written, their deeds could be compressed into homely statistics. And this leads us to inquire what was the sum of their achievement. It has been variously estimated. It is not an uncommon statement that thirty thousand witches were hanged in England during the rule of Parliament, and this wild guess has been copied by reputable authors. In other works the number has been estimated at three thousand, but this too is careless guesswork. Stearne himself boasted that he knew of two hundred executions, and Stearne ought to have known. It is indeed possible that his estimate was too high. He had a careless habit of confusing condemnations with executions that makes us suspect that in this estimate he may have been thinking rather of the number of convictions than of the hangings. Yet his figures are those of a man who was on the ground, and cannot be lightly discounted. Moreover, James Howell, writing in 1648, says that "within the compass of two years, near upon three hundred Witches were arraign'd and the major part executed in Essex and Suffolk only." If these estimates be correct—or even if they approach correctness—a remarkable fact appears. Hopkins and Stearne, in fourteen months' time, sent to the gallows more witches than all the other witch-hunters of England can be proved—so far as our present records go—to have hung in the hundred and sixty years during which the persecution nourished in England. It must occur to the reader that this crusade was extraordinary. Certainly it calls for explanation.

So far as the writer is aware, but one explanation has been offered. It has been repeated until it has become a commonplace in the history of witchcraft that the Hopkins crusade was one of the expressions of the intolerant zeal of the Presbyterian party during its control of Parliament. This notion is largely due to Francis Hutchinson, who wrote the first history of English witchcraft. Hutchinson was an Anglican clergyman, but we need not charge him with partisanship in accusing the Presbyterians. There was no inconsiderable body of evidence to support his point of view. The idea was developed by Sir Walter Scott in his Letters on Demonology, but it was left to Lecky, in his classic essay on witchcraft, to put the case against the Presbyterian Parliament in its most telling form. His interpretation of the facts has found general acceptance since.

It is not hard to understand how this explanation grew up. At a time when Hutchinson was making his study, Richard Baxter, the most eminent Puritan of his time, was still a great name among the defenders of witchcraft. In his pages Hutchinson read how Puritan divines accompanied the witch-magistrates on their rounds and how a "reading parson" was one of their victims. Gaule, who opposed them, he seems to have counted an Anglican. He clearly put some faith in the lines of Hudibras. Probably, however, none of these points weighed so much with him as the general fact of coincidence in time between the great witch persecution and Presbyterian rule. It was hard to escape the conclusion that these two unusual situations must in some way have been connected.

Neither Hutchinson nor those who followed have called attention to a point in support of their case which is quite as good proof of their contention as anything adduced. It was in the eastern counties, where the Eastern Association had flourished and where Parliament, as well as the army, found its strongest backing—the counties that stood consistently against the king—in those counties it was that Hopkins and Stearne carried on their work.

It may seem needless in the light of these facts to suggest any other explanation of the witch crusade. Yet the whole truth has not by any means been told. It has already been noticed that Hutchinson made some mistakes. Parson Lowes, who was hanged as a witch at the instance of his dissatisfied parishioners, was not hanged because he was an Anglican. And the Presbyterian Parliament had not sent down into Suffolk a commission to hang witches, but to check the indiscriminate proceedings that were going on there against witches. Moreover, while it is true that East Anglia and the counties adjacent, the stronghold of the Puritans, were the scene of Hopkins's operations, it is quite as true that in those counties arose that powerful opposition which forced the witchfinders into retirement. We have noticed in another connection that the "malignants" were inclined to mock at the number of witches in the counties friendly to Parliament, but there is nothing to show that the mockers disbelieved the reality of the witchcrafts.

It is easy enough to turn some of Hutchinson's reasoning against him, as well as to weaken the force of other arguments that may be presented on his side. But, when we have done all this, we still have to face the unpleasant facts that the witch persecution coincided in time with Presbyterian rule and in place with Puritan communities. It is very hard to get around these facts. Nor does the writer believe that they can be altogether avoided, even if their edge can be somewhat blunted. It was a time of bitter struggle. The outcome could not yet be forecast. Party feeling was at a high pitch. The situation may not unfairly be compared with that in the summer of 1863 during the American civil war. Then the outbreaks in New York revealed the public tension. The case in 1645 in the eastern counties was similar. Every energy was directed towards the prosecution of the war. The strain might very well have shown itself in other forms than in hunting down the supposed agents of the Devil. As a matter of fact, the apparitions and devils, the knockings and strange noises, that filled up the pages of the popular literature were the indications of an overwrought public mind. Religious belief grew terribly literal under the tension of the war. The Anglicans were fighting for their king, the Puritans for their religion. That religious fervor which very easily deepens into dementia was highly accentuated.

Nevertheless, too much importance may have been given to the part played by Presbyterianism. There is no evidence which makes it certain that the morbidity of the public would have taken the form of witch-hanging, had it not been for the leadership of Hopkins and Stearne. The Manningtree affair started very much as a score of others in other times. It had just this difference, that two pushing men took the matter up and made of it an opportunity. The reader who has followed the career of these men has seen how they seem the backbone of the entire movement. It is true that the town of Yarmouth invited them of its own initiative to take up the work there, but not until they had already made themselves famous in all East Anglia. There is, indeed, too much evidence that their visits were in nearly every case the result of their own deliberate purpose to widen the field of their labors. In brief, two aggressive men had taken advantage of a time of popular excitement and alarm. They were fortunate in the state of the public mind, but they seem to have owed more to their own exertions.

But perhaps to neither factor was their success due so much as to the want of government in England at this time. We have seen in an earlier chapter that Charles I and his privy council had put an end to a witch panic that bade fair to end very tragically. Not that they interfered with random executions here and there. It was when the numbers involved became too large that the government stepped in to revise verdicts. This was what the government of Parliament failed to do. And the reasons are not far to seek. Parliament was intensely occupied with the war. The writer believes that it can be proved that, except in so far as concerned the war, the government of Parliament and the Committee of Both Kingdoms paid little or no attention to the affairs of the realm. It is certainly true that they allowed judicial business to go by the board. The assizes seem to have been almost, if not entirely, suspended during the last half of the year 1645 and the first half of 1646. The justices of the peace, who had always shown themselves ready to hunt down witches, were suffered to go their own gait. To be sure, there were exceptions. The Earl of Warwick held a court at Chelmsford, but he was probably acting in a military capacity, and, inexperienced in court procedure, doubtless depended largely upon the justices of the peace, who, gathered in quarter sessions, were assisting him. It is true too that Parliament had sent down a Commission of Oyer and Terminer to Bury, a commission made up of a serjeant and two clergymen. But these two cases are, so far as we can discover, the sole instances during these two years when the justices of the peace were not left to their own devices. This is significant. Except in Middlesex and in the chartered towns of England, we have, excepting during this time of war, no records that witches were ever sentenced to death, save by the judges of assize.

To put it in a nutshell, England was in a state of judicial anarchy. Local authorities were in control. But local authorities had too often been against witches. The coming of Hopkins and Stearne gave them their chance, and there was no one to say stop.

This explanation fits in well with the fact, to which we shall advert in another chapter, that no small proportion of English witch trials took place in towns possessing separate rights of jurisdiction. This was especially true in the seventeenth century. The cases in Yarmouth, King's Lynn, Newcastle-upon-Tyne, Berwick, and Canterbury, are all instances in point. Indeed, the solitary prosecution in Hopkins's own time in which he had no hand was in one of those towns, Faversham in Kent. There the mayor and "local jurators" sent not less than three to the gallows.

One other aspect of the Hopkins crusade deserves further attention. It has been shown in the course of the chapter that the practice of torture was in evidence again and again during this period. The methods were peculiarly harrowing. At the same time they were methods which the rationale of the witch belief justified. The theory need hardly be repeated. It was believed that the witches, bound by a pact with the Devil, made use of spirits that took animal forms. These imps, as they were called, were accustomed to visit their mistress once in twenty-four hours. If the witch, said her persecutors, could be put naked upon a chair in the middle of the room and kept awake, the imps could not approach her. Herein lay the supposed reasonableness of the methods in vogue. And the authorities who were offering this excuse for their use of torture were not loth to go further. It was, they said, necessary to walk the creatures in order to keep them awake. It was soon discovered that the enforced sleeplessness and the walking would after two or three days and nights produce confessions. Stearne himself describes the matter graphically: "For the watching," he writes, "it is not to use violence or extremity to force them to confesse, but onely the keeping is, first, to see whether any of their spirits or familiars come to or neere them; for I have found that if the time be come, the spirit or Impe so called should come, it will be either visible or invisible, if visible, then it may be discerned by those in the Roome, if invisible, then by the party. Secondly, it is for this end also, that if the parties which watch them, be so carefull that none come visible nor invisible but that may be discerned, if they follow their directions then the party presently after the time their Familiars should have come, if they faile, will presently confesse, for then they thinke they will either come no more or have forsaken them. Thirdly it is also to the end, that Godly Divines and others might discourse with them, for if any of their society come to them to discourse with them, they will never confesse.... But if honest godly people discourse with them, laying the hainousnesse of their sins to them, and in what condition they are in without Repentance, and telling them the subtilties of the Devil, and the mercies of God, these ways will bring them to Confession without extremity, it will make them break into confession hoping for mercy."

Hopkins tells us more about the walking of the witches. In answer to the objection that the accused were "extraordinarily walked till their feet were blistered, and so forced through that cruelty to confesse," "he answered that the purpose was only to keepe them waking: and the reason was this, when they did lye or sit in a chaire, if they did offer to couch downe, then the watchers were only to desire them to sit up and walke about."

Now, the inference might be drawn from these descriptions that the use of torture was a new feature of the witchcraft persecutions characteristic of the Civil War period. There is little evidence that before that time such methods were in use. A schoolmaster who was supposed to have used magic against James I had been put to the rack. There were other cases in which it is conjectured that the method may have been tried. There is, however, little if any proof of such trial.

Such an inference would, however, be altogether unjustified. The absence of evidence of the use of torture by no means establishes the absence of the practice. It may rather be said that the evidence of the practice we possess in the Hopkins cases is of such a sort as to lead us to suspect that it was frequently resorted to. If for these cases we had only such evidence as in most previous cases has made up our entire sum of information, we should know nothing of the terrible sufferings undergone by the poor creatures of Chelmsford and Bury. The confessions are given in full, as in the accounts of other trials, but no word is said of the causes that led to them. The difference between these cases of 1645 and other cases is this, that Hopkins and Stearne accused so large a body of witches that they stirred up opposition. It is through those who opposed them and their own replies that we learn about the tortures inflicted upon the supposed agents of the Devil.

The significance of this cannot be insisted upon too strongly. A chance has preserved for us the fact of the tortures of this time. It is altogether possible—it is almost probable—that, if we had all the facts, we should find that similar or equally severe methods had been practised in many other witch cases.

We have been very minute in our descriptions of the Hopkins crusade, and by no means brief in our attempt to account for it. But it is safe to say that it is easily the most important episode in that series of episodes which makes up the history of English witchcraft. None of them belong, of course, in the larger progress of historical events. It may seem to some that we have magnified the point at which they touched the wider interests of the time. Let it not be forgotten that Hopkins was a factor in his day and that, however little he may have affected the larger issues of the times, he was affected by them. It was only the unusual conditions produced by the Civil Wars that made the great witchfinder possible.

See J. O. Jones, "Matthew Hopkins, Witchfinder," in Thomas Seccombe's Twelve Bad Men (London, 1894).

See Notes and Queries, 1854, II, 285, where a quotation from a parish register of Mistley-cum-Manningtree is given: "Matthew Hopkins, son of Mr. James Hopkins, Minister of Wenham, was buried at Mistley August 12, 1647." See also John Stearne, A Confirmation and Discovery of Witchcraft, 61 (cited hereafter as "Stearne").

Calendar of the Proceedings of the Committee for Advance of Money, 1642-1656, I, 457. Cf. Notes and Queries, 1850, II, 413.

The oft-repeated statement that he had been given a commission by Parliament to detect witches seems to rest only on the mocking words of Butler's Hudibras:

> "Hath not this present Parliament
> A Ledger to the Devil sent,
> Fully empower'd to treat about
> Finding revolted Witches out?"
> (Hudibras, pt. ii, canto 3.)

To these lines an early editor added the note: "The Witch-finder in Suffolk, who in the Presbyterian Times had a Commission to discover Witches." But he names no authority, and none can be found. It is probably a confusion with the Commission appointed for the trial of the witches in Suffolk (see below, p. 178). Even his use of the title "witch-finder-general" is very doubtful. "Witch-finder" he calls himself in his book; only the frontispiece has "Witch Finder Generall." Nor is this title given him by Stearne, Gaule, or any contemporary record. It is perhaps only a misunderstanding of the phrase of Hopkins's title-page, "for the benefit of the whole kingdome"—a phrase which, as the punctuation shows, describes, not the witch-finder, but his book. Yet in County Folk Lore, Suffolk (Folk Lore Soc., 1893), 178, there is an extract about John Lowes from a Brandeston MS.: "His chief accuser was one Hopkins, who called himself Witchfinder-General." But this is of uncertain date, and may rest on Hutchinson.

This is evident enough from his incessant use of Scripture and from the Calvinistic stamp of his theology; but he leaves us no doubt when (p. 54) he describes the Puritan Fairclough as "an able Orthodox Divine."

Matthew Hopkins, The Discovery of Witches (London, 1647), 2—cited hereafter as "Hopkins."

One of them was Sir Harbottle Grimston, a baronet of Puritan ancestry, who had been active in the Long Parliament, but who as a "moderate man" fell now somewhat into the background. The other was Sir Thomas Bowes. Both figure a little later as Presbyterian elders.

Hopkins, 3.

Hopkins, 2; Stearne, 14-16.

It must, however, be noted that the oaths of the four women are put together, and that one of the men deposed merely that he confirmed Stearne's particulars.

Although Hopkins omitted in his testimony the first animal seen by Stearne. He mentioned it later, calling it Holt. Stearne called it Lought. See Hopkins, 2; Stearne, 15. But Stearne calls it Hoult in his testimony as reproduced in the True and exact Relation of the severall Informations, Examinations and Confessions of the Late Witches ... at Chelmesford ... (London, 1645), 3-4.

Despite this record Anne West is described by Stearne (p. 39) as one of the very religious people who make an outward show "as if they had been Saints on earth."

The confession of Rebecca West is indeed dated "21" March 1645, the very day of Elizabeth Clarke's arrest; but all the context suggests that this is an error. In spite of her confessions, which were of the most damaging, Rebecca West was eventually acquitted.

It must not for a moment, however, be forgotten that these confessions had been wrung from tortured creatures.

Richard Carter and Henry Cornwall had testified that Margaret Moone confessed to them. Probably she did, as she was doubtless at that time under torture.

The evidence offered against her well suggests on what slender grounds a witch might be accused. "This Informant saith that the house where this Informante and the said Mary did dwell together, was haunted with a Leveret, which did usually sit before the dore: And this Informant knowing that one Anthony Shalock had an excellent Greyhound that had killed many Hares; and having heard that a childe of the said Anthony was much haunted and troubled, and that the mother of the childe suspected the said Mary to be the cause of it: This Informant went to the said Anthony Shalock and acquainted him that a Leveret did usually come and sit before the dore, where this Informant and the said Mary Greenleife lived, and desired the said Anthony to bring downe his Greyhound to see if he could kill the said Leveret; and the next day the said Anthony did accordingly bring his Greyhound, and coursed it, but whether the dog killed it this Informant knows not: But being a little before coursed by Good-man Merrils dog, the dog ran at it, but the Leveret never stirred, and just when the dog came at it, he skipped over it, and turned about and stood still, and looked on it, and shortly after that dog languished and dyed."

See Bulstrode Whitelocke, Memorials of English Affairs ... (London, 1682; Oxford, 1853), ed. of 1853, I, 501.

"H. F."'s publication is the True and exact Relation cited above (note 11). He seems to have written it in the last of May, but inserted verdicts later in the margin. Arthur Wilson, who was present, says that 18 were executed; Francis Peck, Desiderata Curiosa (London, 1732-1735; 1779), ed. of 1779, II, 476. But Hopkins writes that 29 were condemned at once and Stearne says about 28; quite possibly there were two trials at Chelmsford. There is only one other supposition, i. e., that Hopkins and Stearne confused the number originally accused with the number hanged. For further discussion of the somewhat conflicting evidence as to the number of these Essex witches and the dates of their trial see appendix C, under 1645.

A Diary or an Exact Journall, July 24-31, 1645, pp. 5-6.

A True Relation of the Araignment of eighteene Witches at St. Edmundsbury ... (London, 1645), 9.

Ibid., 6.

Ibid.

John Gaule, Select Cases of Conscience Touching Witches and Witchcrafts (London, 1646), 78, 79.

Queries 8 and 9 answered by Hopkins to the Norfolk assizes confirm Gaule's description. See Hopkins, 5. "Query 8. When these ... are fully discovered, yet that will not serve sufficiently to convict them, but they must be tortured and kept from sleep two or three nights, to distract them, and make them say anything; which is a way to tame a wilde Colt, or Hawke." "Query 9. Beside that unreasonable watching, they were extraordinarily walked, till their feet were blistered, and so forced through that cruelty to confess." Hopkins himself admitted the keeping of Elizabeth Clarke from sleep, but is careful to insert "upon command from the Justice." Hopkins, 2-3. On p. 5 he again refers to this point. Stearne, 61, uses the phrase "with consent of the justices."

Suffolk Institute of Archæology, Proceedings, X, 378. Baxter seems to have started the notion that Lowes was a "reading parson," or Anglican.

Ibid.

See A Magazine of Scandall, or a heape of wickednesse of two infamous Ministers (London, 1642), where there is a deposition, dated August 4, 1641, that Lowes had been twice indicted and once arraigned for witchcraft, and convicted by law as "a common Barrettor" at the assizes in Suffolk. Stearne, 23, says he was charged as a "common imbarritor" over thirty years before.

This account of the torture is given, in a letter to Hutchinson, by a Mr. Rivet, who had "heard it from them that watched with him." It is in some measure confirmed by the MS. history of Brandeston quoted in County Folk Lore, Suffolk (Folk Lore Soc.), 178, which adds the above-quoted testimony as to his litigiousness.

Stearne, 24.

A True Relation of the Araignment of eighteene Witches, 5; Moderate Intelligencer, September 4-11, 1645.

See Samuel Clarke, Lives of sundry Eminent Persons ... (London, 1683), 172. In writing the life of Samuel Fairclough, Clarke used Fairclough's papers; see ibid., 163.

Fairclough was a Non-Conformist, but not actively sympathetic with Presbyterianism. Calamy was counted a Presbyterian.

Hopkins, 5-6; Stearne, 18.

One of these was Lowes.

A True Relation of the Araignment of eighteene Witches.

Stearne, 14.

A True Relation of the Araignment of eighteene Witches, 5.

Ibid.; Stearne, 25.

Hutchinson speaks of repeated sessions. Stearne, 25, says: "by reason of an Allarum at Cambridge, the gaol delivery at Burie St. Edmunds was adjourned for about three weeks." As a matter of fact, the king's forces seem not to have got farther east than Bedford and Cambridge. See Whitelocke, Memorials, I, 501

Stearne, 11, speaks of 68 condemnations. On p. 14 he tells of 18 who were executed at Bury, but this may have referred to the first group only. A MS. history of Brandeston quoted in County Folk Lore, Suffolk (Folk Lore Soc.), 178, says that Lowes was executed with 59 more. It is not altogether certain, however, that this testimony is independent. Nevertheless, it contains pieces of information not in the other accounts, and so cannot be ignored.

Moderate Intelligencer, September 4-11, 1645.

Howell, Familiar Letters (I use the ed. of Joseph Jacobs, London 1890-1892) II, 506, 515, 551. The letters quoted are dated as of Feb., 1646 (1647), and Feb., 1647 (1648 of our calendar); but, as is well known, Howell's dates cannot be trusted. The first was printed in the volume of his letters published in 1647, the others in that published in 1650.

Joseph Hall, Soliloquies (London, 1651), 52-53.

Thomas Ady, Candle in the Dark (London, 1656), 101-105.

The Rev. John Worthington attended the trial. In mentioning it in his diary, he made no comment. Diary and Correspondence of Dr. John Worthington, I (Chetham Soc., no. 13, 1847), 22.

So, at least, says Whitelocke, Memorials, I, 487.

J. G. Nall, Great Yarmouth and Lowestoft (London, 1867), 92, note, quotes from the Yarmouth assembly book. Nall makes very careless statements, but his quotations from the assembly book may be depended upon.

Ibid.

Hist. MSS. Comm. Reports, IX, pt. i, 320.

The Collection of Modern Relations says that sixteen were hanged, but this compilation was published forty-seven years after the events: the number 6 had been changed to 16. One witch seems to have suffered later, see Stearne, 53. The statement about the 16 witches hanged at Yarmouth may be found in practically all accounts of English witchcraft, e. g., see the recent essay on Hopkins by J. O. Jones, in Seccombe's Twelve Bad Men, 60. They can all be traced back through various lines to this source.

H. Manship, History of Great Yarmouth, continued by C. J. Palmer (Great Yarmouth, 1854-1856), where the Yarmouth records about Hopkins are given in full. See also H. Harrod, in Norfolk Archæology (Norfolk and Norwich Arch. Soc., 1847-1864), IV, 249.

The Lawes against Witches and Conjuration ... (London, 1645), 4. J. O. Jones, in his account of Hopkins, loc. cit., says that "many were hanged or burned in Ipswich." I believe that no authority can be cited for this statement.

The first is in, A True Relation of the Araignment of eighteene Witches, 5. We of course do not know that the sentence was carried out.

The master of a ship had been "sutor" for her grandchild; The Lawes against Witches, 8. She was a "professour of Religion, a constant hearer of the Word for these many years."

Ibid.

I. e., The Lawes against Witches (London, 1645). See below, appendix A, § 4.

N. F. Hele, Notes or Jottings about Aldeburgh (Ipswich, 1890), 43-44.

This was doubtless the fee to the executioner. Mr. Richard Browne and Mr. Newgate, who were either the justices of the peace or the local magistrates, received £4 apiece for their services in trying the witches.

A. G. Hollingsworth, History of Stowmarket (Ipswich, 1844), 170.

For a list of these towns, see below, appendix C, under 1645, Suffolk.

Stearne, 45, two instances.

Ibid., 37, 39, 45.

Thomas Ady, A Candle in the Dark, 135.

Stearne, 39.

His whole confession reads like the utterance of a tortured man.

He had previously been found with a rope around his neck. This was of course attributed to witchcraft. Stearne, 35.

Ibid., 11.

John Wynnick and Joane Wallis made effective confessions. The first, when in the heat of passion at the loss of a purse, had signed his soul away (Stearne, 20-21; see also the pamphlet, the dedication of which is signed by John Davenport, entitled, The Witches of Huntingdon, their Examinations and Confessions ... London, 1646, 3). The latter maintained a troop of imps, among whom Blackeman, Grissell, and Greedigut figured most prominently. The half-witted creature could not recall the names on the repetition of her confessions, but this failing does not seem to have awakened any doubt of her guilt. Stearne could not avoid noticing that some of those who suffered were very religious. One woman, who had kept an imp for twenty-one years, "did resort to church and had a desire to be rid of her unhappy burden."

I. e., witches.

This letter is printed by Gaule at the opening of his Select Cases of Conscience Touching Witches and Witchcrafts.

Stearne, 11; cf. below, appendix C, 1646 (pp. 405-406).

That it was done by the justices of the peace is a probable conclusion from Stearne's language. See his account of Joane Wallis, p. 13, also his account of John Wynnick, pp. 20-21. That the examinations were in March and April (see John Davenport's account, The Witches of Huntingdon) and the executions in May is a fact confirmatory of this; see Stearne, 11. But it is more to the point that John Davenport dedicates his pamphlet to the justices of the peace for the county of Huntingdon, and says: "You were present, and Judges at the Tryall and Conviction of them."

The swimming ordeal was perhaps unofficial; see Stearne, 19. Another case was that of Elizabeth Chandler, who was "duckt"; Witches of Huntingdon, 8.

Tilbrooke-bushes, Stearne, 11; Risden, ibid., 31.

This may be inferred from Stearne's words: "but afterward I heard that she made a very large confession," ibid., 31.

Thomas Wright, John Ashton, J. O. Jones, and the other writers who have dealt with Hopkins, speak of the Worcester trials, in 1647, in which four women are said to have been hanged. Their statements are all based upon a pamphlet, The Full Tryals, Examination, and Condemnation of Four Notorious Witches at the Assizes held at Worcester on Tuseday the 4th of March.... Printed for I. W. What seems to have been the first edition of this brochure bears no date. In 1700 another edition was printed for "J. M." in Fleet Street. Some writer on witchcraft gained the notion that this pamphlet belonged in the year 1647 and dealt with events in that year. Wright, John Ashton, and W. H. Davenport Adams (Witch, Warlock, and Magician, London, 1889), all accept this date. An examination of the pamphlet shows that it was cleverly put together from the True and Exact Relation of 1645. The four accused bear the names of four of those accused at Chelmsford, and make, with a few differences, the same confessions. See below, appendix A, § 4, for a further discussion of this pamphlet. It is strange that so careful a student as Thomas Wright should have been deceived by this pamphlet, especially since he noticed that the confessions were "imitations" of those in Essex.

A. Gibbons, ed., Ely Episcopal Records (Lincoln, 1891), 112-113.

Stearne, 37.

That there were assizes is proved by the statement that "Moore's wife" confessed before the "Judge, Bench, and Country," ibid., 21-22, as well as by the reference in the Ely Episcopal Records, 113, to the "assizes."

Stearne, 17, 21-22.

For a clear statement of this point of view, see ibid., 40-50.

Stearne, 46-47.

Ibid., 50.

Ibid., 17.

Ibid., 13.

Ibid., 14.

Hopkins, 5. But Hopkins was not telling the exact truth here. When he was at Aldeburgh in September (8th) the accused were watched day and night. See chamberlain's accounts, in N. F.

Hele, Notes or Jottings about Aldeburgh, 43.

Hopkins, 7.

Hopkins, 9.

Stearne, 18. Hopkins did not attempt to deny the use of the ordeal. He supported himself by quoting James; see Hopkins, 6.

Stearne, 18. He means, of course, Serjeant Godbolt.

See Stearne, in his preface to the reader, also p. 61; and see also the complete title of Hopkins's book as given in appendix A (p. 362).

A similar case was that of Anne Binkes, to whom Stearne refers on p. 54. He says she confessed to him her guilt. "Was this woman fitting to live?... I am sure she was living not long since, and acquitted upon her trial."

Not until after Stearne was already busy elsewhere. Stearne, 58.

It would seem, too, that Stearne was sued for recovery of sums paid him. "Many rather fall upon me for what hath been received; but I hope such suits will be disannulled." Stearne, 60.

Hopkins, 11.

County Folk Lore, Suffolk (Folk Lore Soc.) 176, quoting from J. T. Varden in the East Anglian Handbook for 1885, p. 89.

James Howell, Familiar Letters, II, 551. Howell, of course, may easily have counted convictions as executions. Moreover, it was a time when rumors were flying about, and Howell would not have taken the pains to sift them. Yet his agreement with Stearne in numbers is remarkable. Somewhat earlier, (the letter is dated February 3, 1646/7) Howell had written that "in Essex and Suffolk there were above two hundred indicted within these two years and above the one half executed" (ibid., 506). But, as noted above, his dates are not to be trusted.

See his History of Rationalism.

A name no greater, however, than that of Glanvill, who was a prominent Anglican.

It does not belong in this connection, but it should be stated, that one of the strongest reasons for supposing the Presbyterian party largely responsible for the persecution of witches lies in the large number of witches in Scotland throughout the whole period of that party's ascendancy. This is an argument that can hardly be successfully answered. Yet it is a legitimate question whether the witch-hunting proclivities of the north were not as much the outcome of Scottish laws and manners as of Scottish religion.

The Magazine of Scandall, speaking of Lowes and another man, says: "Their Religion is either none, or else as the wind blows: If the ceremonies be tending to Popery, none so forward as they, and if there be orders cleane contrary they shall exceed any Round-head in the Ile of great Brittain." See also above, pp. 175-177.

Yet it must not be overlooked that Stearne himself, who must have known well the religious sympathies of his opponents, asks, p. 58, "And who are they that have been against the prosecution ... but onely such as (without offence I may speak it) be enemies to the Church of God?" He dares not mention names, "not onely for fear of offence, but also for suits of Law."

Scott has pictured this very well in Woodstock. For a good example of it see The [D]lvell in

Kent, or His strange Delusions at Sandwitch (London, 1647).

See below, note 107.

The witches of Aldeburgh were tried at the "sessions," N. F. Hele, op. cit., 43-44. Mother Lakeland was probably condemned by the justices of the peace; see The Lawes against Witches. The witches of Huntingdon were tried by the justices of the peace; see above, note 73. As for the trials in Norfolk, Northamptonshire, Bedfordshire, and Cambridgeshire, it is fairly safe to reason that they were conducted by the justices of the peace from other evidence which we have that there were no assizes during the last half of 1645 and the first five months of 1646; see Whitelocke, Memorials, II, 31, 44, 64.

For a few of the evidences of this situation during these years see James Thompson, Leicester (Leicester, 1849), 401; Hist. MSS. Comm. Reports, Various, I, 109-110, 322; XIII, 4, p. 216 (note gaps in the records); Whitelocke, Memorials, I, 436; II, 31, 44, 64, 196; III, 152. Innumerable other references could be added to prove this point. F. A. Inderwick in his Interregnum (London, 1891), 153, goes so far as to say that "from the autumn of 1642 to the autumn of 1646 no judges went the circuits." This seems rather a sweeping statement.

See The Examination, Confession, etc. (London, 1645). Joan Williford, Joan Cariden, and Jane Hott were tried. The first two quickly confessed to the keeping of imps. Not so Jane Hott, who urged the others to confess and "stoode to it very perversely that she was cleare." When put to the swimming test she floated, and is said to have then declared that the Devil "had sat upon a Cross beame and laughed at her." Elizabeth Harris was examined, and gave some damaging evidence against herself. She named several goodwives who had very loose tongues.

Stearne, 13, 14.

CHAPTER IX.: Witchcraft during the Commonwealth and Protectorate.

We have, in the last chapter, traced the history of witchcraft in England through the Hopkins episode of 1645-1647. From the trials at Ely in the autumn of 1647 to the discoveries at Berwick in the summer of 1649 there was a lull in the witch alarms. Then an epidemic broke out in the north of England. We shall, in this chapter, describe that epidemic and shall carry the narrative of the important cases from that time to the Restoration. In doing this we shall mark off two periods, one from 1649 to 1653, when the executions were still numerous, and a second from 1653 to 1659 when there was a rapid falling off, not only in death penalties for witchcraft, but even in accusations. To be sure, this division is somewhat artificial, for there was a gradual decline of the attack throughout the two periods, but the year 1653 more nearly than any other marks the year when that decline became visible.

The epidemic of 1649 came from Scotland. Throughout the year the northern kingdom had been "infested." From one end of that realm to the other the witch fires had been burning. It was not to be supposed that they should be suddenly extinguished when they reached the border. In July the guild of Berwick had invited a Scotchman who had gained great fame as a "pricker" to come to Berwick, and had promised him immunity from all violence. He came and proceeded to apply his methods of detection. They rested upon the assumption that a witch had insensible spots on her body, and that these could be found by driving in a pin. By such processes he discovered thirty witches, who were sent to gaol. Some of them made confessions but refused to admit that they had injured any one. On the contrary, they had assisted Cromwell, so some of the more ingenious of them claimed, at the battle of Preston. Whether this helped their case we do not know, for we are not told the outcome. It seems almost certain, however, that few, if any, of them suffered death. But the pricker went back to Scotland with thirty pounds, the arrangement having been that he was to receive twenty shillings a witch.

He was soon called upon again. In December of the same year the town of Newcastle underwent a scare. Two citizens, probably serjeants, applied the test with such success that in March (1649/50) a body of citizens petitioned the common council that some definite steps be taken about the witches. The council accepted the suggestion and despatched two serjeants, doubtless the men already engaged in the work, to Scotland to engage the witch-pricker. He was brought to Newcastle with the definite contract that he was to have his passage going and coming and twenty shillings apiece for every witch he found. The magistrates did everything possible to help him. On his arrival in Newcastle they sent the bellman through the town inviting every one to make complaints. In this business-like way they collected thirty women at the town hall, stripped them, and put them to the pricking test. This cruel, not to say indelicate, process was carried on with additions that must have proved highly diverting to the base-minded prickers and onlookers. Fourteen women and one man were tried (Gardiner says by the assizes) and found guilty. Without exception they asserted their innocence; but this availed not. In August of 1650 they were executed on the town moor of Newcastle.

The witchfinder continued his activities in the north, but a storm was rising against him. Henry

Ogle, a late member of Parliament, caused him to be jailed and put under bond to answer the sessions. Unfortunately the man got away to Scotland, where he later suffered death for his deeds, probably during the Cromwellian regime in that country.

We have seen that Henry Ogle had driven the Scotch pricker out of the country. He participated in another witch affair during this same period which is quite as much to his credit. The children of George Muschamp, in Northumberland, had been troubled for two years (1645-1647) with strange convulsions. The family suspected Dorothy Swinow, who was the wife of Colonel Swinow. It seems that the colonel's wife had, at some time, spoken harshly to one of the children. No doubt the sick little girl heard what they said. At any rate her ravings began to take the form of accusations against the suspected woman. The family consulted John Hulton, "who could do more then God allowed," and he accused Colonel Swinow's wife. But unfortunately for him the child had been much better during his presence, and he too was suspected. The mother of the children now rode to a justice of the peace, who sent for Hulton, but not for Mistress Swinow. Then the woman appealed to the assizes, but the judge, "falsely informed," took no action. Mrs. Muschamp was persistent, and in the town of Berwick she was able, at length, to procure the arrest of the woman she feared. But Dorothy Swinow was not without friends, who interfered successfully in her behalf. Mrs. Muschamp now went to a "counsellor," who refused to meddle with the matter, and then to a judge, who directed her to go to Durham. She did so and got a warrant; but it was not obeyed. She then procured a second warrant, and apparently succeeded in getting an indictment. But it did her little good: Dorothy Swinow was not apprehended.

One can hardly refrain from smiling a little at the unhappy Mrs. Muschamp and her zealous assistants, the "physician" and the two clergymen. But her poor daughters grew worse, and the sick child, who had before seen angels in her convulsions, now saw the colonel's wife and cried out in her ravings against the remiss judge. The case is at once pathetic and amusing, but it has withal a certain significance. It was not only Mrs. Swinow's social position that saved her, though that doubtless carried weight. It was the reluctance of the north-country justices to follow up accusations. Not that they had done with trials. Two capital sentences at Durham and another at Gateshead, although perhaps after-effects of the Scotch pricker's activity, showed that the witch was still feared; but such cases were exceptions. In general, the cases resulted in acquittals. We shall see, in another chapter, that the discovery which alarmed Yorkshire and Northumberland in 1673 almost certainly had this outcome; and the cases tried at that time formed the last chapter in northern witchcraft.

But, if hanging witches was not easy in the north, there were still districts in the southwest of England where it could be done, with few to say nay. Anne Bodenham, of Fisherton Anger in Wiltshire, had not the social position of Dorothy Swinow, but she was the wife of a clothier who had lived "in good fashion," and in her old age she taught children to read. She had, it seems, been in earlier life an apt pupil of Dr. Lambe, and had learned from him the practice of magic lore. She drew magic circles, saw visions of people in a glass, possessed numerous charms and incantations, and, above all, kept a wonderful magic book. She attempted to find lost money, to tell the future, and to cure disease; indeed, she had a varied repertoire of occult performances.

Now, Mistress Bodenham did all these things for money and roused no antagonism in her community until she was unfortunate enough to have dealings with a maid-servant in a Wiltshire family. It is impossible to get behind the few hints given us by the cautious writer. The members of the family, evidently one of some standing in Wiltshire, became involved in a quarrel among themselves. It was believed, indeed, by neighbors that there had been a conspiracy on the part of some of the family to poison the mother-in-law. At all events, a maid in the family was imprisoned for participation in such a plot. It was then that Anne Bodenham first came into the story. The maid, to judge from the few data we have, in order to distract attention from her own doings, made a confession that she had signed a book of the Devil's with her own blood, all at the instigation of Anne Bodenham. Moreover, Anne, she said, had offered to send her to London in two hours. This was communicated to a justice of the peace, who promptly took the accused woman into custody. The maid-servant, successful thus far, began to simulate fits and to lay the blame for them on Mistress Anne. Questioned as to what she conceived her condition, she replied, "Oh very damnable, very wretched." She could see the Devil, she said, on the housetop looking at her. These fancies passed as facts, and the accused woman was put to the usual humiliations. She was searched, examined, and urged to confess. The narrator of the story made effort after effort to wring from her an admission of her guilt, but she slipped out of all his traps. Against her accuser she was very bitter. "She hath undone me ... that am an honest woman, 'twill break my Husband's heart, he grieves to see me in these Irons: I did once live in good fashion."

The case was turned over by the justices of the peace to the assizes at Salisbury, where Chief Baron John Wylde of the exchequer presided. The testimony of the maid was brought in, as well as the other proofs. All we know of the trial is that Anne was condemned, and that Judge Wylde was so well satisfied with his work that he urged Edmund Bower, who had begun an account of the case, but had hesitated to expose himself to "this Censorious Age," to go on with his booklet. That detestable individual had followed the case closely. After the condemnation he labored with the woman to make her confess. But no acknowledgment of guilt could be wrung from the high-spirited Mistress Bodenham, even when the would-be father confessor held out to her the false hope of mercy. She made a will giving gifts to thirty people, declared she had been robbed by her maids in prison, lamented over her husband's sorrow, and requested that she be buried under the gallows. Like the McPherson who danced so wantonly and rantingly beneath the gallows tree, she remained brave-hearted to the end. When the officer told her she must go with him to the place of execution, she replied, "Be you ready, I am ready." The narrator closes the account with some moral reflections. We may close with the observation that there is no finer instance of womanly courage in the annals of witchcraft than that of Anne Bodenham. Doubtless she had used charms, and experimented with glasses; it had been done by those of higher rank than she.

As for the maid, she had got herself well out of trouble. When Mistress Bodenham had been hanged, the fits ceased, and she professed great thankfulness to God and a desire to serve him.

The case of Joan Peterson, who was tried at the Old Bailey in 1652, is another instance of the struggle of a spirited woman against too great odds. Joan, like Mistress Bodenham, kept various kinds of powders and prescribed physic for ailing neighbors. It was, however, if we may believe her defender, not on account of her prescriptions, but rather on account of her refusal to swear falsely, that her downfall came. One would be glad to know the name of the vigorous defender who after her execution issued A Declaration in Answer to severall lying Pamphlets concerning the Witch of Wapping. His narrative of the plot against the accused woman offers a plausible explanation of the affair and is not improbably trustworthy. As he tells the story, there were certain relatives of Lady Powell who had been disappointed that her estate had been bequeathed to Mrs. Anne Levingston. They conspired to get rid of the heiress, went to a cunning woman, and offered to pay her liberally if she would swear that Mrs. Levingston had used sorcery to take away the life of Lady Powell. Unfortunately for the conspirators, the cunning woman betrayed their schemes. Not discouraged, however, they employed another woman, who, as their representative, went to Joan Peterson and offered her a hundred pounds to swear that Mrs. Levingston had procured from her "certain powders and bags of seeds." Joan refused the proposition, and the plotters, fearing a second exposure of their plans, determined that Mistress Peterson should also be put out of the way. They were able to procure a warrant to have her arrested and searched. Great pressure was put upon her to confess enough to implicate Mrs. Levingston and she was given to understand that if she would do so she would herself be spared. But Joan refused their proffers and went to her trial. If the narrative may be at all trusted there was little effort to give her a fair hearing. Witnesses against her were purchased in advance, strangers were offered money to testify against her, and those who were to have given evidence on her side were most of them intimidated into staying away from the trial. Four physicians and two surgeons signed a certificate that Lady Powell had died from perfectly natural causes. It was of no avail. Joan was convicted and died bravely, denying her guilt to the end. Her defender avers that some of the magistrates in the case were involved in the conspiracy against her. One of these was Sir John Danvers, a member of Cromwell's council. In the margin of his account the pamphleteer writes: "Sir John Danvers came and dined at the Sessions house and had much private discourse with the Recorder and many of the Justices and came and sate upon the Bench at her Trial, where he hath seldom or never been for these many years."

In July of 1652 occurred another trial that attracted notice in its own time. Six Kentish women were tried at the assizes at Maidstone before Peter Warburton. We know almost nothing of the evidence offered by the prosecution save that there was exhibited in the Swan Inn at Maidstone a piece of flesh which the Devil was said to have given to one of the accused, and that a waxen image of a little girl figured in the evidence. Some of the accused confessed that they had used it in order to kill the child. Search was instituted for it, and it was found, if the narrator may be trusted, under the door where the witches had said it would be. The six were all condemned and suffered execution. Several others were arraigned, but probably escaped trial.

If the age was as "censorious" of things of this nature as Edmund Bower had believed it to be, it is rather remarkable that "these proceedings," which were within a short distance of London, excited so little stir in that metropolis. Elias Ashmole, founder of the Ashmolean Museum at Oxford and delver in astrology, attended the trials, with John Tradescant, traveller and gardener.

He left no comments. The Faithful Scout, in its issue of July 30-August 7, mentioned the trial and the confessions, but refrained from any expression of opinion.

There were other trials in this period; but they must be passed over rapidly. The physicians were quite as busy as ever in suggesting witchcraft. We can detect the hand of a physician in the attribution of the strange illness of a girl who discharged great quantities of stones to the contrivance of Catherine Huxley, who was, in consequence, hanged at Worcester. In a case at Exeter the physician was only indirectly responsible. When Grace Matthews had consulted him about her husband's illness, he had apparently given up the case, and directed her to a wise woman. The wise woman had warned Mistress Matthews of a neighbor "tall of stature and of a pale face and blinking eye," against whom it would be well to use certain prescribed remedies. Mrs. Matthews did so, and roused out the witch, who proved to be a butcher's wife, Joan Baker. When the witch found her spells thwarted, she turned them against Mrs. Matthews's maid-servant, who in consequence died. This was part of the evidence against Joan, and it was confirmed by her own kinsfolk: her father-in-law had seen her handling toads. She was committed, but we hear no more of the case.

That random accusations were not feared as they had been was evidenced by the boldness of suspected parties in bringing action against their accusers, even if boldness was sometimes misjudged. We have two actions of this sort.

Joan Read of Devizes had been reported to be a witch, and on that account had been refused by the bakers the privilege of using their bakeries for her dough. She threw down the glove to her accusers by demanding that they should be brought by warrant to accuse her. No doubt she realized that she had good support in her community, and that her challenge was not likely to be accepted. But a woman near Land's End in Cornwall seems to have overestimated the support upon which she could count. She had procured a warrant against her accusers to call the case before the mayor. The court sided with the accusers and the woman was brought to trial. Caught herself, she proceeded to ensnare others. As a result, eight persons were sent to Launceston, and some probably suffered death.

We have already seen what a tangled web Mrs. Muschamp wove when she set out to imprison a colonel's wife. It would be easy to cite cases to show the same reluctance to follow up prosecution. Four women at Leicester searched Ann Chettle and found no evidence of guilt. In Durham a case came up before Justice Henry Tempest. Mary Sykes was accused. Sara Rodes, a child, awakening from sleep in a fright, had declared to her mother that "Sikes' wife" had come in "att a hole att the bedd feete" and taken her by the throat. Of course Sara Rodes fell ill. Moreover, the witch had been seen riding at midnight on the back of a cow and at another time flying out of a "mistall windowe." But the woman, in spite of the unfavorable opinion of the women searchers, went free. There were cases that seem to have ended the same way at York, at Leeds, and at Scarborough. They were hints of what we have already noticed, that the northern counties were changing their attitude. But a case in Derbyshire deserves more attention because the justice, Gervase Bennett, was one of the members of Cromwell's council. The case itself was not in any way unusual. A beggar woman, who had been liberally supported by those who feared her, was on trial for witchcraft. Because of Bennett's close relation to the government, we should be glad to know what he did with the case, but the fact that the woman's conviction is not among the records makes it probable that she was not bound over to the assizes.

We come now to examine the second of the sub-periods into which we have divided the Interregnum. We have been dealing with the interval between the war and the establishment of the Protectorate, a time that shaded off from the dark shadows of internecine struggle towards the high light of steady peace and security. By 1653 the equilibrium of England had been restored. Cromwell's government was beginning to run smoothly. The courts were in full swing. None of those conditions to which we have attributed the spread of the witch alarms of the Civil Wars were any longer in operation. It is not surprising, then, that the Protectorate was one of the most quiet periods in the annals of witchcraft. While the years 1648-1653 had witnessed thirty executions in England, the period of the Protectorate saw but half a dozen, and three of these fell within the somewhat disturbed rule of Richard Cromwell. In other words, there was a very marked falling off of convictions for witchcraft, a falling off that had indeed begun before the year 1653. Yet this diminution of capital sentences does not by any means signify that the realm was rid of superstition. In Middlesex, in Somerset and Devon, in York, Northumberland, and Cumberland, the attack upon witches on the part of the people was going on with undiminished vigor. If no great discoveries were made, if no nests of the pestilent creatures were unearthed, the justices of the peace were kept quite as busy with examinations as ever before.

To be sure, an analysis of cases proves that a larger proportion of those haled to court were light offenders, "good witches" whose healing arts had perhaps been unsuccessful, dealers in magic who had aroused envy or fear. The court records of Middlesex and York are full of complaints against the professional enchanters. In most instances they were dismissed. Now and then a woman was sent to the house of correction, but even this punishment was the exception.

Two other kinds of cases appeared with less frequency. We have one very clear instance at Wakefield, in York, where a quarrel between two tenant farmers over their highway rights became so bitter that a chance threat uttered by the loser of the lawsuit, "It shall be a dear day's work for you," occasioned an accusation of witchcraft. In another instance the debt of a penny seems to have been the beginning of a hatred between two impecunious creatures, and this brought on a charge.

The most common type of case, of course, was that where strange disease or death played a part. In Yorkshire, in Hertfordshire, and in Cornwall there were trials based upon a sort of evidence with which the reader is already quite familiar. It was easy for the morbid mother of a dead child to recall or imagine angry words spoken to her shortly before the death of her offspring. It was quite as natural for a sick child to be alarmed at the sight of a visitor and go into spasms. There was no fixed rule, however, governing the relation of the afflicted children and the possible witches. When William Wade was named, Elizabeth Mallory would fly into fits. When Jane Brooks entered the room, a bewitched youth of Chard would become hysterical. It was the opposite way with a victim in Exeter, who remained well only so long as the witch who caused the trouble stayed with him.

Closely related to these types of evidence was what has been denominated spectral evidence, a form of evidence recurrent throughout the history of English witchcraft. In the time of the Protectorate we have at least three cases of the kind. The accused woman appeared to the afflicted individual now in her own form, again in other shapes, as a cat, as a bee, or as a dog. The identification of a particular face in the head of a bee must have been a matter of some difficulty, but there is no ground for supposing that any objection was made to this evidence in court. At all events, the testimony went down on the official records in Yorkshire. In Somerset the Jane Brooks case, already referred to, called forth spectral evidence in a form that must really have been very convincing. When the bewitched boy cried out that he saw the witch on the wall, his cousin struck at the place, upon which the boy cried out, "O Father, Coz Gibson hath cut Jane Brooks's hand, and 'tis bloody." Now, according to the story, the constable proceeded to the woman's house and found her hand cut.

As to the social status of the people involved in the Protectorate trials there is little to say, other than has been said of many earlier cases. By far the larger number of those accused, as we have already pointed out, were charmers and enchanters, people who made a penny here and twopence there, but who had at best a precarious existence. Some of them, no doubt, traded on the fear they inspired in their communities and begged now a loaf of bread and now a pot of beer. They were the same people who, when begging and enchanting failed, resorted to stealing. In one of the Yorkshire depositions we have perhaps a hint of another class from which the witches were recruited. Katherine Earle struck a Mr. Frank between the shoulders and said, "You are a pretty gentleman; will you kisse me?" When the man happened to die this solicitation assumed a serious aspect.

Witchcraft was indeed so often the outcome of lower-class bickering that trials involving the upper classes seem worthy of special record. During the Protectorate there were two rather remarkable trials. In 1656 William and Mary Wade were accused of bewitching the fourteen-year-old daughter of Elizabeth Mallory of Studley Hall. The Mallorys were a prominent family in Yorkshire. The grandfather of the accusing child had been a member of Parliament and was a well known Royalist colonel. When Mistress Elizabeth declared that her fits would not cease until Mary Wade had said that she had done her wrong, Mary Wade was persuaded to say the words. Elizabeth was well at once, but Mary withdrew her admission and Elizabeth resumed her fits, indeed "she was paste holdinge, her extreamaty was such." She now demanded that the two Wades should be imprisoned, and when they were "both in holde" she became well again. They were examined by a justice of the peace, but were probably let off.

The story of Diana Crosse at Exeter is a more pathetic one. Mrs. Crosse had once kept a girls' school—could it be that there was some connection between teaching and witchcraft?—had met with misfortune, and had at length been reduced to beggary. We have no means of knowing whether the suspicion of witchcraft antedated her extreme poverty or not, but it seems quite clear that the former school-teacher had gained an ill name in the community. She resented bitterly the attitude of the people, and at one time seems to have appealed to the mayor. It was perhaps by this very act that she focussed the suspicion of her neighbors. To go over the details of the trial is not worth while. Diana Crosse probably escaped execution to eke out the remainder of her life in beggary.

The districts of England affected by the delusion during this period have already been indicated. While there were random cases in Suffolk, Hertfordshire, Wiltshire, Somerset, Cumberland, and Northumberland, by far the greatest activity seems to have been in Middlesex, Cornwall, and Yorkshire. To a layman it looks as if the north of England had produced the greater part of its folk-lore. Certain it is that the witch stories of Yorkshire, as those of Lancaster at another time, by their mysterious and romantic elements made the trials of the south seem flat, stale, and unprofitable. Yet they rarely had as serious results.

To the historian the Middlesex cases must be more interesting because they should afford some index of the attitude of the central government. Unhappily we do not know the fate of the Yorkshire witches, though it has been surmised, in the absence of evidence to the contrary, that they all escaped execution. In Middlesex we know that during this period only one woman, so far as our extant records go, was adjudged guilty. All the rest were let go free. Now, this may be significant and it may not. It does not seem unreasonable to suppose that the Middlesex quarter sessions were in harmony with the central government. Yet this can be no more than a guess. It is not easy to take bearings which will locate the position of the Cromwellian government. The protector himself was occupied with weightier matters, and, so far as we know, never uttered a word on the subject. He was almost certainly responsible for the pardon of Margaret Gyngell at Salisbury in 1655, yet we cannot be sure that he was not guided in that case by special circumstances as well as by the recommendation of subordinates.

We have but little more evidence as to the attitude of his council of state. It was three years before the Protectorate was put into operation that the hesitating sheriff of Cumberland, who had some witches on his hands, was authorized to go ahead and carry out the law. But on the other hand it was in the same period that the English commissioners in Scotland put a quietus on the witch alarms in that kingdom. In fact, one of their first acts was to take over the accused women from the church courts and demand the proof against them. When it was found that they had been tortured into confessions, the commission resolved upon an enquiry into the conduct of the sheriff, ministers, and tormentors who had been involved. Several women had been accused. Not one was condemned. The matter was referred to the council of state, where it seems likely that the action of the commissioners was ratified. Seven or eight years later, in the administration of Richard Cromwell, there was an instance where the council, apparently of its own initiative, ordered a party of soldiers to arrest a Rutlandshire witch. The case was, however, dismissed later.

To draw a definite conclusion from these bits of evidence would be rash. We can perhaps reason somewhat from the general attitude of the government. Throughout the Protectorate there was a tendency, which Cromwell encouraged, to mollify the rigor of the criminal law. Great numbers of pardons were issued; and when Whitelocke suggested that no offences should be capital except murder, treason, and rebellion, no one arose in holy horror to point out the exception of witchcraft, and the suggestion, though never acted upon, was favorably considered.

When we consider this general attitude towards crime in connection with what we have already indicated about the rapid decline in numbers of witch convictions, it seems a safe guess that the Cromwellian government, while not greatly interested in witchcraft, was, so far as interested, inclined towards leniency.

Whitelocke, Memorials, III, 63, 97, 99, 113.

See an extract from the Guild Hall Books in John Fuller, History of Berwick (Edinburgh, 1799), 155-156.

Thomas Widdrington's letter to Whitelocke (Whitelocke, Memorials, III, 99). Widdrington said the man professed himself "an artist that way." The writer was evidently somewhat skeptical.

Ibid.

Ralph Gardiner, England's Grievance Discovered in Relation to the Coal Trade (London, 1655), 108.

Ibid.

See John Brand, History and Antiquities of ... Newcastle (London, 1789), II, 478, or the Chronicon Mirabile (London, 1841), 92, for an extract from the parish registers, giving the names. A witch of rural Northumberland was executed with them.

The witches of 1649 were not confined to the north. Two are said to have been executed at St. Albans, a man and a woman; one woman was tried in Worcestershire, one at Gloucester, and two in Middlesex. John Palmer and Elizabeth Knott, who suffered at St. Albans, had gained some notoriety. Palmer had contracted with the Devil and had persuaded his kinswoman to assist him in procuring the death of a woman by the use of clay pictures. Both were probably practitioners in magic. Palmer, even when in prison, claimed the power of transforming men into beasts. The woman seems to have been put to the swimming test. Both were condemned. Palmer, at his execution, gave information about a "whole colledge of witches," most of them, no doubt, practisers like himself, but his random accusations were probably passed over. See The Divels Delusions or A faithfull relation of John Palmer and Elizabeth Knott ... (1649).

Ralph Gardiner, op. cit., 109.

See ibid. At his execution, Gardiner says, he confessed that he had been the death of 220 witches in Scotland and England. Either the man was guilty of unseemly and boastful lying, which is very likely, or Scotland was indeed badly "infested." See above, note 1.

This narrative is contained in Wonderfull News from the North, Or a True Relation of the Sad and Grievous Torments Inflicted upon ... three Children of Mr. George Muschamp ... (London, 1650).

The story of the case was sent down to London and there published, where it soon became a classic among the witch-believing clergy.

See the two pamphlets by Edmond Bower described below in appendix A, § 5, and Henry More, Antidote against Atheisme, bk. III, ch. VII.

Wylde was not well esteemed as a judge. On the institution of the protectorate he was not reappointed by Cromwell.

Aubrey (who had it from an eye-witness) tells us that "the crowd of spectators made such a noise that the judge could not heare the prisoner, nor the prisoner the judge; but the words were handed from one to the other by Mr. R. Chandler and sometimes not truly repeated." John Aubrey, Remaines of Gentilisme and Judaisme ... (ed. J. Britten, Folk Lore Soc. Publications, IV, 1881), 261.

For the case see The Tryall and Examinations of Mrs. Joan Peterson ...; The Witch of Wapping, or an Exact ... Relation of the ... Practises of Joan Peterson ...; A Declaration in Answer to severall lying Pamphlets concerning the Witch of Wapping ..., (as to these pamphlets, all printed at London in 1652, see below, appendix A, § 5); French Intelligencer, April 6-13, 1652; Weekly Intelligencer, April 6-13, 1652; The Faithful Scout, April 9-16, 1652; Mercurius Democritus, April 7-17, 1652.

The French Intelligencer tells us the story of her execution: "She seemed to be much dejected, having a melancholy aspect; she seemed not to be much above 40 years of age, and was not in the least outwardly deformed, as those kind of creatures usually are."

For an account of this affair see A Prodigious and Tragicall History of the ... Condemnation of six Witches at Maidstone ... (London, 1652).

It was "supposed," says the narrator, that nine children, besides a man and a woman, had suffered at their hands, £500 worth of cattle had been lost, and much corn wrecked at sea. Two of the women made confession, but not to these things.

See Ashmole's diary as given in Charles Burman, Lives of Elias Ashmole, Esq., and Mr. William Lilly, written by themselves ... (London, 1774), 316.

In his Certainty of the World of Spirits (London, 1691), 44, 45, Richard Baxter, who is by no means absolutely reliable, tells us about this case. It should be understood that it is only a guess of the writer that the physician was to blame for the accusation; but it much resembles other cases where the physician started the trouble.

William Cotton, Gleanings from the Municipal and Cathedral Records Relative to the History of the City of Exeter (Exeter, 1877), 149-150.

Hist. MSS. Comm. Reports, Various, I, 127.

Mercurius Politicus, November 24-December 2, 1653. One of these witches was perhaps the one mentioned as from Launceston in Cornwall in R. and O. B. Peter, The Histories of Launceston and Dunheved (Plymouth, 1885), 285: "the grave in wch the wich was buryed."

Richard Burthogge, An Essay upon Reason and the Nature of Spirits (London, 1694), 196, writes that he has the confessions in MS. of "a great number of Witches (some of which were Executed) that were taken by a Justice of Peace in Cornwall above thirty Years agoe." It does not seem impossible that this is a reference to the same affair as that mentioned by the Launceston record.

Leicestershire and Rutland Notes and Queries (Leicester, 1891, etc.), I, 247.

James Raine, ed., A Selection from the Depositions in Criminal Cases taken before the Northern Magistrates, from the Originals preserved in York Castle (Surtees Soc., no. 40, 1861), 28-30. Cited hereafter as York Depositions.

Yet in 1650 there had been a scare at Gateshead which cost the rate payers £2, of which a significant item was 6 d. for a "grave for a witch." Denham Tracts (Folk Lore Soc.), II, 338. At Durham, in 1652, two persons were executed. Richardson, Table Book (London, 1841), I, 286.

J. C. Cox, Three Centuries of Derbyshire Annals (London, 1890), II, 88. Cox, however, thinks it probable that she was punished.

It is of course not altogether safe to reason from the absence of recorded executions, and it is least safe in the time of the Civil Wars and the years of recovery.

Middlesex County Records, ed. by J. C. Jeaffreson (London, 1892), III, 295; Hist. MSS. Comm. Reports, Various, I, 129.

York Depositions, 74.

Hertfordshire County Sessions Rolls, compiled by W. J. Hardy (Hertford, 1905), I, 126. It is not absolutely certain in the second case that the committal was to the house of correction.

York Depositions, 76-77.

Joseph Glanvill, Sadducismus Triumphatus (London, 1681), pt. ii, 122.

Cotton, Gleanings ... relative to the History of ... Exeter, 152.

In the famous Warboys case of 1593 it was the witch's presence that relieved the bewitched of their ailments.

York Depositions, 64-67.

Glanvill, Sadducismus Triumphatus, pt. ii, 120-121.

Hist. MSS. Comm. Reports, Various, I, 120.

York Depositions, 69.

Ibid., 75-78.

See the story of Anne Bodenham.

Cotton, Gleanings ... Relative to the History of ... Exeter, 150-152.

James Raine, editor of York Depositions, writes that he has found no instance of the conviction of a witch. Preface, xxx. The Criminal Chronology of York Castle, with a Register of Criminals capitally Convicted and Executed (York, 1867), contains not a single execution for witchcraft.

Inderwick, Interregnum, 188-189.

Cal. St. P., Dom., 1650, 159.

There are several secondary accounts of this affair. See F. Legge in Scottish Review, XVIII, 267. But a most important primary source is a letter from Clarke to Speaker Lenthall, published by the Scottish History Society in its volume on Scotland and the Commonwealth (Edinburgh, 1895), 367-369. See also a tract in Brit. Mus. Thomason collection, Two Terrible Sea Fights (London, 1652). See, too, the words of Thomas Ady, A Candle in the Dark, 105.

Cal. St. P., Dom., 1658-1659, 169.

When the council of state, however, in 1652 had issued an act of general pardon, witchcraft had been specifically reserved, along with murder, treason, piracy, etc. Cal. St. P., Dom., 1651-1652, 106.

Inderwick, Interregnum, 231.

CHAPTER X.: The Literature of Witchcraft from 1603 to 1660.

No small part of our story has been devoted to the writings of Scot, Gifford, Harsnett, and King James. It is impossible to understand the significance of the prosecutions without some acquaintance with the course of opinion on the subject. In this chapter we shall go back as far as the opening of the reign of James and follow up to the end of the Commonwealth the special discussions of witchcraft, as well as some of the more interesting incidental references. It will be recalled that James's Dæmonologie had come out several years before its author ascended the English throne. With the coming of the Scottish king to Westminster the work was republished at London. But, while James by virtue of his position was easily first among those who were writing on the subject, he by no means occupied the stage alone. Not less than four other men gained a hearing within the reign and for that reason deserve consideration. They were Perkins, Cotta, Roberts, and Cooper.

William Perkins's Discourse of the Damned Art of Witchcraft came first in order, indeed it was written during the last years of Elizabeth's reign; but it was not published until 1608, six years after the author's death. William Perkins was a fellow of Christ's College at Cambridge and an eminent preacher in that university. He holds a high place among Puritan divines. His sermons may still be found in the libraries of older clergymen and citations from them are abundant in commentaries. It was in the course of one of his university sermons that he took up the matter of witchcraft. In what year this sermon was preached cannot definitely be said. That he seems to have read Scot, that however he does not mention King James's book, are data which lead us to guess that he may have uttered the discourse between 1584 and 1597. His point of view was strictly theological and his convictions grounded—as might be expected—upon scriptural texts. Yet it seems not unfair to suppose that he was an exponent of opinion at Cambridge, where we have already seen evidences of strong faith in the reality of witchcraft. It seems no less likely that a perusal of Reginald Scot's Discoverie prompted the sermon. Witches nowadays, he admitted, have their patrons. His argument for the existence of witches was so thoroughly biblical that we need not go over it. He did not, however, hold to all current conceptions of them. The power of the evil one to transform human beings into other shapes he utterly repudiated. The scratching of witches and the testing of them by water he thought of no value. In this respect it will be seen that he was in advance of his royal contemporary. About the bodily marks, the significance of which James so emphasized, Perkins seems to have been less decided. He believed in the death penalty, but he warned juries to be very careful as to evidence. Evidence based upon the accusations of "good witches," upon the statements of the dying, or upon the charges of those who had suffered ill after threats, he thought ought to be used with great caution. It is evident that Perkins—though he doubtless would not have admitted it himself—was affected by the reading of Scot. Yet it is disappointing to find him condoning the use of torture in extreme instances.

A Cambridge man who wrote about a score of years after Perkins put forth opinions a good deal farther advanced. John Cotta was a "Doctor in Physicke" at Northampton who had taken his

B. A. at Cambridge in 1595, his M. A. the following year, and his M. D. in 1603. Nine years after leaving Cambridge he had published A Short Discoverie of the Unobserved Dangers, in which he had devoted a very thoughtful chapter to the relation between witchcraft and sickness. In 1616 he elaborated his notions in The Triall of Witchcraft, published at London. Like Perkins he disapproved of the trial by water. He discredited, too, the evidence of marks, but believed in contracts with the Devil, and cited as illustrious instances the cases of Merlin and "that infamous woman," Joan of Arc. But his point of view was of course mainly that of a medical man. A large number of accusations of witchcraft were due to the want of medical examination. Many so-called possessions could be perfectly diagnosed by a physician. He referred to a case where the supposed witches had been executed and their victim had nevertheless fallen ill again. Probably this was the case of Mistress Belcher, on whose account two women had been hanged at Northampton.

Yet Cotta believed that there were real witches and arraigned Scot for failing to distinguish the impostors from the true. It was indeed, he admitted, very hard to discover, except by confession; and even confession, as he had pointed out in his first work, might be a "meane, poore and uncertain proofe," because of the Devil's power to induce false confession. Here the theologian— it was hard for a seventeenth-century writer not to be a theologian—was cropping out. But the scientific spirit came to the front again when he made the point that imagination was too apt to color observations made upon bewitched and witch. The suggestion that coincidence explained many of the alleged fulfillments of witch predictions was equally in advance of his times.

How, then, were real cases of bewitchment to be recognized? The best assurance on such matters, Cotta answered, came "whensoever ... the Physicion shall truely discover a manifest transcending power." In other words, the Northampton physician believed that his own profession could best determine these vexed matters. One who has seen the sorry part played by the physicians up to this time can hardly believe that their judgment on this point was saner than that of men in other professions. It may even be questioned if they were more to be depended upon than the so superstitious clergy.

In the same year as Cotta's second book, Alexander Roberts, "minister of God's word at King's Lynn" in Norfolk, brought out A Treatise of Witchcraft as a sort of introduction to his account of the trial of Mary Smith of that town and as a justification of her punishment. The work is merely a restatement of the conventional theology of that time as applied to witches, exactly such a presentation of it as was to be expected from an up-country parson who had read Reginald Scot, and could wield the Scripture against him.

The following year saw the publication of a work equally theological, The Mystery of Witchcraft, by the Reverend Thomas Cooper, who felt that his part in discovering "the practise of Anti-Christ in that hellish Plot of the Gunpowder-treason" enabled him to bring to light other operations of the Devil. He had indeed some experience in this work, as well as some acquaintance with the writers on the subject. But he adds nothing to the discussion unless it be the coupling of the disbelief in witchcraft with the "Atheisme and Irreligion that overflows the land." Five years later the book was brought out again under another title, Sathan transformed into an Angell of Light, ... [ex]emplified specially in the Doctrine of Witchcraft.

In the account of the trials for witchcraft in the reign of James I the divorce case of the Countess of Essex was purposely omitted, because in it the question of witchcraft was after all a subordinate matter. In the history of opinion, however, the views about witchcraft expressed by the court that passed upon the divorce can by no means be ignored. It is not worth while to rehearse the malodorous details of that singular affair. The petitioner for divorce made the claim that her husband was unable to consummate the marriage with her and left it to be inferred that he was bewitched. It will be remembered that King James, anxious to further the plans of his favorite, Carr, was too willing to have the marriage annulled and brought great pressure to bear upon the members of the court. Archbishop Abbot from the beginning of the trial showed himself unfavorable to the petition of the countess, and James deemed it necessary to resolve his doubts on the general grounds of the divorce. On the matter of witchcraft in particular the king wrote: "for as sure as God is, there be Devils, and some Devils must have some power, and their power is in this world That the Devil's power is not so universal against us, that I freely confess; but that it is utterly restrained quoad nos, how was then a minister of Geneva bewitched to death, and were the witches daily punished by our law. If they can harm none but the papists, we are too charitable for avenging of them only." This was James's opinion in 1613, and it is worthy of note that he was much less certain of his ground and much more on the defensive about witchcraft than the author of the Dæmonologie had been. It can hardly be doubted that he had already been affected by the more liberal views of the ecclesiastics who surrounded him. Archbishop Bancroft, who had waged through his chaplain the war on the exorcists, was not long dead. That chaplain was now Bishop of Chichester and soon to become Archbishop of York. It would be strange if James had not been affected to some degree by their opinions. Moreover, by this time he had begun his career as a discoverer of impostors.

The change in the king's position must, however, not be overrated. He maintained his belief in witches and seemed somewhat apprehensive lest others should doubt it. Archbishop Abbot, whom he was trying to win over to the divorce, would not have denied James's theories, but he was exceedingly cautious in his own use of the term maleficium. Abbot was wholly familiar with the history of the Anglican attitude towards exorcism. There can be little doubt that he was in sympathy with the policy of his predecessor. It is therefore interesting to read his carefully worded statement as to the alleged bewitchment of the Earl of Essex. In his speech defending his refusal and that of three colleagues to assent to the divorce, he wrote: "One of my lords (my lord of Winchester) hath avowed it, that he dislikes that maleficium; that he hath read Del Rio, the Jesuit, writing upon that argument, and doth hold him an idle and fabulous fellow.... Another of my lords (my lord of Ely) hath assented thereunto, and maleficium must be gone. Now I for my part will not absolutely deny that witches by God's permission may have a power over men, to hurt all, or part in them, as by God they shall be limited; but how shall it appear that this is such a thing in the person of a man." This was not, of course, an expression of disbelief in the reality or culpability of witchcraft. It was an expression of great reluctance to lay much stress upon charges of witchcraft—an expression upon the part of the highest ecclesiastical authority in England.

In the reign of Charles I prior to the Civil Wars we have to analyze but a single contribution to the literature of our subject, that made by Richard Bernard. Bernard had preached in Nottinghamshire and had gone from there to Batcombe in Somerset. While yet in Nottinghamshire, in the early years of James's reign, he had seen something of the exorcizers. Later he had had to do with the Taunton cases of 1626; indeed, he seems to have had a prominent part in this affair. Presumably he had displayed some anxiety lest the witches should not receive fair treatment, for in his Guide to Grand-Jurymen ... in cases of Witchcraft, published in 1627, he explained the book as a "plaine countery Minister's testimony." Owing to his "upright meaning" in his "painstaking" with one of the witches, a rumor had spread that he favored witches or "were of Master Scots erroneous opinion that Witches were silly Melancholikes." He had undertaken in consequence to familiarize himself with the whole subject and had read nearly all the discussions in English, as well as all the accounts of trials published up to that time. His work he dedicated to the two judges at Taunton, Sir John Walter and Sir John Denham, and to the archdeacon of Wells and the chancellor of the Bishop of Bath and Wells. The book was, indeed, a truly remarkable patchwork. All shades of opinion from that of the earnestly disbelieving Scot to that of the earnestly believing Roberts were embodied. Nevertheless Bernard had a wholesome distrust of possessions and followed Cotta in thinking that catalepsy and other related diseases accounted for many of them. He thought, too, that the Devil very often acted as his own agent without any intermediary. Like Cotta, he was skeptical as to the water ordeal; but, strange to say, he accepted the use of a magical glass to discover "the suspected." He was inclined to believe that the "apparition of the party suspected, whom the afflicted in their fits seem to see," was a ground for suspicion. The main aim of his discourse was, indeed, to warn judges and jurors to be very careful by their questions and methods of inquiring to separate the innocent from the guilty. In this contention, indeed in his whole attitude, he was very nearly the mouthpiece of an age which, while clinging to a belief, was becoming increasingly cautious of carrying that belief too far into judicial trial and punishment.

It is a jump of seventeen years from Bernard of Batcombe to John Gaule. It cannot be said that Gaule marks a distinct step in the progress of opinion beyond Bernard. His general position was much the same as that of his predecessor. His warnings were perhaps more earnest, his skepticism a little more apparent. In an earlier chapter we have observed the bold way in which the indignant clergyman of Huntingdonshire took up Hopkins's challenge in 1646. It was the Hopkins crusade that called forth his treatise. His little book was in large part a plea for more caution in the use of evidence. Suspicion was too lightly entertained against "every poore and peevish olde Creature." Whenever there was an extraordinary accident, whenever there was a disease that could not be explained, it was imputed to witchcraft. Such "Tokens of Tryall" he deemed "altogether unwarrantable, as proceeding from ignorance, humor, superstition." There were other more reliable indications by which witches could sometimes be detected, but those indications were to be used with exceeding caution. Neither the evidence of the fact—that is, of a league with the Devil—without confession nor "confession without fact" was to be accounted as certain proof. On the matter of confession Gaule was extraordinarily skeptical for his time. It was to be considered whether the party confessing were not diabolically deluded, whether the confession were not forced, or whether it were not the result of melancholy. Gaule went even a little further. Not only was he inclined to suspect confession, but he had serious doubts about a great part of witch lore. There were stories of metamorphoses, there were narratives of "tedious journeys upon broomes," and a hundred other tales from old authors, which the wise Christian would, he believed, leave with the writers. To believe nothing of them, however, would be to belittle the Divine attributes. As a matter of fact there was a very considerable part of the witch theory that Gaule accepted. His creed came to this: it was unsafe to pronounce such and such to be witches. While not one in ten was guilty, the tenth was still to be accounted for. The physician Cotta would have turned the matter over to the physicians; the clergyman Gaule believed that it belonged to the province of the "Magistracy and Ministery."

During the period of the Commonwealth one would have supposed that intellectual men would be entirely preoccupied with more weighty matters than the guilt of witches. But the many executions that followed in the wake of Hopkins and Stearne had invested the subject with a new interest and brought new warriors into the fray. Half a dozen writers took up the controversy. On the conservative side three names deserve mention, two of them not unknown in other connections, Henry More and Meric Casaubon. For the defence of the accused witches appeared two men hardly so well known in their time, Robert Filmer and Thomas Ady.

More was a young Cambridge scholar and divine who was to take rank among the English philosophers of the seventeenth century. Grounded in Plato and impregnated with Descartes, he became a little later thoroughly infected with the Cabalistic philosophy that had entered Europe from the East. It was the point of view that he acquired in the study of this mystic Oriental system that gave the peculiar turn to his witchcraft notions, a turn which through his own writings and those of Glanvill found wide acceptance. It was in 1653 that More issued An Antidote to Atheisme. The phenomena of witchcraft he reckoned as part of the evidence for the reality of the spirit world and used them to support religion, quite in the same manner as Sir Oliver Lodge or Professor Hyslop would today use psychical research to establish immortality. More had made investigations for himself, probably at Maidstone. In his own town of Cambridge there was a story—doubtless a college joke, but he referred to it in all seriousness—of "Old Strangridge," who "was carried over Shelford Steeple upon a black Hogge and tore his breeches upon the weather-cock." He believed that he had absolute proof of the "nocturnal conventicles" of witches. He had, however, none of that instinct for scientific observation that had distinguished Scot, and his researches did not prevent his being easily duped. His observations are not by any means so entertaining as are his theories. His effort to account for the instantaneous transportation of witches is one of the bright spots in the prosy reasonings of the demonologists. More was a thoroughgoing dualist. Mind and matter were the two separate entities. Now, the problem that arose at once was this: How can the souls of witches leave their bodies? "I conceive," he says, "the Divell gets into their body and by his subtile substance more operative and searching than any fire or putrifying liquor, melts the yielding Campages of the body to such a consistency ... and makes it plyable to his imagination: and then it is as easy for him to work it into what shape he pleaseth." If he could do that, much more could he enable men to leave their bodies. Then arose the problem: How does this process differ from death? The writer was puzzled apparently at his own question, but reasoned that death was the result of the unfitness of the body to contain the soul. But no such condition existed when the Devil was operating; and no doubt the body could be anointed in such fashion that the soul could leave and return.

Meric Casaubon, son of the eminent classical scholar and himself a well known student, was skeptical as to the stories told about the aerial journeys of witches which More had been at such pains to explain. It was a matter, he wrote in his Treatise concerning Enthusiasme, of much dispute among learned men. The confessions made were hard to account for, but he would feel it very wrong to condemn the accused upon that evidence. We shall meet with Casaubon again.

Nathaniel Homes, who wrote from his pastoral study at Mary Stayning's in London, and dedicated his work to Francis Rous, member of Parliament, was no halfway man. He was a thoroughgoing disciple of Perkins. His utmost admission—the time had come when one had to make some concessions—was that evil spirits performed many of their wonders by tricks of juggling. But he swallowed without effort all the nonsense about covenants, and was inclined to see in the activities of the Devil a presage of the last days.

The reader can readily see that More, Casaubon, and Homes were all on the defensive. They were compelled to offer explanations of the mysteries of witchcraft, they were ready enough to make admissions; but they were nevertheless sticking closely to the main doctrines. It is a pleasure to turn to the writings of two men of somewhat bolder stamp, Robert Filmer and Thomas Ady. Sir Robert Filmer was a Kentish knight of strong royalist views who had written against the limitations of monarchy and was not afraid to cross swords with Milton and Hobbes on the origin of government. In 1652 he had attended the Maidstone trials, where, it will be remembered, six women had been convicted. As Scot had been stirred by the St. Oses trials, so Filmer was wrought up by what he had seen at Maidstone, and in the following year he published his Advertisement to the Jurymen of England. He set out to overturn the treatise of Perkins. As a consequence he dealt with Scripture and the interpretation of the well known passages in the Old Testament. The Hebrew witch, Filmer declared, was guilty of nothing more than "lying prophecies." The Witch of Endor probably used "hollow speaking." In this suggestion Filmer was following his famous Kentish predecessor. But Filmer's main interest, like Bernard's and Gaule's before him, was to warn those who had to try cases to be exceedingly careful. He felt that a great part of the evidence used was worth little or nothing.

Thomas Ady's Candle in the Dark was published three years later. Even more than Filmer, Ady was a disciple of Scot. But he was, indeed, a student of all English writers on the subject and set about to answer them one by one. King James, whose book he persistently refused to believe the king's own handiwork, Cooper, who was a "bloudy persecutor," Gifford, who "had more of the spirit of truth in him than many," Perkins, the arch-enemy, Gaule, whose "intentions were godly," but who was too far "swayed by the common tradition of men," all of them were one after another disposed of. Ady stood eminently for good sense. It was from that point of view that he ridiculed the water ordeal and the evidence of marks, and that he attacked the cause and effect relation between threats and illness. "They that make this Objection must dwell very remote from Neighbours."

Yet not even Ady was a downright disbeliever. He defended Scot from the report "that he held an opinion that Witches are not, for it was neither his Tenent nor is it mine." Alas, Ady does not enlighten us as to just what was his opinion. Certainly his witches were creatures without power. What, then, were they? Were they harmless beings with malevolent minds? Mr. Ady does not answer.

A hundred years of witchcraft history had not brought to light a man who was willing to deny in a printed work the existence of witches. Doubtless such denial might often have been heard in the closet, but it was never proclaimed on the housetop. Scot had not been so bold—though one imagines that if he had been quietly questioned in a corner he might have denied the thing in toto—and those who had followed in his steps never ventured beyond him.

The controversy, indeed, was waged in most of its aspects along the lines laid down by the first aggressor. Gifford, Cotta, and Ady had brought in a few new arguments to be used in attacking superstition, but in general the assailants looked to Scot. On the other side, only Perkins and More had contributed anything worth while to the defence that had been built up. Yet, the reader will notice that there had been progress. The centre of struggle had shifted to a point within the outer walls. The water ordeal and the evidence of marks were given up by most, if not all. The struggle now was over the transportation of witches through the air and the battle was going badly for the defenders.

We turn now to the incidental indications of the shifting of opinion. In one sense this sort of evidence means more than the formal literature. Yet its fragmentary character at best precludes putting any great stress upon it.

If one were to include all the references to witchcraft in the drama of the period, this discussion might widen out into a long chapter. Over the passages in the playwrights we must pass with haste; but certain points must be noted. Shakespeare, in Macbeth, which scholars have usually placed at about 1606, used a great body of witch lore. He used it, too, with apparent good faith, though to conclude therefrom that he believed in it himself would be a most dangerous step. Thomas Middleton, whose Witch probably was written somewhat later, and who is thought to have drawn on Shakespeare for some of his witch material, gives absolutely no indication in that play that he did not credit those tales of witch performances of which he availed himself. The same may be said of Dekker and of those who collaborated with him in writing The Witch of Edmonton.

We may go further and say that in none of these three plays is there any hint that there were disbelievers. But when we come to Ben Jonson we have a different story. His various plays we cannot here take up. Suffice it to say, on the authority of careful commentators, that he openly or covertly ridiculed all the supposedly supernatural phenomena of his time. Perhaps a search through the obscurer dramatists of the period might reveal other evidences of skepticism. Such a search we cannot make. It must, however, be pointed out that Thomas Heywood, in The late

Lancashire Witches a play which is described at some length in an earlier chapter, makes a character say: "It seemes then you are of opinion that there are witches. For mine own part I can hardly be induc'd to think there is any such kinde of people." The speech is the more notable because Heywood's own belief in witchcraft, as has been observed in another connection, seems beyond doubt.

The interest in witchcraft among literary men was not confined to the dramatists. Three prose writers eminent in their time dealt with the question. Burton, in his Anatomy of Melancholy admits that "many deny witches at all, or, if there be any, they can do no harm." But he says that on the other side are grouped most "Lawyers, Divines, Physitians, Philosophers." James Howell, famous letter-writer of the mid-century, had a similar reverence for authority: "I say ... that he who denies there are such busy Spirits and such poor passive Creatures upon whom they work, which commonly are call'd Witches ... shews that he himself hath a Spirit of Contradiction in him." There are, he says, laws against witches, laws by Parliament and laws in the Holy Codex.

Francis Osborne, a literary man whose reputation hardly survived his century, but an essayist of great fame in his own time, was a man who made his fortune by sailing against rather than with the wind. It was conventional to believe in witches and Osborne would not for any consideration be conventional. He assumed the skeptical attitude, and perhaps was as influential as any one man in making that attitude fashionable.

From these lesser lights of the literary world we may pass to notice the attitude assumed by three men of influence in their own day, whose reputations have hardly been dimmed by time, Bacon, Selden, and Hobbes. Not that their views would be representative of their times, for each of the three men thought in his own way, and all three were in many respects in advance of their day. At some time in the reign of James I Francis Bacon wrote his Sylva Sylvarum and rather incidentally touched upon witchcraft. He warned judges to be wary about believing the confessions of witches and the evidence against them. "For the witches themselves are imaginative and believe oft-times they do that which they do not; and people are credulous in that point, and ready to impute accidents and natural operations to witchcraft. It is worthy the observing, that ... the great wonders which they tell, of carrying in the air, transporting themselves into other bodies, &c., are still reported to be wrought, not by incantations, or ceremonies, but by ointments, and anointing themselves all over. This may justly move a man to think that these fables are the effects of imagination."

Surely all this has a skeptical sound. Yet largely on the strength of another passage, which has been carelessly read, the great Bacon has been tearfully numbered among the blindest leaders of the blind. A careful comparison of his various allusions to witchcraft will convince one that, while he assumed a belief in the practice, partly perhaps in deference to James's views, he inclined to explain many reported phenomena from the effects of the imagination and from the operation of "natural causes" as yet unknown.

Bacon, though a lawyer and man of affairs, had the point of view of a philosopher. With John Selden we get more directly the standpoint of a legal man. In his Table Talk that eminent jurist wrote a paragraph on witches. "The Law against Witches," he declared, "does not prove there be any; but it punishes the Malice of those people that use such means to take away mens Lives. If one should profess that by turning his Hat thrice and crying Buz, he could take away a man's life (though in truth he could do no such thing) yet this were a just Law made by the State, that whosoever should turn his Hat thrice and cry Buz, with an intention to take away a man's life, shall be put to death." As to the merits of this legal quip the less said the better; but it is exceedingly hard to see in the passage anything but downright skepticism as to the witch's power.

It is not without interest that Selden's point of view was exactly that of the philosopher Hobbes. There is no man of the seventeenth century, unless it be Oliver Cromwell or John Milton, whose opinion on this subject we would rather know than that of Hobbes. In 1651 Hobbes had issued his great Leviathan. It is unnecessary here to insist upon the widespread influence of that work. Let it be said, however, that Hobbes was not only to set in motion new philosophies, but that he had been tutor to Prince Charles and was to become a figure in the reign of that prince. Hobbes's work was directed against superstition in many forms, but we need only notice his statement about witchcraft, a statement that did not by any means escape his contemporaries. "As for Witches," he wrote, "I think not that their witchcraft is any reall power; but yet that they are justly punished for the false beliefe they have that they can do such mischief, joined with their purpose to do it if they can." Perhaps the great philosopher had in mind those pretenders to diabolic arts who had suffered punishment, and was so defending the community that had rid itself of a preying class. In any case, while he defended the law, he put himself among the disbelievers in witchcraft.

From these opinions of the great we may turn to mark the more trivial indications of the shifting of opinion to be found in the pamphlet literature. It goes without saying that the pamphlet-writers believed in that whereof they spoke. It is not in their outspoken faith that we are interested, but rather in their mention of those opponents at whose numbers they marvelled, and whose incredulity they undertook to shake. Nowhere better than in the prefaces of the pamphleteers can evidence be found of the growing skepticism. The narrator of the Northampton cases in 1612 avowed it his purpose in writing to convince the "many that remaine yet in doubt whether there be any Witches or no." That ardent busybody, Mr. Potts, who reported the Lancaster cases of 1612, very incidentally lets us know that the kinsfolk and friends of Jennet Preston, who, it will be remembered, suffered at York, declared the whole prosecution to be an act of malice. The Yorkshire poet and gentleman, Edward Fairfax, who made such an ado about the sickness of his two daughters in 1622 and would have sent six creatures to the gallows for it, was very frank in describing the opposition he met. The accused women found supporters among the "best able and most understanding." There were, he thought, three kinds of people who were doubters in these matters: those who attributed too much to natural causes and who were content to call clear cases of bewitchment convulsions, those who when witchcraft was broached talked about fairies and "walking ghosts," and lastly those who believed there were no witches. "Of this opinion I hear and see there be many, some of them men of worth, religious and honest."

The pamphlet-writers of James's reign had adjusted themselves to meet opposition. Those of the Civil Wars and the Commonwealth were prepared to meet ridicule. "There are some," says the narrator of a Yorkshire story, "who are of opinion that there are no Divells nor any witches.... Men in this Age are grown so wicked, that they are apt to believe there are no greater Divells than themselves." Another writer, to bolster up his story before a skeptical public, declares that he is "very chary and hard enough to believe passages of this nature."

We have said that the narrators of witch stories fortified themselves against ridicule. That ridicule obviously must have found frequent expression in conversation, but sometimes it even crept into the newspapers and tracts of the day. The Civil Wars had developed a regular London press. We have already met with expressions of serious opinion from it. But not all were of that sort. In 1654 the Mercurius Democritus, the Punch of its time, took occasion to make fun of the stories of the supernatural then in circulation. There was, it declared, a strange story of a trance and apparition, a ghost was said to be abroad, a woman had hanged herself in a tobacco pipe. With very broad humor the journal took off the strange reports of the time and concluded with the warning that in "these distempered times" it was not safe for an "idle-pated woman" to look up at the skies.

The same mocking incredulity had manifested itself in 1648 in a little brochure entitled, The Devil seen at St. Albans, Being a true Relation how the Devill was seen there in a Cellar, in the likeness of a Ram; and how a Butcher came and cut his throat, and sold some of it, and dressed the rest for himselfe, inviting many to supper, who did eat of it. The story was a clever parody of the demon tracts that had come out so frequently in the exciting times of the wars. The writer made his point clear when he declared that his story was of equal value with anything that "Britannicus" ever wrote. The importance of these indications may be overestimated. But they do mean that there were those bold enough to make fun. A decade or two later ridicule became a two-edged knife, cutting superstition right and left. But even under the terribly serious Puritans skepticism began to avail itself of that weapon, a weapon of which it could hardly be disarmed.

In following the history of opinion we must needs mention again some of the incidents of certain cases dealt with in earlier chapters, incidents that indicate the growing force of doubt. The reader has hardly forgotten the outcome of the Lancashire cases in 1633. There Bishop Bridgeman and the king, if they did not discredit witchcraft, discredited its manifestation in the particular instance. As for William Harvey, he had probably given up his faith in the whole business after the little incident at Newmarket. When we come to the time of the Civil Wars we cannot forget that Stearne and Hopkins met opposition, not alone from the Huntingdon minister, but from a large party in Norfolk, who finally forced the witchfinder to defend himself in court. Nor can we forget the witch-pricker of Berwick who was sent a-flying back to his native northern soil, nor the persistent Mrs. Muschamp who tramped over Northumberland seeking a warrant and finding none.

The course of opinion is a circuitous one. We have followed its windings in and out through more than half a century. We have listened as respectfully as possible to the vagaries of country parsons and university preachers, we have heard from scholars, from gentlemen, from jurists and men of affairs, from physicians and philosophers. It matters little now what they thought or said, but it did matter then. We have seen how easy a thing it was to fall into the error that a middle course was nearest truth. Broad was the way and many there were that walked therein. Yet even those who travelled that highway found their direction shifting. For there was progress in opinion. With every decade the travellers, as well those who strayed aside as those who followed the crowd, were getting a little nearer to truth.

"Printed by Cantrel Legge, Printer to the Universitie of Cambridge" (1608, 1610).

See Discourse of the Damned Art of Witchcraft, ch. VII, sect. I.

His literary executor, Thomas Pickering, late of Emmanuel College, Cambridge, and now "Minister of Finchingfield in Essex," who prepared the Discourse for the press (both in its separate form and as a part of Perkins's collected works), and who dedicates it to Sir Edward Coke, is, however, equally silent as to James, though in his preface he mentions Scot by name.

Ibid., ch. IV, sect. I. See also ch. II.

Ibid., ch. VII, sect. II.

Ibid., ch. VI.

Ibid., ch. VII, sect. II.

Ibid., ch. VII, sect. II.

James Mason, "Master of Artes," whose Anatomie of Sorcerie ("printed at London by John Legatte, Printer to the Universitie of Cambridge," 1612), puts him next to Perkins in chronological order, needs only mention in passing. He takes the reality of sorcery for granted, and devotes himself to argument against its use.

... Shewing the True and Right Methode of the Discovery. Cotta was familiar with the more important trials of his time. He knew of the Warboys, Lancaster, and York trials and he probably had come into close contact with the Northampton cases. He had read, too, several of the books on the subject, such as Scot, Wier, and Perkins. His omission of King James's work is therefore not only curious but significant. A second edition of his book was published in 1625.

See Triall of Witchcraft, ch. XIV.

See ibid., p. 48.

Ibid., 66-67.

See ibid., ch. VI. Cotta speaks of the case as six years earlier.

Ibid., 62, 66.

A Short Discoverie, 70.

Triall of Witchcraft, 83-84.

A Short Discoverie, 51-53.

Triall of Witchcraft, 70.

Roberts's explanation of the proneness of women to witchcraft deserves mention in passing. Women are more credulous, more curious, "their complection is softer," they have "greater facility to fall," greater desire for revenge, and "are of a slippery tongue." Treatise of Witchcraft, 42-43.

"In Cheshire and Coventry," he tells us. "Hath not Coventrie," he asks (p. 16), "beene usually haunted by these hellish Sorcerers, where it was confessed by one of them, that no lesse than three-score were of that confedracie?... And was I not there enjoyned by a necessity to the discoverie of this Brood?"

For the whole case see Howell, State Trials, II.

See article on Bernard in Dict. Nat. Biog.

See below, appendix C, list of witch cases, under 1626.

See Guide to Grand-Jurymen, Dedication.

Ibid., 11-12.

Ibid., 53.

Ibid., 214.

This he did on the authority of a repentant Mr. Edmonds, of Cambridge, who had once been questioned by the University authorities for witchcraft. Ibid., 136-138.

Guide to Grand-Jurymen, 22-28.

He was "for the law, but agin' its enforcement."

Select Cases of Conscience Touching Witches and Witchcraft (London, 1646).

Ibid., 92.

Ibid., 94, 97. That Gaule was a Puritan, as has been asserted, appears from nothing in his book. If he dedicated his Select Cases to his townsman Colonel Walton, a brother-in-law of Cromwell, and his Mag-astro-mancer (a later diatribe against current superstitions) to Oliver himself, there is nothing in his prefatory letters to show him of their party. Nor does the tone of his writings suggest a Calvinist. That in 1649 we find Gaule chosen to preach before the assizes of Huntingdon points perhaps only to his popularity as a leader of the reaction against the work of Hopkins.

Antidote to Atheisme, 129.

Ibid., 127-130.

Ibid., ch. VIII, 134.

Ibid., 135.

See p. 118. This Treatise was first published in 1655. Four years later, in 1659, he published A True and faithful Relation of what passed ... between Dr. John Dee, ... and some spirits. In the preface to this he announced his intention of writing the work which he later published as Of Credulity and Incredulity.

In passing we must mention Richard Farnworth, who in 1655 issued a pamphlet called Witchcraft Cast out from the Religious Seed and Israel of God. Farnworth was a Quaker, and wrote merely to warn his brethren against magic and sorcery. He never questioned for a moment the facts of witchcraft and sorcery, nor the Devil's share in them. As for the witches, they were doomed everlastingly to the lake of fire.

Dæmonologie and Theologie. The first, the Malady ..., The Second, The Remedy (London, 1650).

Ibid., 42.

Ibid., 16.

See the Introduction to the Advertisement.

Filmer noted further that the Septuagint translates the Hebrew word for witch as "an Apothecary, a Druggister, one that compounds poysons."

London, 1656.

In Ady's second edition, A Perfect Discovery of Witches (1661), 134, Gaule's book having meanwhile come into his hands, he speaks of Gaule as "much inclining to the Truth" and yet swayed by traditions and the authority of the learned. He adds, "Mr. Gaule, if this work of mine shall come to your hand, as yours hath come to mine, be not angry with me for writing God's Truth."

"... few men or women being tied hand and feet together can sink quite away till they be drowned" (Candle in the Dark, 100); "... very few people in the World are without privie Marks" (Ibid., 127).

Ibid., 129.

In giving "The Reason of the Book" he wrote, "The Grand Errour of these latter Ages is ascribing power to Witches."

See a recent discussion of a nearly related topic by Professor Elmer Stoll in the Publications of the Modern Language Association, XXII, 201-233. Of the attitude of the English dramatists before Shakespeare something may be learned from Mr. L. W. Cushman's The Devil and the Vice in the English Dramatic Literature before Shakespeare (Halle, 1900).

About 1622 or soon after.

See, for instance, Mr. W. S. Johnson's introduction to his edition of The Devil is an Ass (New York, 1905).

1634. This play was written, of course, in cooperation with Brome; see above, pp. 158-160. For other expressions of Heywood's opinions on witchcraft see his Hierarchie of the Blessed Angels, 598, and his ΓΥΝΑΙΚΕΙΟΝ: or Nine Books of Various History concerning Women (London, 1624), lib. viii, 399, 407, etc.

Act I, scene 1.

In another part of the same scene: "They that thinke so dreame," i. e. they who believe in witchcraft.

First published in 1621—I use, however, Shilleto's ed. of London, 1893, which follows that of 1651-1652; see pt. I, sect. II, memb. I, sub-sect. 3.

James Howell, Familiar Letters, II, 548.

His Advice to a Son, first published in 1656-1658, went through edition after edition. It is very entertaining. His strongly enforced advice not to marry made a sensation among young Oxford men.

Works of Francis Osborne (London, 1673), 551-553.

Works of Bacon (ed. Spedding, London, 1857-1858), II, 642-643.

"The ointment that witches use is reported to be made of the fat of children digged out of their graves; of the juices of smallage, wolf-bane, and cinque-foil, mingled with the meal of fine wheat; but I suppose that the soporiferous medicines are likest to do it." See Sylva Sylvarum, cent. X, 975, in Works, ed. Spedding, II, 664. But even this passage shows Bacon a skeptic. His suggestion that the soporiferous medicines are likest to do it means that he thinks the delusions of witches subjective and produced by drugs. For other references to the subject see Works, II, 658, 660; VII, 738.

De Argumentis, bk. II, ch. II, in Works, IV, 296; see also ibid., III, 490.

Advancement of Learning, bk. II; ibid., III, 490.

Works, IV, 400-401.

Ibid., IV, 296.

Selden, Table Talk (London, 1689). The book is supposed to have been written during the last twenty years of Selden's life, that is, between 1634 and 1654.

Selden, Table Talk, s. v. "Witches."

Nor did Selden believe in possessions. See his essay on Devils in the Table Talk.

See article on Hobbes in Dict. Nat. Biog.

See, for example, Bishop Burnet's History of his Own Time (Oxford, 1823), I, 172, 322-323.

Leviathan (1651), 7. See also his Dialogue of the Common Laws of England, in Works (ed. of London, 1750), 626: "But I desire not to discourse of that subject; for, though without doubt there is some great Wickedness signified by those Crimes, yet have I ever found myself too dull to conceive the nature of them, or how the Devil hath power to do many things which Witches have been accused of." See also his chapter on Dæmonology in the Leviathan, in Works, 384.

He continues, "Some doe maintaine (but how wisely let the wiser judge) that all Witchcraft spoken of either by holy writers, or testified by other writers to have beene among the heathen or in later daies, hath beene and is no more but either meere Cousinage [he had been reading Scot], or Collusion, so that in the opinion of those men, the Devill hath never done, nor can do anything by Witches." The Witches of Northamptonshire, ... A 4.

Potts, The Wonderfull Discoverie ..., X 4 verso.

Fairfax, A Discourse of Witchcraft (Philobiblon Soc.), 12.

Ibid., 20.

One notable instance must be mentioned. "H. F.," the narrator of the Essex affair of 1645 (A true and exact Relation) not only recognized the strong position of those who doubted, but was by no means extreme himself. "I doubt not," he wrote, "but these things may seeme as incredible unto some, as they are matter of admiration unto others.... The greatest doubt and question will be, whether it be in the power of the Devil to perform such asportation and locall translation of the bodies of Witches.... And whether these supernaturall works, which are above the power of man to do, and proper only to Spirits, whether they are reall or only imaginary and fained." The writer concludes that the Devil has power to dispose and transport bodies, but, as to changing them into animals, he thinks these are "but jugling transmutations."

The most true and wonderfull Narration of two women bewitched in Yorkshire; ... (1658).

"Relation of a Memorable Piece of Witchcraft at Welton near Daventry," in Glanvill, Sadducismus Triumphatus (London, 1681), pt. ii, 263-268.

See above, pp. 179-180, for an expression about the persecution in 1645.

Mercurius Democritus, February 8-15, 1654.

1648. This must be distinguished from The Divels Delusion ..., 1649, (see above, ch. IX, note 8), which deals with two witches executed at St. Alban's.

The truth is that the newspapers, pamphlets, etc., were full of such stories. And they were believed by many intelligent men. He who runs through Whitelocke's Memorials may read that the man was exceeding superstitious. Whether it be the report of the horseman seen in the air or the stories of witches at Berwick, Whitelocke was equally interested. While he was merely recording the reports of others, there is not a sign of skepticism.

See above, pp. 152-157.

See above, pp. 160-162.

CHAPTER XI.: Witchcraft under Charles II and James II.

No period of English history saw a wider interest in both the theory and the practice of witchcraft than the years that followed the Restoration. Throughout the course of the twenty-eight years that spanned the second rule of the Stuarts, the Devil manifested himself in many forms and with unusual frequency. Especially within the first half of that régime his appearances were so thrilling in character that the enemies of the new king might very well have said that the Evil One, like Charles, had come to his own again. All over the realm the witches were popping up. If the total number of trials and of executions did not foot up to the figures of James I's reign or to those of the Civil War, the alarm was nevertheless more widely distributed than ever before. In no less than twenty counties of England witches were discovered and fetched to court. Up to this time, so far at any rate as the printed records show, the southwestern counties had been but little troubled. Now Somerset, Devon, and Cornwall were the storm centre of the panic. In the north Yorkshire began to win for itself the reputation as a centre of activity that had long been held by Lancashire. Not that the witch was a new criminal in Yorkshire courts. During the Civil Wars and the troubled years that followed the discoverers had been active. But with the reign of Charles II their zeal increased mightily. Yet, if they had never before fetched in so many "suspected parties" to the court of the justice of the peace, they had never before been so often baffled by the outcome. Among the many such cases known to us during this time there is no mention of a conviction. In Kent there was a flickering revival of the old hatred of witches. In the year that Charles gained the throne the city of Canterbury sent some women to the gibbet. Not so in Essex. In that county not a single case during this period has been left on record. In Middlesex, a county which from the days of Elizabeth through to the Restoration had maintained a very even pace—a stray conviction now and then among many acquittals—the reign of Charles II saw nothing more serious than some commitments and releases upon bail. In the Midland counties, where superstition had flourished in the days of James I, there were now occasional tales of possession and vague charges which rarely reached the ears of the assize judges. Northampton, where an incendiary witch was sentenced, constituted the single exception. In East Anglia there was just enough stir to prove that the days of Matthew Hopkins had not been forgotten.

It needs no pointing out that a large proportion of the cases were but a repetition of earlier trials. If a difference is discernible, it is in the increased number of accusations that took their start in strange diseases called possessions. Since the close of the sixteenth century and the end of John Darrel's activities, the accounts of possession had fallen off sensibly, but the last third of the seventeenth century saw a distinct revival of this tendency to assign certain forms of disease to the operation of the Devil. We have references to many cases, but only in exceptional instances are the details given. Oliver Heywood, one of the eminent Dissenters of northern England, fasted and prayed with his co-workers over the convulsive and hysterical boys and girls in the West Riding. Nathan Dodgson was left after long fastings in "a very sensible melting frame," but the troubles returned and led, as we shall see in another connection, to very tragic results. The Puritan clergymen do not seem, however, to have had any highly developed method of exorcism or to have looked upon cases of possession in a light very different from that in which they would have looked upon ordinary illnesses.

Among the Baptists of Yorkshire there was a possession that roused wide comment. Mary Hall of Little Gaddesden in Hertfordshire, daughter of a smith, was possessed in the fall of 1663 with two spirits who were said to have come to her riding down the chimney upon a stick. The spirits declared through the girl that Goodwife Harwood had sent them, and when that suspected woman was brought into the girl's presence the spirits cried out, "Oh, Goodwife Harwood, are you come?—that is well; ... we have endeavored to choak her but cannot," and, when Mistress Harwood left, the spirits begged to go with her

In Southwark James Barrow, the son of John Barrow, was long possessed, and neither "doctors, astrologers, nor apothecaries" could help him. He was taken to the Catholics, but to no purpose. Finally he was cast among a "poor dispirited people whom the Lord owned as instruments in his hand to do this great work." By the "poor dispirited people" the Baptists were almost certainly meant. By their assistance he seems to have been cured. So also was Hannah Crump of Warwick, who had been afflicted by witchcraft and put in a London hospital. Through prayer and fasting she was entirely recovered.

Mary Hall had been taken to Doctor Woodhouse of Berkhampstead, "a man famous for curing bewitched persons." Woodhouse's name comes up now and again in the records of his time. He was in fact a very typical specimen of the witch doctor. When Mary Hall's case had been submitted to him he had cut off the ends of her nails and "with somewhat he added" hung them in the chimney over night before making a diagnosis. He professed to find stolen goods as well and fell foul of the courts in one instance, probably because the woman who consulted him could not pay the shilling fee. He was arraigned and spent a term in prison. No doubt many of the witch physicians knew the inside of prisons and had returned afterwards to successful practice. Redman, "whom some say is a Conjurer, others say, He is an honest and able phisitian," had been in prison, but nevertheless he had afterwards "abundance of Practice" and was much talked about "in remote parts," all this in spite of the fact that he was "unlearned in the languages."

Usually, of course, the witch doctor was a poor woman who was very happy to get a penny fee now and then, but who ran a greater risk of the gallows than her male competitors. Her reputation, which brought her a little money from the sick and from those who had lost valuables, made her at the same time a successful beggar. Those whom she importuned were afraid to refuse her. But she was in constant peril. If she resented ill treatment, if she gave in ill wishes as much as she took, she was sure to hear from it before a stern justice of the peace. It can hardly be doubted that a large proportion, after the Restoration as in every other period, of those finally hanged for witchcraft, had in fact made claims to skill in magic arts. Without question some of them had even traded on the fear they inspired. Not a few of the wretched creatures fetched to York castle to be tried were "inchanters."

Very often, indeed, a woman who was nothing more than a midwife, with some little knowledge of medicine perhaps, would easily be classed by the public among the regular witch doctors and so come to have a bad name. Whether she lived up to her name or not—and the temptation to do so would be great—she would from that time be subject to suspicion, and might at length become a prey to the justice of the peace. Mrs. Pepper was no more than a midwife who made also certain simple medical examinations, but when one of her patients was "strangely handled" she was taken to court. Margaret Stothard was probably, so far as we can piece together her story, a woman who had been successful in calming fretful children and had so gained for herself a reputation as a witch. Doubtless she had acquired in time a few of the charmer's tricks that enhanced her reputation and increased her practice. This was all very well until one of her patients happened to die. Then she was carried to Newcastle and would probably have suffered death, had it not been for a wise judge.

These are typical cases. The would-be healer of the sick ran a risk, and it was not always alone from failure to cure. If a witch doctor found himself unable to bring relief to a patient, it was easy to suggest that some other witch doctor—and such were usually women—was bewitching the patient. There are many instances, and they are not confined to the particular period with which we are dealing, in which one "good witch" started the run on the other's reputation. Even the regular physician may sometimes have yielded to the temptation to crush competition.

Of course, when all the cases are considered, only a very small part of the "good witches" ever fell into the clutches of the law. The law prescribed very definite penalties for their operations, but in most instances no action was taken until after a long accumulation of "suspicious circumstances," and, even if action was taken, the chances, as we have seen, were by this time distinctly in favor of the accused.

This is not to say, by any means, that the judges and juries of England had come over to the side of the witch. The period with which we are dealing was marked by a variety of decision which betrays the perplexity of judges and juries. It is true, indeed, that out of from eighty to one hundred cases where accusations are on record less than twenty witches were hanged. This does not mean that six times out of every seven the courts were ruling against the fact of witchcraft. In the case of the six released there was no very large body of evidence against them to be considered, or perhaps no strong popular current to be stemmed. In general, it may be said that the courts were still backing up the law of James I.

To show this, it is only necessary to run over some of the leading trials of the period. We shall briefly take up four trials conducted respectively by Justice Archer, Chief Baron Hale, Justice Rainsford, and Justice Raymond.

Julian Cox, who was but one of the "pestilent brood" of witches ferreted out in Somerset by the aggressive justice, Robert Hunt, was tried in 1663 at Taunton before Justice Archer. The charges against her indeed excited such interest all over England, and elicited, upon the part of disbelievers, so much derision, that it will be worth our while to go over the principal points of evidence. The chief witness against her was a huntsman who told a strange tale. He had started a hare and chased it behind a bush. But when he came to the bush he had found Julian Cox there, stooped over and quite out of breath. Another witness had a strange story to tell about her. She had invited him to come up on her porch and take a pipe of tobacco with her. While he was with her, smoking, he saw a toad between his legs. On going home he had taken out a pipe and smoked again and had again seen what looked to be the same toad between his legs. "He took the Toad out to kill it, and to his thinking cut it in several pieces, but returning to his Pipe the Toad still appeared.... At length the Toad cryed, and vanish'd." A third witness had seen the accused fly in at her window "in her full proportion." This tissue of evidence was perhaps the absurdest ever used against even a witch, but the jury brought in a verdict of guilty. It is not unpleasant to know that Justice Archer met with a good deal of criticism for his part in the affair.

In the following year occurred the trials at Bury St. Edmunds, which derive their interest and importance largely from the position of the presiding judge, Sir Matthew Hale, who was at this time chief baron of the exchequer, and was later to be chief justice of the king's bench. He was allowed, according to the admission of one none too friendly to him, "on all hands to be the most profound lawyer of his time." Hale had been a Puritan from his youth, though not of the rigid or theologically minded sort. In the Civil Wars and the events that followed he had remained non-partisan. He accepted office from Cromwell, though without doubt mildly sympathizing with the king. One of those who had assisted in recalling Charles II, he rose shortly to be chief baron of the exchequer. Famous for his careful and reasoned interpretation of law, he was to leave behind him a high reputation for his justice and for the exceptional precision of his judgments. It is not too much to say that he was one of the greatest legal figures of his century and that his decisions served in no small degree to fix the law.

We should like to know how far he had been brought into contact with the subject of witchcraft, but we can do no more than guess. His early career had been moulded in no small degree by Selden, who, as has been noted in an earlier chapter, believed in the punishment of those who claimed to be witches. It is not unreasonable to suppose that the Puritans with whom he had been thrown were all of them ready to quote Scripture against the minions of Satan. We know that he had read some of the works of Henry More, and, whether or not familiar with his chapters on witchcraft, would have deduced from that writer's general philosophy of spirits the particular application.

The trial concerned two women of Lowestoft, Amy Duny and Rose Cullender. The first had been reputed a witch and a "person of very evil behaviour." She was in all probability related to some of those women who had suffered at the hands of Hopkins, and to that connection owed her ill name. Some six or seven years before the date of the trial she had got herself into trouble while taking care of the child of a tradesman in Lowestoft. It would seem that, contrary to the orders of the mother, she had suckled the child. The child had that same night been attacked by fits, and a witch doctor of Yarmouth, who was consulted, had prescribed for it. The reader will note that this "suspicious circumstance" happened seven years earlier, and a large part of the evidence presented in court concerned what had occurred from five to seven years before.

We can not go into the details of a trial which abounded in curious bits of evidence. The main plot indeed was an old one. The accused woman, after she had been discharged from employment and reproved, had been heard to mutter threats, close upon which the children of those she cursed, who were now the witnesses against her, had fallen ill. Two of the children had suffered severely and were still afflicted. They had thrown up pins and even a two-penny nail. The nail, which was duly offered as an exhibit in court, had been brought to one of the children by a bee and had been forced into the child's mouth, upon which she expelled it. This narrative was on a level with the other, that flies brought crooked pins to the child. Both flies and bee, it will be understood, were the witches in other form. A similar sort of evidence was that a toad, which had been found as the result of the witch doctor's directions, had been thrown into the fire, upon which a sharp crackling noise ensued. When this incident was testified to in the court the judge interrupted to ask if after the explosion the substance of the toad was not to be seen in the fire. He was answered in the negative. On the next day Amy Duny was found to have her face and body all scorched. She said to the witness that "she might thank her for it." There can be no doubt in the world that this testimony of the coincident burning of the woman and the toad was regarded as damning proof, nor is there any reason to believe that the court deemed it necessary to go behind the mere say-so of a single witness for the fact. Along with this sort of unsubstantial testimony there was presented a monotonous mass of spectral evidence. Apparitions of the witches were the constant occasions for the paroxysms of the children. In another connection it will be observed that this form of proof was becoming increasingly common in the last part of the seventeenth century. It can hardly be doubted that in one way or another the use of such evidence at Bury influenced other trials and more particularly the Salem cases in the New World, where great importance was attached to evidence of this sort.

The usual nauseating evidence as to the Devil's marks was introduced by the testimony of the mother of one of the children bewitched. She had been, a month before, a member of a jury of matrons appointed by a justice of the peace to examine the body of the accused. Most damning proof against the woman had been found. It is very hard for us to understand why Hale allowed to testify, as one of the jury of examining matrons, a woman who was at the same time mother of one of the bewitched children upon whom the prosecution largely depended.

So far the case for the prosecution had been very strong, but it was in the final experiments in court, which were expected to clinch the evidence, that a very serious mishap occurred. A bewitched child, eleven years old, had been fetched into court. With eyes closed and head reclining upon the bar she had remained quiet until one of the accused was brought up, when she at once became frantic in her effort to scratch her. This was tried again and again and in every instance produced the same result. The performance must have had telling effect. But there happened to be present at the trial three Serjeants of the law. One of them, Serjeant John Kelyng, a few years later to become chief justice of the king's bench, was "much dissatisfied." He urged the point that the mere fact that the children were bewitched did not establish their claim to designate the authors of their misfortune. There were others present who agreed with Kelyng in suspecting the actions of the girl on the stand. Baron Hale was induced, at length, to appoint a committee of several gentlemen, including Serjeant Kelyng, to make trial of the girl with her eyes covered. An outside party was brought up to her and touched her hand. The girl was expecting that Amy Duny would be brought up and flew into the usual paroxysms. This was what the committee had expected, and they declared their belief that the whole transaction was a mere imposture. One would have supposed that every one else must come to the same conclusion, but Mr. Pacy, the girl's father, offered an explanation of her mistake that seems to have found favor. The maid, he said, "might be deceived by a suspicion that the Witch touched her when she did not." One would suppose that this subtle suggestion would have broken the spell, and that Mr. Pacy would have been laughed out of court. Alas for the rarity of humor in seventeenth-century court rooms! Not only was the explanation received seriously, but it was, says the court reporter, afterwards found to be true.

In the mean time expert opinion had been called in. It is hard to say whether Dr. Browne had been requisitioned for the case or merely happened to be present. At all events, he was called upon to render his opinion as a medical man. The name of Thomas Browne is one eminent in English literature and not unknown in the annals of English medicine and science. More than twenty years earlier he had expressed faith in the reality of witchcraft. In his Commonplace Book, a series of jottings made throughout his life, he reiterated his belief, but uttered a doubt as to the connection between possession and witchcraft.

We should be glad to know at what time Browne wrote this deliverance; for, when called upon at Bury, he made no application of his principles of caution. He gave it as his opinion that the bewitchment of the two girls was genuine. The vomiting of needles and nails reminded him very much of a recent case in Denmark. For the moment the physician spoke, when he said that "these swounding Fits were Natural." But it was the student of seventeenth-century theology who went on: they were "heightened to a great excess by the subtilty of the Devil, co-operating with the Malice of these which we term Witches, at whose Instance he doth these Villanies."

No doubt Browne's words confirmed the sentiment of the court room and strengthened the case of the prosecution. But it will not be overlooked by the careful reader that he did not by any means commit himself as to the guilt of the parties at the bar.

When the judge found that the prisoners had "nothing material" to say for themselves he addressed the jury. Perhaps because he was not altogether clear in his own mind about the merits of the case, he refused to sum up the evidence. It is impossible for us to understand why he did not carry further the tests which had convinced Kelyng of the fraud, or why he did not ask questions which would have uncovered the weakness of the testimony. One cannot but suspect that North's criticism of him, that he had a "leaning towards the Popular" and that he had gained such "transcendent" authority as not easily to bear contradiction, was altogether accurate. At all events he passed over the evidence and went on to declare that there were two problems before the jury: (1) were these children bewitched, (2) were the prisoners at the bar guilty of it? As to the existence of witches, he never doubted it. The Scriptures affirmed it, and all nations provided laws against such persons.

On the following Sunday Baron Hale composed a meditation upon the subject. Unfortunately it was simply a dissertation on Scripture texts and touched upon the law at no point.

It is obvious enough to the most casual student that Sir Matthew Hale had a chance to anticipate the work of Chief Justice Holt and missed it. In the nineties of the seventeenth century, as we shall see, there was a man in the chief justiceship who dared to nullify the law of James I.

It is not too much to say that Matthew Hale by a different charge to the jury could as easily have made the current of judicial decisions run in favor of accused witches all over England. His weight was thrown in the other direction, and the witch-triers for a half-century to come invoked the name of Hale.

There is an interesting though hardly trustworthy story told by Speaker Onslow—writing a century later—that Hale "was afterwards much altered in his notions as to this matter, and had great concern upon him for what had befallen these persons." This seems the more doubtful because there is not a shred of proof that Hale's decisions occasioned a word of criticism among his contemporaries. So great, indeed, was the spell of his name that not even a man like John Webster dared to comment upon his decision. Not indeed until nearly the middle of the eighteenth century does anyone seem to have felt that the decision called for apology.

The third noteworthy ruling in this period anent the crime of witchcraft was made a few years later in Wiltshire by Justice Rainsford. The story, as he himself told it to a colleague, was this: "A Witch was brought to Salisbury and tried before him. Sir James Long came to his Chamber, and made a heavy Complaint of this Witch, and said that if she escaped, his Estate would not be worth any Thing; for all the People would go away. It happen'd that the Witch was acquitted, and the Knight continued extremely concern'd; therefore the Judge, to save the poor Gentleman's Estate, order'd the Woman to be kept in Gaol, and that the Town should allow her 2s. 6d. per Week; for which he was very thankful. The very next Assizes, he came to the Judge to desire his lordship would let her come back to the Town. And why? They could keep her for 1s. 6d. there; and, in the Gaol, she cost them a shilling more." Another case before Justice Rainsford showed him less lenient. By a mere chance we have a letter, written at the time by one of the justices of the peace in Malmesbury, which sheds no little light on this affair and on the legal status of witchcraft at that time. A certain Ann Tilling had been taken into custody on the complaint of Mrs. Webb of Malmesbury. The latter's son had swooning fits in which he accused Ann of bewitching him. Ann Tilling made voluble confession, implicating Elizabeth Peacock and Judith Witchell, who had, she declared, inveigled her into the practice of their evil arts. Other witches were named, and in a short time twelve women and two men were under accusation. But the alderman of Malmesbury, who was the chief magistrate of that town, deemed it wise before going further to call in four of the justices of the peace in that subdivision of the county. Three of these justices of the peace came and listened to the confessions, and were about to make out a mittimus for sending eleven of the accused to Salisbury, when the fourth justice arrived, the man who has given us the story. He was, according to his own account, not "very credulous in matters of Witchcraft," and he made a speech to the other justices. "Gentlemen, what is done at this place, a Borough remote from the centre of this large County, and almost forty miles from Salisbury, will be expended [sic] both by the Reverend Judges, the learned Counsayle there ..., and the Gentry of the body of the County, so that if anything be done here rashly, it will be severely censured." He went on to urge the danger that the boy whose fits were the cause of so much excitement might be an impostor, and that Ann Tilling, who had freely confessed, might be in confederacy with the parents. The skeptical justice, who in spite of his boasted incredulity was a believer in the reality of witchcraft, was successful with his colleagues. All the accused were dismissed save Tilling, Peacock, and Witchell. They were sent to Salisbury and tried before Sir Richard Rainsford. Elizabeth Peacock, who had been tried on similar charges before, was dismissed. The other two were sentenced to be hanged.

Ten years later came a fourth remarkable ruling against witchcraft, this time by Justice Raymond at Exeter. During the intervening years there had been cases a-plenty in England and a few hangings, but none that had attracted comment. It was not until the summer of 1682, when three Devonshire women were arraigned, tried, and sent to the gallows by Justice Raymond, that the public again realized that witchcraft was still upheld by the courts.

The trials in themselves had no very striking features. At least two of the three women had been beggars; the other, who had been the first accused and who had in all probability involved her two companions, had on two different occasions before been arraigned but let off. The evidence submitted against them consisted of the usual sworn statements made by neighbors to the justice of the peace, as well as of hardly coherent confessions by the accused. The repetition of the Lord's Prayer was gone through with and the results of examinations by a female jury were detailed ad nauseam. The poor creatures on trial were remarkably stupid, even for beings of their grade. Their several confessions tallied with one another in hardly a single point.

Sir Thomas Raymond and Sir Francis North were the judges present at the Exeter assizes. Happily the latter has left his impressions of this trial. He admits that witch trials worried him because the evidence was usually slight, but the people very intent upon a verdict of guilty. He was very glad that at Exeter his colleague who sat upon the "crown side" had to bear the responsibilities. The two women (he seems to have known of no more) were scarce alive as to sense and understanding, but were "overwhelm'd with melancholy and waking Dreams." Barring confessions, the other evidence he considered trifling, and he cites the testimony of a witness that "he saw a cat leap in at her (the old woman's) window, when it was twilight; and this Informant farther saith that he verily believeth the said Cat to be the Devil, and more saith not." Raymond, declares his colleague, made no nice distinctions as to the possibility of melancholy women contracting an opinion of themselves that was false, but left the matter to the jury.

We have already intimated that the rulings of the courts were by no means all of them adverse to the witches. Almost contemporaneous with the far-reaching sentence of Sir Matthew Hale at Bury were the trials in Somerset, where flies and nails and needles played a similar part, but where the outcome was very different. A zealous justice of the peace, Robert Hunt, had for the last eight years been on the lookout for witches. In 1663 he had turned Julian Cox over to the tender mercies of Justice Archer. By 1664 he had uncovered a "hellish knot" of the wicked women and was taking depositions against them, wringing confessions from them and sending them to gaol with all possible speed. The women were of the usual class, a herd of poor quarrelsome, bickering females who went from house to house seeking alms. In the numbers of the accused the discovery resembled that at Lancaster in 1633-1634, as indeed it did in other ways. A witch meeting or conventicle was confessed to. The county was being terrified and entertained by the most horrible tales, when suddenly a quietus was put upon the affair "by some of them in authority." A witch chase, which during the Civil Wars would have led to a tragedy, was cut short, probably through the agency of a privy council less fearful of popular sentiment than the assize judges.

The Mompesson case was of no less importance in its time, although it belongs rather in the annals of trickery than in those of witchcraft. But the sensation which it caused in England and the controversy waged over it between the upholders of witchcraft and the "Sadducees," give the story a considerable interest and render the outcome of the trial significant. The only case of its sort in its time, it was nevertheless most typical of the superstition of the time. A little town in Wiltshire had been disturbed by a stray drummer. The self-constituted noise-maker was called to account by a stranger in the village, a Mr. Mompesson of Tedworth, who on examining the man's license saw that it had been forged and took it away from him. This, at any rate, was Mr. Mompesson's story as to how he had incurred the ill will of the man. The drummer took his revenge in a singular way. Within a few days the Mompesson family at Tedworth began to be annoyed at night by strange noises or drummings on the roofs. All the phenomena and manifestations which we associate with a modern haunted-house story were observed by this alarmed family of the seventeenth century. The little girls were knocked about in their beds at night, a stout servant was forcibly held hand and foot, the children's shoes were thrown about, the chairs glided about the room. It would seem that all this bold horse-play must soon have been exposed, but it went on merrily. Whenever any tune was called for, it was given on the drum. The family Bible was thrown upside down into the ashes. For three weeks, however, the spirits ceased operations during the lying-in of Mrs. Mompesson. But they sedulously avoided the family servants, especially when those retainers happened to be armed with swords. Well they might, for we are told that on one occasion, after a pistol shot had been fired at the place where they were heard, blood was found on the spot. In another instance, according to Mr. Mompesson's own account, there were seen figures, "in the shape of Men, who, as soon as a Gun was discharg'd, would shuffle away together into an Arbour."

It is clear enough that a somewhat clumsy fraud was being imposed upon Mr. Mompesson. A contemporary writer tells us he was told that it was done by "two Young Women in the House with a design to scare thence Mr. Mompesson's Mother." From other sources it is quite certain that the injured drummer had a hand in the affair. A very similar game had been played at Woodstock in 1649, and formed a comedy situation of which Scott makes brilliant use in his novel of that name. Indeed, it is quite possible that the drummer, who had been a soldier of Cromwell's, was inspired by a memory of that affair.

But there was no one to detect the fraud, as at Woodstock. Tedworth became a Mecca for those interested in the supernatural. One of the visitors was Joseph Glanvill, at this time a young man of twenty-seven, later to become a member of the Royal Society and chaplain in ordinary to the king. The spirits were less noisy; they were always somewhat restrained before visitors, but scratched on bed sheets and panted in dog fashion, till Glanvill was thoroughly taken in. For the rest of his life this psychic experimenter fought a literary war over this case with those who made fun of it. While we cannot prove it, we may guess with some confidence that this episode was the beginning of the special interest in the supernatural upon Glanvill's part which was later to make him the arch-defender of the witchcraft superstition in his generation.

How wide an interest the matter evoked may be judged from the warm discussions upon it at Cambridge, and from the royal interest in it which induced Charles to send down a committee of investigation. Curiously enough, the spirits were singularly and most extraordinarily quiet when the royal investigators were at work, a fact to which delighted skeptics pointed with satisfaction.

One wonders that the drummer, who must have known that his name would be connected with the affair, failed to realize the risk he was running from the witch hunters. He was indicted on minor felonies of another sort, but the charges which Mompesson brought against him seem to have been passed over. The man was condemned for stealing and was transported. With his departure the troubles at Tedworth ceased. But the drummer, in some way, escaped and returned to England. The angry Mompesson now brought him to the assizes as a felon on the strength of the statute of James I. Unhappily we have no details of this trial, nor do we know even the name of the judge; but we do know that the jury gave a verdict of acquittal.

In 1671 Cornwall was stirred up over a witch whose crimes were said to be directed against the state. She had hindered the English fleet in their war against the Dutch, she had caused a bull to kill one of the enemies in Parliament of the Non-Conformists, she had been responsible for the barrenness of the queen. And for all these political crimes the chief evidence was that some cats had been seen playing ("dancing") near her house. She was committed, along with several other women who were accused. Although at the assizes they were all proved to have had cats and rats about them, they went free.

In 1682, the same year in which the three women of Devonshire had been condemned, there was a trial at Southwark, just outside of London, which resulted in a verdict of acquittal. The case had many of the usual features, but in two points was unique. Joan Butts was accused of having bewitched a child that had been taken with fits. Nineteen or twenty witnesses testified against the witch. One of the witnesses heard her say that, if she had not bewitched the child, if all the devils in hell could help her, she would bewitch it. Joan admitted the words, but said that she had spoken them in passion. She then turned on one of the witnesses and declared that he had given himself to the Devil, body and soul. Chief Justice Pemberton was presiding, and he called her to order for this attack on a witness, and then catechized her as to her means of knowing the fact. The woman had thoughtlessly laid herself open by her own words to the most serious suspicion. In spite of this, however, the jury brought her in not guilty, "to the great amazement of some, ... yet others who consider the great difficulty in proving a Witch, thought the jury could do no less than acquit her."

This was, during the period, the one trial in or near London of which we have details. There can be no doubt that the courts in London and the vicinity were beginning to ignore cases of witchcraft. After 1670 there were no more trials of the sort in Middlesex.

The reader will remember that Justice North had questioned the equity of Justice Raymond's decision at Exeter. He has told us the story of a trial at Taunton-Dean, where he himself had to try a witch. A ten-year-old girl, who was taking strange fits and spitting out pins, was the witness against an old man whom she accused of bewitching her. The defendant made "a Defence as orderly and well expressed as I ever heard spoke." The judge then asked the justice of the peace who had committed the man his opinion. He said that he believed the girl, "doubling herself in her Fit, as being convulsed, bent her Head down close to her Stomacher, and with her Mouth, took Pins out of the Edge of that, and then, righting herself a little, spit them into some By-stander's Hands." "The Sum of it was Malice, Threatening, and Circumstances of Imposture in the Girl." As the judge went downstairs after the man had been acquitted, "an hideous old woman" cried to him, "My Lord, Forty Years ago they would have hang'd me for a Witch, and they could not; and now they would have hang'd my poor Son."

The five cases we have cited, while not so celebrated as those on the other side, were quite as representative of what was going on in England. It is to be regretted that we have not the records by which to compute the acquittals of this period. In a large number of cases where we have depositions we have no statement of the outcome. This is particularly true of Yorkshire. As has been pointed out in the earlier part of the chapter, we can be sure that most of these cases were dismissed or were never brought to trial.

When we come to the question of the forms of evidence presented during this period, we have a story that has been told before. Female juries, convulsive children or child pretenders, we have met them all before. Two or three differences may nevertheless be noted. The use of spectral evidence was becoming increasingly common. The spectres, as always, assumed weird forms. Nicholas Rames's wife (at Longwitton, in the north) saw Elizabeth Fenwick and the Devil dancing together. A sick boy in Cornwall saw a "Woman in a blue Jerkin and Red Petticoat with Yellow and Green patches," who was quickly identified and put in hold. Sometimes the spectres were more material. Jane Milburne of Newcastle testified that Dorothy Stranger, in the form of a cat, had leaped upon her and held her to the ground for a quarter of an hour. A "Barber's boy" in Cambridge had escaped from a spectral woman in the isle of Ely, but she followed him to Cambridge and killed him with a blow. "He had the exact mark in his forehead, being dead, where the Spiritual Woman did hit him alive." It is unnecessary to multiply cases. The Collection of Modern Relations is full of the same sort of evidence.

It has been seen that in nearly every epoch of witch history the voluntary and involuntary confessions of the accused had greatly simplified the difficulties of prosecution. The witches whom Matthew Hopkins discovered were too ready to confess to enormous and unnatural crimes. In this respect there is a marked change in the period of the later Stuarts. Elizabeth Style of Somerset in 1663 and the three Devonshire witches of 1682 were the only ones who made confessions. Elizabeth Style had probably been "watched," in spite of Glanvill's statement to the contrary, perhaps somewhat in the same torturing way as the Suffolk witches whom Hopkins "discovered," and her wild confession showed the effect. The Devonshire women were half-witted creatures, of the type that had always been most voluble in confession; but such were now exceptions.

This means one of two things. Either the witches of the Restoration were by some chance a more intelligent set, or they were showing more spirit than ever before because they had more supporters and fairer treatment in court. It is quite possible that both suppositions have in them some elements of truth. As the belief in the powers of witches developed in form and theory, it came to draw within its radius more groups of people. In its earlier stages the attack upon the witch had been in part the community's way of ridding itself of a disreputable member. By the time that the process of attack had been developed for a century, it had become less impersonal. Personal hatreds were now more often the occasion of accusation. Individual malice was playing a larger rôle. In consequence those who were accused were more often those who were capable of fighting for themselves or who had friends to back them. And those friends were more numerous and zealous because the attitude of the public and of the courts was more friendly to the accused witch. This explanation is at best, however, nothing more than a suggestion. We have not the material for confident generalization.

One other form of evidence must be mentioned. The town of Newcastle, which in 1649 had sent to Scotland for a witchfinder, was able in 1673 to make use of home-grown talent. In this instance it was a woman, Ann Armstrong, who implicated a score of her neighbors and at length went around pointing out witches. She was a smooth-witted woman who was probably taking a shrewd method of turning off charges against herself. Her testimony dealt with witch gatherings or conventicles held at various times and places. She told whom she had seen there and what they had said about their crimes. She told of their feasts and of their dances. Poor woman, she had herself been compelled to sing for them while they danced. Nor was this the worst. She had been terribly misused. She had been often turned into a horse, then bridled and ridden.

It would not be worth while to go further into Ann Armstrong's stories. It is enough to remark that she offered details, as to harm done to certain individuals in certain ways, which tallied closely with the sworn statements of those individuals as to what had happened to them at the times specified. The conclusion cannot be avoided that the female witchfinder had been at no small pains to get even such minute details in exact form. She had gathered together all the witch stories of that part of Northumberland and had embodied them in her account of the confessions made at the "conventicles."

What was the ruling of the court on all this evidence we do not know. We have only one instance in which any evidence was ruled out. That was at the trial of Julian Cox in 1663. Justice Archer tried an experiment in that trial, but before doing so he explained to the court that no account was to be taken of the result in making up their verdict. He had heard that a witch could not repeat the petition in the Lord's Prayer, "Lead us not into temptation." The witch indeed failed to meet the test.

In the course of this period we have two trials that reveal a connection between witchcraft and other crimes. Perhaps it would be fairer to say that the charge of witchcraft was sometimes made when other crimes were suspected, but could not be proved. The first case concerned a rich farmer in Northamptonshire who had gained the ill will of a woman named Ann Foster. Thirty of his sheep were found dead with their "Leggs broke in pieces, and their Bones all shattered in their Skins." A little later his house and barns were set on fire. Ann Foster was brought to trial for using witchcraft against him, confessed to it, and was hanged.

The other case was at Brightling in Sussex, not far from London. There a woman who was suspected as the one who had told a servant that Joseph Cruther's house would be burned—a prophecy which came true very shortly—was accused as a witch. She had been accused years before at the Maidstone assizes, but had gone free. This time she was "watched" for twenty-four hours and four ministers kept a fast over the affair.

These cases are worth something as an indication that the charge of witchcraft was still a method of getting rid of people whom the community feared.

At the beginning of this chapter the years 1660 to 1688 were marked off as constituting a single epoch in the history of the superstition. Yet those years were by no means characterized by the same sort of court verdicts. The sixties saw a decided increase over the years of the Commonwealth in the number of trials and in the number of executions. The seventies witnessed a rapid dropping off in both figures. Even more so the eighties. By the close of the eighties the accounts of witchcraft were exceedingly rare. The decisions of the courts in the matter were in a state of fluctuation. Two things were happening. The justices of the peace were growing much more reluctant to send accused witches to the assize courts; and the itinerant judges as a body were, in spite of the decisions of Hale and Raymond, more careful in witch trials than ever before, and more likely to withstand public sentiment.

The changes of opinion, as reflected in the literature of the time, especially in the literature of the subject, will show the same tendencies. We shall take them up in the next chapter.

See Raine, ed., York Depositions (Surtees Soc.), preface, xxx.

Joseph Hunter, Life of Heywood (London, 1842), 167, and Heywood's Diaries, ed. J. H. Turner (Brighouse, 1881-1885), I, 199; III, 100. Heywood, who was one of the leading Dissenters of his time, must not be credited with extreme superstition. In noting the death of a boy whom his parents believed bewitched, he wrote, "Oh that they saw the lords hand." Diary, I, 287.

William Drage, Daimonomageia (London, 1665), 32-38.

The Lord's Arm Stretched Out, ... or a True Relation of the wonderful Deliverance of James Barrow ... (London, 1664).

Compare Drage, op. cit., 36, 39, 42, with The Lord's Arm Stretched Out, 17. Mary Hall, whose cure Drage celebrates, had friends among the Baptists. Drage seems to connect her case with those of Barrow and Hannah Crump, both of whom were helped by that "dispirited people" whom the author of The Lord's Arm Stretched Out exalts.

Drage, op. cit., 34.

Yorkshire Notes and Queries, I (Bradford, 1885), 26. But a physician in Winchester Park, whom Hannah Crump had consulted, had asked five pounds to unbewitch her.

Drage, op. cit., 39.

York Depositions, 127.

See E. Mackenzie, History of Northumberland (Newcastle, 1825), II, 33-36. We do not know that the woman was excused, but the case was before Henry Ogle and we may fairly guess the outcome.

Glanvill, Sadducismus Triumphatus, pt. ii, 191-209.

This is the estimate of him by North, who adds: "and he knew it." Roger North, Life of the Rt. Hon. Francis North, Baron of Guilford ... (London, 1742), 62-63.

Diary and Correspondence of Dr. John Worthington, II, pt. I (Chetham Soc., no. 36, 1855), 155.

In his Religio Medici. See Sir Thomas Browne's Works (ed. S. Wilkin, London, 1851-1852), II, 43.

Ibid., IV, 389.

Roger North, op. cit., 61.

Inderwick has given a good illustration of Hale's weakness of character: "I confess," he says, "to a feeling of pain at finding him in October, 1660, sitting as a judge at the Old Bailey, trying and condemning to death batches of the regicides, men under whose orders he had himself acted, who had been his colleagues in parliament, with whom he had sat on committees to alter the law." Interregnum, 217-218.

Hist. MSS. Comm. Reports, XIV, 9, p. 480.

Bishop Burnet, in his Life and Death of Sir Matthew Hale (London, 1682), does not seem to have felt called upon to mention the Bury trial at all. See also Lord Campbell, Lives of the Chief Justices (London, 1849), I, 563-567.

Roger North, op. cit., 130, 131. The story, as here told, ascribes the event to the year preceding Lord Guilford's first western circuit—i. e., to 1674. But this perhaps need not be taken too exactly, and the witch was probably that Elizabeth Peacock who was acquitted in 1670 and again in the case of 1672 described above. At least the list of "Indictments for witchcraft on the Western Circuit from 1670 to 1712," published by Inderwick in his Sidelights on the Stuarts (London, 1888), shows no other acquittal in Wiltshire during this decade.

For this letter see the Gentleman's Magazine, 1832, pt. I, 405-410, 489-402. The story is confirmed in part by Inderwick's finds in the western Gaol Delivery records. As to the trustworthiness of this unknown justice of the peace, see above, pp. 160, 162, and notes.

That the judge was Sir Richard Rainsford appears from Inderwick's list, mentioned above, note 20.

A True and Impartial Relation of the Informations against ... Temperance Lloyd, Mary Trembles, and Susanna Edwards (London, 1682). And The Tryal, Condemnation and Execution of Three Witches ... (London, 1682). See also below, note 26, and appendix A, § 6.

Roger North, op. cit., 130.

At a trial at the York assizes in 1687 Sir John Reresby seems to have played about the same part that North played at Exeter. Serjeant Powell, later to be chief justice, was presiding over the case. "An old woman was condemned for a witch. Those who were more credulous in points of this nature than myself, conceived the evidence to be very strong against her. The boy she was said to have bewitched fell down on a sudden before all the court when he saw her, and would then as suddenly return to himself again, and very distinctly relate the several injuries she had done him: but in all this it was observed the boy was free from any distortion; that he did not foam at the mouth, and that his fits did not leave him gradually, but all at once; so that, upon the whole, the judge thought it proper to reprieve her." Memoirs and Travels of Sir John Reresby (London, 1813), 329.

There is indeed some evidence that Raymond wished not to condemn the women, but yielded nevertheless to public opinion. In a pamphlet published five years later it is stated that the judge "in his charge to the jury gave his Opinion that these three poor Women (as he supposed) were weary of their Lives, and that he thought it proper for them to be carryed to the Parish from whence they came, and that the Parish should be charged with their Maintainance; for he thought their oppressing Poverty had constrained them to wish for Death." Unhappily the neighbors made such an outcry that the women were found guilty and sentenced. This is from a later and somewhat untrustworthy account, but it fits in well with what North says of the case. The Life and Conversation of Temperance Floyd, Mary Lloyd [sic], and Susanna Edwards: ... (London, 1687).

The second part of Glanvill's Sadducismus Triumphatus is full of these depositions.

For a full account of this affair see Glanvill's Sadducismus Triumphatus, pt. ii, preface and Relation I. Glanvill had investigated the matter and had diligently collected all the evidence. He was familiar also with what the "deriders" had to say, and we can discover their point of view from his answers. See also John Beaumont, An Historical, Physiological and Theological Treatise of Spirits, Apparitions, Witchcrafts, and other Magical Practices (London, 1705), 307-309.

Ibid., 309.

Cal. St. P., Dom., 1671, 105, 171.

We have two accounts of this affair: Strange and Wonderful News from Yowell in Surry (1681), and An Account of the Tryal and Examination of Joan Buts (1682).

Roger North, op. cit., 131-132.

York Depositions, 247.

A True Account ... of one John Tonken, of Pensans in Cornwall ... (1686). For other examples of spectral evidence see York Depositions, 88; Roberts, Southern Counties (London, 1856), 525-526; Gentleman's Magazine, 1832, pt. II, 489.

York Depositions, 112, 113.

Drage, Daimonomageia, 12.

For an account of her case, see Glanvill, Sadducismus Triumphatus, pt. ii, 127-146.

York Depositions, 191-201.

For a complete account of the Julian Cox case see Glanvill, Sadducismus Triumphatus, pt. ii, 191-209.

A Full and True Relation of the Tryal ... of Ann Foster ... (London, 1674).

Sussex Archaeological Collections, XVIII, 111-113.

CHAPTER XII.: Glanvill and Webster and the Literary War over Witchcraft, 1660-1688.

In an earlier chapter we followed the progress of opinion from James I to the Restoration. We saw that in the course of little more than a half-century the centre of the controversy had been considerably shifted: we noted that there was a growing body of intelligent men who discredited the stories of witchcraft and were even inclined to laugh at them. It is now our purpose to go on with the history of opinion from the point at which we left off to the revolution of 1688. We shall discover that the body of literature on the subject was enormously increased. We shall see that a larger and more representative group of men were expressing themselves on the matter. The controversialists were no longer bushwhackers, but crafty warriors who joined battle after looking over the field and measuring their forces. The groundworks of philosophy were tested, the bases of religious faith examined. The days of skirmishing about the ordeal of water and the test of the Devil's marks were gone by. The combatants were now to fight over the reality or unreality of supernatural phenomena. We shall observe that the battle was less one-sided than ever before and that the assailants of superstition, who up to this time had been outnumbered, now fought on at least even terms with their enemies. We shall see too that the non-participants and onlookers were more ready than ever before to join themselves to the party of attack.

The struggle was indeed a miniature war and in the main was fought very fairly. But it was natural that those who disbelieved should resort to ridicule. It was a form of attack to which their opponents exposed themselves by their faith in the utterly absurd stories of silly women. Cervantes with his Don Quixote laughed chivalry out of Europe, and there was a class in society that would willingly have laughed witchcraft out of England. Their onslaught was one most difficult to repel. Nevertheless the defenders of witchcraft met the challenge squarely. With unwearying patience and absolute confidence in their cause they collected the testimonies for their narratives and then said to those who laughed: Here are the facts; what are you going to do about them?

The last chapter told of the alarms in Somerset and in Wilts and showed what a stir they produced in England. In connection with those affairs was mentioned the name of that brave researcher, Mr. Glanvill. The history of the witch literature of this period is little more than an account of Joseph Glanvill, of his opinions, of his controversies, of his disciples and his opponents. It is not too much to say that in Glanvill the superstition found its ablest advocate. In acuteness of logical distinction, in the cleverness and brilliance of his intellectual sword-play, he excelled all others before and after who sought to defend the belief in witchcraft. He was a man entitled to speak with some authority. A member of Exeter College at Oxford, he had been in 1664 elected a fellow of the recently founded Royal Society and was in sympathy with its point of view. At the same time he was a philosopher of no small influence in his generation.

His intellectual position is not difficult to determine. He was an opponent of the Oxford scholasticism and inclined towards a school of thought represented by Robert Fludd, the two Vaughans, Henry More, and Van Helmont, men who had drunk deeply of the cabalistic writers, disciples of Paracelsus and Pico della Mirandola. It would be foolhardy indeed for a layman to attempt an elucidation of the subtleties either of this philosophy or of the processes of Glanvill's philosophical reasoning. His point of view was partially unfolded in the Scepsis Scientifica, published in 1665 and dedicated to the Royal Society. In this treatise he pointed out our present ignorance of phenomena and our inability to determine their real character, owing to the subjectivity of our perceptions of them, and insisted consequently upon the danger of dogmatism. He himself had drawn but a cockle-shell of water from the ocean of knowledge. His notion of spirit—if his works on witchcraft may be trusted—seems to have been that it is a light and invisible form of matter capable of detachment from or infusion into more solid substances—precisely the idea of Henry More. Religiously, it would not be far wrong to call him a reconstructionist—to use a much abused and exceedingly modern term. He did not, indeed, admit the existence of any gap between religion and science that needed bridging over, but the trend of his teaching, though he would hardly have admitted it, was to show that the mysteries of revealed religion belong in the field of unexplored science. It was his confidence in the far possibilities opened by investigation in that field, together with the cabalistic notions he had absorbed, which rendered him so willing to become a student of psychical phenomena.

Little wonder, then, that he found the Mompesson and Somerset cases material to his hand and that he seized upon them eagerly as irrefutable proof of demoniacal agency. His first task, indeed, was to prove the alleged facts; these once established, they could be readily fitted into a comprehensive scheme of reasoning. In 1666 he issued a small volume, Some Philosophical Considerations touching Witches and Witchcraft. Most of the first edition was burned in the fire of London, but the book was reprinted. Already by 1668 it had reached a fourth impression. In this edition the work took the new title A Blow at Modern Sadducism, and it was republished again in 1681 with further additions as Sadducismus Triumphatus, which might be translated "Unbelief Conquered." The work continued to be called for faster than the publisher could supply the demand, and went through several more revisions and reimpressions. One of the most popular books of the generation, it proved to be Glanvill's greatest title to contemporary fame. The success of the work was no doubt due in large measure to the collection of witch stories; but these had been inserted by the author as the groundwork of his argument. He recognized, as no one on his side of the controversy had done before, the force of the arguments made by the opposition. They were good points, but to them all he offered one short answer—the evidence of proved fact. That such transformations as were ascribed to the witches were ridiculous, that contracts between the Devil and agents who were already under his control were absurd, that the Devil would never put himself at the nod and beck of miserable women, and that Providence would not permit His children to be thus buffeted by the evil one: these were the current objections; and to them all Glanvill replied that one positive fact is worth a thousand negative arguments. Innumerable frauds had been exposed. Yes, he knew it, but here were well authenticated cases that were not fraud. Glanvill put the issue squarely. His confidence in his case at once wins admiration. He was thoroughly sincere. The fly in the ointment was of course that his best authenticated cases could not stand any careful criticism. He had been furnished the narratives which he used by "honest and honourable friends." Yet, if this scientific investigator could be duped, as he had been at Tedworth, much more those worthy but credulous friends whom he quoted.

From a simple assertion that he was presenting facts Glanvill went on to make a plea used often nowadays in another connection by defenders of miracles. If the ordinary mind, he said, could not understand "every thing done by Mathematics and Mechanical Artifice," how much more would even the most knowing of us fail to understand the power of witches. This proposition, the reader can see, was nothing more than a working out of one of the principles of his philosophy. There can be no doubt that he would have taken the same ground about miracles, a position that must have alarmed many of his contemporaries.

In spite of his emphasis of fact, Glanvill was as ready as any to enter into a theological disquisition. Into those rarefied regions of thought we shall not follow him. It will perhaps not be out of order, however, to note two or three points that were thoroughly typical of his reasoning. To the contention that, if a wicked spirit could work harm by the use of a witch, it should be able to do so without any intermediary and so to harass all of mankind all of the time, he answered that the designs of demons are levelled at the soul and can in consequence best be carried on in secret. To the argument that when one considers the "vileness of men" one would expect that the evil spirits would practise their arts not on a few but on a great many, he replied that men are not liable to be troubled by them till they have forfeited the "tutelary care and oversight of the better spirits," and, furthermore, spirits find it difficult to assume such shapes as are necessary for "their Correspondencie with Witches." It is a hard thing for spirits "to force their thin and tenuious bodies into a visible consistence.... For, in this Action, their Bodies must needs be exceedingly compress'd." To the objection that the belief in evil beings makes it plausible that the miracles of the Bible were wrought by the agency of devils, he replied that the miracles of the Gospel are notoriously contrary to the tendency, aims, and interests of the kingdom of darkness. The suggestion that witches would not renounce eternal happiness for short and trivial pleasures here, he silenced by saying that "Mankind acts sometimes to prodigious degrees of brutishness."

It is needless to go further in quoting his arguments. Doubtless both questions and answers seem quibbles to the present-day reader, but the force of Glanvill's replies from the point of view of his contemporaries must not be underestimated. He was indeed the first defender of witchcraft who in any reasoned manner tried to clear up the problems proposed by the opposition. His answers were without question the best that could be given.

It is easy for us to forget the theological background of seventeenth-century English thought. Given a personal Devil who is constantly intriguing against the kingdom of God (and who would then have dared to deny such a premise?), grant that the Devil has supernatural powers (and there were Scripture texts to prove it), and it was but a short step to the belief in witches. The truth is that Glanvill's theories were much more firmly grounded on the bedrock of seventeenth-century theology than those of his opponents. His opponents were attempting to use common sense, but it was a sort of common sense which, however little they saw it, must undermine the current religious convictions.

Glanvill was indeed exceedingly up-to-date in his own time. Not but that he had read the learned old authors. He was familiar with what "the great Episcopius" had to say, he had dipped into Reginald Scot and deemed him too "ridiculous" to answer. But he cared far more about the arguments that he heard advanced in every-day conversation. These were the arguments that he attempted to answer. His work reflected the current discussions of the subject. It was, indeed, the growing opposition among those whom he met that stirred him most. Not without sadness he recognized that "most of the looser Gentry and small pretenders to Philosophy and Wit are generally deriders of the belief of Witches and Apparitions." Like an animal at bay, he turned fiercely on them. "Let them enjoy the Opinion of their own Superlative Judgements" and run madly after Scot, Hobbes, and Osborne. It was, in truth, a danger to religion that he was trying to ward off. One of the fundamentals of religion was at stake. The denial of witchcraft was a phase of prevalent atheism. Those that give up the belief in witches, give up that in the Devil, then that in the immortality of the soul. The question at issue was the reality of the spirit world.

It can be seen why the man was tremendously in earnest. One may indeed wonder if his intensity of feeling on the matter was not responsible for his accepting as bona fide narratives those which his common sense should have made him reject. In defending the authenticity of the remarkable stories told by the accusers of Julian Cox, he was guilty of a degree of credulity that passes belief. Perhaps the reader will recall the incident of the hunted rabbit that vanished behind a bush and was transformed into a panting woman, no other than the accused Julian Cox. This tale must indeed have strained Glanvill's utmost capacity of belief. Yet he rose bravely to the occasion. Determined not to give up any well-supported fact, he urged that probably the Devil had sent a spirit to take the apparent form of the hare while he had hurried the woman to the bush and had presumably kept her invisible until she was found by the boy. It was the Nemesis of a bad cause that its greatest defender should have let himself indulge in such absurdities.

In truth we may be permitted to wonder if the philosopher was altogether true to his own position. In his Scepsis Scientifica he had talked hopefully about the possibility that science might explain what as yet seemed supernatural. This came perilously near to saying that the realms of the supernatural, when explored, would turn out to be natural and subject to natural law. If this were true, what would become of all those bulwarks of religion furnished by the wonders of witchcraft? It looks very much as if Glanvill had let an inconsistency creep into his philosophy.

It was two years after Glanvill's first venture that Meric Casaubon issued his work entitled Of Credulity and Incredulity in Things Natural, Civil, and Divine. On account of illness, however, as he tells the reader in his preface, he had been unable to complete the book, and it dealt only with "Things Natural" and "Things Civil." "Things Divine" became the theme of a separate volume, which appeared in 1670 under the title Of Credulity and Incredulity in Things Divine and Spiritual: wherein ... the business of Witches and Witchcraft, against a late Writer, [is] fully Argued and Disputed. The interest of this scholar in the subject of witchcraft was, as we have seen, by no means recent. When a young rector in Somerset he had attended a trial of witches, quite possibly the identical trial that had moved Bernard to appeal to grand jurymen. We have noted in an earlier chapter that Casaubon in 1654, writing on Enthusiasm, had touched lightly upon the subject. It will be recalled that he had come very near to questioning the value of confessions. Five years later, in prefacing a Relation of what passed between Dr. Dee and some Spirits, he had anticipated the conclusions of his Credulity and Incredulity. Those conclusions were mainly in accord with Glanvill. With a good will he admitted that the denying of witches was a "very plausible cause." Nothing was more liable to be fraud than the exhibitions given at trials, nothing less trustworthy than the accounts of what witches had done. Too many cases originated in the ignorance of ministers who were on the look-out "in every wild notion or phansie" for a "suggestion of the Devil." But, like Glanvill, and indeed like the spiritualists of to-day, he insisted that many cases of fraud do not establish a negative. There is a very large body of narratives so authentic that to doubt them would be evidence of infidelity. Casaubon rarely doubted, although he sought to keep the doubting spirit. It was hard for him not to believe what he had read or had been told. He was naturally credulous, particularly when he read the stories of the classical writers. For this attitude of mind he was hardly to be censured. Criticism was but beginning to be applied to the tales of Roman and Greek writers. Their works were full of stories of magic and enchantment, and it was not easy for a seventeenth-century student to shake himself free from their authority. Nor would Casaubon have wished to do so. He belonged to the past both by religion and raining, and he must be reckoned among the upholders of superstition.

In the next year, 1669, John Wagstaffe, a graduate of Oriel College who had applied himself to "the study of learning and politics," issued a little book, The Question of Witchcraft Debated. Wagstaffe was a university man of no reputation. "A little crooked man and of a despicable presence," he was dubbed by the Oxford wags the little wizard. Nevertheless he had something to say and he gained no small hearing. Many of his arguments were purely theological and need not be repeated. But he made two good points. The notions about witches find their origin in "heathen fables." This was an undercutting blow at those who insisted on the belief in witchcraft as an essential of Christian faith; and Wagstaffe, moreover, made good his case. His second argument was one which no less needed to be emphasized. Coincidence, he believed, accounts for a great deal of the inexplicable in witchcraft narratives.

Within two years the book appeared again, much enlarged, and it was later translated into German. It was answered by two men—by Casaubon in the second part of his Credulity and by an author who signed himself "R. T." Casaubon added nothing new, nor did "R. T.," who threshed over old theological straw. The same can hardly be said of Lodowick Muggleton, a seventeenth-century Dowie who would fain have been a prophet of a new dispensation. He put out an exposition of the Witch of Endor that was entirely rationalistic. Witches, he maintained, had no spirits but their own wicked imaginations. Saul was simply the dupe of a woman pretender.

An antidote to this serious literature may be mentioned in passing. There was published at London, in 1673, A Pleasant Treatise of Witches, in which a delightful prospect was opened to the reader: "You shall find nothing here of those Vulgar, Fabulous, and Idle Tales that are not worth the lending an ear to, nor of those hideous Sawcer-eyed and Cloven-Footed Divels, that

Grandmas affright their children withal, but only the pleasant and well grounded discourses of the Learned as an object adequate to thy wise understanding." An outline was offered, but it was nothing more than a thread upon which to hang good stories. They were tales of a distant past. There were witches once, of course there were, but that was in the good old days. Such was the author's implication.

Alas that such light treatment was so rare! The subject was, in the minds of most, not one for laughter. It called for serious consideration. That point of view came to its own again in The Doctrine of Devils proved to be the grand apostacy of these later Times. The Dutch translator of this book tells us that it was written by a New England clergyman. If that be true, the writer must have been one of the least provincial New Englanders of his century, for he evinces a remarkable knowledge of the witch alarms and witch discussions in England. Some of his opinions betray the influence of Scot, as for instance his interpretation of Christ's casting out of devils. The term "having a devil" was but a phrase for one distracted. The author made, however, some new points. He believed that the importance of the New Testament miracles would be overshadowed by the greater miracles wrought by the Devil. A more telling argument, at least to a modern reader, was that the solidarity of society would be endangered by a belief that made every man afraid of his neighbor. The writer commends Wagstaffe's work, and writes of Casaubon, "If any one could possibly have bewitcht me into the Belief of Witchcraft, this reverend person, of all others, was most like to have done it." He decries the "proletarian Rabble," and "the great Philosophers" (More and Glanvill, doubtless), who call themselves Christians and yet hold "an Opinion that Butchers up Men and Women without Fear or Witt, Sense or Reason, Care or Conscience, by droves;" but he praises "the reverend judges of England, now ... much wiser than before," who "give small or no encouragement to such accusations."

We come now to the second great figure among the witch-ologists of the Restoration, John Webster. Glanvill and Webster were protagonist and antagonist in a drama where the others played somewhat the rôle of the Greek chorus. It was in 1677 that Webster put forth The Displaying of Supposed Witchcraft. A Non-Conformist clergyman in his earlier life, he seems to have turned in later years to the practice of medicine. From young manhood he had been interested in the subject of witchcraft. Probably that interest dates from an experience of his one Sunday afternoon over forty years before he published his book. It will be recalled that the boy Robinson, accuser of the Lancashire women in 1634, had been brought into his Yorkshire congregation at an afternoon service and had come off very poorly when cross-questioned by the curious minister. From that time Webster had been a doubter. Now and again in the course of his Yorkshire and Lancashire pastorates he had come into contact with superstition. He was no philosopher, this Yorkshire doctor of souls and bodies, nor was he more than a country scientist, and his reasoning against witchcraft fell short—as Professor Kittredge has clearly pointed out—of scientific rationalism. That was a high mark and few there were in the seventeenth century who attained unto it. But it is not too much to say that John Webster was the heir and successor to Scot. He carried weight by the force of his attack, if not by its brilliancy. He was by no means always consistent, but he struck sturdy blows. He was seldom original, but he felled his opponents.

Many of his strongest arguments, of course, were old. It was nothing new that the Witch of Endor was an impostor. It was Muggleton's notion, and it went back indeed to Scot. The emphasizing of the part played by imagination was as old as the oldest English opponent of witch persecution. The explanation of certain strange phenomena as ventriloquism—a matter that Webster had investigated painstakingly—this had been urged before. Webster himself did not believe that new arguments were needed. He had felt that the "impious and Popish opinions of the too much magnified powers of Demons and Witches, in this Nation were pretty well quashed and silenced" by various writers and by the "grave proceedings of many learned judges." But it was when he found that two "beneficed Ministers," Casaubon and Glanvill, had "afresh espoused so bad a cause" that he had been impelled to review their grounds.

As the reader may already have guessed, Webster, like so many of his predecessors, dealt largely in theological and scriptural arguments. It was along this line, indeed, that he made his most important contribution to the controversy then going on. Glanvill had urged that disbelief in witchcraft was but one step in the path to atheism. No witches, no spirits, no immortality, no God, were the sequences of Glanvill's reasoning. In answer Webster urged that the denial of the existence of witches—i. e., of creatures endued with power from the Devil to perform supernatural wonders—had nothing to do with the existence of angels or spirits. We must rely upon other grounds for a belief in the spirit world. Stories of apparitions are no proof, because we cannot be sure that those apparitions are made or caused by spirits. We have no certain ground for believing in a spirit world but the testimony of Scripture.

But if we grant the existence of spirits—to modernize the form of Webster's argument—we do not thereby prove the existence of witches. The New Testament tells of various sorts of "deceiving Imposters, Diviners, or Witches," but amongst them all "there were none that had made a visible league with the Devil." There was no mention of transformation into cats, dogs, or wolves. It is hard to see how the most literal students of the Scriptures could have evaded this argument. The Scriptures said a great deal about the Devil, about demoniacs, and about witches and magicians—whatever they might mean by those terms. Why did they not speak at all of the compacts between the Devil and witches? Why did they leave out the very essential of the witch-monger's lore?

All this needed to be urged at a time when the advocates of witchcraft were crying "Wolf! wolf!" to the Christian people of England. In other words, Webster was rendering it possible for the purely orthodox to give up what Glanvill had called a bulwark of religion and still to cling to their orthodoxy.

It is much to the credit of Webster that he spoke out plainly concerning the obscenity of what was extorted from the witches. No one who has not read for himself can have any notion of the vile character of the charges and confessions embodied in the witch pamphlets. It is an aspect of the question which has not been discussed in these pages. Webster states the facts without exaggeration: "For the most of them are not credible, by reason of their obscenity and filthiness; for chast ears would tingle to hear such bawdy and immodest lyes; and what pure and sober minds would not nauseate and startle to understand such unclean stories ...? Surely even the impurity of it may be sufficient to overthrow the credibility of it, especially among Christians." Professor Burr has said that "it was, indeed, no small part of the evil of the matter, that it so long debauched the imagination of Christendom."

We have said that Webster denied the existence of witches, that is, of those who performed supernatural deeds. But, like Scot, he explicitly refrained from denying the existence of witches in toto. He was, in fact, much more satisfactory than Scot; for he explained just what was his residuum of belief. He believed that witches were evil-minded creatures inspired by the Devil, who by the use of poisons and natural means unknown to most men harmed and killed their fellow-beings. Of course he would have insisted that a large proportion of all those charged with being such were mere dealers in fraud or the victims of false accusation, but the remainder of the cases he would have explained in this purely natural way.

Now, if this was not scientific rationalism, it was at least straight-out skepticism as to the supernatural in witchcraft. Moreover there are cases enough in the annals of witchcraft that look very much as if poison were used. The drawback of course is that Webster, like Scot, had not disabused his mind of all superstition. Professor Kittredge in his discussion of Webster has pointed this out carefully. Webster believed that the bodies of those that had been murdered bleed at the touch of the murderer. He believed, too, in a sort of "astral spirit," and he seems to have been convinced of the truth of apparitions. These were phenomena that he believed to be substantiated by experience. On different grounds, by a priori reasoning from scriptural premises, he arrived at the conclusion that God makes use of evil angels "as the executioners of his justice to chasten the godly, and to restrain or destroy the wicked."

This is and was essentially a theological conception. But there was no small gap between this and the notion that spirits act in supernatural ways in our every-day world. And there was nothing more inconsistent in failing to bridge this gap than in the position of the Christian people today who believe in a spirit world and yet discredit without examination all that is offered as new evidence of its existence.

The truth is that Webster was too busy at destroying the fortifications of his opponents to take the trouble to build up defences for himself. But it is not too much to call him the most effective of the seventeenth century assailants of witch persecution in England. He had this advantage over all who had gone before, that a large and increasing body of intelligent people were with him. He spoke in full consciousness of strong support. It was for his opponents to assume the defensive.

We have called John Webster's a great name in the literature of our subject, and we have given our reasons for so thinking. Yet it would be a mistake to suppose that he created any such sensation in his time as did his arch-opponent, Glanvill. His work never went into a second edition. There are but few references to it in the writings of the time, and those are in works devoted to the defence of the belief. Benjamin Camfield, a Leicestershire rector, wrote an unimportant book on Angels and their Ministries, and in an appendix assailed Webster. Joseph Glanvill turned fiercely upon him with new proofs of what he called facts, and bequeathed the work at his death to Henry More, who in the several following editions of the Sadducismus Triumphatus attacked him with no little bitterness.

We may skip over three lesser writers on witchcraft. During the early eighties John Brinley, Henry Hallywell, and Richard Bovet launched their little boats into the sea of controversy. Brinley was a bold plagiarist of Bernard, Hallywell a logical but dull reasoner from the Bible, Bovet a weakened solution of Glanvill.

We turn now from the special literature of witchcraft to a sketch of the incidental evidences of opinion. Of these we have a larger body than ever before, too large indeed to handle in detail. It would be idle to quote from the chap-books on witch episodes their raisons d'être. It all comes to this: they were written to confute disbelievers. They refer slightingly and even bitterly to those who oppose belief, not however without admitting their numbers and influence. It will be more to our purpose to examine the opinions of men as they uttered them on the bench, in the pulpit, and in the other walks of practical life.

We have already had occasion to learn what the judges were thinking. We listened to Matthew Hale while he uttered the pronouncement that was heard all over England and even in the North American colonies. The existence of witches, he affirmed solemnly, is proved by Scripture and by the universality of laws against them. Justice Rainsford in the following years and Justice Raymond about twenty years later seem to have taken Hale's view of the matter. On the other side were to be reckoned Sir John Reresby and Francis North. Neither of them was quite outspoken, fearing the rage of the people and the charge of atheism. Both sought to save the victims of persecution, but rather by exposing the deceptions of the accusers than by denying witchcraft itself. From the vast number of acquittals in the seventies and the sudden dropping off in the number of witch trials in the eighties we know that there must have been many other judges who were acquitting witches or quietly ignoring the charges against them. Doubtless Kelyng, who, as a spectator at Bury, had shown his skepticism as to the accusations, had when he later became a chief justice been one of those who refused to condemn witches.

From scientific men there were few utterances. Although we shall in another connection show that a goodly number from the Royal Society cherished very definite beliefs—or disbeliefs—on the subject, we have the opinions of but two men who were professionally scientists, Sir Thomas Browne and Sir Robert Boyle. Browne we have already met at the Bury trial. It may reasonably be questioned whether he was really a man of science. Certainly he was a physician of eminence. The attitude he took when an expert witness at Bury, it will be recalled, was quite consistent with the opinion given in his Commonplace Book. "We are noways doubtful," he wrote, "that there are witches, but have not always been satisfied in the application of their witchcrafts." So spoke the famous physician of Norwich. But a man whose opinion was of much more consequence was Sir Robert Boyle. Boyle was a chemist and "natural philosopher." He was the discoverer of the air pump, was elected president of the Royal Society, and was altogether one of the greatest non-political figures in the reign of Charles II. While he never, so far as we know, discussed witchcraft in the abstract, he fathered a French story that was brought into England, the story of the Demon of Mascon. He turned the story over to Glanvill to be used in his list of authentic narratives; and, when it was later reported that he had pronounced the demon story an imposture, he took pains to deny the report in a letter to Glanvill.

Of literary men we have, as of scientists, but two. Aubrey, the "delitescent" antiquarian and Will Wimble of his time, still credited witchcraft, as he credited all sorts of narratives of ghosts and apparitions. It was less a matter of reason than of sentiment. The dramatist Shadwell had the same feeling for literary values. In his preface to the play, The Lancashire Witches, he explained that he pictured the witches as real lest the people should want "diversion," and lest he should be called "atheistical by a prevailing party who take it ill that the power of the Devil should be lessen'd." But Shadwell, although not seriously interested in any side of the subject save in its use as literary material, included himself among the group who had given up belief.

What philosophers thought we may guess from the all-pervading influence of Hobbes in this generation. We have already seen, however, that Henry More, whose influence in his time was not to be despised, wrote earnestly and often in support of belief. One other philosopher may be mentioned. Ralph Cudworth, in his True Intellectual System, touched on confederacies with the Devil and remarked in passing that "there hath been so full an attestation" of these things "that those our so confident Exploders of them, in this present Age, can hardly escape the suspicion of having some Hankring towards Atheism." This was Glanvill over again. It remains to notice the opinions of clergymen. The history of witch literature has been in no small degree the record of clerical opinion. Glanvill, Casaubon, Muggleton, Camfield, and Hallywell were all clergymen. Fortunately we have the opinions of at least half a dozen other churchmen. It will be remembered that Oliver Heywood, the famous Non-Conformist preacher of Lancashire, believed, though not too implicitly, in witchcraft. So did Samuel Clarke, Puritan divine and hagiographer. On the same side must be reckoned Nathaniel Wanley, compiler of a curious work on The Wonders of the Little World. A greater name was that of Isaac Barrow, master of Trinity, teacher of Isaac Newton, and one of the best preachers of his time. He declared that to suppose all witch stories fictions was to "charge the world with both extreme Vanity and Malignity." We can cite only one divine on the other side. This was Samuel Parker, who in his time played many parts, but who is chiefly remembered as the Bishop of Oxford during the troubles of James II with the university. Parker was one of the most disliked ecclesiastics of his time, but he deserves praise at any rate for his stand as to witchcraft. We do not know the details of his opinions; indeed we have nothing more than the fact that in a correspondence with Glanvill he questioned the opinions of that distinguished protagonist of witchcraft.

By this time it must be clear that there is possible no hard and fast discrimination by groups between those that believed in witchcraft and those that did not. We may say cautiously that through the seventies and eighties the judges, and probably too the justices of the peace, were coming to disbelieve. With even greater caution we may venture the assertion that the clergy, both Anglican and Non-Conformist, were still clinging to the superstition. Further generalization would be extremely hazardous. It looks, however, from the evidence already presented, as well as from some to be given in another connection—in discussing the Royal Society—as if the scientists had not taken such a stand as was to be expected of them.

When we examine the attitude of those who scoffed at the stories vouched for by Glanvill and More it becomes evident that they assumed that practically all thinking men were with them. In other words, they believed that their group comprised the intellectual men of the time. Now, it would be easy to rush to the conclusion that all men who thought in conventional ways would favor witchcraft, and that those who took unconventional views would be arrayed on the other side, but this would be a mistake. Glanvill was an exceedingly original man, while Muggleton was uncommonly commonplace; and there were numbered among those who held to the old opinion men of high intelligence and brilliant talents.

We must search, then, for some other basis of classification. Glanvill gives us an interesting suggestion. In withering tone he speaks of the "looser gentry and lesser pretenders to wit." Here is a possible line of cleavage. Might it be that the more worldly-minded among the county families, that those too who comprised what we may call, in the absence of a better term, the "smart set," and the literary sets of London, were especially the "deriders" of superstition? It is not hard to believe that Shadwell, the worldly Bishop Parker, and the polished Sir William Temple would fairly reflect the opinions of that class. So too the diarist Pepys, who found Glanvill "not very convincing." We can conceive how the ridicule of the supernatural might have become the fad of a certain social group. The Mompesson affair undoubtedly possessed elements of humor; the wild tales about Amy Duny and Rose Cullender would have been uncommonly diverting, had they not produced such tragic results. With the stories spun about Julian Cox the witch accusers could go no farther. They had reached the culmination of nonsense. Now, it is conceivable that the clergyman might not see the humor of it, nor the philosopher, nor the scholar; but the worldly-minded Londoner, who cared less about texts in Leviticus than did his father, who knew more about coffee-houses and plays, and who cultivated clever people with assiduity, had a better developed sense of humor. It was not strange that he should smile quizzically when told these weird stories from the country. He may not have pondered very deeply on the abstract question nor read widely—perhaps he had seen Ady's book or glanced over Scot's—but, when he met keen men in his group who were laughing quietly at narratives of witchcraft, he laughed too. And so, quite unobtrusively, without blare of trumpets, skepticism would slip into society. It would be useless for Glanvill and More to call aloud, or for the people to rage. The classes who mingled in the worldly life of the capital would scoff; and the country gentry who took their cue from them would follow suit.

Of course this is theory. It would require a larger body of evidence than we can hope to gather on this subject to prove that the change of opinion that was surely taking place spread at first through the higher social strata and was to reach the lower levels only by slow filtration. Yet such an hypothesis fits in nicely with certain facts. It has already been seen that the trials for witchcraft dropped off very suddenly towards the end of the period we are considering. The drop was accounted for by the changed attitude of judges and of justices of the peace. The judges avoided trying witches, the justices were less diligent in discovering them. But the evidence that we had about men of other occupations was less encouraging. It looked as if those who dispensed justice were in advance of the clergy, of the scholars, physicians, and scientists of their time. Had the Master of Trinity, or the physician of Norwich, or the discoverer of the air pump been the justices of the peace for England, it is not incredible that superstition would have flourished for another generation. Was it because the men of the law possessed more of the matter-of-factness supposed to be a heritage of every Englishman? Was it because their special training gave them a saner outlook? No doubt both elements help to explain the difference. But is it not possible to believe that the social grouping of these men had an influence? The itinerant justices and the justices of the peace were recruited from the gentry, as none of the other classes were. Men like Reresby and North inherited the traditions of their class; they spent part of the year in London and knew the talk of the town. Can we doubt that their decisions were influenced by that fact? The country justice of the peace was removed often enough from metropolitan influences, but he was usually quick to catch the feelings of his own class.

If our theory be true that the jurists were in advance of other professions and that they were sprung of a higher stock, it is of course some confirmation of the larger theory that witchcraft was first discredited among the gentry. Yet, as we have said before, this is at best a guess as to how the decline of belief took place and must be accepted only provisionally. We have seen that there are other assertions about the progress of thought in this period that may be ventured with much confidence. There had been great changes of opinion. It would not be fair to say that the movement towards skepticism had been accelerated. Rather, the movement which had its inception back in the days of Reginald Scot and had found in the last days of James I a second impulse, which had been quietly gaining force in the thirties, forties, and fifties, was now under full headway. Common sense was coming into its own.

Ferris Greenslet, Joseph Glanvill (New York, 1900), 153. The writer wishes to acknowledge his indebtedness to Mr. Greenslet's excellent book on Glanvill.

The Scepsis Scientifica was really The Vanity of Dogmatising (1661) recast.

See, for example, the introductory essay by John Owen in his edition (London, 1885), of the Scepsis Scientifica, xxvii, xxix. See also Sadducismus Triumphatus (citations are all from the edition of 1681), 7, 13.

So at least says Leslie Stephen, Dict. Nat. Biog. Glanvill himself, in Essays on Several Important Subjects (1676), says that the sixth essay, "Philosophical Considerations against Modern Sadducism," had been printed four times already, i. e., before 1676. The edition of 1668 had been revised.

This edition was dedicated to Charles, Duke of Richmond and Lenox, since His Grace had been "pleased to commend the first and more imperfect Edition."

Sadducismus Triumphatus, Preface, F 3 verso, F 4; see also p. 10. In the second part see Preface, Aa 2—Aa 3. In several other places he has insisted upon this point.

See ibid., 9 ff., 18 ff., 21 ff., 34 ff.

Ibid., 32, 34.

Ibid., 11-13.

See, for example, ibid., 88-89.

Ibid., 25-27.

Sadducismus Triumphatus, 39.

Ibid., 52-53.

To the argument that witches are not mentioned in the New Testament he retorted that neither is North America (ibid., 82).

Ibid., 78.

Nevertheless he took up some of Scot's points.

Sadducismus Triumphatus, Preface.

Sadducismus Triumphatus, pt. ii, 3.

See ibid., pt. ii, Relation VIII.

Scepsis Scientifica (ed. of 1885), 179.

London, 1668. It was reprinted in 1672 with the title A Treatise proving Spirits, Witches, and Supernatural Operations by pregnant instances and evidences.

See above, pp. 239-240.

Of Credulity and Incredulity, 29, 30.

He characterizes Reginald Scot as an illiterate wretch, but admits that he had never read him. It was Wierus whom he chiefly sought to confute.

He was given also to "strong and high tasted liquors." Anthony à Wood, Athenae Oxonienses (London, 1691-1692; 3d ed., with additions, London, 1813-1820), ed. of 1813-1820, III, 11-14.

The Question of Witchcraft Debated (London, 1669), 64.

1670 (see above, p. 293).

The Opinion of Witchcraft Vindicated. In an Answer to a Book Intituled The Question of Witchcraft Debated (London, 1670).

A True Interpretation of the Witch of Endor (London, 1669).

"By a Pen neer the Convent of Eluthery."

London, 1676.

To Professor Burr I owe my knowledge of this ascription. The translator (the English Quaker, William Sewel, all his life a resident of Holland), calls him "N. Orchard, Predikant in Nieuw-Engeland."

See Doctrine of Devils, chaps. VII, VIII, and cf. Scot, Discoverie of Witchcraft, 512-514.

Glanvill had answered a somewhat similar argument, that the miracles of the Bible were wrought by the agency of the Devil.

He said also that, if the Devil could take on "men's shapes, forms, habits, countenances, tones, gates, statures, ages, complexions ... and act in the shape assumed," there could be absolutely no certainty about the proceedings of justice.

The book had been written four years earlier.

See G. L. Kittredge, "Notes on Witchcraft," in American Antiquarian Soc., Proceedings, n. s., XVIII (1906-1907), 169-176.

There is, however, no little brilliance and insight in some of Webster's reasoning.

Displaying of Supposed Witchcraft, 38-41.

Displaying of Supposed Witchcraft, 53.

Ibid., 68.

The Witch-Persecutions (University of Pennsylvania Translations and Reprints, vol. III, no. 4), revised ed. (Philadelphia, 1903), p. 1.

Displaying of Supposed Witchcraft, 247-248.

Displaying of Supposed Witchcraft, 308, 312 ff. The astral spirit which he conceived was not unlike More's and Glanvill's "thin and tenuous substance."

Ibid., 294 ff.

Ibid., 219-228.

The author of The Doctrine of Devils (see above, note 32), was thorough-going enough, but his work seems to have attracted much less attention.

London, 1678.

John Brinley, "Gentleman," brought out in 1680 A Discovery of the Impostures of Witches and Astrologers. Portions of his book would pass for good thinking until one awakens to the feeling that he has read something like this before. As a matter of fact Brinley had stolen the line of thought and much of the phrasing from Richard Bernard (1627, see above, pp. 234-236), and without giving any credit. A second edition of Brinley's work was issued in 1686. It was the same in every respect save that the dedication was omitted and the title changed to A Discourse Proving by Scripture and Reason and the Best Authors Ancient and Modern that there are Witches.

Henry Hallywell, a Cambridge master of arts and sometime fellow of Christ's College, issued in 1681 Melampronoea, or a Discourse of the Polity and Kingdom of Darkness, Together with a Solution of the chiefest Objections brought against the Being of Witches. Hallywell was another in the long list of Cambridge men who defended superstition. He set about to assail the "over-confident Exploders of Immaterial Substances" by a course of logical deductions from Scripture. His treatise is slow reading.

Richard Bovet, "Gentleman," gave the world in 1684 Pandæmonium, or the Devil's Cloyster; being a further Blow to Modern Sadduceism. There was nothing new about his discussion, which he dedicates to Dr. Henry More. His attitude was defensive in the extreme. He was consumed with indignation at disbelievers: "They oppose their simple ipse dixit against the most unquestionable Testimonies"; they even dare to "affront that relation of the Dæmon of Tedworth." He was indeed cast down over the situation. He himself relates a very patent instance of witchcraft in Somerset; yet, despite the fact that numerous physicians agreed on the matter, no "justice was applyed." One of Bovet's chief purposes in his work was to show "the Confederacy of several Popes and Roman Priests with the Devil." He makes one important admission in regard to witchcraft; namely, that the confessions of witches might sometimes be the result of "a Deep Melancholy, or some Terrour that they may have been under."

Works, ed. of 1835-1836, IV, 389.

For Boyle's opinions see also Webster, Displaying of Supposed Witchcraft, 248.

He says also: "For my part I am ... somewhat cotive of belief. The evidences I have represented are natural, viz., slight, and frivolous, such as poor old women were wont to be hang'd upon."

The play may be found in all editions of Shadwell's works. I have used the rare privately printed volume in which, under the title of The Poetry of Witchcraft (Brixton Hill, 1853), J. O. Halliwell [-Phillips] united this play of Shadwell's with that of Heywood and Brome on The late Lancashire Witches. These two plays, so similar in title, that of Heywood and Brome in 1634, based on the case of 1633, and that of Shadwell in 1682, based on the affair of 1612, must not be confused. See above pp. 121, 158-160, 244-245.

See above, pp. 238-239.

The True Intellectual System of the Universe (London, 1678), 702.

See above, p. 256 and note.

See his Lives of Sundry Eminent Persons (London, 1683), 172; also his Mirrour or Looking Glass, Both for Saints and Sinners (London, 1657-1671), I, 35-38; II, 159-183.

London, 1678; see pp. 515-518.

Works (ed. of Edinburgh, 1841), II, 162.

Glanvill, Sadducismus Triumphatus, 80.

By the eighties it is very clear that the justices were ceasing to press charges against witches.

In an article to be published separately.

See his essay "Of Poetry" in his Works (London, 1814), III, 430-431.

Justice Jeffreys and Justice Herbert both acquitted witches according to F. A. Inderwick, Sidelights on the Stuarts (2d ed., London, 1891), 174.

CHAPTER XIII.: The Final Decline.

In the history of witchcraft the years from 1688 to 1718 may be grouped together as comprising a period. This is not to say that the year of the Revolution marked any transition in the course of the superstition. It did not. But we have ventured to employ it as a convenient date with which to bound the influences of the Restoration. The year 1718 derives its importance for us from the publication, in that year, of Francis Hutchinson's Historical Essay on Witchcraft, a book which, it is not too much to say, gave the final blow to the belief in England.

We speak of fixing a date by which to bound the influences of the Restoration. Now, as a matter of fact, there is something arbitrary about any date. The influences at work during the previous period went steadily on. The heathen raged, and the people imagined a vain thing. The great proletariat hated witches as much as ever. But the justices of the peace and the itinerant judges were getting over their fear of popular opinion and were refusing to listen to the accusations that were brought before them. The situation was in some respects the same as it had been in the later seventies and throughout the eighties. Yet there were certain features that distinguished the period. One of them was the increased use of exorcism. The expelling of evil spirits had been a subject of great controversy almost a century before. The practice had by no means been forgotten in the mean time, but it had gained little public notice. Now the dispossessors of the Devil came to the front again long enough to whet the animosity between Puritans and Anglicans in Lancashire. But this never became more than a pamphlet controversy. The other feature of the period was far more significant. The last executions for witchcraft in England were probably those at Exeter in 1682. For a whole generation the courts had been frowning on witch prosecution. Now there arose in England judges who definitely nullified the law on the statute-book. By the decisions of Powell and Parker, and most of all by those of Holt, the statute of the first year of James I was practically made obsolete twenty-five or fifty years before its actual repeal in 1736. We shall see that the gradual breaking down of the law by the judges did not take place without a struggle. At the famous trial in Hertford in 1712 the whole subject of the Devil and his relation to witches came up again in its most definite form, and was fought out in the court room and at the bar of public opinion. It was, however, but the last rallying and counter-charging on a battle-field where Webster and Glanvill had led the hosts at mid-day. The issue, indeed, was now very specific. Over the abstract question of witchcraft there was nothing new to be said. Here, however, was a specific instance. What was to be done with it? Over that there was waged a merry war. Of course the conclusion was foregone. It had indeed been anticipated by the action of the bench.

We shall see that with the nullification of the law the common people began to take the law into their own hands. We shall note that, as a consequence, there was an increase in the number of swimming ordeals and other illegal procedures.

The story of the Lancashire demonomania is not unlike the story of William Somers in Nottingham a century before. In this case there was no John Darrel, and the exorcists were probably honest but deluded men. The affair started at the village of Surey, near to the superstition-brewing Pendle Forest. The possessed boy, Richard Dugdale, was a gardener and servant about nineteen years of age. In April, 1689, he was seized with fits in which he was asserted to speak Latin and Greek and to preach against the sins of the place. Whatever his pretensions were, he seemed a good subject for exorcism. Some of the Catholics are said to have tampered with him, and then several Puritan clergymen of the community took him in hand. For eight months they held weekly fasts for his recovery; but their efforts were not so successful as they had hoped. They began to suspect witchcraft and were about to take steps towards the prosecution of the party suspected. This came to nothing, but Dugdale at length grew better. He was relieved of his fits; and the clergymen, who had never entirely given up their efforts to cure him, hastened to claim the credit. More than a dozen of the dissenting preachers, among them Richard Frankland, Oliver Heywood, and other well known Puritan leaders in northern England, had lent their support to Thomas Jollie, who had taken the leading part in the praying and fasting. From London, Richard Baxter, perhaps the best known Puritan of his time, had sent a request for some account of the wonder, in order to insert it in his forthcoming book on the spirit world. This led to a plan for printing a complete narrative of what had happened; but the plan was allowed to lapse with the death of Baxter. Meantime, however, the publication in London of the Mathers' accounts of the New England trials of 1692 caused a new call for the story of Richard Dugdale. It was prepared and sent to London; and there in some mysterious way the manuscript was lost. It was, however, rewritten and appeared in 1697 as The Surey Demoniack, or an Account of Strange and Dreadful Actings in and about the Body of Richard Dugdale. The preface was signed by six ministers, including those already named; but the book was probably written by Thomas Jollie and John Carrington. The reality of the possession was attested by depositions taken before two Lancashire justices of the peace. The aim of the work was, of course, to add one more contemporary link to the chain of evidence for the supernatural. It was clear to the divines who strove with the possessed boy that his case was of exactly the same sort as those in the New Testament. Moreover, his recovery was a proof of the power of prayer.

Now Non-Conformity was strong in Lancashire, and the Anglican church as well as the government had for many years been at no little pains to put it down. Here was a chance to strike the Puritans at one of their weakest spots, and the Church of England was not slow to use its opportunity. Zachary Taylor, rector of Wigan and chaplain to the Bishop of Chester, had already familiarized himself with the methods of the exorcists. In the previous year he had attacked the Catholics of Lancashire for an exorcism which they claimed to have accomplished within his parish. Pleased with his new rôle, he found in Thomas Jollie a sheep ready for the shearing. He hastened to publish The Surey Impostor, in which, with a very good will, he made an assault upon the reality of Dugdale's fits, charged that he had been pre-instructed by the Catholics, and that the Non-Conformist clergymen were seeking a rich harvest from the miracles they should work. Self-glorification was their aim. He made fun of the several divines engaged in the affair, and accused them of trickery and presumption in their conduct of the case.

Of course Taylor was answered, and with a bitterness equal to his own. Thomas Jollie replied in A Vindication of the Surey Demoniack. "I will not foul my Paper," wrote the mild Jollie, "and offend my reader with those scurrilous and ridiculous Passages in this Page. O, the Eructations of an exulcerated Heart! How desperately wicked is the Heart of Man!"

We shall not go into the details of the controversy, which really degenerated into a sectarian squabble. The only discussion of the subject that approached fairness was by an anonymous writer, who professed himself impartial and of a different religious persuasion from Jollie. To be sure, he was a man who believed in possession by spirits. It may be questioned, too, whether his assumption of fair dealing towards the Church of England was altogether justified. But, at any rate, his work was free from invective and displayed moderation. He felt that the Dissenting clergymen were probably somewhat deluded. But they had acted, he believed, under good motives in attempting to help one who had appealed to them. Some of them were not only "serious good Men," but men well known in the nation. This, indeed, was true. The Dissenters had laid themselves open to attack, and doubtless some of them saw and regretted their mistake. At least, it seems not without significance that neither Oliver Heywood nor Richard Frankland nor any other of the Dissenters was sure enough of his ground to support Jollie in the controversy into which he had been led.

We have gone into some detail about the Dugdale affair because of its importance in its time, and because it was so essentially characteristic of the last era of the struggle over the power of the Devil. There were cases of possession not only in Lancashire but in Somersetshire and in and around London. Not without a struggle was His Satanic Majesty surrendering his hold.

We turn from this controversy to follow the decisions of those eminent judges who were nullifying the statute against witches. We have already mentioned three names, those of Holt, Powell, and Parker. This is not because they were the only jurists who were giving verdicts of acquittal—we know that there must have been others—but because their names are linked with significant decisions. Without doubt Chief Justice Holt did more than any other man in English history to end the prosecution of witches. Justice Powell was not so brave a man, but he happened to preside over one of the most bitterly contested of all trials, and his verdict served to reaffirm the precedents set by Holt. It was Justice Parker's fortune to try the last case of witchcraft in England.

Holt became chief justice of the king's bench on the accession of William and Mary. Not one of the great names in English judicial rolls, his decided stand against superstition makes him great in the history of witchcraft. Where and when he had acquired his skeptical attitude we do not know. The time was past when such an attitude was unusual. In any case, from the moment he assumed the chief justiceship he set himself directly against the punishment of witchcraft. As premier of the English judiciary his example meant quite as much as his own rulings. And their cumulative effect was not slight. We know of no less than eleven trials where as presiding officer he was instrumental in securing a verdict of acquittal. In London, at Ipswich, at Bury, at Exeter, in Cornwall, and in other parts of the realm, these verdicts were rendered, and they could not fail to influence opinion and to affect the decisions of other judges. Three of the trials we shall go over briefly—those at Bury, Exeter, and Southwark.

In 1694 he tried Mother Munnings at Bury St. Edmunds, where his great predecessor Hale had condemned two women. Mother Munnings had declared that a landlord should lie nose upward in the church-yard before the next Saturday, and, sure enough, her prophecy had come true. Nevertheless, in spite of this and other testimony, she was acquitted. Two years later Holt tried Elizabeth Horner at Exeter, where Raymond had condemned three women in 1682. Bishop Trelawny of Exeter had sent his sub-dean, Launcelot Blackburne (later to be Archbishop of York), to look into the case, and his report adds something to the account which Hutchinson has given us. Elizabeth was seen "three nights together upon a large down in the same place, as if rising out of the ground." It was certified against her by a witness that she had driven a red-hot nail "into the witche's left foot-step, upon which she went lame, and, being search'd, her leg and foot appear'd to be red and fiery." These testimonies were the "most material against her," as well as the evidence of the mother of some possessed children, who declared that her daughter had walked up a wall nine feet high four or five times backwards and forwards, her face and the fore part of her body parallel to the ceiling, saying that Betty Horner carried her up. In closing the narrative the archdeacon wrote without comment: "My Lord Chief Justice by his questions and manner of hemming up the evidence seem'd to me to believe nothing of witchery at all, and to disbelieve the fact of walking up the wall which was sworn by the mother." He added, "the jury brought her in not guilty."

The case of Sarah Moordike of London versus Richard Hathaway makes even clearer the attitude of Holt. Sarah Moordike, or Morduck, had been accused years before by a Richard Hathaway of causing his illness. On several occasions he had scratched her. Persecuted by the rabble, she had betaken herself from Southwark to London. Thither Richard Hathaway followed her and soon had several churches praying for his recovery. She had appealed to a magistrate for protection, had been refused, and had been tried at the assizes in Guildford, where she was acquitted. By this time, however, a good many people had begun to think Hathaway a cheat. He was arrested and put under the care of a surgeon, who watched him closely and soon discovered that the fasts which were a feature of his pretended fits were false. This was not the first time that he had been proved an impostor. On an earlier occasion he had been trapped into scratching a woman whom he erroneously supposed to be Sarah Morduck. In spite of all exposures, however, he stuck to his pretended fits and was at length brought before the assizes at Southwark on the charge of attempting to take away the life of Sarah Moordike for being a witch. It is refreshing to know that a clergyman, Dr. Martin, had espoused the cause of the witch and had aided in bringing Hathaway to judgment. Chief Justice Holt and Baron Hatsell presided over the court, and there seems to have been no doubt about the outcome. The jury "without going from the bar" brought Hathaway in guilty. The verdict was significant. Pretenders had got themselves into trouble before, but were soon out. The Boy of Bilston had been reproved; the young Robinson, who would have sent to the gallows a dozen fellow-creatures, thought it hard that he was kept a few months confined in London. A series of cases in the reign of Charles I had shown that it was next to impossible to recover damages for being slandered as a witch, though in the time of the Commonwealth one woman had come out of a suit with five shillings to her credit. Of course, when a man of distinction was slandered, circumstances were altered. At some time very close to the trial of Hathaway, Elizabeth Hole of Derbyshire was summoned to the assizes for accusing Sir Henry Hemloke, a well known baronet, of witchcraft. Such a charge against a man of position was a serious matter. But the Moordike-Hathaway case was on a plane entirely different from any of these cases. Sarah Morduck was not a woman of position, yet her accuser was punished, probably by a long imprisonment. It was a precedent that would be a greater safeguard to supposed witches than many acquittals.

Justice Powell was not to wield the authority of Holt: yet he made one decision the effects of which were far-reaching. It was in the trial of Jane Wenham at Hertford in 1712. The trial of this woman was in a sense her own doing. She was a widow who had done washing by the day. For a long time she had been suspected of witchcraft by a neighboring farmer, so much so that, when a servant of his began to act queerly, he at once laid the blame on the widow. Jane applied to Sir Henry Chauncy, justice of the peace, for a warrant against her accuser. He was let off with a fine of a shilling, and she was instructed by Mr. Gardiner, the clergyman, to live more peaceably. So ended the first act. In the next scene of this dramatic case a female servant of the Reverend Mr. Gardiner's, a maid just getting well of a broken knee, was discovered alone in a room undressed "to her shift" and holding a bundle of sticks. When asked to account for her condition by Mrs. Gardiner, she had a curious story to tell. "When she was left alone she found a strange Roaming in her head, ... her Mind ran upon Jane Wenham and she thought she must run some whither ... she climbed over a Five-Bar-Gate, and ran along the Highway up a Hill ... as far as a Place called Hackney-Lane, where she look'd behind her, and saw a little Old Woman Muffled in a Riding-hood." This dame had asked whither she was going, had told her to pluck some sticks from an oak tree, had bade her bundle them in her gown, and, last and most wonderful, had given her a large crooked pin. Mrs. Gardiner, so the account goes, took the sticks and threw them into the fire. Presto! Jane Wenham came into the room, pretending an errand. It was afterwards found out that the errand was fictitious.

All this raised a stir. The tale was absolutely original, it was no less remarkable. A maid with a broken knee had run a half-mile and back in seven minutes, very good time considering the circumstances. On the next day the maid, despite the knee and the fits she had meantime contracted, was sent out on an errand. She met Jane Wenham and that woman quite properly berated her for the stories she had set going, whereupon the maid's fits were worse than ever. Then, while several people carefully watched her, she repeated her former long distance run, leaping over a five-bar gate "as nimbly as a greyhound."

Jane Wenham was now imprisoned by the justice of the peace, who collected with all speed the evidence against her. In this he was aided by the Reverend Francis Bragge, rector of Walkerne, and the Reverend Mr. Strutt, vicar of Audley. The wretched woman asked the justice to let her submit to the ordeal of water, but he refused, pronouncing it illegal and unjustifiable. Meantime, the Rev. Mr. Strutt used the test of the Lord's Prayer, a test that had been discarded for half a century. She failed to say the prayer aright, and alleged in excuse that "she was much disturbed in her head," as well she might be. But other evidence came in against her rapidly. She had been caught stealing turnips, and had quite submissively begged pardon, saying that she had no victuals that day and no money to buy any. On the very next day the man who gave this evidence had lost one of his sheep and found another "taken strangely, skipping and standing upon its head." There were other equally silly scraps of testimony. We need not go into them. The two officious clergymen busied themselves with her until one of them was able to wring some sort of a confession from her. It was a narrative in which she tried to account for the strange conduct of Anne Thorne and made a failure of it. A few days later, in the presence of three clergymen and a justice of the peace, she was urged to repeat her confession but was "full of Equivocations and Evasions," and when pressed told her examiners that they "lay in wait for her Life."

Bragge and Strutt had shown a great deal of energy in collecting evidence. Yet, when the case came to trial, the woman was accused only of dealing with a spirit in the shape of a cat. This was done on the advice of a lawyer. Unfortunately we have no details about his reasons, but it would look very much as if the lawyer recognized that the testimony collected by the ministers would no longer influence the court, and believed that the one charge of using a cat as a spirit might be substantiated. The assizes were largely attended. "So vast a number of People," writes an eye-witness, "have not been together at the Assizes in the memory of Man." Besides the evidence brought in by the justice of the peace, who led the prosecution with vigor, the Rev. Mr. Bragge, who was not to be repressed because the charges had been limited, gave some most remarkable testimony about the stuffing of Anne Thorne's pillow. It was full of cakes of small feathers fastened together with some viscous matter resembling much the "ointment made of dead men's flesh" mentioned by Mr. Glanvill. Bragge had done a piece of research upon the stuff and discovered that the particles were arranged in geometrical forms with equal numbers in each part. Justice Powell called for the pillow, but had to be content with the witness's word, for the pillow had been burnt. Arthur Chauncy, who was probably a relative of the justice of the peace, offered to show the judge pins taken from Anne Thorne. It was needless, replied the judge, he supposed they were crooked pins. The leaders of the prosecution seem to have felt that the judge was sneering at them throughout the trial. When Anne Thorne was in a fit, and the Reverend Mr. Chishull, being permitted to pray over her, read the office for the visitation of the sick, Justice Powell mockingly commented "That he had heard there were Forms of Exorcism in the Romish Liturgy, but knew not that we had any in our Church." It must have been a great disappointment to these Anglican clergymen that Powell took the case so lightly. When it was testified against the accused that she was accustomed to fly, Powell is said to have said to her, "You may, there is no law against flying." This indeed is quite in keeping with the man as described by Swift: "an old fellow with grey hairs, who was the merriest old gentleman I ever saw, spoke pleasing things, and chuckled till he cried again."

In spite of Powell's obvious opinion on the trial, he could not hinder a conviction. No doubt the jury were greatly swayed by the crowds. The judge seems to have gone through the form of condemning the woman, but took pains to see that she was reprieved. In the mean time her affair, like that of Richard Dugdale, had become a matter of sectarian quarrel. It was stated by the enemies of Jane Wenham that she was supported in prison by the Dissenters, although they said that up to this time she had never been a church-going woman. It was the Dugdale case over again, save that the parties were reversed. Then Puritans had been arrayed on the side of superstition; now some of the Anglicans seem to have espoused that cause. Of course the stir produced was greater. Mistress Jane found herself "the discourse of the town" in London, and a pamphlet controversy ensued that was quite as heated as that between Thomas Jollie and Zachary Taylor. No less than ten brochures were issued. The justice of the peace allowed his story of the case to be published and the Reverend Mr. Bragge rushed into print with a book that went through five editions. Needless to say, the defenders of Jane Wenham and of the judge who released her were not hesitant in replying. A physician who did not sign his name directed crushing ridicule against the whole affair, while a defender of Justice Powell considered the case in a mild-mannered fashion: he did not deny the possibility of witchcraft, but made a keen impeachment of the trustworthiness of the witnesses against the woman.

But we cannot linger over the details of this controversy. Justice Powell had stirred up a hornets' nest of opposition, but it meant little. The insects could buzz; but their stingers were drawn.

The last trial for witchcraft was conducted in 1717 at Leicester by Justice Parker. Curiously enough, the circumstances connected with it make it evident that crudest forms of superstition were still alive. Decency forbids that we should narrate the details of the methods used to demonstrate the guilt of the suspected parties. No less than twenty-five people banded themselves against "Old woman Norton and daughter" and put them through tests of the most approved character. It need hardly be said that the swimming ordeal was tried and that both creatures "swam like a cork." The persecutors then set to work to "fetch blood of the witches." In this they had "good success," but the witches "would be so stubborn, that they were often forced to call the constable to bring assistance of a number of persons to hold them by force to be blooded." The "old witch" was also stripped and searched "publickly before a great number of good women." The most brutal and illegal of all forms of witch procedure had been revived, as if to celebrate the last appearance of the Devil. But the rest of the story is pleasanter. When the case came before the grand jury at the assizes, over which Justice Parker was presiding, "the bill was not found."

With this the story of English trials comes to an end. The statute of James I had been practically quashed, and, though it was not to be taken from the law books for nineteen years, it now meant nothing. It was very hard for the great common people to realize what had happened. As the law was breaking down they had shown an increasing tendency to take justice into their own hands. In the case with which we have just been dealing we have seen the accusers infringing the personal rights of the individual, and calling in the constables to help them in their utterly unlawful performances. This was not new. As early as 1691, if Hutchinson may be trusted, there were "several tried by swimming in Suffolk, Essex, Cambridgeshire, and Northamptonshire and some were drowned." It would be easy to add other and later accounts, but we must be content with one. The widow Coman, in Essex, had recently lost her husband; and her pastor, the Reverend Mr. Boys, went to cheer her in her melancholy. Because he had heard her accounted a witch he questioned her closely and received a nonchalant admission of relations with the Devil. That astounded him. When he sought to inquire more closely, he was put off. "Butter is eight pence a pound and Cheese a groat a pound," murmured the woman, and the clergyman left in bewilderment. But he came back in the afternoon, and she raved so wildly that he concluded her confession was but "a distraction in her head." Two women, however, worried from her further and more startling confessions. The minister returned, bringing with him "Mr. Goldsmith and Mr. Grimes," two of the disbelieving "sparks of the age." The rest of the story may be told as it is given in another account, a diary of the time. "July 3d, 1699, the widow Coman was put into the river to see if she would sinke, ... and she did not sinke but swim, ... and she was tryed again July 19, and then she swam again. July 24 the widow was tryed a third time by putting her into the river and she swam. December 27. The widow Coman that was counted a witch was buried." The intervening links need hardly be supplied, but the Reverend Mr. Boys has given them: "whether by the cold she got in the water, or by some other means, she fell very ill and dyed."

It must have been very diverting, this experimentation by water, and it had become so popular by the beginning of the eighteenth century that Chief Justice Holt is said to have ruled that in the future, where swimming had fatal results, those responsible would be prosecuted for murder. Such a declaration perhaps caused some disuse of the method for a time, but it was revived in the second third of the eighteenth century.

Popular feeling still arrayed itself against the witch. If the increasing use of the swimming ordeal was the answer to the non-enforcement of the Jacobean statute, it was the answer of the ignorant classes. Their influence was bound to diminish. But another possible consequence of the breaking down of the law may be suggested. Mr. Inderwick, who has looked much into English witchcraft, says that "from 1686 to 1712 ... the charges and convictions of malicious injury to property in burning haystacks, barns, and houses, and malicious injuries to persons and to cattle increased enormously." This is very interesting, if true, and it seems quite in accord with the history of witchcraft that it should be true. Again and again we have seen that the charge of witchcraft was a weapon of prosecutors who could not prove other suspected crimes. As the charges of witchcraft fell off, accusations for other crimes would naturally be multiplied; and, now that it was no longer easy to lay everything to the witch of a community, the number of the accused would also grow.

We are now at the end of the witch trials. In another chapter we shall trace the history of opinion through this last period. With the dismissal of the Norton women at Leicester, the courts were through with witch trials.

See below, pp. 342-343.

We are assuming that the cases at Northampton in 1705 and at Huntingdon in 1716 have no basis of fact. At Northampton two women, according to the pamphlet account, had been hanged and burnt; at Huntingdon, according to another account, a woman and her daughter. It is possible that these pamphlets deal with historical events; but the probabilities are all against that supposition. For a discussion of the matter in detail see below, appendix A, § 10.

For his early history see The Surey Demoniack, ... or, an Account of Satan's ... Actings, In and about the Body of Richard Dugdale.... (London, 1697).

The Catholics do not seem, so far as the account goes, to have said anything about witchcraft.

The Surey Demoniack, 49; Zachary Taylor, The Surey Impostor, being an answer to a ... Pamphlet, Entituled The Surey Demoniack (London, 1697), 21-22.

"N. N.," The Lancashire Levite Rebuked, or a Vindication of the Dissenters from Popery.... (London, 1698), 3-4; see also the preface of The Surey Demoniack.

Ibid.

The Wonders of the Invisible World: being an Account of the Tryals of ... Witches ... in New England (London, 1693), by Cotton Mather, and A Further Account of the Tryals of the New-England Witches (London, 1693), by Increase Mather. See preface to The Surey Demoniack.

Thomas Jollie told a curious tale about how the manuscript had been forcibly taken from the man who was carrying it to the press by a group of armed men on the Strand. See ibid.

Alexander Gordon in his article on Thomas Jollie, Dict. Nat. Biog., says that the pamphlet was drafted by Jollie and expanded by Carrington. Zachary Taylor, in his answer to it (The Surey Impostor), constantly names Mr. Carrington as the author. "N. N.," in The Lancashire Levite Rebuked, also assumes that Carrington was the author.

The Devil Turned Casuist, or the Cheats of Rome Laid open in the Exorcism of a Despairing Devil.... By Zachary Taylor, ... (London, 1696).

It is interesting that Zachary Taylor's father was a Non-Conformist; see The Lancashire Levite Rebuked, 2.

London, 1697.

The Devil Turned Casuist.

A Vindication of the Surey Demoniack, 17.

Taylor replied to Jollie's Vindication of the Surey Demoniack in 1698 with a pamphlet entitled Popery, Superstition, Ignorance and Knavery ... very fully proved ... in the Surey Imposture. Then came The Lancashire Levite Rebuked, by the unknown writer, "N. N.," whose views we give in the text. Taylor seems to have answered in a letter to "N. N." which called forth a scathing reply (1698) in The Lancashire Levite Rebuked, or a Farther Vindication of the Dissenters.... Taylor's reply, which came out in 1699, was entitled Popery, Superstition, Ignorance, and Knavery Confess'd and fully Proved on the Surey Dissenters....

"N. N." The Lancashire Levite Rebuked. The Rev. Alexander Gordon, in his article on Zachary Taylor, Dict. Nat. Biog., says that Carrington probably wrote this book. This seems impossible. The author of the book, in speaking of Mr. Jollie, Mr. R. Fr. [Frankland], and Mr. O. H. [Oliver Heywood], refers to Mr. C. as having "exposed himself in so many insignificant Fopperies foisted into his Narrative"—proof enough that Carrington did not write The Lancashire Levite Rebuked.

Several dissenting clergymen had opposed the publication of The Surey Demoniack, and had sought to have it suppressed. See The Lancashire Levite Rebuked, 2.

For an account of this case see Francis Hutchinson, Historical Essay on Witchcraft (London, 1718), 43. Hutchinson had made an investigation of the case when in Bury, and he had also

Holt's notes of the trial.

Hutchinson had Holt's notes on this case, as on the preceding; ibid., 45. Blackburne's letter is printed in Notes and Queries, 1st series, XI, 498-499, and reprinted in Brand, Popular Antiquities (1905), II, 648-649.

See The Tryal of Richard Hathaway, ... For endeavouring to take away the Life of Sarah Morduck, For being a Witch ... (London, 1702), and A Full and True Account of the Apprehending and Taking of Mrs. Sarah Moordike, ... accused ... for having Bewitched one Richard Hetheway ...; see also Hutchinson, op. cit., 224-228.

Ibid., 226.

A somewhat similar case at Hammersmith met with the same treatment, if the pamphlet account may be trusted. Susanna Fowles pretended to be possessed in such a way that she could not use the name of God or Christ. The application of a red-hot iron to her head in the midst of her fits was drastic but effectual. She cried out "Oh Lord," and so proved herself a "notorious Lyar." She was sent to the house of correction, where, reports the unfeeling pamphleteer, "She is now beating hemp." Another pamphlet, however, gives a very different version. According to this account, Susan, under Papist influences, pretended to be possessed in such a way that she was continually blaspheming. She was indicted for blasphemy, fined, and sentenced to stand in the pillory. (For the graphic titles of these contradictory pamphlets and of a folio broadside on the same subject, see appendix A, § 7).

Probably not by any court verdict, but through the privy council.

See J. C. Cox, Three Centuries of Derbyshire Annals (London, 1890), II, 90.

Jane Wenham (broadside); see also A Full and Impartial Account of the Discovery of Sorcery and Witchcraft, Practis'd by Jane Wenham ... (London, 1712).

This narrative is given in great detail in A Full and Impartial Account. It is of course referred to in nearly all the other pamphlets.

Jane Wenham (broadside) see also A Full and Impartial Account, 12.

Jane Wenham (broadside); see also A Full and Impartial Account, 10.

Jane Wenham (broadside); see also A Full and Impartial Account, 14.

Ibid., 14.

It was suggested by some who did not believe Jane guilty, that she confessed from unhappiness and a desire to be out of the world, Witchcraft Farther Display'd. Containing (I) An Account of the Witchcraft practis'd by Jane Wenham, ... An Answer to ... Objections against the Being and Power of Witches ... (London, 1712), 37.

A Full and Impartial Account, 24.

An Account of the Tryal, Examination and Condemnation of Jane Wenham.

A Full and Impartial Account, 27.

A Full and Impartial Account, 26.

Ibid., 25.

For this story I have found no contemporary testimony. The earliest source that I can find is Alexander Chalmers's Biographical Dictionary (London, 1812-1827), XXV, 248 (s. v. Powell).

After her release she was taken under the protection of Colonel Plummer of Gilston, who had followed the trial. Hutchinson, Historical Essay on Witchcraft, 130. On his death she was supported by the Earl and Countess of Cowper, and lived until 1730. Robert Clutterbuck, History and Antiquities of the County of Hertford (London, 1815-1827), II, 461, note.

Witchcraft Farther Displayed, introduction.

See the dedication to Justice Powell in The Case of the Hertfordshire Witchcraft Consider'd (London, 1712).

A Full Confutation of Witchcraft: More particularly of the Depositions against Jane Wenham.... In a Letter from a Physician in Hertfordshire, to his Friend in London (London, 1712).

The Case of the Hertfordshire Witchcraft Consider'd. For more as to these discussions see below, ch. XIV.

It seems, however, that the efforts of Lady Frances —— to bring about Jane's execution in spite of the judge were feared by Jane's friends. See The Impossibility of Witchcraft, ... In which the Depositions against Jane Wenham ... are Confuted ... (London, 1712), 2d ed. (in the Bodleian), 36.

See Brit. Mus., Add. MSS., 35,838, f. 404.

They could "get no blood of them by Scratching so they used great pins and such Instruments for that purpose."

See Hist. MSS. Comm. Reports, Various, I, 160; see also C. J. Bilson, County Folk Lore, Leicestershire and Rutland (Folk Lore Soc., 1895), 51-52.

The Case of Witchcraft at Coggeshall, Essex, in the year 1699. Being the narrative of the Rev. J. Boys ... (London, 1901).

By some Parker is given the credit. I cannot find the original authority.

Inderwick, Sidelights on the Stuarts, 174, 175.

CHAPTER XIV.: The Close of the Literary Controversy.

In the last chapter we mentioned the controversy over Jane Wenham. In attempting in this chapter to show the currents and cross-currents of opinion during the last period of witch history in England, we cannot omit some account of the pamphlet war over the Hertfordshire witch. It will not be worth while, however, to take up in detail the arguments of the upholders of the superstition. The Rev. Mr. Bragge was clearly on the defensive. There were, he admitted sadly, "several gentlemen who would not believe that there are any witches since the time of our Saviour Jesus Christ." He struck the same note when he spoke of those who disbelieved "on the prejudices of education only." With great satisfaction the clergyman quoted the decision of Sir Matthew Hale in 1664.

The opinions of the opposition are more entertaining, if their works did not have so wide a sale. The physician who wrote to his friend in London poked fun at the witchmongers. It was dangerous to do so, he admitted, "especially in the Country, where to make the least Doubt is a Badge of Infidelity." As for him, he envied the privileges of the town. He proceeded to take up the case of Anne Thorne. Her seven-minute mile run with a broken knee was certainly puzzling. "If it was only a violent Extention of the Rotula, something might be allow'd: but it is hard to tell what this was, your Country Bone-Setters seldom plaguing their heads with Distinctions." The "Viciousness of Anne Thorn's opticks," the silly character of the clergyman's evidence, and the spiritual juggles at exorcism, all these things roused his merriment. As for Jane's confession, it was the result of ensnaring questions. He seemed to hold the clergy particularly responsible for witch cases and advised them to be more conversant with the history of diseases and to inquire more narrowly into the physical causes of things.

A defender of Justice Powell, probably Henry Stebbing, later an eminent divine but now a young Cambridge master of arts, entered the controversy. He was not altogether a skeptic about witchcraft in general, but his purpose was to show that the evidence against Jane Wenham was weak. The two chief witnesses, Matthew Gilston and Anne Thorne, were "much disturbed in their Imaginations." There were many absurdities in their stories. He cited the story of Anne Thorne's mile run in seven minutes. Who knew that it was seven minutes? There was no one timing her when she started. How was it known that she went half a mile? And, supposing these narratives were true, would they prove anything? The writer took up piece after piece of the evidence in this way and showed its absurdity. Some of his criticisms are amusing—he attacked silly testimony in such a solemn way—yet he had, too, his sense of fun. It had been alleged, he wrote, that the witch's flesh, when pricked, emitted no blood, but a thin watery matter. "Mr. Chauncy, it is like, expected that Jane Wenham's Blood shou'd have been as rich and as florid as that of Anne Thorne's, or of any other Virgin of about 16. He makes no difference, I see, between the Beef and Mutton Regimen, and that of Turnips and Water-gruel." Moreover, he urges, it is well known that fright congeals the blood.

We need not go further into this discussion. Mr. Bragge and his friends re-entered the fray at once, and then another writer proved with elaborate argument that there had never been such a thing as witchcraft. The controversy was growing dull, but it had not been without value. It had been, on the whole, an unconventional discussion of the subject and had shown very clearly the street-corner point of view. But we must turn to the more formal treatises. Only three of them need be noticed, those of Richard Baxter, John Beaumont, and Richard Boulton. All of these writers had been affected by the accounts of the Salem witchcraft in New England. The opinions of Glanvill and Matthew Hale had been carried to America and now were brought back to fortify belief in England. Richard Baxter was most clearly influenced by the accounts of what had happened in the New World. The Mathers were his friends and fellow Puritans, and their testimony was not to be doubted for a minute. But Baxter needed no convincing. He had long preached and written about the danger of witches. In a sermon on the Holy Ghost in the fifties he had shown a wide acquaintance with foreign works on demonology. In a Defence of the Christian Religion, written several years later, he recognized that the malice of the accusers and the melancholy of the accused were responsible for some cases, but such cases were exceptions. If any one doubted that there were bona fide cases, let him talk to the judges and ministers yet living in Suffolk, Norfolk, and Essex. They could tell him of many of the confessions made in the Hopkins period. Baxter had not only talked on witchcraft with Puritan ministers, but had corresponded as well with Glanvill, with whom, although Glanvill was an Anglican, he seems to have been on very friendly terms. Nor is it likely that in the many conversations he held with his neighbor, Sir Matthew Hale, the evidence from witchcraft for a spiritual world had been neglected. The subject must have come up in his conversations with another friend, Robert Boyle. Boyle's interest in such matters was of course a scientific one. Baxter, like Glanvill, looked at them from a religious point of view. In the classic Saint's Everlasting Rest he drew his fourth argument for the future happiness and misery of man from the Devil's compact with witches. To this point he reverted in his Dying Thoughts. His Certainty of the World of Spirits, in which he took up the subject of witchcraft in more detail, was written but a few months before his death. "When God first awakened me, to think with preparing seriousness of my Condition after Death, I had not any observed Doubts of the Reality of Spirits.... But, when God had given me peace of Conscience, Satan Assaulted me with those worse Temptations.... I found that my Faith of Supernatural Revelation must be more than a Believing Man and that if it had not a firm foundation, ... even sure Evidence of Verity, ... it was not like ... to make my Death to be safe and comfortable.... I tell the Reader, that he may see why I have taken this Subject as so necessary, why I am ending my Life with the publication of these Historical Letters and Collections, which I dare say have such Evidence as will leave every Sadduce that readeth them, either convinced, or utterly without excuse."

By the "Collection" he meant, of course, the narratives brought out in his Certainty of the World of Spirits—published in 1691. It is unnecessary to review its arguments here. They were an elaboration of those already used in earlier works. Too much has been made of this book. Baxter had the fever for publication. It was a lean year when he dashed off less than two works. His wife told him once that he would write better if he wrote less. Probably she was thinking of his style, and she was doubtless right. But it was true, too, of his thinking; and none of his productions show this more than his hurried book on, spirits and witches.

Beaumont and Boulton may be passed over quickly. Beaumont had read widely in the witch literature of England and other countries; he had read indeed with some care, as is evidenced by the fact that he had compared Hopkins's and Stearne's accounts of the same events and found them not altogether consistent. Nevertheless Beaumont never thought of questioning the reality of witchcraft phenomena, and his chief aim in writing was to answer The World Bewitched, the great work of a Dutch theologian, Balthazar Bekker, "who laughs at all these things of this Nature as done by Humane contrivance." Bekker's bold book was indeed gaining wide notice; but this reply to it was entirely commonplace. Richard Boulton, sometime of Brasenose College, published ten years later, in 1715, A Compleat History of Magic. It was a book thrown together in a haphazard way from earlier authors, and was written rather to sell than to convince. Seven years later a second edition was brought out, in which the writer inserted an answer to Hutchinson.

Before taking up Hutchinson's work we shall turn aside to collect those stray fragments of opinion that indicate in which direction the wind was blowing. Among those who wrote on nearly related topics, one comparatively obscure name deserves mention. Dr. Richard Burthogge published in 1694 an Essay upon Reason and the Nature of Spirits, a book which was dedicated to John Locke. He touched on witchcraft in passing. "Most of the relations," he wrote, "do, upon impartial Examination, prove either Impostures of Malicious, or Mistakes of Ignorant and Superstitious persons; yet some come so well Attested that it were to bid defiance to all Human Testimony to refuse them belief."

This was the last stand of those who still believed. Shall we, they asked, discredit all human testimony? It was practically the belief of Bishop William Lloyd of Worcester, who, while he urged his clergy to give up their notions about witches, was inclined to believe that the Devil still operates in the Gentile world and among the Pagans. Joseph Addison was equally unwilling to take a radical view. "There are," he wrote in the Spectator for July 14, 1711, "some opinions in which a man should stand neuter.... It is with this temper of mind that I consider the subject of witchcraft.... I endeavour to suspend my belief till I hear more certain accounts.... I believe in general that there is, and has been, such a thing as witchcraft; but at the same time can give no credit to any particular instance of it." The force of credulity among the country people he fully recognized. His Sir Roger de Coverley, who was a justice of the peace, and his chaplain were, he said, too often compelled to put an end to the witch-swimming experiments of the people.

If this was belief, it was at least a harmless sort. It was almost exactly the position of James Johnstone, former secretary for Scotland, who, writing from London to the chancellor of Scotland, declared his belief in the existence of witches, but called attention to the fact that the parliaments of France and other judicatories had given up the trying of them because it was impossible to distinguish possession from "nature in disorder."

But there were those who were ready to assert a downright negative. The Marquis of Halifax in the Political, Moral and Miscellaneous Thoughts and Reflections which he wrote (or, at least, completed) in 1694, noted "It is a fundamental ... that there were witches—much shaken of late."

Secretary of State Vernon and the Duke of Shrewsbury were both of them skeptical about the confessions of witches. Sir Richard Steele lampooned the belief. "Three young ladies of our town," he makes his correspondent relate, "were indicted for witchcraft. One by spirits locked in a bottle and magic herbs drew hundreds of men to her; the second cut off by night the limbs of dead bodies and, muttering words, buried them; the third moulded pieces of dough into the shapes of men, women, and children and then heated them." They "had nothing to say in their own defence but downright denying the facts, which," the writer remarks, "is like to avail very little when they come upon their trials." "The parson," he continued, "will believe nothing of all this; so that the whole town cries out: 'Shame! that one of his cast should be such an atheist.'"

The parson had at length assimilated the skepticism of the jurists and the gentry. It was, as has been said, an Anglican clergyman who administered the last great blow to the superstition. Francis Hutchinson's Historical Essay on Witchcraft, published in 1718 (and again, enlarged, in 1720), must rank with Reginald Scot's Discoverie as one of the great classics of English witch literature. Hutchinson had read all the accounts of trials in England—so far as he could find them—and had systematized them in chronological order, so as to give a conspectus of the whole subject. So nearly was his point of view that of our own day that it would be idle to rehearse his arguments. A man with warm sympathies for the oppressed, he had been led probably by the case of Jane Wenham, with whom he had talked, to make a personal investigation of all cases that came at all within the ken of those living. Whoever shall write the final story of English witchcraft will find himself still dependent upon this eighteenth-century historian.

Hutchinson's work was the last chapter in the witch controversy. There was nothing more to say.

Witchcraft Farther Displayed.

A Full Confutation of Witchcraft, 4.

Ibid., 11.

Ibid., 38.

Ibid., 5.

Ibid., 23-24.

The Case of the Hertfordshire Witchcraft Consider'd, 72.

If certain phrases may be trusted, this writer was interested in the case largely because it had become a cause of sectarian combat and he hoped to strike at the church.

See Baxter's Works (London, 1827-1830), XX, 255-271.

See ibid., XXI, 87.

W. Orme in his Life of Richard Baxter (London, 1830), I, 435, says that the Baxter MSS. contain several letters from Glanvill to Baxter.

See Memoirs of Richard Baxter by Dr. Bates (in Biographical Collections, or Lives and Characters from the Works of the Reverend Mr. Baxter and Dr. Bates, 1760), II, 51, 73.

Ibid., 26; see also Baxter's Dying Thoughts, in Works, XVIII, 284, where he refers to the Demon of Mascon, a story for which Boyle, as we have seen, had stood sponsor in England.

Ch. VII, sect. iv, in Works, XXII, 327.

Certainty of the World of Spirits (London, 1691), preface.

Two other collectors of witch stories deserve perhaps a note here, for each prefaced his collection with a discussion of witchcraft. The London publisher Nathaniel Crouch, who wrote much for his own press under the pseudonym of "R. B." (later expanded to "Richard Burton"), published as early as 1688 (not 1706, as says the Dict. Nat. Biog.) The Kingdom of Darkness: or The History of Dæmons, Specters, Witches, ... Containing near Fourscore memorable Relations, ... Together with a Preface obviating the common Objections and Allegations of the Sadduces [sic] and Atheists of the Age, ... with Pictures. Edward Stephens, first lawyer, then clergyman, but always a pamphleteer, brought out in 1693 A Collection of Modern Relations concerning Witches and Witchcraft, to which was prefaced Sir Matthew Hale's Meditations concerning the Mercy of God in preserving us from the Malice and Power of Evil Angels and a dissertation of his own on Questions concerning Witchcraft.

An Historical, Physiological, and Theological Treatise of Spirits, Apparitions, Witchcraft and other Magical Practices (London, 1705). Dedicated to "John, Earl of Carbury."

See for example, ibid., 63, 70, 71, 75, 130-135, 165, 204, 289, 306.

Balthazar Bekker's De Betoverde Weereld (Leeuwarden and Amsterdam, 1691-1693), was a most telling attack upon the reality of witchcraft, and, through various translations, was read all over Europe. The first part was translated and published in London in 1695 as The World Bewitched, and was republished in 1700 as The World Turn'd upside down.

Essay upon Reason and the Nature of Spirits, 195.

G. P. R. James, ed., Letters Illustrative of the Reign of William III, ... addressed to the Duke of Shrewsbury, by James Vernon, Esq. (London, 1841), II, 302-303.

Spectator, no. 117.

Hist. MSS. Comm. Reports, XIV, 3, p. 132.

H. C. Foxcroft, ed., Life and Letters of Sir George Savile, Marquis of Halifax (London, 1898), II, 493.

G. P. R. James, ed., op. cit., II, 300. Shrewsbury's opinion may be inferred from Vernon's reply to him.

See the Tatler, no. 21, May 28, 1709.

APPENDICES.: A.—PAMPHLET LITERATURE.: § 1.—Witchcraft under Elizabeth (see ch. II).

A large part of the evidence for the trials of Elizabeth's reign is derived from the pamphlets issued soon after the trials. These pamphlets furnish a peculiar species of historical material, and it is a species so common throughout the history of English witchcraft that it deserves a brief examination in passing. The pamphlets were written of course by credulous people who easily accepted what was told them and whose own powers of observation were untrained. To get at the facts behind their marvellous accounts demands the greatest care and discrimination. Not only must the miraculous be ruled out, but the prejudices of the observer must be taken into account. Did the pamphleteer himself hear and see what he recorded, or was his account at second hand? Did he write soon after the events, when they were fresh in his memory? Does his narrative seem to be that of a painstaking, careful man or otherwise? These are questions to be answered. In many instances, however, the pamphlets were not narrative in form, but were merely abstracts of the court proceedings and testimony. In this case, too, care must be taken in using them, for the testimony damaging to the accused was likely to be accented, while the evidence on the other side, if not suppressed, was not emphasized. In general, however, these records of depositions are sources whose residuum of fact it is not difficult to discover. Both in this and in the narrative material the most valuable points may be gleaned from the incidental references and statements. The writer has made much use of this incidental matter. The position of the witch in her community, the real ground of the feeling against her upon the part of her neighbors, the way in which the alarm spread, the processes used to elicit confession—inferences of this sort may, the writer believes, be often made with a good deal of confidence. We have taken for granted that the pamphlets possess a substratum of truth. This may not always be the case. The pamphleteer was writing to sell. A fictitious narrative of witchcraft or of a witch trial was almost as likely to sell as a true narrative. More than once in the history of witch literature absolutely imaginary stories were foisted upon the public. It is necessary to be constantly on guard against this type of pamphlet. Fortunately nine-tenths of the witch accounts are corroborated from other sources. The absence of such corroboration does not mean that an account should be barred out, but that it should be subjected to the methods of historical criticism, and that it should be used cautiously even if it pass that test. Happily for us, the plan of making a witch story to order does not seem to have occurred to the Elizabethan pamphleteers. So far as we know, all the pamphlets of that time rest upon actual events. We shall take them up briefly in order.

The first was The examination and confession of certaine Wytches at Chensforde in the Countie of Essex before the Quenes maiesties Judges, the XXVI daye of July Anno 1566. The only original copy of this pamphlet is in the Lambeth Palace library at London and its binding bears the initials of R. B. [Richard Bancroft]. The versified introduction is signed by John Phillips, who presumably was the author. The pamphlet—a black letter one—was issued, in three parts, from the press of William Powell at London, two of them on August 13, the third on August 23, 1566. It has since been reprinted by H. Beigel for the Philobiblon Society, London,

1864-1865. It gives abstracts of the confessions and an account of the court interrogatories. There is every reason to believe that it is in the main an accurate account of what happened at the Chelmsford trials in 1566. Justice Southcote, Dr. Cole, Master Foscue, and Attorney-General Gerard are all names we can identify. Moreover, the one execution narrated is confirmed by the pamphlet dealing with the trials at Chelmsford in 1579.

The second pamphlet, also in black letter, deals with the Abingdon cases of 1579. It is entitled A Rehearsall both straung and true of hainous and horrible actes committed by Elizabeth Stile, alias Rockingham, Mother Dutten, Mother Devell, Mother Margaret. Fower notorious Witches apprehended at Winsore in the Countie of Barks, and at Abington arraigned, condemned and executed on the 28 daye of Februarie last anno 1579. This pamphlet finds confirmation by a reference in the privy council records to the same event (Acts P. C., n. s., XI, 22). Reginald Scot, in his Discoverie of Witchcraft, 17, 543, mentions another, a book of "Richard Gallis of Windesor" "about certaine witches of Windsore executed at Abington." This would seem to have been a different account of the Abingdon affair, because Scot also on p. 51 speaks of some details of the Abingdon affair as to be found "in a little pamphlet of the acts and hanging of foure witches in anno 1579." It is perhaps the one described by Lowndes, Bibliographer's Manual of English Literature (p. 2959) under the title The horrible Acts of Eliz. Style, alias Rockingham, Mother Dutton, Mother Dovell, and Mother Margaret, 4 Witches executed at Abingdon, 26 Feb. upon Richard Galis (London, 1579) or that mentioned in the Stationers' Registers, II (London, 1875), 352, under date of May 4, 1579, as A brief treatise conteyninge the most strange and horrible crueltye of Elizabeth Sule [sic] alias Bockingham [sic] and hir confederates executed at Abingdon upon Richard Galis etc.

The second Chelmsford trials were also in 1579. The pamphlet account was called A Detection of damnable driftes, practised by three Witches arraigned at Chelmsforde in Essex at the last Assizes there holden, whiche were executed in Aprill 1579. There are three references in this pamphlet to people mentioned in the earlier Chelmsford pamphlet, so that the two confirm each other.

The third Chelmsford trials came in 1589 and were narrated in a pamphlet entitled The apprehension and confession of three notorious Witches arraigned and by Justice condemnede in the Countye of Essex the 5 day of Julye last past. Joan Cunny was convicted, largely on the evidence of the two bastard sons of one of her "lewde" daughters. The eldest of these boys, who was not over ten or twelve, told the court that he had seen his grandmother cause an oak to be blown up by the roots during a calm. The charges against Joan Upney concerned chiefly her dealings with toads, those against Joan Prentice, who lived in an Essex almshouse, had to do with ferrets. The three women seem to have been brought first before justices of the peace and were then tried together and condemned by the "judge of the circuit." This narrative has no outside confirmation, but the internal evidence for its authenticity is good. Three men mentioned as sheriff, justice, and landowner can all be identified as holding those respective positions in the county.

The narrative of the St. Oses case appeared in 1582. It was called A True and just Recorde of the Information, Examination and Confession of all the Witches taken at St. Oses in the countie of Essex: whereof some were executed, and other some entreated according to the determination of Lawe.... Written orderly, as the cases were tryed by evidence, by W. W. The pamphlet is merely a record of examinations. It is dedicated to Justice Darcy; and from slips, where the judge in describing his action breaks into the first person, it is evident that it was written by the judge himself. Scot, who wrote two years later, had read this pamphlet, and knew of the case (Discoverie, 49, 542). There are many references to the case by later writers on witchcraft.

Eleven years later came the trials which brought out the pamphlet: The most strange and admirable discoverie of the three Witches of Warboys, arraigned, convicted and executed at the last assises at Huntingdon ..., London, 1593. Its contents are reprinted by Richard Boulton, in his Compleat History of Magick, Sorcery, and Witchcraft (London, 1715), I, 49-152. There can be no doubt as to the historical character of this pamphlet. The Throckmortons, the Cromwells, and the Pickerings were all well known in Huntingdonshire. An agreement is still preserved in the archives of the Huntingdon corporation providing that the corporation shall pay £40 to Queen's College, Cambridge, in order that a sermon shall be preached on witchcraft at Huntingdon each Lady day. This was continued for over two hundred years. One of the last sermons on this endowment was preached in 1795 and attacked the belief in witchcraft. The record of the contract is still kept in Queen's College, Brit. Mus. MSS., 5,849, fol. 254. For mention of the affair see Darrel, Detection of that sinnful ... discours of Samuel Harshnet, 36, 39, 110; also Harsnett, Discovery of the Fraudulent Practises, 93, 97. Several Jacobean writers refer to the case. What seems to be another edition is in the Bodleian: A True and Particular Observation of a notable Piece of Witchcraft—which is the inside heading of the first edition. The text is the same, but there are differences in the paging.

Perhaps the most curious of all Elizabethan witch pamphlets is entitled The most wonderfull and true Storie of a certaine Witch named Alse Gooderidge of Stapenhill, who was arraigned and convicted at Darbie, at the Assizes there. As also a true Report of the strange Torments of Thomas Darling, a boy of thirteen years of age, that was possessed by the Devill, with his horrible Fittes and terrible apparitions by him uttered at Burton upon Trent, in the Countie of Stafford, and of his marvellous deliverance, London, 1597. There are two copies of this—the only ones of which the writer knows—in Lambeth Palace library. They are exactly alike, page for page, except for the last four lines of the last page, where the wording differs. The pamphlet is clearly one written by John Denison as an abstract of an account by Jesse Bee. Harsnett, Discovery of the Fraudulent Practices of John Darrel, 266-269, tells how these two books were written. Denison is quoted as to certain insertions made in his manuscript after it left his hands, insertions which are to be found, he says, on pages 15 and 39. The insertions complained of by Denison are indeed to be found on the pages indicated of The most wonderfull and true Storie of ... Alse Gooderidge, thus establishing his authorship of the pamphlet. The account by Bee, of which this is an abstract, I have not seen. Alse Gooderidge was put through many examinations and finally died in prison. "She should have been executed, but that her spirit killed her in prison." John Darrel was one of those who sought to help the boy who had been bewitched by

Alice. Darrel, however, receives only passing mention from the author of this pamphlet. The narrative does not agree very well in matters of detail with the Darrel tracts, although in the main outlines it is similar to them. It is very crudely put together, and, while it was doubtless a sincere effort to present the truth, must not be too implicitly depended upon.

Two pamphlets are hidden away in the back of the Triall of Maist. Dorrel (see below, § 2). The first (pp. 92-98) deals with the trial of Doll Bartham of Shadbrook in Suffolk. She was tried by the chief justice and hanged the 12th of July, 1599. The second (pp. 99-103) narrates the trial of Anne Kerke before "Lorde Anderson," the 30th of December, 1599. She also went to the gallows.

There are other pamphlets referred to in Lowndes, etc., which we have been unable to find. One of them is The Arraignment and Execution of 3 detestable Witches, John Newell, Joane his wife, and Hellen Calles; two executed at Barnett, and one at Braynford, 1 Dec. 1595. A second bears the title The severall Facts of Witchcrafte approved on Margaret Haskett of Stanmore. 1585. Black letter. Another pamphlet in the same year deals with what is doubtless the same case. It is An Account of Margaret Hacket, a notorious Witch, who consumed a young Man to Death, rotted his Bowells and back bone asunder, who was executed at Tiborn, 19 Feb. 1585. London, 1585. A fourth pamphlet is The Examination and Confession of a notorious Witch named Mother Arnold, alias Whitecote, alias Glastonbury, at the Assise of Burntwood in July, 1574: who was hanged for Witchcraft at Barking. 1575.

The title The case of Agnes Bridges and Rachel Pinder, created by Hazlitt, Collections and Notes, 1867-1876, out of the mention by Holinshed of a printed account, means but The discloysing, etc. (see p. 351). The case—see Holinshed, Chronicles (London, 1808), IV, 325, and Stow, Annales (London, 1631), p. 678, who put the affair in 1574—was not of witchcraft, but of pretended possession. See above, p. 59.

To this period must belong also A true report of three Straunge Witches, lately found at Newnham Regis, mentioned by Hazlitt (Handbook, p. 230). I have not seen it; but the printer is given as "J. Charlewood," and Charlewood printed between 1562 and 1593. The Stationers' Registers, 1570-1587 (London; Shakespeare Soc., 1849), II, 32, mention also the licensing in 1577 of The Booke of Witches—whatever that may have been.

Among pamphlets dealing with affairs nearly related to witchcraft may be mentioned the following:

A short treatise declaringe the detestable wickednesse of magicall sciences, as Necromancie, Coniuration of Spirites, Curiouse Astrologie and such lyke.... Made by Francis Coxe. [London, 1561.] Black letter. Coxe had been pardoned by the Queen.

The Examination of John Walsh, before Master Thomas Williams, Commissary to the Reverend father in God, William, bishop of Excester, upon certayne Interrogatories touchyng Wytch-crafte and Sorcerye, in the presence of divers gentlemen and others, the XX of August, 1566. 1566. Black letter. John Ashton (The Devil in Britain and America, London, 1896, p. 202) has called this the "earliest English printed book on witchcraft pure and simple"; but it did not deal with witches and it was preceded by the first Chelmsford pamphlet.

The discloysing of a late counterfeyted possession by the devyl in two maydens within the Citie of London. [1574.] Black letter. The case is that of Agnes Bridges and Rachel Pinder, mentioned above (pp. 59, 351).

The Wonderfull Worke of God shewed upon a Chylde, whose name is William Withers, being in the Towne of Walsam ... Suffolk, who, being Eleven Yeeres of age, laye in a Traunce the Space of Tenne Days ... and hath continued the Space of Three Weeks, London, 1581. Written by John Phillips. This pamphlet is mentioned by Sidney Lee in his article on John Phillips in the Dict. Nat. Biog.

A Most Wicked worke of a Wretched Witch (the like whereof none can record these manie yeares in England) wrought on the Person of one Richard Burt, servant to Maister Edling of Woodhall in the Parrish of Pinner in the Countie of Myddlesex, a myle beyond Harrow. Latelie committed in March last, An. 1592 and newly recognized acording to the truth. By G. B. maister of Artes. [London, 1593.] See Hazlitt, Collections and Notes, 1867-1877. The pamphlet may be found in the library of Lambeth Palace. The story is a curious one; no action seems to have been taken.

A defensative against the poyson of supposed prophecies, not hitherto confuted by the penne of any man; which being eyther uppon the warrant and authority of old paynted bookes, expositions of dreames, oracles, revelations, invocations of damned spirits ... have been causes of great disorder in the commonwealth and chiefly among the simple and unlearned people. Henry Howard, afterwards Earl of Northampton, was the author of this "defensative." It appeared about 1581-1583, and was revised and reissued in 1621.

Three Elizabethan ballads on witches are noted by Hazlitt, Bibliographical Collections and Notes, 2d series (London, 1882): A warnynge to wytches, published in 1585, The scratchinge of the wytches, published in 1579, and A lamentable songe of Three Wytches of Warbos, and executed at Huntingdon, published in 1593. Already in 1562-3 "a boke intituled A poosye in forme of a visyon, agaynste wytche Crafte, and Sosyrye," written "in myter" by John Hall, had been published (Stationers' Registers, 1557-1570, p. 78).

Some notion of the first step in the Elizabethan procedure against a witch may be gathered from the specimens of "indictments" given in the old formula book of William West, Simboleography (pt. ii, first printed in 1594). Three specimens are given; two are of indictments "For killing a man by witchcraft upon the statute of Anno 5. of the Queene," the third is "For bewitching a Horse, whereby he wasted and became worse." As the documents in such bodies of models are usually genuine papers with only a suppression of the names, it is probable that the dates assigned to the indictments noted—the 34th and 35th years of Elizabeth—are the true ones, and that the initials given, "S. B. de C. in comit. H. vidua," "Marg' L. de A. in com' E. Spinster," and "Sara B. de C. in comitatu Eb. vidua," are those of the actual culprits and of their residences. Yorkshire is clearly one of the counties meant. It was, moreover, West's own county.

§ 2.—The Exorcists (see ch. IV).

The account of Elizabethan exorcism which we have given is necessarily one-sided. It deals only with the Puritan movement—if Darrel's work may be so called—and does not treat the Catholic exorcists. We have omitted the performances of Father Weston and his coadjutors because they had little or no relation to the subject of witchcraft. Those who wish to follow up this subject can find a readable discussion of it by T. G. Law in the Nineteenth Century for March, 1894, "Devil Hunting in Elizabethan England."

It is a rather curious fact that the Puritan exorcist has never, except for a few pages by S. R. Maitland, in his Puritan Thaumaturgy (London, 1842), been made a study. Without doubt he, his supporters, and his enemies were able between them to make a noise in their own time. To be convinced of that one need only read the early seventeenth-century dramatists. It may possibly be that Darrel was not the mere impostor his enemies pictured him. Despite his trickery it may be that he had really a certain hypnotic control over William Somers and perhaps over Katherine Wright.

Whatever else Darrel may have been, he was a ready pamphleteer. His career may easily be traced in the various brochures put forth, most of them from his own pen. Fortunately we have the other side presented by Samuel Harsnett, and by two obscure clergymen, John Deacon and John Walker. The following is a tentative list of the printed pamphlets dealing with the subject:

A Breife Narration of the possession, dispossession, and repossession of William Sommers: and of some proceedings against Mr. John Dorrel preacher, with aunsweres to such objections.... Together with certaine depositions taken at Nottingham ..., 1598. Black letter. This was written either by Darrel or at his instigation.

An Apologie, or defence of the possession of William Sommers, a yong man of the towne of Nottingham.... By John Darrell, Minister of Christ Jesus.... [1599?] Black letter. This work is undated, but, to judge from the preface, it was probably written soon after both Darrel and More were imprisoned. It is quite clear too that it was written before Harsnett's Discovery of the Fraudulent Practices of John Darrel, for Darrel says that he hears that the Bishop of London is writing a book against him.

The Triall of Maist. Dorrel, or A Collection of Defences against Allegations.... 1599. This seems written by Darrel himself; but the Huth catalogue (V, 1643) ascribes it to James Bamford.

A brief Apologie proving the possession of William Sommers. Written by John Dorrel, a faithful Minister of the Gospell, but published without his knowledge.... 1599.

A Discovery of the Fraudulent Practises of John Darrel, Bacheler of Artes ..., London, 1599. The "Epistle to the Reader" is signed "S. H.," i. e., Samuel Harsnett, then chaplain to the Bishop of London. The book is an exposure, in 324 pages, of Darrel's various impostures, and is based mainly on the depositions given in his trial at Lambeth.

A True Narration of the strange and grevous Vexation by the Devil of seven persons in Lancashire ..., 1600. Written by Darrel. Reprinted in 1641 with the title A True Relation of the grievous handling of William Somers of Nottingham. It is again reprinted in the Somers Tracts,

III, and is the best known of the pamphlets.

A True Discourse concerning the certaine possession and dispossession of 7 persons in one familie in Lancashire, which also may serve as part of an Answere to a fayned and false Discoverie.... By George More, Minister and Preacher of the Worde of God ..., 1600. More was Darrel's associate in the Cleworth performances and suffered imprisonment with him.

A Detection of that sinnful, shamful, lying, and ridiculous discours of Samuel Harshnet. 1600. This is Darrel's most abusive work. He takes up Harsnett's points one by one and attempts to answer them.

Dialogicall Discourses of Spirits and Divels by John Deacon [and] John Walker, Preachers, London, 1601.

A Summarie Answere to al the Material Points in any of Master Darel his bookes, More especiallie to that one Booke of his, intituled, the Doctrine of the Possession and Dispossession of Demoniaks out of the word of God. By John Deacon [and] John Walker, Preachers, London, 1601. The "one Booke" now answered is a part of Darrel's A True Narration. The Discourses are dedicated to Sir Edmund Anderson and other men eminent in the government and offer in excuse that "the late bred broyles ... doe mightilie over-runne the whole Realme."

A Survey of Certaine Dialogical Discourses, written by John Deacon and John Walker ... By John Darrell, minister of the gospel ..., 1602.

The Replie of John Darrell, to the Answer of John Deacon, and John Walker concerning the doctrine of the Possession and Dispossession of Demoniakes ..., 1602.

Harsnett's second work must not be omitted from our account. In his famous Declaration of Egregious Popish Impostures, 1603 and 1605, he shows to even better advantage than in the earlier work his remarkable talents as an exposer and gives freer play to his wicked humor.

A True and Breife Report of Mary Glover's Vexation, and of her deliverance by the meanes of fastinge and prayer.... By John Swan, student in Divinitie ..., 1603.

This narrates another exorcism in which a number of clergymen participated. Swan, the author, in his dedication to the king, takes up the cudgels vigorously against Harsnett. Elizabeth Jackson was accused of having bewitched her, and was indicted. Justice Anderson tried the case and showed himself a confirmed believer in witchcraft. But the king was of another mind and sent, to examine the girl, a physician, Dr. Edward Jorden, who detected her imposture and explained it in his pamphlet, A briefe discourse of a disease called the Suffocation of the Mother, Written uppon occasion which hath beene of late taken thereby, to suspect possession of an evill spirit.... (London, 1603). He was opposed by the author of a book still unprinted, "Mary Glover's late woefull case ... by Stephen Bradwell.... 1603" (Brit. Mus., Sloane, 831). But see also below, appendix C, under 1602-1603.

One other pamphlet dealing with this same episode must be mentioned. Hutchinson, Historical Essay on Witchcraft, and George Sinclar, Satan's Invisible World Discovered (Edinburgh, 1685), had seen an account by the Rev. Lewis Hughes (in his Certaine Grievances) of the case of Mother Jackson, who was accused of bewitching Mary Glover. Although Hughes's tale was not here published until 1641-2, the events with which it deals must all have taken place in 1602 or

1603. Sir John Crook is mentioned as recorder of London and Sir Edmund Anderson as chief justice. "R. B.," in The Kingdom of Darkness (London, 1688), gives the story in detail, although misled, like Hutchinson, into assigning it to 1642.

It remains to mention certain exorcist pamphlets of which we possess only the titles:

A history of the case of Catherine Wright. No date; written presumably by Darrel and given by him to Mrs. Foljambe, afterwards Lady Bowes. See C. H. and T. Cooper, Athenae Cantabrigienses (Cambridge, 1858-1861), II, 381.

Darrel says that there was a book printed about "Margaret Harrison of Burnham-Ulpe in Norfolk and her vexation by Sathan." See Detection of that sinnfull ... discours of Samuel Harshnet, 36, and Survey of Certaine Dialogical Discourses, 54.

The strange Newes out of Sommersetshire, Anno 1584, tearmed, a dreadfull discourse of the dispossessing of one Margaret Cooper at Ditchet, from a devill in the likenes of a headlesse beare. Referred to by Harsnett, Discovery of the Fraudulent Practises of John Darrel, 17.

A ballad seems to have been written about the Somers case. Extracts from it are given by Harsnett, ibid., 34, 120.

§ 3.—James I and Witchcraft and Notable Jacobean Cases (see chs. V, VI).

The Most Cruell and Bloody Murther committed by an Innkeepers Wife called Annis Dell, and her Sonne George Dell, Foure Yeares since.... With the severall Witch-crafts and most damnable practices of one Iohane Harrison and her Daughter, upon several persons men and women at Royston, who were all executed at Hartford the 4 of August last past 1606. So far as the writer knows, there is no contemporary reference to confirm the executions mentioned in this pamphlet. The story itself is a rather curious one with a certain literary flavor. This, however, need not weigh against it. It seems possible rather than probable that the narrative is a fabrication.

The severall notorious and lewd Cosenages of Iohn West and Alice West, falsely called the King and Queene of Fayries ... convicted ... 1613, London, 1613. This might pass in catalogues as a witch pamphlet. It is an account of two clever swindlers and of their punishment.

The Witches of Northamptonshire.
Mary Barber
Who were all executed at Northampton the 22. of July last. 1612.

Concerning this same affair there is an account in MS., "A briefe abstract of the arraignment of nine witches at Northampton, July 21, 1621" (Brit. Mus., Sloane, 972). This narrative has, in common with the printed narrative, the story of Mistress Belcher's and Master Avery's sufferings from witchcraft. It mentions also Agnes Brown and Joan Brown (or Vaughan) who, according to the other account, were hanged. All the other names are different. But it is nevertheless not hard to reconcile the two accounts. The "briefe abstract" deals with the testimony taken before the justices of the peace on two charges; the Witches of Northamptonshire with the final outcome at the assizes. Three of those finally hanged were not concerned in the first accusations and were brought in from outlying districts. On the other hand, most of those who were first accused by Belcher and Avery seem not to have been indicted.

The Wonderfull Discoverie of Witches in the countie of Lancaster. With the Arraignement and Triall of Nineteene notorious Witches, at the Assizes and generall Gaole deliverie, holden at the Castle of Lancaster, upon Munday, the seventeenth of August last, 1612. Before Sir James Altham, and Sir Edward Bromley.... Together with the Arraignement and Triall of Jennet Preston, at the Assizes holden at the Castle of Yorke, the seven and twentieth day of Julie last past.... Published and set forth by commandement of his Majesties Justices of Assize in the North Parts. By Thomas Potts, Esq. London, 1613. Reprinted by the Chetham Soc, J. Crossley, ed., 1845. Thomas Potts has given us in this book the fullest of all English witch accounts. No other narrative offers such an opportunity to examine the character of evidence as well as the court procedure. Potts was very superstitious, but his account is in good faith.

Witches Apprehended, Examined and Executed, for notable villanies by them committed both by Land and Water. With a strange and most true trial how to know whether a woman be a Witch or not. London, 1613. Bodleian.

A Booke of the Wytches Lately condemned and executed at Bedford, 1612-1613. I have seen no copy of this pamphlet, the title of which is given by Edward Arber, Transcript of the Registers of the Company of Stationers of London, 1554-1640 (London, 1875-1894), III, 234b.... The story is without doubt the same as that told in the preceding pamphlet. We have no absolutely contemporary reference to this case. Edward Fairfax, who wrote in 1622, had heard of the case—probably, however, from the pamphlet itself. But we can be quite certain that the narrative was based on an actual trial and conviction. Some of the incidental details given are such as no fabricator would insert.

In the MS., "How to discover a witch," Brit. Mus., Add. MSS., 36,674, f. 148, there is a reference to a detail of Mother Sutton's ordeal not given in the pamphlet I have used.

A Treatise of Witchcraft.... With a true Narration of the Witchcrafts which Mary Smith, wife of Henry Smith, Glover, did practise ... and lastly, of her death and execution ... By Alexander Roberts, B. D. and Preacher of Gods Word at Kings-Linne in Norffolke. London, 1616. The case of Mary Smith is taken up at p. 45. This account was dedicated to the "Maior" and aldermen, etc., of "Kings Linne" and was no doubt semi-official. It is reprinted in Howell, State Trials, II.

The Wonderful Discoverie of the Witchcrafts of Margaret and Phillip Flower, daughters of Joan Flower neere Bever Castle: executed at Lincolne, March 11, 1618. Who were specially arraigned and condemned before Sir Henry Hobart and Sir Edward Bromley, Judges of Assize, for confessing themselves actors in the destruction of Henry, Lord Rosse, with their damnable practises against others the Children of the Right Honourable Francis Earle of Rutland. Together with the severall Examinations and Confessions of Anne Baker, Joan Willimot, and Ellen Greene, Witches in Leicestershire, London, 1619. For confirmation of the Rutlandshire witchcraft see Cal. St. P., Dom., 1619-1623, 129; Hist. MSS. Comm. Reports, Rutland, IV, 514. See also Gentleman's Magazine, LXXIV, pt. ii, 909: "On the monument of Francis, sixth earl of Rutland, in Bottesford church, Leicestershire, it is recorded that by his second lady he had 'two Sons, both which died in their infancy by wicked practices and sorcery.'"

Another pamphlet seems to have been issued about the affair: Strange and wonderfull Witchcrafts, discovering the damnable Practises of seven Witches against the Lives of certain noble Personages and others of this Kingdom; with an approved Triall how to find out either Witch or any Apprentice to Witchcraft, 1621. Another edition in 1635; see Lowndes.

The Wonderfull discoverie of Elizabeth Sawyer ... late of Edmonton, her conviction, condemnation and Death.... Written by Henry Goodcole, Minister of the word of God, and her continuall Visiter in the Gaole of Newgate.... 1621. The Reverend Mr. Goodcole wrote a plain, unimaginative story, the main facts of which we cannot doubt. They are supported moreover by Dekker and Ford's play, The Witch of Edmonton, which appeared within a year. Goodcole refers to the "ballets" written about this case.

The Boy of Bilson: or A True Discovery of the Late Notorious Impostures of Certaine Romish Priests in their pretended Exorcisme, or expulsion of the Divell out of a young Boy, named William Perry.... London, 1622. Preface signed by Ryc. Baddeley. This is an account of a famous imposture. It is really a pamphlet against the Catholic exorcists. On pp. 45-54 is given a reprint of the Catholic account of the affair; on pp. 55-75 the exposure of the imposture is related. We can confirm this account by Arthur Wilson, Life and Reign of James I, 107-111, and by John Webster, Displaying of Supposed Witchcraft, 274.

A Discourse of Witchcraft As it was acted in the Family of Mr. Edward Fairfax of Fuystone in the County of York, in the year 1621. Edited by R. Monckton Milnes (the later Lord Houghton) for vol. V of Miscellanies of the Philobiblon Soc. (London, 1858-1859, 299 pages). The editor says the original MS. is still in existence. Edward Fairfax was a natural brother of Sir Thomas Fairfax of Denton. He translated into English verse Tasso's Jerusalem Delivered, and accomplished other poetic feats. His account of his children's bewitchment and of their trances is very detailed. The book was again published at Harrogate in 1882, under the title of Dæmonologia: a Discourse on Witchcraft, with an introduction and notes by William Grainge.

§ 4.—Matthew Hopkins (see ch. VIII).

A Most certain, strange and true Discovery of a Witch, Being overtaken by some of the Parliament Forces, as she was standing on a small Planck-board and sayling on it over the River of Newbury, Together with the strange and true manner of her death. 1643. The tale told here is a curious one. The soldiers saw a woman crossing the river on a plank, decided that she was a witch, and resolved to shoot her. "She caught their bullets in her hands and chew'd them." When the "veines that crosse the temples of the head" were scratched so as to bleed, she lost her power and was killed by a pistol shot just below the ear. It is not improbable that this distorted tale was based on an actual happening in the war. See Mercurius Civicus, September 21-28, 1643.

A Confirmation and Discovery of Witch-craft ... together with the Confessions of many of those executed since May 1645.... By John Stearne ... London, 1648.

The Examination, Confession, Triall, and Execution of Joane Williford, Joan Cariden and Jane Hott: who were executed at Feversham, in Kent ... all attested under the hand of Robert Greenstreet, Maior of Feversham. London, 1645. This pamphlet has no outside evidence to confirm its statements, but it has every appearance of being a true record of examinations.

A true and exact Relation of the severall Informations, Examinations, and Confessions of the late Witches arraigned and executed in the County of Essex. Who were arraigned and condemned at the late Sessions, holden at Chelmsford before the Right Honorable Robert, Earle of Warwicke, and severall of his Majesties Justices of Peace, the 29 of July 1645.... London, 1645. Reprinted London, 1837; also embodied in Howell, State Trials. This is a very careful statement of the court examinations, drawn up by "H. F." In names and details it has points of coincidence with the True Relation about the Bury affair; see next paragraph below. It is supported, too, by Arthur Wilson's account of the affair; see Francis Peck, Desiderata Curiosa (ed. of London, 1779), II, 476.

A True Relation of the Araignment of eighteene Witches at St. Edmundsbury, 27th August 1645.... As also a List of the names of those that were executed. London, 1645. There is abundance of corroborative evidence for the details given in this pamphlet. It fits in with the account of the Essex witches; its details are amplified by Stearne, Confirmation of Witchcraft, Clarke, Lives of sundry Eminent Persons, John Walker, Suffering of the Clergy ... in the Grand Rebellion (London, 1714), and others. The narrative was written in the interim between the first and second trials at Bury.

Strange and fearfull newes from Plaisto in the parish of Westham neere Bow foure miles from London, London, 1645. Unimportant.

The Lawes against Witches and Conjuration, and Some brief Notes and Observations for the Discovery of Witches. Being very Usefull for these Times wherein the Devil reignes and prevailes.... Also The Confession of Mother Lakeland, who was arraigned and condemned for a Witch at Ipswich in Suffolke.... By authority. London, 1645. The writer of this pamphlet acknowledges his indebtedness to Potts, Discoverie of Witches in the countie of Lancaster (1613), and to Bernard, Guide to Grand Jurymen (1627). These books had been used by Stearne and doubtless by Hopkins. This pamphlet expresses Hopkins's ideas, it is written in Hopkins's style—so far as we know it—and it may have been the work of the witchfinder himself. That might explain, too, the "by authority" of the title.

Signes and Wonders from Heaven.... Likewise a new discovery of Witches in Stepney Parish. And how 20. Witches more were executed in Suffolk this last Assise. Also how the Divell came to Soffarn to a Farmers house in the habit of a Gentlewoman on horse backe. London, [1645]. Mentions the Chelmsford, Suffolk, and Norfolk trials.

The Witches of Huntingdon, their Examinations and Confessions ..., London, 1646. This work is dedicated to the justices of the peace for the county of Huntingdon; the dedication is signed by John Davenport. Three of the witches whose accusations are here presented are mentioned by Stearne (Confirmation of Witchcraft, 11, 13, 20-21, 42).

The Discovery of Witches: in answer to severall Queries, lately Delivered to the Judges of Assize for the County of Norfolk. And now published by Matthew Hopkins, Witchfinder. For the Benefit of the Whole Kingdome.... London, 1647. Hopkins's and Stearne's accounts fit into each other and are the two best sources for ch. VIII.

The [D]Ivell in Kent, or His strange Delusions at Sandwitch, London, 1647. Has nothing to do with witches; shows the spirit of the times.

A strange and true Relation of a Young Woman possest with the Devill. By name Joyce Dovey dwelling at Bewdley neer Worcester ... as it was certified in a Letter from Mr. James Dalton unto Mr. Tho. Groome, Ironmonger over against Sepulchres Church in London.... Also a Letter from Cambridge, wherein is related the late conference between the Devil (in the shape of a Mr. of Arts) and one Ashbourner, a Scholler of S. Johns Colledge ... who was afterwards carried away by him and never heard of since onely his Gown found in the River, London, 1647. In the first narrative a woman after hearing a sermon fell into fits. The second narrative was probably based upon a combination of facts and rumor.

The Full Tryals, Examination and Condemnation of Four Notorious Witches, At the Assizes held in Worcester on Tuseday the 4th of March ... As also Their Confessions and last Dying Speeches at the place of Execution, with other Amazing Particulars ..., London, printed by "I. W.," no date. Another edition of this pamphlet (in the Bodleian) bears the date 1700 and was printed for "J. M." in Fleet street. This is a most interesting example of a made-to-order witch pamphlet. The preface makes one suspect its character: "the following narrative coming to my hand." The accused were Rebecca West, Margaret Landis, Susan Cook, and Rose Hallybread. Now, all these women were tried at Chelmsford in 1645, and their examinations and confessions printed in A true and exact Relation. The wording has been changed a little, several things have been added, but the facts are similar; see A true and exact Relation,10, 11, 13-15, 27. When the author of the Worcester pamphlet came to narrate the execution he wandered away from his text and invented some new particulars. The women were "burnt at the stak." They made a "yelling and howling." Two of them were very "stubborn and refractory." Cf. below, § 10.

The Devill seen at St. Albans, Being a true Relation How the Devill was seen there in a Cellar, in the likenesse of a Ram; and how a Butcher came and cut his throat, and sold some of it, and dressed the rest for himselfe, inviting many to supper ..., 1648. A clever lampoon.

§ 5.—Commonwealth and Protectorate (see ch. IX).

The Divels Delusions or A faithfull relation of John Palmer and Elizabeth Knott two notorious Witches lately condemned at the Sessions of Oyer and Terminer in St. Albans ..., 1649. The narrative purports to be taken from a letter sent from St. Alban's. It deals with the practices of two good witches who were finally discovered to be black witches. The tale has no outside confirmation.

Wonderfull News from the North, Or a True Relation of the Sad and Grievous Torments Inflicted upon the Bodies of three Children of Mr. George Muschamp, late of the County of Northumberland, by Witchcraft, ... As also the prosecution of the sayd Witches, as by Oaths, and their own Confessions will appear and by the Indictment found by the Jury against one of them, at the Sessions of the Peace held at Alnwick, the 24 day of April 1650, London, 1650. Preface signed: "Thine, Mary Moore." This pamphlet bears all through the marks of a true narrative. It is written evidently by a friend of the Mistress Muschamp who had such difficulty in persuading the north country justices, judges, and sheriffs to act. The names and the circumstances fit in with other known facts.

The strange Witch at Greenwich haunting a Wench, 1650. Unimportant.

A Strange Witch at Greenwich, 1650.

The last two pamphlets are mentioned by Lowndes. The second pamphlet I have not seen; as, however, Lowndes cites the title of the first incorrectly, it is very possible that he has given two titles for the same pamphlet.

The Witch of Wapping, or an Exact and Perfect Relation of the Life and Devilish Practises of Joan Peterson, who dwelt in Spruce Island, near Wapping; Who was condemned for practising Witchcraft, and sentenced to be Hanged at Tyburn, on Munday the 11th of April 1652, London, 1652.

A Declaration in Answer to several lying Pamphlets concerning the Witch of Wapping, ... shewing the Bloudy Plot and wicked Conspiracy of one Abraham Vandenhemde, Thomas Crompton, Thomas Collet, and others, London, 1652. This pamphlet is described above, pp. 214-215.

The Tryall and Examinations of Mrs. Joan Peterson before the Honourable Bench at the Sessions house in the Old Bayley yesterday. [1652]. This states the case against Mistress Joan in the title, but (unless the British Museum copy is imperfect) gives no details.

Doctor Lamb's Darling, or Strange and terrible News from Salisbury; Being A true, exact, and perfect Relation of the great and wonderful Contract and Engagement made between the Devil, and Mistris Anne Bodenham; with the manner how she could transform herself into the shape of a Mastive Dog, a black Lyon, a white Bear, a Woolf, a Bull, and a Cat.... The Tryal, Examinations, and Confession ... before the Lord Chief Baron Wild.... By James [Edmond?] Bower, Cleric, London, 1653. This is the first account of the affair and is a rather crude one.

Doctor Lamb Revived, or, Witchcraft condemn'd in Anne Bodenham ... who was Arraigned and Executed the Lent Assizes last at Salisbury, before the Right Honourable the Lord Chief

Baron Wild, Judge of the Assize.... By Edmond Bower, an eye and ear Witness of her Examination and Confession, London, 1653. Bower's second and more detailed account. It is dedicated to the judge by the writer, who had a large part in the affair and frequently interviewed the witch. He does not present a record of examinations, but gives a detailed narrative of the entire affair. He throws out hints about certain phases of the case and rouses curiosity without satisfying it. His story of Anne Bodenham is, however, clear and interesting. The celebrated Aubrey refers to the case in his Remaines of Gentilisme and Judaisme, 261. His account, which tallies well with that of Bower, he seems to have derived from Anthony Ettrick "of the Middle Temple," who was a "curious observer of the whole triall."

A Prodigious and Tragicall History of the Arraignment, Tryall, Confession, and Condemnation of six Witches at Maidstone, in Kent, at the Assizes there held in July, Fryday 30, this present year, 1652. Before the Right Honourable, Peter Warburton.... Collected from the Observations of E. G. Gent, a learned person, present at their Conviction and Condemnation, and digested by H. F. Gent., London, 1652. It is a pity that the digesting was not omitted. The account, however, is trustworthy. Mention is made of this trial by Elias Ashmole in his Diary (London, 1717) and by The Faithful Scout, July 30-August 7, 1652.

The most true and wonderfull Narration of two women bewitched in Yorkshire: Who camming to the Assizes at York to give in Evidence against the Witch after a most horrible noise to the terror and amazement of all the beholders, did vomit forth before the Judges, Pins, wool.... Also a most true Relation of a young Maid ... who ... did ... vomit forth wadds of straw, with pins a crosse in them, iron Nails, Needles, ... as it is attested under the hand of that most famour Phisitian Doctor Henry Heers, ... 1658. In the Bodleian. The writer of this pamphlet had little information to give and seems to have got it at second or third hand.

A more Exact Relation of the most lamentable and horrid Contract which Lydia Rogers, living in Pump-Ally in Wapping, made with the Divel.... Together with the great pains and prayers of many eminent Divines, ... 1658. In the Bodleian. This is a "Relation of a woman who heretofore professing Religion in the purity thereof fel afterwards to be a sectary, and then to be acquainted with Astrologers, and afterwards with the Divel himself." A poor woman "naturally inclin'd to melancholy" believed she had made a contract with the Devil. "Many Ministers are dayly with her."

The Snare of the Devill Discovered: Or, A True and perfect Relation of the sad and deplorable Condition of Lydia the Wife of John Rogers House Carpenter, living in Greenbank in Pumpe alley in Wappin.... Also her Examination by Mr. Johnson the Minister of Wappin, and her Confession. As also in what a sad Condition she continues.... London, 1658. Another tract against the Baptists. In spite of Lydia Rogers's supposed contract with the Devil, she does not seem to have been brought into court.

Strange and Terrible Newes from Cambridge, being A true Relation of the Quakers bewitching of Mary Philips ... into the shape of a Bay Mare, riding her from Dinton towards the University. With the manner how she became visible again ... in her own Likeness and Shape, with her sides all rent and torn, as if they had been spur-galled, ... and the Names of the Quakers brought to tryal on Friday last at the Assises held at Cambridge ..., London, 1659. This is mentioned by John Ashton in the bibliographical appendix to his The Devil in Britain and America.

The Just Devil of Woodstock, or a true narrative of the severall apparitions, the frights and punishments inflicted upon the Rumpish commissioners sent thither to survey the manors and houses belonging to His Majesty. 1660. Wood, Athenae Oxonienses (ed. of 1817), III, 398, ascribes this to Thomas Widdowes. It was on the affair described in this pamphlet that Walter Scott based his novel Woodstock. The story given in the pamphlet may be found in Sinclar's Satan's Invisible World Discovered. The writer has not seen the original pamphlet.

§ 6.—Charles II and James II (see ch. XI).

The Power of Witchcraft, Being a most strange but true Relation of the most miraculous and wonderful deliverance of one Mr. William Harrison of Cambden in the County of Gloucester, Steward to the Lady Nowel ..., London, 1662.

A True and Perfect Account of the Examination, Confession, Tryal, Condemnation and Execution of Joan Perry and her two Sons ... for the supposed murder of William Harrison, Gent ..., London, 1676. These are really not witchcraft pamphlets. Mr. Harrison disappears, three people are charged with his murder and hanged. Mr. Harrison comes back from Turkey in two years and tells a story of his disappearance which leads to the supposition that he was transported thither by witchcraft.

A Tryal of Witches at the assizes held at Bury St. Edmonds for the County of Suffolk; on the tenth day of March, 1664, London, 1682; another edition, 1716. The writer of this tract writes in introducing it: "This Tryal of Witches hath lain a long time in a private Gentleman's Hands in the Country, it being given to him by the Person that took it in the Court for his own satisfaction." This is the much quoted case before Sir Matthew Hale. The pamphlet presents one of the most detailed accounts of the court procedure in a witch case.

The Lord's Arm Stretched Out in an Answer of Prayer or a True Relation of the wonderful Deliverance of James Barrow, the Son of John Barrow of Olaves Southwark, London, 1664. This seems to be a Baptist pamphlet.

The wonder of Suffolke, being a true relation of one that reports he made a league with the Devil for three years, to do mischief, and now breaks open houses, robs people daily, ... and can neither be shot nor taken, but leaps over walls fifteen feet high, runs five or six miles in a quarter of an hour, and sometimes vanishes in the midst of multitudes that go to take him. Faithfully written in a letter from a solemn person, dated not long since, to a friend in Ship-yard, near Temple-bar, and ready to be attested by hundreds ..., London, 1677. This is mentioned in the Gentleman's Magazine, 1829, pt. ii, 584. I have not seen a copy of the pamphlet.

Daimonomageia: a small Treatise of Sicknesses and Diseases from Witchcraft and Supernatural Causes.... Being useful to others besides Physicians, in that it confutes Atheistical, Sadducistical, and Sceptical Principles and Imaginations ..., London, 1665. Though its title-page bears no name, the author was undoubtedly that "William Drage, D. P. [Doctor of Physic] at Hitchin," in Hertfordshire, to whose larger treatise on medicine (first printed in 1664 as A Physical Nosonomy, then in 1666 as The Practice of Physick, and again in 1668 as Physical Experiments) it seems to be a usual appendage. It is so, at least, in the Cornell copy of the first edition and in the Harvard copy of the third, and is so described by the Dict. Nat. Biog. and by the British Museum catalogue.

Hartford-shire Wonder. Or, Strange News from Ware, Being an Exact and true Relation of one Jane Stretton ... who hath been visited in a strange kind of manner by extraordinary and unusual fits ..., London, 1669. The title gives the clue to this story. The narrator makes it clear that a certain woman was suspected of the bewitchment.

A Magicall Vision, Or a Perfect Discovery of the Fallacies of Witchcraft, As it was lately represented in a pleasant sweet Dream to a Holysweet Sister, a faithful and pretious Assertor of the Family of the Stand-Hups, for preservation of the Saints from being tainted with the heresies of the Congregation of the Doe-Littles, London, 1673. I have not seen this. It is mentioned by Hazlitt, Bibliographical Collections, fourth series, s. v. Witchcraft.

A Full and True Relation of The Tryal, Condemnation, and Execution of Ann Foster ... at the place of Execution at Northampton. With the Manner how she by her Malice and Witchcraft set all the Barns and Corn on Fire ... and bewitched a whole Flock of Sheep ..., London, 1674. This narrative has no confirmation from other sources, yet its details are so susceptible of natural explanation that they warrant a presumption of its truth.

Strange News from Arpington near Bexby in Kent: Being a True Narrative of a yong Maid who was Possest with several Devils ..., London, 1679.

Strange and Wonderful News from Yowell in Surry; Giving a True and Just Account of One Elisabeth Burgess, Who was most strangely Bewitched and Tortured at a sad rate, London, 1681.

An Account of the Tryal and Examination of Joan Buts, for being a Common Witch and Inchantress, before the Right Honourable Sir Francis Pemberton, Lord Chief Justice, at the Assizes ... 1682. Single leaf.

The four brochures next to be described deal with the same affair and substantially agree.

The Tryal, Condemnation, and Execution of Three Witches, viz. Temperance Floyd, Mary Floyd, and Susanna Edwards. Who were Arraigned at Exeter on the 18th of August, 1682.... London, 1682. Confirmed by the records of the gaol deliveries examined by Mr. Inderwick (Side-Lights on the Stuarts, p. 192).

A True and Impartial Relation of the Informations against Three Witches, viz. Temperance Lloyd, Mary Trembles, and Susanna Edwards, who were Indicted, Arraigned, and Convicted at the Assizes holden ... at ... Exon, Aug. 14, 1682. With their several Confessions ... as also Their ... Behaviour, at the ... Execution on the Twenty fifth of the said Month, London, 1682. This, the fullest account (40 pp.), gives correctly the names of these three women, whom I still believe the last put to death for witchcraft in England.

Witchcraft discovered and punished. Or the Tryals and Condemnation of three Notorious Witches, who were Tryed the last Assizes, holden at the Castle of Exeter ... where they received sentence of Death, for bewitching severall Persons, destroying Ships at Sea, and Cattel by Land. To the Tune of Doctor Faustus; or Fortune my Foe. In the Roxburghe Collection at the British Museum. Broadside. A ballad of 17 stanzas (4 lines each) giving the story of the affair.

The Life and Conversation of Temperance Floyd, Mary Lloyd and Susanna Edwards ...; Lately Condemned at Exeter Assizes; together with a full Account of their first Agreement with the Devil: With the manner how they prosecuted their devilish Sorceries ..., London, 1687.

A Full and True Account of the Proceedings at the Sessions of Oyer and Terminer ... which began at the Sessions House in the Old Bayley on Thursday, June 1st, and Ended on Fryday, June 2nd, 1682. Wherein is Contained the Tryal of many notorious Malefactors ... but more especially the Tryall of Jane Kent for Witchcraft. This pamphlet is a brief summary of several cases just finished and has every evidence of being a faithful account. It is to be found in the library of Lincoln's Inn.

Strange and Dreadful News from the Town of Deptford in the County of Kent, Being a Full, True, and Sad Relation of one Anne Arthur. 1684/5. One leaf, folio.

Strange newes from Shadwell, being a ... relation of the death of Alice Fowler, who had for many years been accounted a witch. London, 1685. 4 pp. In the library of the Earl of Crawford. I have not seen it.

A True Account of a Strange and Wonderful Relation of one John Tonken, of Pensans in Cornwall, said to be Bewitched by some Women: two of which on Suspition are committed to Prison, London, 1686. In the Bodleian. This narrative is confirmed by Inderwick's records.

News from Panier Alley; or a True Relation of Some Pranks the Devil hath lately play'd with a Plaster Pot there, London, 1687. In the Bodleian. A curious tract. No trial.

§ 7.—The Final Decline, Miscellaneous Pamphlets (see ch. XIII).

A faithful narrative of the ... fits which ... Thomas Spatchet ... was under by witchcraft ..., 1693. Unimportant.

The Second Part of the Boy of Bilson, Or a True and Particular Relation of the Imposter Susanna Fowles, wife of John Fowles of Hammersmith in the Co. of Midd., who pretended herself to be possessed, London, 1698.

A Full and True Account Both of the Life: And also the Manner and Method of carrying on the Delusions, Blasphemies, and Notorious Cheats of Susan Fowls, as the same was Contrived, Plotted, Invented, and Managed by wicked Popish Priests and other Papists.

The trial of Susannah Fowles, of Hammersmith, for blaspheming Jesus Christ, and cursing the Lord's Prayer ..., London, 1698.

These three pamphlets tell the story of a woman who was "an impostor and Notorious Lyar"; they have little to do with witchcraft. See above, ch. XIII, note 23.

The Case of Witchcraft at Coggeshall, Essex, in the year 1699. Being the Narrative of the Rev. J. Boys, Minister of the Parish. Printed from his manuscript in the possession of the publisher (A. Russell Smith), London, 1901.

A True and Impartial Account of the Dark and Hellish Power of Witchcraft, Lately Exercised on the Body of the Reverend Mr. Wood, Minister of Bodmyn. In a Letter from a Gentleman there, to his Friend in Exon, in Confirmation thereof, Exeter, 1700.

A Full and True Account of the Apprehending and Taking of Mrs. Sarah Moordike, Who is accused for a Witch, Being taken near Paul's Wharf ... for haveing Bewitched one Richard Hetheway.... With her Examination before the Right Worshipful Sir Thomas Lane, Sir Owen Buckingham, and Dr. Hambleton in Bowe-lane. 1701. This account can be verified and filled out from the records of the trial of Hathaway, printed in Howell, State Trials, XIV, 639-696.

A short Account of the Trial held at Surry Assizes, in the Borough of Southwark; on an Information against Richard Hathway ... for Riot and Assault, London, 1702.

The Tryal of Richard Hathaway, upon an Information For being a Cheat and Impostor, For endeavouring to take away The Life of Sarah Morduck, For being a Witch at Surry Assizes ..., London, 1702.

A Full and True Account of the Discovering, Apprehending and taking of a Notorious Witch, who was carried before Justice Bateman in Well-Close on Sunday, July the 23. Together with her Examination and Commitment to Bridewel, Clerkenwell, London, 1704. Signed at the end, "Tho. Greenwel." Single page.

An Account of the Tryals, Examination, and Condemnation of Elinor Shaw and Mary Phillips ..., 1705.

The Northamptonshire Witches ..., 1705.

The second of these is the completer account. They are by the same author and are probably fabrications; see below, § 10.

The Whole Trial of Mrs. Mary Hicks and her Daughter Elizabeth ..., 1716. See below, § 10.

§ 8.—The Surey Pamphlets (see ch. XIII).

The Devil Turned Casuist, or the Cheats of Rome Laid open in the Exorcism of a Despairing Devil at the House of Thomas Pennington in Oriel.... By Zachary Taylor, M. A., Chaplain to the Right reverend Father in God, Nicholas, Lord Bishop of Chester, and Rector of Wigan, London, 1696.

The Surey Demoniack, Or an Account of Satan's Strange and Dreadful Actings, In and about the Body of Richard Dugdale of Surey, near Whalley in Lancashire. And How he was Dispossest by Gods blessing on the Fastings and Prayers of divers Ministers and People, London, 1697. Fishwick, Notebook of Jollie (Chetham Soc.), p. xxiv says this was written by Thomas Jollie and John Carrington. The preface is signed by "Thomas Jolly" and five other clergymen. Probably Jollie wrote the pamphlet and Carrington revised it. See above, ch. XIII, note 10. Jollie disclaimed the sole responsibility for it. See his Vindication, 7. Taylor in The Surey Impostor assumes that Carrington wrote The Surey Demoniack; see e. g. p. 21.

The Surey Imposter, being an answer to a late Fanatical Pamphlet, entituled The Surey Demoniack. By Zachary Taylor. London, 1697.

A Vindication of the Surey Demoniack as no Imposter: Or, A Reply to a certain Pamphlet publish'd by Mr. Zach. Taylor, called The Surey Imposter.... By T. J., London, 1698. Written by Jollie.

Popery, Superstition, Ignorance and Knavery very unjustly by a letter in the general pretended; but as far as was charg'd very fully proved upon the Dissenters that were concerned in the Surey Imposture. 1698. Written by Zachary Taylor.

The Lancashire Levite Rebuked, or a Vindication of the Dissenters from Popery, Superstition, Ignorance, and Knavery, unjustly Charged on them by Mr. Zachary Taylor.... London, 1698. Signed "N. N.;" see above ch. XIII, note 17.

The Lancashire Levite Rebuked, or a Farther Vindication, 1698. This seems to have been an answer to a "letter to Mr. N. N." which Taylor had published. We have, however, no other mention of such a letter.

Popery, Superstition, Ignorance, and Knavery, Confess'd and fully Proved on the Surey Dissenters, from a Second Letter of an Apostate Friend, to Zach. Taylor. To which is added a Refutation of T. Jollie's Vindication ..., London, 1699. Written by Zachary Taylor.

A Refutation of Mr. T. Jolly's Vindication of the Devil in Dugdale; Or, The Surey Demoniack, London, 1699.

It is not worth while to give any critical appraisement of these pamphlets. They were all controversial and all dealt with the case of Richard Dugdale. Zachary Taylor had the best of it. The Puritan clergymen who backed up Thomas Jollie in his claims seem gradually to have withdrawn their support.

§ 9.—The Wenham Pamphlets (see ch. XIII).

An Account of the Tryal, Examination, and Condemnation of Jane Wenham, on an Indictment of Witchcraft, for Bewitching of Matthew Gilston and Anne Thorne of Walcorne, in the County of Hertford.... Before the Right Honourable Mr. Justice Powell, and is ordered for Execution on Saturday come Sevennight the 15th. One page.

A Full and Impartial Account of the Discovery of Sorcery and Witchcraft, Practis'd by Jane Wenham of Walkerne in Hertfordshire, upon the bodies of Anne Thorn, Anne Street, &c.... till she ... receiv'd Sentence of Death for the same, March 4, 1711-12, London, 1712. Anonymous, but confessedly written by Francis Bragge. 1st ed. in Cornell library and Brit. Mus.; 2d ed. in Brit. Mus.; 3d ed. in Brit. Mus. (Sloane, 3,943), and Bodleian; 4th ed. in Brit. Mus.; 5th ed. in Harvard library: all published within the year.

Witchcraft Farther Display'd, Containing (I) An Account of the Witchcraft practis'd by Jane Wenham of Walkerne, in Hertfordshire, since her Condemnation, upon the bodies of Anne Thorne and Anne Street.... (II) An Answer to the most general Objections against the Being and Power of Witches: With some Remarks upon the Case of Jane Wenham in particular, and on Mr. Justice Powel's procedure therein.... London, 1712. Introduction signed by "F. B." [Francis Bragge], who was the author.

A Full Confutation of Witchcraft: More particularly of the Depositions against Jane Wenham, Lately Condemned for a Witch; at Hertford. In which the Modern Notions of Witches are overthrown, and the Ill Consequences of such Doctrines are exposed by Arguments; proving that, Witchcraft is Priestcraft.... In a Letter from a Physician in Hertfordshire, to his Friend in London. London, 1712.

The Impossibility of Witchcraft, Plainly Proving, From Scripture and Reason, That there never was a Witch; and that it is both Irrational and Impious to believe there ever was. In which the Depositions against Jane Wenham, Lately Try'd and Condemn'd for a Witch, at Hertford, are Confuted and Expos'd, London, 1712. 1st ed. in Brit. Mus.; 2d ed., containing additional material, in the Bodleian. The author of this pamphlet in his preface intimates that its substance had earlier been published by him in the Protestant Post Boy.

The Belief of Witchcraft Vindicated: proving from Scripture, there have been Witches; and from Reason, that there may be Such still. In answer to a late Pamphlet, Intituled, The Impossibility of Witchcraft ..., By G. R., A. M., London, 1712.

The Case of the Hertfordshire Witchcraft Consider'd. Being an Examination of a Book entitl'd, A Full and Impartial Account ..., London, 1712. Dedicated to Sir John Powell. In the Cornell copy of this booklet a manuscript note on the title-page, in an eighteenth century hand, ascribes it to "The Rector of Therfield in Hertfordshire, or his Curate," while at the end of the dedication what seems the same hand has signed the names, "Henry Stebbing or Thomas Sherlock." But Stebbing was in 1712 still a fellow at Cambridge, and Sherlock, later Bishop of London, was Master of the Temple and Chaplain to Queen Anne. See Dict. Nat. Biog.

A Defense of the Proceedings against Jane Wenham, wherein the Possibility and Reality of

Witchcraft are Demonstrated from Scripture.... In Answer to Two Pamphlets, Entituled: (I) The Impossibility of Witchcraft, etc. (II) A Full Confutation of Witchcraft, By Francis Bragge, A. B., ... London, 1712.

The Impossibility of Witchcraft Further Demonstrated, Both from Scripture and Reason ... with some Cursory Remarks on two trifling Pamphlets in Defence of the existence of Witches. By the Author of The Impossibility of Witchcraft, 1712. In the Bodleian.

Jane Wenham. Broadside. The writer of this leaflet claims to have transcribed his account from an account in "Judge Chancy's own hand". Chauncy was the justice of the peace who with Bragge stood behind the prosecution.

It is very hard to straighten out the authorship of these various pamphlets. The Rev. Mr. Bragge wrote several. The Rev. Mr. Gardiner and the Rev. Mr. Strutt, who were active in the case, may have written two of them. The topographer Gough, writing about 1780, declared that the late Dr. Stebbing had as a young man participated in the controversy. Francis Hutchinson was an interested spectator, but probably did not contribute to the literature of the subject.

A short secondary account is that of W. B. Gerish, A Hertfordshire Witch; or the Story of Jane Wenham, the "Wise Woman of Walkern."

In the Brit. Mus., Sloane MSS., 3,943, there is a continuation of the pamphlet discussion, based chiefly, however, upon Glanvill and other writers.

§ 10.—Criticism of the Northampton and Huntingdon Pamphlets of 1705 and 1716 (see ch. XIII, note 10).

An Account of The Tryals, Examination and Condemnation of Elinor Shaw and Mary Phillips (Two notorious Witches) on Wednesday the 7th of March 1705, for Bewitching a Woman, and two children.... With an Account of their strange Confessions. This is signed, at the end, "Ralph Davis, March 8, 1705." It was followed very shortly by a completer account, written after the execution, and entitled:

The Northamptonshire Witches, Being a true and faithful account of the Births, Educations, Lives, and Conversations of Elinor Shaw and Mary Phillips (The two notorious Witches) That were Executed at Northampton on Saturday, March the 17th, 1705 ... with their full Confession to the Minister, and last Dying Speeches at the place of Execution, the like never before heard of.... Communicated in a Letter last Post, from Mr. Ralph Davis of Northampton, to Mr. William Simons, Merchantt in London, London, 1705.

With these two pamphlets we wish to compare another, which was apparently published in 1716 and was entitled: The Whole Trial and Examination of Mrs. Mary Hicks and her Daughter Elizabeth, But of Nine Years of Age, who were Condemn'd the last Assizes held at Huntingdon for Witchcraft, and there Executed on Saturday, the 28th of July 1716 ... the like never heard before; their Behaviour with several Divines who came to converse with 'em whilst under their sentence of Death; and last Dying Speeches and Confession at the place of execution, London, 1716. There is a copy in the Bodleian Library.

The two Northamptonshire pamphlets and the Huntingdonshire pamphlet have been set by themselves because they appear to have been written by one hand. Moreover, it looks very much as if they were downright fabrications foisted upon the public by a man who had already in 1700 made to order an unhistorical pamphlet. To show this, it will be necessary to review briefly the facts about the Worcester pamphlet described above, § 4. What seems to be the second edition of a pamphlet entitled The full Tryalls, Examinations and Condemnations of Four Notorious Witches, At the Assizes held at Worcester on Tuseday the 4th of March, was published at London with the date 1700. It purports to tell the story of one of the cases that came up during Matthew Hopkins's career in 1645-1647. It has been universally accepted—even by Thomas Wright, Ashton, W. H. D. Adams, and Inderwick. An examination shows, however, that it was made over from the Chelmsford pamphlet of 1645. The author shows little ingenuity, for he steals not only the confessions of four witches at that trial, but their names as well. Rebecca West, Margaret Landis, Susan Cock, and Rose Hallybread had all been hanged at Chelmsford and could hardly have been rehanged at Worcester. Practically all that the writer of the Worcester pamphlet did was to touch over the confessions and add thrilling details about their executions.

Now, it looks very much as if the same writer had composed the Northamptonshire pamphlets of 1705 and the Huntingdonshire pamphlets of 1716. The verbal resemblances are nothing less than remarkable. The Worcester pamphlet, in its title, tells of "their Confessions and Last Dying

Speeches at the place of execution." The second of the two Northamptonshire pamphlets (the first was issued before the execution) speaks of "their full Confession to the Minister, and last Dying Speeches at the place of Execution." The Huntingdonshire pamphlet closes the title with "last Dying Speeches and Confession at the place of Execution." The Worcester pamphlet uses the phrase "with other amazing Particulars"; the Northamptonshire pamphlet the phrase "the particulars of their amazing Pranks." The Huntingdon pamphlet has in this case no similar phrase but the Huntingdon and Northamptonshire pamphlets have another phrase in common. The Northamptonshire pamphlet says: "the like never before heard of"; the Huntingdon pamphlet says: "the like never heard before."

These resemblances are in the titles. The Northampton and the fabricated Worcester pamphlets show other similarities in their accounts. The Northampton women were so "hardened in their Wickedness that they Publickly boasted that their Master (meaning the Devil) would not suffer them to be Executed but they found him a Lyer." The Worcester writer speaks of the "Devil who told them to the Last that he would secure them from Publick Punishment, but now too late they found him a Lyer as he was from the beginning of the World." In concluding their narratives the Northamptonshire and Worcestershire pamphleteers show an interesting similarity of treatment. The Northampton witches made a "howling and lamentable noise" on receiving their sentences, the Worcester women made a "yelling and howling at their executions."

These resemblances may be fairly characterized as striking. If it be asked whether the phrases quoted are not conventional in witch pamphlets, the answer must be in the negative. So far as the writer knows, these phrases occur in no other of the fifty or more witch pamphlets. The word "notorious," which occurs in the titles of the Worcester and Northampton pamphlets, is a common one and would signify nothing. The other phrases mentioned are characteristic and distinctive. This similarity suggests that the three pamphlets were written by the same hand. Since we know that one of the three is a fabrication, we are led to suspect the credibility of the other two.

There are, indeed, other reasons for doubting the historicity of these two. A close scrutiny of the Northampton pamphlet shows that the witchcrafts there described have the peculiar characteristics of the witchcrafts in the palmy days of Matthew Hopkins and that the wording of the descriptions is much the same. The Northampton pamphlet tells of a "tall black man," who appeared to the two women. A tall black man had appeared to Rebecca West at Chelmsford in 1645. A much more important point is that the prisoners at Northampton had been watched at night in order to keep their imps from coming in. This night-watching was a process that had never, so far as our records go, been used since the Hopkins alarm, of which it had been the characteristic feature. Were there no other resemblance between the Northampton cases and those at Chelmsford, this similarity would alone lead us to suspect the credibility of the Northampton pamphlet. Unfortunately the indiscreet writer of the Northampton narrative lets other phrases belonging to 1645 creep into his account.

When the Northampton women were watched, a "little white thing about the bigness of a Cat" had appeared. But a "white thing about the bignesse of a Cat" had appeared to the watchers at

Chelmsford in 1645. This is not all. The Northampton witches are said to have killed their victims by roasting and pricking images, a charge which had once been common, but which, so far as the writer can recall, had not been used since the Somerset cases of 1663. It was a charge very commonly used against the Chelmsford witches whom Matthew Hopkins prosecuted. Moreover the Northampton witches boasted that "their Master would not suffer them to be executed." No Chelmsford witch had made that boast; but Mr. Lowes, who was executed at Bury St. Edmunds (the Bury trial was closely connected with that at Chelmsford, so closely that the writer who had read of one would probably have read of the other), had declared that he had a charm to keep him from the gallows.

It will be seen that these are close resemblances both in characteristic features and in wording. But the most perfect resemblance is in a confession. The two Northampton women describing their imps—creatures, by the way, that had figured largely in the Hopkins trials—said that "if the Imps were not constantly imploy'd to do Mischief, they [the witches] had not their healths; but when they were imploy'd they were very Heathful and Well." This was almost exactly what Anne Leech had confessed at Chelmsford. Her words were: "And that when This Examinant did not send and employ them abroad to do mischief, she had not her health, but when they were imploy'd, she was healthfull and well."

We cannot point out the same similarity between the Huntingdonshire witchcrafts of 1716 and the Chelmsford cases. The narrative of the Huntingdon case is, however, somewhat remarkable. Mr. Hicks was taking his nine-year-old daughter to Ipswich one day, when she, seeing a sail at sea, took a "basin of water," stirred it up, and thereby provoked a storm that was like to have sunk the ship, had not the father made the child cease. On the way home, the two passed a "very fine Field of Corn." "Quoth the child again, 'Father, I can consume all this Corn in the twinkling of an Eye.' The Father supposing it not in her Power to do so, he bid to shew her infernal skill." The child did so, and presently "all the Corn in the Field became Stubble." He questioned her and found that she had learned witchcraft from her mother. The upshot of it was that at Mr. Hicks's instance his wife and child were prosecuted and hanged. The story has been called remarkable. Yet it is not altogether unique. In 1645 at Bury St. Edmunds just after the Chelmsford trial there were eighteen witches condemned, and one of them, it will be remembered, was Parson Lowes of Brandeston in Suffolk, who confessed that "he bewitched a ship near Harwidge; so that with the extreme tempestuous Seas raised by blusterous windes the said ship was cast away, wherein were many passengers, who were by this meanes swallowed up by the merciless waves." It will be observed that the two stories are not altogether similar. The Huntingdon narrative is a better tale, and it would be hardly safe to assert that it drew its inspiration from the earlier story. Yet, when it is remembered how unusual is the story in English witch-lore, the supposition gains in probability. There is a further resemblance in the accounts. The Hicks child had bewitched a field of corn. One of the Bury witches, in the narrative which tells of parson Lowes, "confessed that She usually bewitcht standing corne, whereby there came great loss to the owners thereof." The resemblance is hardly close enough to merit notice in itself. When taken, however, in connection with the other resemblances it gives cumulative force to the supposition that the writer of the Huntingdon pamphlet had gone to the narratives of the Hopkins cases for his sources.

There are, however, other reasons for doubting the Huntingdon story. A writer in Notes and Queries, 2d series, V, 503-504, long ago questioned the narrative because of the mention of a "Judge Wilmot," and showed that there was no such judge on the bench before 1755. An examination of the original pamphlet makes it clear, however, that in this form the objection is worth nothing. The tract speaks only of a "Justice Wilmot," who, from the wording of the narrative, would seem to have conducted the examination preliminary to the assizes as a justice of the peace would. A justice of the peace would doubtless, however, have belonged to some Huntingdonshire county family. Now, the writer has searched the various records and histories of Huntingdonshire—unfortunately they are but too few—and among the several hundred Huntingdonshire names he has found no Wilmots (and, for that matter, no Hickes either). This would seem to make the story more improbable.

In an earlier number of Notes and Queries (1st series, V, 514), James Crossley, whose authority as to matters relating to witchcraft is of the highest, gives cogent reasons why the Huntingdonshire narrative could not be true. He recalls the fact that Hutchinson, who made a chronological table of cases, published his work in 1718. Now Hutchinson had the help of two chief-justices, Parker and King, and of Chief-Baron Bury in collecting his cases; and yet he says that the last execution for the crime in England was in 1682. Crossley makes the further strong point that the case of Jane Wenham in 1712 attracted wide attention and was the occasion of numerous pamphlets. "It is scarcely possible," he continues, "that in four years after two persons, one only nine years old, ... should have been tried and executed for witchcraft without public attention being called to the circumstance." He adds that neither the Historical Register for 1716 nor the files of two London newspapers for that year, though they enumerate other convictions on the circuit, record the supposed cases.

It will be seen that exactly the same arguments apply to the Northampton trials of 1705. Hutchinson had been at extraordinary pains to find out not only about Jane Wenham, but about the Moordike case of 1702. It is inconceivable that he should have quite overlooked the execution of two women at Northampton.

We have observed that the Northampton, Huntingdon, and Worcester pamphlets have curious resemblances in wording to one another (resemblances that point to a common authorship), that the Worcester narrative can be proved to be fictitious, and that the Huntingdon narrative almost certainly belongs in the same category. We have shown, further, that the Northampton and Huntingdon stories present features of witchcraft characteristic of the Chelmsford and Bury cases of 1645, from the first of which the material of the Worcester pamphlet is drawn; and this fact points not only to the common authorship of the three tracts, but to the imaginary character of the Huntingdon and Northampton cases.

Against these facts there is to be presented what at first blush seems a very important piece of evidence. In the Northamptonshire Historical Collections, 1st series (Northampton, 1896), there is a chapter on witchcraft in Northamptonshire, copied from the Northamptonshire Handbook for

1867. That chapter goes into the trials of 1705 in detail, making copious extracts from the pamphlets. In a footnote the writers say: "To show that the burning actually took place in 1705, it may be important to mention that there is an item of expense entered in the overseers' accounts for St. Giles parish for faggots bought for the purpose." This in itself seems convincing. It seems to dispose of the whole question at once. There is, however, one fact that instantly casts a doubt upon this seemingly conclusive evidence. In England, witches were hanged, not burned. There are not a half-dozen recorded exceptions to this rule. Mother Lakeland in 1645 was burned. That is easy to explain. Mother Lakeland had by witchcraft killed her husband. Burning was the method of execution prescribed by English law for a woman who killed her husband. The other cases where burnings are said to have taken place were almost certainly cases that came under this rule. But it does not seem possible that the Northampton cases came under the rule. The two women seem to have had no husbands. "Ralph Davis," the ostensible writer of the account, who professed to have known them from their early years, and who was apparently glad to defame them in every possible way, accused them of loose living, but not of adultery, as he would certainly have done, had he conceived of them as married. It is hard to avoid the conclusion that they could not have been burned.

There is a more decisive answer to this argument for the authenticity of the pamphlet. The supposed confirmation of it in the St. Giles parish register is probably a blunder. The Reverend R. M. Serjeantson of St. Peter's Rectory has been kind enough to examine for the writer the parish register of St. Giles Church. He writes: "The St. Giles accounts briefly state that wood was bought from time to time—probably for melting the lead. There is no mention of faggots nor witches in the Church wardens' overseers-for-the-poor accounts. I carefully turned out the whole contents of the parish chest." Mr. Serjeantson adds at the close this extract: "1705 P'd for wood 5/ For taking up the old lead 5/." It goes without saying that Mr. Serjeantson's examination does not prove that there never was a mention of the faggots bought for burning witches; but, when all the other evidence is taken into consideration, this negative evidence does establish a very strong presumption to that effect. Certainly the supposed passage from the overseers' accounts can no longer be used to confirm the testimony of the pamphlet. It looks very much as if the compilers of the Northamptonshire Handbook for 1867 had been careless in their handling of records.

It seems probable, then, that the pamphlet of 1705 dealing with the execution of Mary Phillips and Elinor Shaw is a purely fictitious narrative. The matter derives its importance from the fact that, if the two executions in 1705 be disproved, the last known execution in England is put back to 1682, ten years before the Salem affair in Massachusetts. This would of course have some bearing on a recent contention (G. L. Kittredge, "Notes on Witchcraft," Am. Antiq. Soc., Proc., XVIII), that "convictions and executions for witchcraft occurred in England after they had come to an end in Massachusetts."

B.—LIST OF PERSONS SENTENCED TO DEATH FOR WITCHCRAFT DURING THE REIGN OF JAMES I.: 1.—Charged with Causing Death.

1603. Yorkshire.
Mary Pannel.
1606. Hertford.
Johanna Harrison and her daughter.
1612. Northampton.
Helen Jenkinson, Arthur Bill, Mary Barber.
1612. Lancaster.
Chattox, Eliz. Device, James Device, Alice Nutter, Katherine Hewitt, Anne Redfearne.
1612. York.
Jennet Preston.
1613. Bedford.
Mother Sutton and Mary Sutton.
1616. Middlesex.
Elizabeth Rutter.
1616. Middlesex.
Joan Hunt.
1619. Lincoln.
Margaret and Philippa Flower.
1621. Edmonton.
Elizabeth Sawyer.

C.—LIST OF CASES OF WITCHCRAFT, 1558-1718, WITH REFERENCES TO SOURCES AND LITERATURE.[1]

1558. John Thirkle, "taylour, detected of conjuringe," to be examined. Acts of Privy Council, n. s., VII, 6. ---- Several persons in London charged with conjuration to be sent to the Bishop of London for examination. Ibid., 22.

1559. Westminster. Certain persons examined on suspicion, including probably Lady Frances Throgmorton. Cal. St. P., Dom., 1547-1580, 142.

c. 1559. Lady Chandos's daughter accused and imprisoned with George Throgmorton. Brit Mus., Add. MSS., 32,091, fol. 176.

1560. Kent. Mother Buske of St. John's suspected by the church authorities. Visitations of Canterbury in Archæologia Cantiana, XXVI, 31.

1561. Coxe, alias Devon, a Romish priest, examined for magic and conjuration, and for celebrating mass. Cal. St. P., Dom., 1547-1580, 173.

---- London. Ten men brought before the queen and council on charge of "trespass, contempt, conjuration and sorceries." Punished with the pillory and required to renounce such practices for the future. From an extract quoted in Brit. Mus., Sloane MSS., 3,943, fol. 19.

1565. Dorset. Agnes Mondaye to be apprehended for bewitching Mistress Chettell. Acts P. C., n. s., VII, 200-201.

1565-1573. Durham. Jennet Pereson accused to the church authorities. Depositions ... from ... Durham (Surtees Soc.), 99.

1566. Chelmsford, Essex. Mother Waterhouse hanged; Alice Chandler hanged, probably at this time; Elizabeth Francis probably acquitted. The examination and confession of certaine Wytches at Chensforde. For the cases of Elizabeth Francis and Alice Chandler see also A detection of damnable driftes, A iv, A v, verso.

---- Essex. "Boram's wief" probably examined by the archdeacon. W. H. Hale, A Series of Precedents and Proceedings in Criminal Causes, 1475-1640, extracted from the Act Books of Ecclesiastical Courts in the Diocese of London (London, 1847), 147.

1569. Lyme, Dorset. Ellen Walker accused. Roberts, Southern Counties, 523.

1570. Essex. Malter's wife of Theydon Mount and Anne Vicars of Navestock examined by Sir Thomas Smith. John Strype, Life of Sir Thomas Smith (ed. of Oxford, 1820), 97-100.

1570-1571. Canterbury. Several witches imprisoned. Mother Dungeon presented by the grand jury. Hist. MSS. Comm. Reports, IX, pt. 1, 156 b; Wm. Welfitt, "Civis," Minutes collected from the Ancient Records of Canterbury (Canterbury, 1801-1802), no. VI.

---- —— Folkestone, Kent. Margaret Browne, accused of "unlawful practices," banished from town for seven years, and to be whipped at the cart's tail if found within six or seven miles of town. S. J. Mackie, Descriptive and Historical Account of Folkestone (Folkestone, 1883), 319.

1574. Westwell, Kent. "Old Alice" [Norrington?] arraigned and convicted. Reginald Scot, Discoverie of Witchcraft, 130-131.

---- Middlesex. Joan Ellyse of Westminster convicted on several indictments for witchcraft and sentenced to be hanged. Middlesex County Records, I, 84.

c. 1574. Jane Thorneton accused by Rachel Pinder, who however confessed to fraud. Discloysing of a late counterfeyted possession.

1575. Burntwood, Staffordshire. Mother Arnold hanged at Barking. From the title of a pamphlet mentioned by Lowndes: The Examination and Confession of a notorious Witch named Mother Arnold, alias Whitecote, alias Glastonbury, at the Assise of Burntwood in July, 1574; who was hanged for Witchcraft at Barking, 1575. Mrs. Linton, Witch Stories, 153, says that many were hanged at this time, but I cannot find authority for the statement.

---- Middlesex. Elizabeth Ducke of Harmondsworth acquitted. Middlesex County Records, I, 94.

---- Great Yarmouth, Norfolk. Katharine Smythe acquitted. Henry Harrod, "Notes on the Records of the Corporation of Great Yarmouth," in Norfolk Archæology, IV, 248.

1577. Seaford, Sussex. Joan Wood presented by the grand jury. M. A. Lower, "Memorials of Seaford," in Sussex Archæological Soc., Collections, VII, 98.

---- Middlesex. Helen Beriman of Laleham acquitted. Middlesex County Records, I, 103.

---- Essex. Henry Chittam of Much Barfield to be tried for coining false money and conjuring. Acts P. C., n. s., IX, 391; X, 8, 62.

1578. Prescall, Sanford, and "one Emerson, a preiste," suspected of conjuration against the queen. The first two committed. Id., X, 382; see also 344, 373.

---- Evidence of the use of sorcery against the queen discovered. Cal. St. P., Spanish, 1568-1579, 611; see also note to Ben Jonson's Masque of Queenes (London, Shakespeare Soc., 1848), 71.

---- Sussex. "One Tree, bailiff of Lewes, and one Smith of Chinting" to be examined. Acts P. C., n. s., X, 220.

1579. Chelmsford, Essex. Three women executed. Mother Staunton released because "no manslaughter objected against her." A Detection of damnable driftes.

---- Abingdon, Berks. Four women hanged; at least two others and probably more were apprehended. A Rehearsall both straung and true of ... acts committed by Elisabeth Stile ...; Acts P. C., n. s., XI, 22; Scot, Discoverie of Witchcraft, 10, 51, 543.

---- Certain persons suspected of sorcery to be examined by the Bishop of London. Acts P. C., n. s., XI, 36.

---- Salop, Worcester, and Montgomery. Samuel Cocwra paid for "searching for certen persons suspected for conjuracion." Ibid., 292.

---- Southwark. Simon Pembroke, a conjurer, brought to the parish church of St. Saviour's to be tried by the "ordinarie judge for those parties," but falls dead before the opening of the trial. Holinshed, Chronicles (ed. of 1586-1587), III, 1271.

---- Southampton. Widow Walker tried by the leet jury, outcome unknown. J. S. Davies, History of Southampton (Southampton, 1883), 236.

1579-1580. Shropshire. Mother Garve punished in the corn market. Owen and Blakeway, History of Shrewsbury, I, 562.

1580. Stanhope, Durham. Ann Emerson accused by the church officials. Injunctions ... of ... Bishop of Durham (Surtees Soc.), 126.

---- Bucks. John Coleman and his wife examined by four justices of the peace at the command of the privy council. They were probably released. Acts P. C., n. s., XI, 427; XII, 29.

---- Kent. Several persons to be apprehended for conjuration. Id., XII, 21-23.

---- Somerset. Henry Harrison and Thomas Wadham, suspected of conjuration, to appear before the privy council. Ibid., 22-23.

---- Somerset. Henry Fize of Westpenner, detected in conjuration, brought before the privy council. Ibid., 34.

---- Essex. "Sondery persons" charged with sorceries and conjuration. Acts P. C., XII, 29, 34.

1581. Randoll and four others accused for "conjuring to know where treasure was hid in the earth." Randoll and three others found guilty. Randoll alone executed. Holinshed, Chronicles (London, 1808), IV, 433.

1581. Padstow, Cornwall. Anne Piers accused of witchcraft. Examination of witnesses. Cal. St. P., Dom., 1581-1590, 29. See also Acts P. C., n. s., XIII, 228.

1581. Rochester, Kent. Margaret Simmons acquitted. Scot, Discoverie, 5.

1581-82. Colchester, Essex. Annis Herd accused before the "spiritual Courte." Witches taken at St. Oses, 1582.

1582. St. Osyth, Essex. Sixteen accused, one of whom was a man. How many were executed uncertain. It seems to have been a tradition that thirteen were executed. Scot wrote that seventeen or eighteen were executed. Witches taken at St. Oses, 1582; Scot, Discoverie, 543.

1582 (or before). "T. E., Maister of Art and practiser both of physicke, and also in times past, of certeine vaine sciences," condemned for conjuration, but reprieved. Scot, Discoverie, 466-469.

1582. Middlesex. Margery Androwes of Clerkenwell held in bail. Middlesex County Records, I, 133.

1582. Durham. Alison Lawe of Hart compelled to do penance. Denham Tracts (Folk-Lore Soc.), II, 332.

1582. Kent. Goodwife Swane of St. John's suspected by the church authorities. Archæol. Cant., XXVI, 19.

1582-83. Nottingham. A certain Batte examined before the "Meare" of Nottingham. Hist. MSS. Comm. Reports, XII, pt. 4, 147.

1582-83. King's Lynn. Mother Gabley probably hanged. Excerpt from parish register of Wells in Norfolk, in the Gentleman's Magazine, LXII (1792), 904.

1583. Kingston-upon-Hull, Yorkshire. Three women tried, one sentenced to a year's imprisonment and the pillory. J. J. Sheahan, History of Kingston-upon-Hull (London, 1864), 86.

1583. Colchester, Essex. Two women sentenced to a year in prison and to four appearances in the pillory. E. L. Cutts, Colchester (London, 1888), 151. Henry Harrod, Report on the Records of Colchester (Colchester, 1865), 17; App., 14.

1583. St. Peter's, Kent. Ellen Bamfield suspected by the church authorities. Archæol. Cant., XXVI, 45.

1584. Great Yarmouth, Norfolk. Elizabeth Butcher (punished before) and Joan Lingwood condemned to be hanged. C. J. Palmer, History of Great Yarmouth, I, 273.

1584. Staffordshire. An indictment preferred against Jeffrey Leach. Cal. St. P., Dom., 1581-1590, 206.

1584. "The oulde witche of Ramsbury" and several other "oulde witches and sorcerers" suspected. Cal. St. P., Dom., 1581-1590, 220.

1584. York. Woman, indicted for witchcraft and "high treason touching the supremacy," condemned. Cal. St. P., Dom., Add. 1580-1625, 120-121.

1584. Middlesex. Elizabeth Bartell of St. Martin's-in-the-Fields acquitted. Middlesex County Records, I, 145.

1585. Middlesex. Margaret Hackett of Stanmore executed. From titles of two pamphlets mentioned by Lowndes, The severall Facts of Witchcrafte approved on Margaret Haskett ... 1585, and An Account of Margaret Hacket, a notorious Witch ... 1585.

1585. Middlesex. Joan Barringer of "Harroweelde" (Harrow Weald) acquitted. Middlesex County Records, I, 157.

1585. Dorset. John Meere examined. Cal. St. P., Dom., 1581-90, 246-247.

1585-86. Alnwick, Northumberland. Two men and two women committed to prison on suspicion of killing a sheriff. Denham Tracts, II, 332; Cal. S. P., Dom., Add. 1580-1625, 168.

1586. Eckington, Derbyshire. Margaret Roper accused. Discharged. Harsnett, Discovery of the Fraudulent Practises of John Darrel, 310.

1586. Faversham, Kent. Jone Cason [Carson] tried before the mayor, executed. Holinshed, Chronicles (1586-1587), III, 1560.

1587. Great Yarmouth, Norfolk. Helena Gill indicted. C. J. Palmer, History of Great Yarmouth, 273. H. Harrod in Norfolk Archæology, IV, 248, assigns this to 1597, but it is probably a mistake.

c. 1588. A woman at R. H. said to have been imprisoned and to have died before the assizes. Gifford, Dialogue (London, 1603), C.

1589. Chelmsford, Essex. Three women hanged. The apprehension and confession of three notorious Witches.

1589. Several persons to be examined about their dealings in conjuration with an Italian friar. Acts P. C., n. s., XVII, 31-32.

1589. Mrs. Deir brought into question for sorcery against the queen. Charge dismissed. Strype, Annals of the Reformation (London, 1709-1731), IV, 7-8.

1590. Mrs. Dewse suspected of attempting to make use of conjurors. Cal. St. P., Dom., 1581-1590, 644.

1590. John Bourne, a "sorcerer and seducer," arrested. Acts P. C., n. s., XVIII, 373.

1590. Berwick. A Scottish witch imprisoned. John Scott, History of Berwick (London, 1888), 180; Archæologia, XXX, 172.

1590. Norfolk. Margaret Grame accused before justice of the peace. Neighbors petition in her behalf. Hist. MSS. Comm. Reports, Various, II, 243-244.

1590. King's Lynn. Margaret Read burnt. Benjamin Mackerell, History and Antiquities ... of King's Lynn, (London, 1738), 231.

1590. Edmonton, Middlesex. Certain men taken for witchcraft and conjuring. Bloodhound used in pursuit of them. Cal. St. P., Dom., 1581-1590, 689.

1590-91. Hertfordshire. Indictment of Joan White for killing. Hertfordshire County Session Rolls, I, 4.

1591. John Prestall suspected. Cal. St. P., Dom., 1591-1594, 17-19.

1591. Middlesex. Stephen Trefulback of Westminster given penalty of statute, i. e., probably pillory. Middlesex County Records, I, 197.

1592. Colchester, Essex. Margaret Rand indicted by grand jury. Brit. Mus., Stowe MSS., 840, fol. 42.

1592. Yorkshire. "Sara B. de C." examined. West, Symboleography, pt. II (London, 1594), ed. of 1611, fol. 134 verso (reprinted in County Folk-Lore, Folk-Lore Soc., 135). Whether the "S. B. de C. in comit. H." whose indictment in the same year is printed also by West may possibly be the same woman can not be determined.

1592. Yorkshire. Margaret L. de A. examined. Ibid.

1593. Warboys, Huntingdonshire. Mother, daughter and father Samuel executed. The most strange and admirable discoverie of the three Witches of Warboys. 1593. See also John Darrel, A Detection of that sinnful ... discours of Samuel Harshnet, 20-21, 39-40, 110. Harsnett, Discovery of the Fraudulent Practises of John Darrel, 93, 97.

1594. Jane Shelley examined for using sorcerers to find the time of the queen's death. Hist. MSS. Comm., Cecil., pt. V, 25.

1595. St. Peter's Kent. Two women presented by the church authorities. Still suspected in 1599. Archæol. Cant., XXVI, 46.

1595. Woodbridge, Suffolk. Witches put in the pillory. County Folk-Lore, Suffolk (Folk-Lore Soc., London, 1895), 193.

1595. Jane Mortimer pardoned for witchcraft. Bodleian, Tanner MSS., CLXVIII, fol. 29.

1595. Near Bristol, Somerset. Severall committed for the Earl of Derby's death. Hist. MSS. Comm. Reports, IV, app., 366 b. See also E. Baines's Lancaster (London, 1870), 273-274 and note.

1595. Barnet and Braynford, Herts. Three witches executed. From title of pamphlet mentioned by Lowndes, The Arraignment and Execution of 3 detestable Witches, John Newell, Joane his wife, and Hellen Calles: two executed at Barnett and one at Braynford, 1 Dec. 1595.

1596 (or before). Derbyshire. Elizabeth Wright (mother of Alice Gooderidge) several times summoned before the justice of the peace on suspicion. The most wonderfull and true Storie of ... Alse Gooderidge (1597).

1596. Burton-upon-Trent, Derbyshire. Alice Gooderidge tried at Derby, convicted. Died in prison. Harsnett, Discovery of the fraudulent Practises of John Darrel; John Darrel, Detection of that sinnful ... discours of Samuel Harshnet, 38, 40; The most wonderfull and true Storie of ... Alse Gooderidge (1597).

1596-1597. Leicester. Mother Cooke hanged. Mary Bateson, Records of the Borough of Leicester (Cambridge, 1899), III, 335.

1596-1597. Lancaster. Hartley condemned and executed. John Darrel, True Narration (in the Somers Tracts, III), 175, 176; George More, A True Discourse concerning the certaine possession ... of 7 persons ... in Lancashire, 18-22; John Darrel, Detection of that sinnful ... discours of Samuel Harshnet, 40.

1597. Nottingham. Thirteen or more accused by Somers, at least eight of whom were put in gaol. All but two discharged. Alice Freeman tried at the assizes and finally acquitted. John Darrel, Detection of that sinnful ... discours of Samuel Harshnet, 109-111; An Apologie or defence of the possession of William Sommers, L-L 3; Samuel Harsnett, Discovery of the Fraudulent Practises of John Darrel, 5, 102, 140-141, 320-322.

1597. St. Lawrence, Kent. Sibilla Ferris suspected by the church authorities. Archæol. Cant., XXVI, 12.

1597. Nottingham. William Somers accused of witchcraft as a ruse to get him into the house of correction. Darrel, A True Narration of the ... Vexation ... of seven persons in Lancashire, in Somers Tracts, III, 184; also his Brief Apologie (1599), 17.

1597. Yorkshire. Elizabeth Melton of Collingham condemned, pardoned. Cal. St. P., Dom., 1595-1597, 400.

1597. Lancashire. Alice Brerely of Castleton condemned, pardoned. Ibid., 406.

1597. Middlesex. Agnes Godfrey of Enfield held by the justice of the peace on £10 bail. Middlesex County Records, I, 237.

1597. St. Andrew's in Holborne, Middlesex. Josia Ryley arraigned. "Po se mortuus in facie curie," i. e. Posuit se moriturum. Ibid., 225.

1597. Middlesex. Helen Spokes of St. Giles-in-the-Fields acquitted. Ibid., 239.

1598. Berwick. Richard Swynbourne's wife accused. John Scott, History of Berwick (London, 1888), 180.

1598. St. Peter's, Kent. Two women suspected by the church officials; one of them presented again the next year. Archæol. Cant., XXVI, 46.

1598. King's Lynn. Elizabeth Housegoe executed. Mackerell, History and Antiquities of King's Lynn, 232.

1599. Bury St. Edmunds, Suffolk. Jone Jordan of Shadbrook tried. Darrel, A Survey of Certaine Dialogical Discourses, 54.

1599. Bury St. Edmunds, Suffolk. Joane Nayler tried. Ibid.

1599. Bury St. Edmunds, Suffolk. Oliffe Bartham of Shadbrook executed. The Triall of Maist. Dorrel, 92-98.

1599. London. Anne Kerke of Bokes-wharfe executed at "Tiburn." The Triall of Maist. Dorrel, 99-103.

1600. Hertford. A "notable witch" committed to the gaol at Hertford. Hist. MSS. Comm. Reports, Cecil MSS., pt. X, 310.

1600. Rosa Bexwell pardoned. Bodleian, Tanner MSS., CLXVIII, fol. 104.

1600. Norfolk. Margaret Fraunces committed for a long time. Probably released by justice of the peace on new evidence. Hist. MSS. Comm. Reports, X, pt. II (Gawdy MSS.), 71. See also below, pp. 400, 401.

1600. Ipswich, Suffolk. Several conjurers suspected. Cal. St. P., Dom., 1598-1601, 523.

1601. Bishop Burton, York. Two women apprehended for bewitching a boy. Brit. Mus., Add. MSS., 32,496, fol. 42 b.

1601. Middlesex. Richard Nelson of St. Katharine's arraigned. Middlesex County Records, I, 260.

1601. Nottingham. Ellen Bark presented at the sessions. Records of the Borough of Nottingham, IV, 260-261.

1602. Middlesex. Elizabeth Roberts of West Drayton indicted on three charges, acquitted. Middlesex County Records, I, 212.

1602. Saffron Walden, Essex. Alice Bentley tried before the quarter sessions. Case probably dismissed. Darrel, A Survey of Certaine Dialogical Discourses, 54.

temp. Eliz. Northfleet, Kent. Pardon to Alice S. for bewitching a cow and pigs. Bodleian, Rawlinson MSS., C 404, fol. 205 b.

temp. Eliz. Woman condemned to prison and pillory. Gifford, Dialogue concerning Witches (1603), L 4 verso.

temp. Eliz. Cambridge. Two women perhaps hanged at this time. Henry More, Antidote to Atheisme, III. But see 1605, Cambridge.

temp. Eliz. Mother W. of W. H. said to have been executed. Gifford, Dialogue concerning Witches, D 4 verso—E.

temp. Eliz. Mother W. of Great T. said to have been hanged. Ibid., C 4.

temp. Eliz. Woman said to have been hanged. Ibid., L 3-L 3 verso.

temp. Eliz. Two women said to have been hanged. Ibid., I 3 verso.

1602-1603. London. Elizabeth Jackson sentenced, for bewitching Mary Glover, to four appearances in the pillory and a year in prison. John Swan, A True and Breife Report of Mary Glover's Vexation; E. Jorden, A briefe discourse of ... the Suffocation of the Mother, 1603; also a MS., Marie Glover's late woefull case ... upon occasion of Doctor Jordens discourse of the Mother, wherein hee covertly taxeth, first the Phisitiones which judged her sicknes a vexation of Sathan and consequently the sentence of Lawe and proceeding against the Witche who was discovered to be a meanes thereof, with A defence of the truthe against D. J. his scandalous Impugnations, by Stephen Bradwell, 1603. Brit. Mus., Sloane MSS., 831. An account by Lewis Hughes, appended to his Certaine Grievances (1641-2), is quoted by Sinclar, Satan's Invisible World Discovered (Edinburgh, 1685), 95-100; and hence Burton (The Kingdom of Darkness) and Hutchinson (Historical Essay concerning Witchcraft) assign a wrong date.

1603. Yorkshire. Mary Pannel executed for killing in 1593. Mayhall, Annals of Yorkshire (London, 1878), I, 58. See also E. Fairfax, A Discourse of Witchcraft, 179-180.

1603. Great Yarmouth, Norfolk. Ales Moore in gaol on suspicion. C. J. Palmer, History of Great Yarmouth, II, 70.

1604. Wooler, Northumberland. Katherine Thompson and Anne Nevelson proceeded against by the Vicar General of the Bishop of Durham. Richardson, Table Book, I, 245; J. Raine, York Depositions, 127, note.

1605. Cambridge. A witch alarm. Letters of Sir Thomas Lake to Viscount Cranbourne, January 18, 1604/5, and of Sir Edward Coke to Viscount Craybourne, Jan. 29, 1604/5, both in Brit. Mus., Add. MSS., 6177, fol. 403. This probably is the affair referred to in Cal. St. P., Dom., 1603-1610, 218. Nor is it impossible that Henry More had this affair in mind when he told of two women who were executed in Cambridge in the time of Elizabeth (see above, temp. Eliz., Cambridge) and was two or three years astray in his reckoning.

1605. Doncaster, York. Jone Jurdie of Rossington examined. Depositions in Gentleman's Magazine, 1857, pt. I, 593-595.

1606. Louth, Lincolnshire. "An Indictment against a Witche." R. W. Goulding, Louth Old Corporation Records (Louth, 1891), 54.

1606. Hertford. Johanna Harrison and her daughter said to have been executed. This rests upon the pamphlet The Most Cruell and Bloody Murther, ... See appendix A, § 3.

1606. Richmond, Yorkshire. Ralph Milner ordered by quarter sessions to make his submission at Mewkarr Church. North Riding Record Society, I, 58.

1607. Middlesex. Alice Bradley of Hampstead arraigned on four bills, acquitted. Middlesex County Records, II, 8.

1607. Middlesex. Rose Mersam of Whitecrosse Street acquitted. Ibid., II, 20.

1607. Bakewell, Derby. Several women said to have been executed here. See Robert Simpson, A Collection of Fragments illustrative of the History and Antiquities of Derby (Derby, 1826), 90; Glover, History of Derby (ed. Thos. Noble, 1833), pt. I, vol. II, p. 613; J. C. Cox, Three Centuries of Derbyshire Annals, II, 88. For what purports to be a detailed account of the affair see W. Andrews, Bygone Derbyshire, 180-184.

1607-11. Rye, Sussex. Two women condemned by local authorities probably discharged upon interference from London. Hist. MSS. Comm. Reports, XIII, pt. 4, 136-137, 139-140, 147-148.

1608. Simon Read pardoned. Cal. St. P., Dom., 1603-1610, 406.

1610. Norfolk. Christian[a] Weech, pardoned in 1604, now again pardoned. Ibid., 96, 598. Was this the Christiana Weekes of Cleves Pepper, Wilts, who in 1651 and 1654 was again and again accused of telling where lost goods were? See Hist. MSS. Comm. Reports, Various, I, 120.

1610. Middlesex. Agnes Godfrey of Enfield, with four bills against her, acquitted on three, found guilty of killing. File containing sentence lost. Middlesex County Records, II, 57-58. Acquitted again in 1621. Ibid., 79, 80.

1610. Leicestershire. Depositions taken by the sheriff concerning Randall and other witches. Hist. MSS. Comm. Reports, XII, pt. 4 (MSS. of the Duke of Rutland), I, 422.

1611. Carnarvon. Story of witchcraft "committed on six young maids." Privy Council orders the Bishop of Bangor and the assize judges to look into it. Cal. St. P., Dom., 1611-1618, 53.

1611. Wm. Bate, indicted twenty years before for practising invocation, etc., for finding treasure, pardoned. Ibid., 29.

1611. Thirsk, Yorkshire. Elizabeth Cooke presented by quarter sessions for slight crime related to witchcraft. North Riding Record Soc., I, 213.

1612. Lancaster. Margaret Pearson, who in 1612 was sentenced to a year's imprisonment and the pillory, had been twice tried before, once for killing, and once for bewitching a neighbor. Potts, Wonderfull Discoverie of Witches in the countie of Lancaster (Chetham Soc., 1845).

1612. Lancaster. Ten persons of Pendle sentenced to death, one to a year's imprisonment; eight acquitted including three women of Salmesbury. Potts, Wonderfull Discoverie of Witches, Chetham Soc., 1845. But cf. Cooper's words (Mystery of Witchcraft, 1617), 15.

1612. York. Jennet Preston sentenced to death. Potts, Wonderfull Discoverie of Witches.

1612. Northampton. At least four women and one man hanged. Many others accused, one of whom died in gaol. The Witches of Northamptonshire, 1612; also Brit Mus., Sloane MSS., 972, fol. 7.

1613. Bedford. Mother Sutton and Mary Sutton, her daughter, of Milton Miles hanged. Witches Apprehended, Examined and Executed, 1613. See app. A, § 3, for mention of another pamphlet on the same subject, A Booke of the Wytches lately condemned and executed. See also The Wonderful Discoverie of ... Margaret and Phillip Flower, preface, and Richard Bernard, Guide to Grand Jurymen, iii.

1613. Wilts. Margaret Pilton of Warminster, accused at quarter sessions, probably released. Hist. MSS. Comm. Reports, Various, I, 86-87.

1614. Middlesex. Dorothy Magick of St. Andrew's in Holborn sentenced to a year's imprisonment and four appearances in the pillory. Middlesex County Records, II, 91, 218.

1615. Middlesex. Joan Hunt of Hampstead, who had been, along with her husband, twice tried and acquitted, and whose accuser had been ordered to ask forgiveness, sentenced to be hanged. Middlesex County Records, II, lii, 95, 110, 217-218.

1616. Leicester. Nine women hanged on the accusation of a boy. Six others accused, one of whom died in prison, five released after the king's examination of the boy. Robert Heyrick's letters from Leicester, July 16 and October 15, 1616, reprinted in the Annual Register, 1800, p. 405. See also Cal. S. P., Dom., 1611-1618, 398, and William Kelly, Royal Progresses in Leicester (Leicester, 1855), pt. II, 15.

1616. King's Lynn, Norfolk. Mary Smith hanged. Alexander Roberts, Treatise of Witchcraft (London, 1616); Mackerell, History and Antiquities of King's Lynn, 233.

1616. Middlesex. Elizabeth Rutter of Finchley, for laming and killing three persons, sentenced to be hanged. Middlesex County Records, II, 108, 218.

1616. Middlesex. Margaret Wellan of London accused "upon suspition to be a witch." Andrew Camfield held in £40 bail to appear against her. Middlesex County Records, II, 124-125.

1617. Middlesex. Agnes Berrye of Enfield sentenced to be hanged. Ibid., 116, 219.

1617. Middlesex. Anne Branche of Tottenham arraigned on four counts, acquitted. Ibid., 219.

1618. Middlesex. Bridget Meakins acquitted. Ibid., 225.

1619. Lincoln. Margaret and Philippa Flower hanged. Their mother, Joan Flower, died on the way to prison. The Wonderful Discoverie of the Witchcrafts of Margaret and Phillip Flower; J.

Nichols, History and Antiquities of the County of Leicester (1795-1815), II, pt. I, 49; Cal. St. P., Dom., 1619-1623, 129; Hist. MSS. Comm. Reports, Rutland MSS., IV, 514.

1619. Leicester. Three women, Anne Baker, Joan Willimot, Ellen Green, accused and confessed. Doubtless executed. The Wonderful Discoverie of the Witchcrafts of Margaret and Phillip Flower.

1619. Middlesex. Agnes Miller of Finchley acquitted. Middlesex County Records, II, 143-144.

1620. London. "One Peacock, sometime a schoolmaster and minister," for bewitching the king, committed to the Tower and tortured. Williams, Court and Times of James I, II, 202; Cal. St. P., Dom., 1619-1623, 125.

1620. Leicester. Gilbert Smith, rector of Swithland, accused of witchcraft among other things. Leicestershire and Rutland Notes and Queries, I, 247.

1620. Padiham, Lancashire. Witches in prison. House and Farm Accounts of the Shuttleworths, pt. II. (Chetham Soc., 1856), 240.

1620. Staffordshire. Woman accused on charges of the "boy of Bilson" acquitted. The Boy of Bilson (London, 1622); Arthur Wilson, Life and Reign of James I, 107-112; Webster, Displaying of Supposed Witchcraft, 274-275.

1621. Edmonton, Middlesex. Elizabeth Sawyer hanged. The wonderfull discoverie of Elizabeth Sawyer, by Henry Goodcole (1621).

1621. Middlesex. Anne Beaver, accused of murder on six counts, acquitted. Middlesex County Records, II, 72-73. Acquitted again in 1625. Ibid., III, 2.

1622. York. Six women indicted for bewitching Edward Fairfax's children. At April assizes two were released upon bond, two and probably four discharged. At the August assizes they were again acquitted. Fairfax, A Discourse of Witchcraft (Philobiblon Soc., London, 1858-1859).

1622. Middlesex. Margaret Russel, alias "Countess," committed to Newgate by Sir Wm. Slingsby on a charge by Lady Jennings of injuring her daughter. Dr. Napier diagnosed the daughter's illness as epilepsy. Brit. Mus., Add. MSS., 36,674, fol. 134.

1623. Yorkshire. Elizabeth Crearey of North Allerton sentenced to be set in the pillory once a quarter. Thirsk Quarter Sessions Records in North Riding Record Society (London, 1885), III, 177, 181.

1624. Bristol. Two witches said to have been executed. John Latimer, The Annals of Bristol in the Seventeenth Century (Bristol, 1900), 91. Latimer quotes from another "annalist."

temp. Jac. I? Two women said to have been hanged. Story doubtful. Edward Poeton, Winnowing of White Witchcraft (Brit. Mus., Sloane MSS., 1,954), 41-42.

temp. Jac. I. Norfolk. Joane Harvey accused for scratching "an olde witche" there, "Mother Francis nowe deade." Mother Francis had before been imprisoned at Norwich. Brit. Mus., Add. MSS., 28,223, fol. 15.

temp. Jac. I. Warwickshire. Coventry haunted by "hellish sorcerers." "The pestilent brood" also in Cheshire. Thomas Cooper, The Mystery of Witchcraft (1617), 13, 16.

temp. Jac. I. Norwich. Witches probably accused for illness of a child. Possibly Mother Francis was one of them. Cooper, ibid., "Epistle Dedicatorie."

1626. Taunton, Somerset. Edmund Bull and Joan Greedie accused. Brit. Mus., Add. MSS., 36,674, fol. 189; Wright, Narratives of Sorcery and Magic, II, 139-143. See also Richard Bernard, Guide to Grand Jurymen, "Epistle Dedicatorie."

1627. Durham. Sara Hathericke and Jane Urwen accused before the Consistory Court. Folk-Lore Journal (London, 1887), V, 158. Quoted by Edward Peacock from the records of the Consistory Court of Durham.

1627. Linneston, Lancaster. Elizabeth Londesdale accused. Certificate of neighbors in her favor. Hist. MSS. Comm. Reports, XIV, pt. 4 (Kenyon MSS.), 36.

1628. Leepish, Northumberland. Jane Robson committed. Mackenzie, History of Northumberland (Newcastle, 1825), 36. Mackenzie copies from the Mickleton MS.

1630. Lancaster. A certain Utley said to have been hanged for bewitching Richard Assheton. E. Baines, Lancaster (ed. of 1868-1870), II, 12.

1630. Sandwich, Kent. Woman hanged. Wm. Boys, Collections for an History of Sandwich in Kent (Canterbury, 1792), 707.

c. 1630. Wilts. "John Barlowes wife" said to have been executed. MS. letter of 1685-86 printed in the Gentleman's Magazine, 1832, pt. I, 405-410.

1633. Louth, Lincolnshire. Witch alarm; two searchers appointed. One witch indicted. Goulding, Louth Old Corporation Records, 54.

c. 1633. Lancaster. The father and mother of Mary Spencer condemned. Cal. S. P., Dom., 1634-1635, 79.

1633. Norfolk. Woman accused. No arrest made. Hist. MSS. Comm. Reports, X, pt. 2 (Gawdy MSS.), p. 144.

1633-34. Lancaster. Several witches, probably seventeen, tried and condemned. Reprieved by the king. For the many references to this affair see above, chap. VII, footnotes.

1634. Yorkshire. Four women of West Ayton presented for telling "per veneficationem vel incantationem" where certain stolen clothes were to be found. Thirsk Quarter Sessions Records in North Riding Record Society, IV, 20.

1635. Lancaster. Four witches condemned. Privy Council orders Bishop Bridgeman to examine them. Two died in gaol. The others probably reprieved. Hist. MSS. Comm. Reports, XII, 2 (Cowper MSS., II), 77, 80.

1635. Leicester. Agnes Tedsall acquitted. Leicestershire and Rutland Notes and Queries, I, 247.

1635. ———. Mary Prowting, who was a plaintiff before the Star Chamber, accused of witchcraft. Accuser, who was one of the defendants, exposed. Cal. St. P., Dom., 1635, 476-477.

c. 1637. Bedford. Goodwife Rose "ducked," probably by officials. Wm. Drage, Daimonomageia (London, 1665), 41.

1637. Staffordshire. Joice Hunniman committed, almost certainly released. Hist. MSS. Comm. Reports, II, App., 48 b.

1637-38. Lathom, Lancashire. Anne Spencer examined and probably committed. Hist. MSS.

Comm. Reports, XIV, 4 (Kenyon MSS.), 55.

1638. Middlesex. Alice Bastard arraigned on two charges. Acquitted. Middlesex County Records, III, 112-113.

1641. Middlesex. One Hammond of Westminster tried and perhaps hanged. John Aubrey, Remaines of Gentilisme and Judaisme (Folk-Lore Soc.), 61.

temp. Carol I. Oxford. Woman perhaps executed. This story is given at third hand in A Collection of Modern Relations (London, 1693), 48-49.

temp. Carol, I. Somerset. One or more hanged. Later the bewitched person, who may have been Edmund Bull (see above, s. v. 1626, Taunton), hanged also as a witch. Meric Casaubon, Of Credulity and Incredulity (London, 1668), 170-171.

temp. Carol. I? Taunton Dean. Woman acquitted. North, Life of North, 131.

1642. Middlesex. Nicholas Culpepper of St. Leonard's, Shoreditch, acquitted. Middlesex County Records, III, 85.

1643. Newbury, Berks. A woman supposed to be a witch probably shot here by the parliament forces. A Most certain, strange and true Discovery of a Witch ... 1643; Mercurius Aulicus, Oct. 1-8, 1643; Mercurius Civicus, Sept. 21-28, 1643; Certaine Informations, Sept. 25-Oct. 2, 1643; Mercurius Britannicus, Oct. 10-17, 1643.

1644. Sandwich, Kent. "The widow Drew hanged for a witch." W. Boys, Collections for an History of Sandwich, 714.

1645 (July). Chelmsford, Essex. Sixteen certainly condemned, probably two more. Possibly eleven or twelve more at another assize. A true and exact Relation ... of ... the late Witches ... at Chelmesford (1645); Arthur Wilson, in Peck, Desiderata Curiosa, II, 76; Hopkins, Discovery of Witches, 2-3; Stearne, Confirmation and Discovery of Witchcraft, 14, 16, 36, 38, 58, etc.; Signes and Wonders from Heaven (1645), 2; "R. B." The Kingdom of Darkness (London, 1688). The fate of the several Essex witches is recorded by the True and Exact Relation in marginal notes printed opposite their depositions (but omitted in the reprint of that pamphlet in Howell's State Trials). "R. B.," in The Kingdom of Darkness, though his knowledge of the Essex cases is ascribed to the pamphlet, gives details as to the time and place of the executions which are often in strange conflict with its testimony.

1645 (July). Norfolk. Twenty witches said to have been executed. Whitelocke, Memorials, I, 487. A Perfect Diurnal (July 21-28, 1645) says that there has been a "tryall of the Norfolke witches, about 40 of them and 20 already executed." Signes and Wonders from Heaven says that "there were 40 witches arraigned for their lives and 20 executed."

1645. Bury St. Edmunds, Suffolk. Sixteen women and two men executed Aug. 27. Forty or fifty more probably executed a few weeks later. A very large number arraigned. A manuscript (Brit. Mus., Add. MSS., 27,402, fol. 104 ff.) mentions over forty true bills and fifteen or more bills not found. A True Relation of the Araignment of eighteene Witches at St. Edmundsbury (1645); Clarke, Lives of Sundry Eminent Persons, 172; County Folk-Lore, Suffolk (Folk-Lore Soc.), 178; Ady, A Candle in the Dark, 104-105, 114; Moderate Intelligencer, Sept. 4-11, 1645; Scottish Dove, Aug. 29-Sept. 6, 1645.

Stearne mentions several names not mentioned in the True Relation—names probably belonging to those in the second group of the accused. Of most of them he has quoted the confession without stating the outcome of the cases. They are Hempstead of Creeting, Ratcliffe of Shelley, Randall of Lavenham, Bedford of Rattlesden, Wright of Hitcham, Ruceulver of Powstead, Greenliefe of Barton, Bush of Barton, Cricke of Hitcham, Richmond of Bramford, Hammer of Needham, Boreham of Sudbury, Scarfe of Rattlesden, King of Acton, Bysack of Waldingfield, Binkes of Haverhill. In addition to these Stearne speaks of Elizabeth Hubbard of Stowmarket. Two others from Stowmarket were tried, "Goody Mils" and "Goody Low." Hollingsworth, History of Stowmarket (Ipswich, 1844), 171.

1645. Melford, Suffolk. Alexander Sussums made confession. Stearne, 36.

1645. Great Yarmouth, Norfolk. At least nine women indicted, five of whom were condemned. Three women acquitted and one man. Many others presented. C. J. Palmer, History of Great Yarmouth, I, 273-274. Hist. MSS. Comm. Reports, IX, App., pt. I, 320 a; Henry Harrod in Norfolk Archæol., IV, 249-251.

1645. Cornwall. Anne Jeffries confined in Bodmin gaol and starved by order of a justice of the peace. She was said to be intimate with the "airy people" and to cause marvellous cures. We do not know the charge against her. Finally discharged. William Turner, Remarkable Providences (London, 1697), ch. 82.

1645. Ipswich, Suffolk. Mother Lakeland burnt. The Lawes against Witches (1645).

1645. King's Lynn, Norfolk. Dorothy Lee and Grace Wright hanged. Mackerell, History and Antiquities of King's Lynn, 236.

1645. Aldeburgh, Norfolk. Seven witches hanged. Quotations from the chamberlain's accounts in N. F. Hele, Notes or Jottings about Aldeburgh, 43-44.

1645. Faversham, Kent. Three women hanged, a fourth tried, by the local authorities. The Examination, Confession, Triall and Execution of Joane Williford, Joan Cariden and Jane Hott (1645).

1645. Rye, Sussex. Martha Bruff and Anne Howsell ordered by the "mayor of Rye and others" to be put to the ordeal of water. Hist. MSS. Comm. Reports, XIII, pt. 4, 216.

1645. Middlesex. Several witches of Stepney accused. Signes and Wonders from Heaven, 2-3.

1645-46. Cambridgeshire. Several accused, at least one or two of whom were executed. Ady, Candle in the Dark, 135; Stearne, 39, 45; H. More, Antidote against Atheisme, 128-129. This may have been what is referred to in Glanvill's Sadducismus Triumphatus, pt. ii, 208-209.

1646. Northamptonshire. Several witches hanged. One died in prison. Stearne, 11, 23, 34-35.

1646. Huntingdonshire. Many accused, of whom at least ten were examined and several executed, among them John Wynnick. One woman swam and was released. John Davenport, Witches of Huntingdon (London, 1646); H. More, Antidote against Atheisme, 125; Stearne, 11, 13, 17, 19, 20-21, 39, 42.

1646. Bedfordshire. Elizabeth Gurrey of Risden made confession. Stearne says a Huntingdonshire witch confessed that "at Tilbrooke bushes in Bedfordshier ... there met above twenty at one time." Huntingdonshire witches seem meant, but perhaps not alone. Stearne, 11,

31.

c. 1646. Yarmouth, Norfolk. Stearne mentions a woman who suffered here. Stearne, 53.

1646. Heptenstall, Yorkshire. Elizabeth Crossley, Mary Midgley, and two other women examined before two justices of the peace. York Depositions, 6-9.

1647. Ely, Cambridgeshire. Stearne mentions "those executed at Elie, a little before Michaelmas last, ... also one at Chatterish there, one at March there, and another at Wimblington there, now lately found, still to be tryed"; and again "one Moores wife of Sutton, in the Isle of Elie," who "confessed her selfe guilty" and was executed; and yet again "one at Heddenham in the Isle of Ely," who "made a very large Confession" and must have paid the penalty. Stearne, 17, 21, 37; Gibbons, Ely Episcopal Records (Lincoln, 1891), 112-113.

1647. Middlesex. Helen Howson acquitted. Middlesex County Records, III, 124.

1648. Middlesex. Bill against Katharine Fisher of Stratford-at-Bow ignored. Middlesex County Records, III, 102.

1648. Norwich, Norfolk. Two women burnt. P. Browne, History of Norwich (Norwich, 1814), 38.

1649. Worcester. A Lancashire witch said to have been tried; perhaps remanded to Lancashire. A Collection of Modern Relations. The writer says that he received the account from a "Person of Quality" who attended the trial.

1649. Middlesex. Elizabeth Smythe of St. Martin's-in-the-Fields acquitted. Middlesex County Records, III, 191.

1649. Middlesex. Dorothy Brumley acquitted. Ibid.

1649. St. Albans. John Palmer and Elizabeth Knott said to have been hanged for witches. The Divels Delusion (1649).

1649. Berwick. Thirty women, examined on the accusation of a Scotch witch-finder, committed to prison. Whitelocke, Memorials, III, 99; John Fuller, History of Berwick (Edinburgh, 1799), 155-156, giving extracts from the Guild Hall Books; John Sykes, Local Records (Newcastle, 1833), I, 103-105.

1649. Gloucester. Witch tried at the assizes. A Collection of Modern Relations, 52.

1649-50. Yorkshire. Mary Sykes and Susan Beaumont committed and searched. The former acquitted, bill against the latter ignored. York Depositions, 28.

1649-50. Durham. Several witches at Gateshead examined, and carried to Durham for trial; "a grave for a witch." Sykes, Local Records, I, 105; or Denham Tracts (Folk-Lore Soc.), II, 338.

1649-50. Newcastle. Thirty witches accused. Fourteen women and one man hanged, together with a witch from the county of Northumberland. Ralph Gardiner, England's Grievance (London, 1655), 108; Sykes, Local Records, I, 103; John Brand, History and Antiquities of Newcastle (London, 1789), II, 477-478; Whitelocke, Memorials, III, 128; Chronicon Mirabile (London, 1841), 92.

1650. Yorkshire. Ann Hudson of Skipsey charged. York Depositions, 38, note.

1650. Cumberland. A "discovery of witches." Sheriff perplexed. Cal. St. P., Dom., 1650, 159.

1650. Derbyshire. Ann Wagg of Ilkeston committed for trial. J. C. Cox, Three Centuries of

Derbyshire Annals, II, 88.

1650. Middlesex. Joan Roberts acquitted. Middlesex County Records, III, 284.

1650. Stratford-at-Bow, Middlesex. Witch said to have been apprehended, but "escaped the law." Glanvill, Sadducismus Triumphatus, pt. ii, Relation XX.

1650. Middlesex. Joan Allen sentenced to be hanged. Middlesex County Records, III, 284. The Weekly Intelligencer, Oct. 7, 1650, refers to the hanging of a witch at the Old Bailey, probably Joan.

1650. Leicester. Anne Chettle searched and acquitted. Tried again two years later. Result unknown. Leicestershire and Rutland Notes and Queries, I, 247; James Thompson, Leicester (Leicester, 1849), 406.

1650. Alnwick. Dorothy Swinow, wife of a colonel, indicted. Nothing further came of it. Wonderfull News from the North (1650).

1650. Middlesex. Elizabeth Smith acquitted. Middlesex County Records, III, 284.

c. 1650-60. St. Alban's, Herts. Two witches suspected and probably tried. Drage, Daimonomageia (1665), 40-41.

1651. Yorkshire. Margaret Morton acquitted. York Depositions, 38.

1651. Middlesex. Elizabeth Lanam of Stepney acquitted. Middlesex County Records, III, 202, 285.

1651. Colchester, Essex. John Lock sentenced to one year's imprisonment and four appearances in the pillory. Brit. Mus., Stowe MSS., 840, fol. 43.

1652. Yorkshire. Hester France of Huddersfield accused before the justice of the peace. York Depositions, 51.

1652. Maidstone, Kent. Six women hanged, others indicted. A Prodigious and Tragicall History of the Arraignment ... of six Witches at Maidstone ... by "H. F. Gent.," 1652; The Faithful Scout, July 30-Aug. 7, 1652; Ashmole's Diary in Lives of Ashmole and Lilly (London, 1774), 316.

1652. Middlesex. Joan Peterson of Wapping acquitted on one charge, found guilty on another, and hanged. Middlesex County Records, III, 287; The Witch of Wapping; A Declaration in Answer to several lying Pamphlets concerning the Witch of Wapping; The Tryall and Examinations of Mrs. Joan Peterson; French Intelligencer, Apr. 6-13, 1652; Mercurius Democritus, Apr. 7-14, 1652; Weekly Intelligencer, April 6-13, 1652; Faithful Scout, Apr. 9-16, 1652.

1652. London. Susan Simpson acquitted. A True and Perfect List of the Names of those Prisoners in Newgate (London, 1652).

1652. Worcester. Catherine Huxley of Evesham, charged with bewitching a nine-year-old girl, hanged. Baxter, Certainty of the World of Spirits (London, 1691), 44-45. Baxter's narrative was sent him by "the now Minister of the place."

1652. Middlesex. Temperance Fossett of Whitechapel acquitted. Middlesex County Records, III, 208, 288.

1652. Middlesex. Margery Scott of St Martin's-in-the-Fields acquitted. Ibid., 209.

1652. Scarborough, Yorkshire. Anne Marchant or Hunnam accused and searched. J. B. Baker, History of Scarborough (London, 1882), 481, using local records.

1652. Durham. Francis Adamson and —— Powle executed. Richardson, Table Book, I, 286.

1652. Exeter, Devonshire. Joan Baker committed. Cotton, Gleanings ... Relative to the History of ... Exeter (Exeter, 1877), 149.

1652. Wilts. William Starr accused and searched. Hist. MSS. Comm. Reports, Various, I, 127.

1652-53. Cornwall. A witch near Land's End accused, and accuses others. Eight sent to Launceston gaol. Some probably executed (see above, p. 218 and footnotes 24, 25). Mercurius Politicus, Nov. 24-Dec. 2, 1653; R. and O. B. Peter, The Histories of Launceston and Dunheved (Plymouth, 1885), 285. See also Burthogge, Essay upon Reason and the Nature of Spirits (London, 1694), 196.

1653. Wilts. Joan Baker of the Devizes makes complaint because two persons have reported her to be a witch. Hist. MSS. Comm. Reports, Various, I, 127. Is this the Joan Baker of Exeter mentioned a few lines above?

1653. Wilts. Joan Price of Malmesbury and Elizabeth Beeman of the Devizes indicted, the latter committed to the assizes. Ibid.

1653. Yorkshire. Elizabeth Lambe accused. York Depositions, 58.

1653. Middlesex. Elizabeth Newman of Whitechapel acquitted on one charge, found guilty on another, and sentenced to be hanged. Middlesex County Records, III, 217, 218, 289.

1653. Middlesex. Barbara Bartle of Stepney acquitted. Ibid., 216.

1653. Leeds, Yorkshire. Isabel Emott indicted for witchcraft upon cattle. Hist. MSS. Comm. Reports, IX, pt. 1, 325 b.

1653. Salisbury, Wilts. Anne Bodenham of Fisherton Anger hanged. Doctor Lamb Revived; Doctor Lamb's Darling; Aubrey, Folk-Lore and Gentilisme (Folk-Lore Soc.), 261; Henry More, An Antidote against Atheisme, bk. III, chap. VII.

1654. Yorkshire. Anne Greene of Gargrave examined. York Depositions, 64-65.

1654. Yorkshire. Elizabeth Roberts of Beverley examined. Ibid., 67.

1654. Wilts. Christiana Weekes of Cleves Pepper, who had been twice before accused in recent sessions, charged with telling where lost goods could be found. "Other conjurers" charged at the same time. Hist. MSS. Comm. Reports, Various, I, 120. See above, 1610, Norfolk.

1654. Exeter. Diana Crosse committed. Cotton, Gleanings ... Relative to the History of ... Exeter, 150.

1654. Wilts. Elizabeth Loudon committed on suspicion. Hist. MSS. Comm. Reports, Various, I, 129.

1654. Whitechapel, Middlesex. Grace Boxe, arraigned on three charges, acquitted. Acquitted again in 1656. Middlesex County Records, III, 223, 293.

1655. Yorkshire. Katherine Earle committed and searched. York Depositions, 69.

1655. Salisbury. Margaret Gyngell convicted. Pardoned by the Lord Protector. F. A. Inderwick, The Interregnum, 188-189.

1655. Bury St. Edmunds, Suffolk. Mother and daughter Boram said to have been hanged.

Hutchinson, An Historical Essay concerning Witchcraft, 38.

1656. Yorkshire. Jennet and George Benton of Wakefield examined. York Depositions, 74.

1656. Yorkshire. William and Mary Wade committed for bewitching the daughter of Lady Mallory. York Depositions, 75-78.

1657. Middlesex. Katharine Evans of Fulham acquitted. Middlesex County Records, III, 263.

1657. Middlesex. Elizabeth Crowley of Stepney acquitted, but detained in the house of correction. Middlesex County Records, III, 266, 295.

1657. Gisborough, Yorkshire. Robert Conyers, "gent.," accused. North Riding Record Society, V, 259.

1658. Exeter. Thomas Harvey of Oakham, Rutlandshire, "apprehended by order of Council by a party of soldiers," acquitted at Exeter assizes, but detained in custody. Cal. St. P., Dom., 1658-1659, 169.

1658. Chard, Somerset. Jane Brooks of Shepton Mallet hanged. Glanvill, Sadducismus Triumphatus (1681), pt. ii, 120-122. (Glanvill used Hunt's book of examinations). J. E. Farbrother, Shepton Mallet; notes on its history, ancient, descriptive and natural (1860), 141.

1658. Exeter. Joan Furnace accused. Cotton, Gleanings ... Relative to the History of ... Exeter, 152.

1658. Yorkshire. Some women said to have been accused by two maids. The woman "cast" by the jury. The judges gave a "respite." Story not entirely trustworthy. The most true and wonderfull Narration of two women bewitched in Yorkshire ... (1658).

1658. Wapping, Middlesex. Lydia Rogers accused. A More Exact Relation of the most lamentable and horrid Contract which Lydia Rogers ... made with the Divel (1658). See app. A, § 5, for another tract.

1658. Northamptonshire. Some witches of Welton said to have been examined. Glanvill, Sadducismus Triumphatus (1681), pt. ii, 263-268.

1658. Salisbury, Wilts. The widow Orchard said to have been executed. From a MS. letter of 1685-86, printed in the Gentleman's Magazine, 1832, pt. I, 405-410.

1659. Norwich, Norfolk. Mary Oliver burnt. P. Brown, History of Norwich, 39. Francis Blomefield, An Essay towards a Topographical History of the County of Norfolk (London, 1805-1810), III, 401.

1659. Middlesex. Elizabeth Kennett of Stepney accused. Middlesex County Records, III, 278, 299.

1659. Hertfordshire. "Goody Free" accused of killing by witchcraft. Hertfordshire County Sessions Rolls, I, 126, 129.

1659-1660. Northumberland. Elizabeth Simpson of Tynemouth accused. York Depositions, 82.

1660. Worcester. Joan Bibb of Rushock received £20 damages for being ducked. Gentleman's Magazine, 1856, pt. I, 39, from a letter of J. Noake of Worcester, who used the Townshend MSS.

1660. Worcester. A widow and her two daughters, and a man, from Kidderminster, tried. "Little proved." Copied from the Townshend MSS. by Nash, in his Collections for the History of Worcestershire (1781-1799), II, 38.

1660. Newcastle. Two suspected women detained in prison. Extracts from the Municipal Accounts of Newcastle-upon-Tyne in M. A. Richardson, Reprints of Rare Tracts ... illustrative of the History of the Northern Counties (Newcastle, 1843-1847), III, 57.

1660. Canterbury, Kent. Several witches said to have been executed. W. Welfitt ("Civis"), Minutes of Canterbury (Canterbury, 1801-1802), no. X.

c. 1660. Sussex. A woman who had been formerly tried at Maidstone watched and searched. MS. quoted in Sussex Archæol. Collections, XVIII, 111-113; see also Samuel Clarke, A Mirrour or Looking Glasse both for Saints and Sinners, II, 593-596.

1661. Hertfordshire. Frances Bailey of Broxbourn complained of abuse by those who believed her a witch. Hertfordshire County Sessions Rolls, I, 137.

1661. Newcastle. Jane Watson examined before the mayor. York Depositions, 92-93.

1661. Newcastle. Margaret Catherwood and two other women examined before the mayor. Ibid., 88.

1663. Somerset. Elizabeth Style died before execution. Glanvill, Sadducismus Triumphatus, pt. ii, 127-146. For copies of three depositions about Elizabeth Style, see Gentleman's Magazine, 1837, pt. ii, 256-257.

1663. Taunton, Somerset. Julian Cox hanged. Glanvill, Sadducismus Triumphatus, pt. ii, 191-198.

1663-64. Newcastle. Dorothy Stranger accused before the mayor. York Depositions, 112-114.

1664. Somerset. A "hellish knot" of witches (Hutchinson says twelve) accused before justice of the peace Robert Hunt. His discovery stopped by "some of them in authority." Glanvill, Sadducismus Triumphatus, pt. ii, 256-257. But see case of Elizabeth Style above.

1664. Somerset. A witch condemned at the assizes. She may have been one of those brought before Hunt. Cal. St. P., Dom., 1663-1664, 552.

1664. Bury St. Edmunds, Suffolk. Rose Cullender and Amy Duny condemned. A Tryal of Witches at ... Bury St. Edmunds (1682).

1664. Newcastle. Jane Simpson, Isabell Atcheson and Katharine Curry accused before the mayor. York Depositions, 124.

1664. York. Alice Huson and Doll Dilby tried. Both made confessions. Copied for A Collection of Modern Relations (see p. 52) from a paper written by the justice of the peace, Corbet.

1665. Wilts. Jone Mereweather of Weeke in Bishop's Cannings committed. Hist. MSS. Comm. Reports, Various, I, 147.

1665. Newcastle. Mrs. Pepper accused before the mayor. York Depositions, 127.

1665. Three persons convicted of murder and executed for killing a supposed witch. Joseph Hunter, Life of Heywood (London, 1842), 167-168, note.

1666. Lancashire. Four witches of Haigh examined, two committed but probably acquitted. Cal. St. P., Dom., 1665-1666, 225.

1667. Newcastle, Northumberland. Emmy Gaskin of Landgate accused before the mayor. York Depositions, 154.

1667. Norfolk. A fortune-teller or conjuror condemned to imprisonment. Cal. St. P., Dom., 1667, 30.

1667. Ipswich, Suffolk. Two witches possibly imprisoned. Story doubtful. Cal. St. P., Dom., 1667-1668, 4.

1667. Devizes, Wilts. "An old woman" imprisoned, charged with bewitching by making and pricking an image. Blagrave, Astrological Practice (London 1689), 90, 103.

1667. Lancashire. Widow Bridge and her sister, Margaret Loy, both of Liverpool, accused. The Moore Rental (Chetham Soc., 1847), 59-60.

1668. Durham. Alice Armstrong of Strotton tried, but almost certainly acquitted. Tried twice again in the next year with the same result. Sykes, Local Records, II, 369.

1668. Warwick. Many witches "said to be in hold." Cal. St. P., Dom., 1668-1669, 25.

1669. Hertfordshire. John Allen of Stondon indicted for calling Joan Mills a witch. Hertfordshire County Sessions Rolls, I, 217.

1670. Yorkshire. Anne Wilkinson acquitted. York Depositions, 176 and note.

1670. Latton Wilts. Jane Townshend accused. Hist. MSS. Comm. Reports, Various. I, 150-151.

1670. Wilts. Elizabeth Peacock acquitted. See Inderwick's list of witch trials in the western circuit, in his Sidelights on the Stuarts (London, 1888), 190-194. Hereafter the reference "Inderwick" will mean this list. See also above, p. 269, note.

1670. Devonshire. Elizabeth Eburye and Aliena Walter acquitted. Inderwick.

1670. Somerset. Anne Slade acquitted on two indictments. Inderwick.

1670. Bucks. Ann Clarke reprieved. Cal. St. P., Dom., 1670, 388.

1671. Devonshire. Johanna Elford acquitted. Inderwick.

1671. Devonshire. Margaret Heddon acquitted on two indictments. Inderwick.

1671. Falmouth. Several witches acquitted. Cal. St. P., Dom., 1671, 105, 171. Perhaps identical with the three, two men and a woman, mentioned by Inderwick as acquitted in Cornwall.

1672. Somerset. Margaret Stevens acquitted on two indictments. Inderwick.

1672. Devonshire. Phelippa Bruen acquitted on four indictments. Inderwick.

1672. Wilts. Elizabeth Mills acquitted on two indictments. Inderwick.

1672. Wilts. Elizabeth Peacock, who had been acquitted two years before, acquitted on five indictments. Judith Witchell acquitted on two, found guilty on a third. She and Ann Tilling sentenced to execution. They must have been reprieved. Inderwick; Gentleman's Magazine, 1832, pt. II, p. 489-492.

1673. Yorkshire, Northumberland, and Durham. At least twenty-three women and six men accused to various justices of the peace by Ann Armstrong, who confessed to being present at witch meetings, and who acted as a witch discoverer. Some of those whom she accused were accused by others. Margaret Milburne, whom she seems not to have mentioned, also accused, York Depositions, 191-202.

1674. Northampton. Ann Foster said to have been hanged for destroying sheep and burning barns by witchcraft. A Full and True Relation of The Tryal, Condemnation, and Execution of Ann Foster (1674).

1674. Middlesex. Elizabeth Row of Hackney held in bail for her appearance at Quarter Sessions. Middlesex County Records, IV, 42-43.

1674. Southton, Somerset. John and Agnes Knipp acquitted. Inderwick.

1674? (see above, p. 269, note). Salisbury. Woman acquitted, but kept in gaol. North, Life of North, 130, 131.

1674-75. Lancashire. Joseph Hinchcliffe and his wife bound over to appear at the assizes. He committed suicide and his wife died soon after. York Depositions, 208; Oliver Heywood's Diary (1881-1885), I, 362.

1675. Southton, Somerset. Martha Rylens acquitted on five indictments. Inderwick.

1676. Devonshire. Susannah Daye acquitted. Inderwick.

1676. Cornwall. Mary Clarkson acquitted. Inderwick.

c. 1679. Ely, Cambridgeshire. Witch condemned, but reprieved. Hutchinson, Historical Essay concerning Witchcraft, 41.

c. 1680. Somerset. Anna Rawlins acquitted. Inderwick.

c. 1680. Derbyshire. Elizabeth Hole of Wingerworth accused and committed for charging a baronet with witchcraft. J. C. Cox, Three Centuries of Derbyshire Annals, II, 90.

1680. Yorkshire, Elizabeth Fenwick of Longwitton acquitted. York Depositions, 247.

1682. London. Jane Kent acquitted. A Full and True Account ... but more especially the Tryall of Jane Kent for Witchcraft (1682).

1682. Surrey. Joan Butts acquitted. Strange and Wonderfull News from Yowell in Surry (1681); An Account of the Tryal and Examination of Joan Buts (1682).

1682. Devonshire. Temperance Lloyd acquitted on one indictment, found guilty on another. Susanna Edwards and Mary Trembles found guilty. All three executed. Inderwick; North, Life of North, 130; see also app. A, § 6, above.

1682-88. Northumberland. Margaret Stothard of Edlingham accused. E. Mackenzie, History of Northumberland, II, 33-36.

1683. London. Jane Dodson acquitted. An Account of the Whole Proceedings at the Sessions Holden at the Sessions House in the Old Baily ... (1683).

1683. Somerset. Elenora, Susannah, and Marie Harris, and Anna Clarke acquitted. Inderwick.

1684. Devonshire. Alicia Molland found guilty. Inderwick.

1685. Devonshire. Jane Vallet acquitted on three indictments. Inderwick.

temp. Carol. II. Devonshire. Agnes Ryder of Woodbury accused, probably committed. A. H. A. Hamilton, Quarter Sessions chiefly in Devon (London, 1878), 220.

temp. Carol. II. Ipswich, Suffolk. A woman in prison. William Drage, Daimonomageia, 11.

temp. Carol. II. Herts. Two suspected witches of Baldock ducked. Ibid., 40.

temp. Carol. II. St. Albans, Herts. Man and woman imprisoned. Woman ducked. Ibid.

temp. Carol. II. Taunton Dean, Somerset. Man acquitted. North, Life of North, 131.

1685-86. Malmesbury, Wilts. Fourteen persons accused, among whom were the three women, Peacock, Tilling and Witchell, who had been tried in 1672. Eleven set at liberty; Peacock, Tilling and Witchell kept in prison awhile, probably released eventually. Gentleman's Magazine, 1832, pt. I, 489-492.

1686. Somerset. Honora Phippan acquitted on two indictments. Inderwick.

1686. Cornwall. Jane Noal, alias Nickless, alias Nicholas, and Betty Seeze committed to Launceston gaol for bewitching a fifteen-year-old boy. We know from Inderwick that Jane Nicholas was acquitted. A True Account of ... John Tonken of Pensans in Cornwall (1686).

1687. York. Witch condemned, probably reprieved. Memoirs and Travels of Sir John Reresby (London, 1812), 329.

1687. Dorset. Dewnes Knumerton and Elizabeth Hengler acquitted. Inderwick. For examination of first see Roberts, Southern Counties, 525-526.

1687. Wilts. M. Parle acquitted. Inderwick.

1687. Devonshire. Abigail Handford acquitted. Inderwick.

1689. Wilts. Margareta Young condemned but reprieved. Christiana Dunne acquitted. Inderwick.

1690. Taunton, Somerset. Elizabeth Farrier (Carrier), Margaret Coombes and Ann Moore committed. Coombes died in prison at Brewton. The other two acquitted at the assizes. Inderwick; Baxter, Certainty of the World of Spirits, 74-75.

1692. Wilts. Woman committed. Hist. MSS. Comm. Reports, Various, I, 160.

1693. Suffolk. Widow Chambers of Upaston committed, died in gaol. Hutchinson, Historical Essay concerning Witchcraft, 42.

1693-94. Devonshire. Dorothy Case acquitted on three indictments. Inderwick.

1693-94. Devonshire. Katherine Williams acquitted. Inderwick.

1694. Bury St. Edmunds, Suffolk. Mother Munnings of Hartis acquitted. Hutchinson, op. cit., 43.

1694. Somerset. Action brought against three men for swimming Margaret Waddam. Hist. MSS. Comm. Reports, Various, I, 160.

1694. Ipswich, Suffolk. Margaret Elnore acquitted. Hutchinson, 44.

1694. Kent. Ann Hart of Sandwich convicted, but went free under a general act of pardon. W. Boys, Collections for an History of Sandwich, 718.

1694-95. Devonshire. Clara Roach acquitted. Inderwick.

1695. Launceston, Cornwall. Mary Guy or Daye acquitted. Hutchinson, 44-45; Inderwick gives the name as Maria Daye (or Guy) and puts the trial in Devonshire in 1696.

1696. Devonshire. Elizabeth Horner acquitted on three indictments, Hutchinson, 45; Inderwick. See also letter from sub-dean Blackburne to the Bishop of Exeter in Brand, Popular Antiquities (ed. of 1905), II, 648-649.

1698-99. Wilts. Ruth Young acquitted. Inderwick.

1700. Dorset. Anne Grantly and Margaretta Way acquitted. Inderwick.

1700-10. Lancashire. A woman of Chowbent searched and committed. Died before the assizes. MS. quoted by Harland and Wilkinson, Lancashire Folk-Lore (London, 1867), 207; also E. Baines, Lancaster, II, 203.

1701. Southwark. Sarah Morduck, who had been before acquitted at Guildford, and who had unsuccessfully appealed to a justice in London against her persecutor, tried and acquitted. Hutchinson, 46. The Tryal of Richard Hathaway (1702); A Full and True Account of the Apprehending and Taking of Mrs. Sarah Moordike (1701); A short Account of the Trial held at Surry Assizes, in the Borough of Southwark (1702). See above, app. A, § 7.

1701. Kingston, Surrey. Woman acquitted. Notes and Queries (April 10, 1909), quoting from the London Post of Aug. 1-4, 1701.

1701-02. Devonshire. Susanna Hanover acquitted. Inderwick.

1702-03. Wilts. Joanna Tanner acquitted. Inderwick.

1704. Middlesex. Sarah Griffiths committed to Bridewell. A Full and True Account ... of a Notorious Witch (London, 1704).

1705. Northampton. Two women said to have been burned here. Story improbable. See above, appendix A, § 10.

1707. Somerset. Maria Stevens acquitted. Inderwick.

1712. Hertford. Jane Wenham condemned, but reprieved. See footnotes to chapter XIII and app. A, § 9.

1716. Huntingdon. Two witches, a mother and daughter, said to have been executed here. Story improbable. See above, app. A, § 10.

1717. Leicester. Jane Clark and her daughter said to have been tried. Leicestershire and Rutland Notes and Queries, I, 247.

1717. Leicester. Mother Norton and her daughter acquitted. Brit. Mus., Add. MSS., 35,838, fol. 404.

I am unwilling to close this work without an expression of my gratitude to the libraries, on both sides of the sea, which have so generously welcomed me to the use of their books and pamphlets on English witchcraft—many of them excessively rare and precious. They have made possible this study. My debt is especially great to the libraries of the British Museum and of Lambeth Palace at London, to the Bodleian Library at Oxford, and in America to the Boston Athenæum and to the university libraries of Yale and Harvard. To the unrivalled White collection at Cornell my obligation is deepest of all.

The references in this list, together with the account, in appendix A, of the pamphlet literature of witchcraft, are designed to take the place of a formal bibliography. That the list of cases here given is complete can hardly be hoped. Crude though its materials compel it to be, the author believes it may prove useful. He hopes in the course of time to make it more complete, and to that end will gladly welcome information respecting other trials.

Made in the USA
Lexington, KY
22 August 2016